THE JEWISH BIBLE

THE SAMUEL & ALTHEA STROUM
LECTURES IN JEWISH STUDIES

Samuel Stroum, businessman, community leader, and philanthropist, by a major gift to the Jewish Federation of Greater Seattle, established the Samuel and Althea Stroum Philanthropic Fund.

In recognition of Mr. and Mrs. Stroum's deep interest in Jewish history and culture, the Board of Directors of the Jewish Federation of Greater Seattle, in cooperation with the Jewish Studies Program at the University of Washington, established an annual lectureship at the University of Washington known as the Samuel and Althea Stroum Lectureship in Jewish Studies. This lectureship makes it possible to bring to the area outstanding scholars and interpreters of Jewish thought, thus promoting a deeper understanding of Jewish history, religion, and culture. Such understanding can lead to an enhanced appreciation of the Jewish contributions to the historical and cultural traditions that have shaped the American nation.

The terms of the gift also provide for the publication from time to time of the lectures or other appropriate materials resulting from or related to the lectures.

THE Jewish Bible

A MATERIAL HISTORY

David Stern

A SAMUEL AND ALTHEA STROUM BOOK

UNIVERSITY OF WASHINGTON PRESS
Seattle and London

The Jewish Bible is published with the assistance of a grant from the Samuel and Althea Stroum Endowed Book Fund.
Additional support was provided by generous grants from the Harvard University Faculty of Arts and Sciences Tenured Faculty Publication Fund, the University of Pennsylvania Research Fund, and the Lucius N. Littauer Foundation.

Printed and bound in South Korea
Composed in Minion, typeface designed by Robert Slimbach
Maps created by C. Scott Walker, Harvard Map Collection
21 20 19 5 4 3 2

UNIVERSITY OF WASHINGTON PRESS
www.washington.edu/uwpress

LIBRARY OF CONGRESS CATALOGING-IN-PUBLICATION DATA
Names: Stern, David, 1949- author.
Title: The Jewish Bible : a material history / David Stern.
Description: First edition. | Seattle : University of Washington Press, [2017] | Series: Samuel and Althea Stroum lectures in Jewish studies | Includes bibliographical references and index.
Identifiers: LCCN 2016049326 | ISBN 9780295741482 (hardcover : alk. paper)
Subjects: LCSH: Bible. Old Testament—History. | Bible. Old Testament—Criticism, interpretation, etc.
Classification: LCC BS1130 .S74 2017 | DDC 221.09—dc23
LC record available at https://lccn.loc.gov/2016049326
ISBN (hardcover): 978-0-295-74148-2
ISBN (paperback): 978-0-295-74617-3
ISBN (ebook): 978-0-295-74149-9

COVER ILLUSTRATIONS (FRONT) Pentateuch (Joshua 1), Prophets, and Hagiographa, Soncino: Joshua Solomon b. Israel Nathan Soncino, 1488. The Bodleian Libraries, University of Oxford. (BACK) Fragment of Bible codex with Palestinian vocalization (Ezekiel 31:4–36:7), Cairo Genizah. Cambridge, T-S 249.5. Syndics of Cambridge University Library. (SPINE) Detail of Torah ark, gold glass, Rome, fourth century CE. Photo © The Israel Museum, by David Harris

The paper used in this publication is acid-free and meets the minimum requirements of American National Standard for Information Sciences—Permanence of Paper for Printed Library Materials, ANSI Z39.48–1984. ∞

For Kathryn, Jonah, Rebecca, and Jesse

CONTENTS

CENTERS OF BOOK PRODUCTION IN THE NEAR EAST AND NORTH AFRICA
Aleppo
BABYLONIA
Tiberias
Mount Gerizim
Jerusalem
Qumran
Baghdad
Alexandria
Cairo
EGYPT
Sana'a
YEMEN
0
300 mi
0
300 km
N

CENTERS OF BOOK PRODUCTION IN EUROPE, 1200–1800 CE
Vilnius
ENGLAND
London
Amsterdam
Berlin
Cologne
Erfurt
Mainz
Wuerzburg
ASHKENAZ
Worms
Frankfurt
Basel
Konstanz
Venice
Ferrara
La Coruña
SEPHARAD
LANGUEDOC
Narbonne
CASTILE
CROWN OF ARAGON
PROVENCE
Florence
Girona
Perpignan
Madrid
Cervera
Rome
Lisbon
Barcelona
Toledo
Hijar
ANDALUSIA
TUNISIA
MOROCCO
LIBYA
0
300 mi
0
300 km
N

ACKNOWLEDGMENTS

In the course of writing this book, I have been supported and assisted by foundations, institutions, and many individuals. The book never would have come into existence in the first place if I had not been invited by my colleagues Hillel Kieval and Martin Jaffee to deliver the Samuel Stroum Lectures at the University of Washington in 1999; I thank both Hillel and Marty for starting me on this project. As I explain in the introduction, the lectures I gave at that time were on three books (the Talmud, the prayer book, and the Haggadah) not covered in this book, but the hospitality, encouragement, and nourishment I received during my visit emboldened me to continue even as I was learning what it meant to do the history of the book. I vividly remember meeting Sam and Althea Stroum when I gave the lectures, and their enormous charm remains very much alive in my memory.

In addition to the lectures, the Stroum Foundation has subsidized the publication of this book by the University of Washington Press. Its large number of illustrations, which make this book so beautiful, were made possible by generous subventions from the Lucius

N. Littauer Foundation, the University of Pennsylvania Research Foundation, and the Harvard University Publications Fund. I thank all these foundations and funds for their support.

Several sections of this book were worked out in the course of writing three lengthy articles, for which I received numerous words of advice and criticism from many colleagues. I have acknowledged them in the notes to the separate articles and, without repeating their names, I wish again to thank all my colleagues for their intellectual and scholarly generosity.

I especially want to thank my good friends and colleagues Edward Breuer and Eva Frojmovic for reading the entirety of an earlier draft of this book and offering numerous points of correction and suggestions for revisions. Sections of the book were also very helpfully read by Jeffrey Tigay, Mark Smith, Jordan Penkower, Sarit Shalev-Eyni, Katrin Kogman-Appel, Alan Mintz, Malachi Beit-Arié, Sharon Lieberman Mintz, and Luis Girón-Negrón, and I wish to acknowledge their assistance and generosity. Last of all, I want to express my gratitude to Raymond Scheindlin, my ideal *magiah*, for reading the entire manuscript at a late stage in its composition and correcting numerous inaccuracies, in addition to offering the wisdom of his massive erudition spanning the entirety of Jewish history. I could not have found a better, keener reader.

In the course of researching this book, the staff of numerous libraries and their special collections also offered me invaluable assistance, specifically César Merchán-Hamman and Rahel Fronda of the Bodleian Library of Oxford University; Ilana Tahan of the British Library; Ben Outhwaite of the Genizah Collection at Cambridge University; Sharon Lieberman Mintz of the Jewish Theological Seminary and Sotheby's (on behalf of the Valmadonna Trust); the Bibliothèque Nationale, and the National Library of Israel. Much of the work for this book was done at the Library of the Herbert Katz Center for Advanced Judaic Studies at the University of Pennsylvania, and I especially wish to thank Seth Jerchower, Bruce Nielsen, and Josef Gulka for their always ready assistance and good humor. Peter Stallybrass and the participants in the Workshop on the History of the Material Text at Penn were a constant source of inspiration for the entire time I wrote this book, and several of the sections in this book originated as seminars I gave at the workshop; as I hope to explain elsewhere, the workshop was the real genesis of this book.

I also want to express my gratitude for their invaluable help in acquiring images to Professor Mauro Perani of the University of Bologna and Professor Justine Landau of Harvard. Harvard Hillel was generous in allowing me to use their Sefer Torah. David and Jemima Jeselsohn were extremely gracious in supplying me with images from their extraordinary collection of books. Most of all, I want to thank Bill Gross, my good friend, personal rabbi, and mentor-in-all-things-Judaica, for his generosity in permitting me to use the various Torah Scroll objects from the Gross Family Collection that I discuss in chapter 1, and for arranging for them to be photographed. Scott Walker of the Harvard

Map Collection produced the two maps in the book with alacrity, skill, and imagination. Hanna Kipnis King was extremely helpful in assisting me in gathering all the images and permissions.

The University of Washington Press and its staff have a patience longer than God's. I wish to thank Larin R. McLaughlin, Beth Fuget, Whitney E. Johnson, and Margaret Sullivan for their support and good humor throughout the very long period of this book's gestation. Elizabeth Berg's rigorous copyediting gave consistency to a manuscript and author very much lacking in it. And last of all, Maria Metzler proofread the text with a vigilant eye and created the multiple indices that readers will appreciate as they search for the pages in this book that truly interest them.

This book is dedicated to my family, whose support, patience, and encouragement has kept me going through all years I have worked on this book—to my dear wife, Kathryn Hellerstein, my love, my partner in writing and scholarship, and my closest reader, in all senses; to our son Jonah, whose visual gifts first inspired me to look at books, not just read them; and to my daughter and my son-in-law, Rebecca and Jesse Wenger, and to their future together, because they will be, we hope, the first in our family to pass the Jewish Bible on to the next generation.

THE JEWISH BIBLE

INTRODUCTION

An oft-quoted rabbinic text tells us, "Yeish shiv'im panim la-torah" (The Torah has seventy faces).[1] In context, this statement refers to the Bible's polysemy, its capacity to hold multiple meanings and sustain innumerable interpretations. But the Torah, the Hebrew Bible, also possesses multiple faces in a more literal sense—that is, actual faces, the changing appearances it has assumed with varying material features, the numerous physical forms and shapes that "the Jewish Bible" has taken through the centuries, from the distant reaches of the ancient Near Eastern past down to the present day. The term *Jewish Bible*—which is my own coinage—refers to the Bibles that Jews have literally held in their hands; it includes the Hebrew Bible as well as translations made by Jews into the various vernaculars they have spoken in the course of their diasporic history. This book is devoted to tracing the history of the material shapes of the Bibles that Jews have held in their hands, to studying the impact the Bible's physical features have had on its reception in the many historical and cultural contexts of Jewish history, and to understanding what the Bible's materiality can tell us about the Bible for Jews as an artifact in its own right, not just as the conveyor of a text.

In the course of pursuing these questions, this book will inevitably touch upon other topics more conventionally associated with biblical scholarship: the Bible's ancient Near Eastern background, the formation of the biblical text in its early and late phases, biblical scribal culture and the process of canonization, the history of scriptural interpretation, and the place of the Bible among the other genres of Jewish literature. I have, however, sought to keep this book's focus as much as possible on the Bible's materiality. To the best of my knowledge, this volume is the first scholarly attempt to trace the history of the physical shape of the Bible through its entire history, even in its broad outlines, and I hope my study will inspire more research on this neglected topic.

The approach to the Bible taken in this book derives from a field of scholarship that has developed over the last half century under the title of "the history of the book." To be sure, this field is not truly new; scholars have been studying the material history of texts in a distinctively modern, critical fashion at least since the nineteenth century and the beginning of analytic bibliography. But the appearance in France in 1976 of Lucien Febvre and Henri-Jean Martin's *L'apparition du livre* (Paris, 1976) introduced a new approach to book *culture*. This approach used the study of the book, initially in its printed form, as a window into understanding the book as both an agent and mirror of historical change in the early and later modern periods. In relatively short order, the new book history turned its attention from print back to manuscript, and then migrated from historical scholarship to other disciplines, like the sociology of knowledge and literary studies, which investigated the complex relationship of text and inscription.[2]

Literary approaches to the study of the book take their impetus from the obvious but profound insight that we do not read "texts." What we read are texts that have been inscribed upon some type of writing material in a particular fashion. Whether it is on a clay tablet, or in a parchment scroll, or inside the covers of a printed book, or on the screen of that more contemporary kind of digital tablet; whether the text is handwritten or printed or electronic; whether it is illustrated with pictures, or decorated with designs, or accompanied by commentaries on the page, or presented in its naked solitary splendor, the concrete specificities of a text's material transmission profoundly affect and shape the way we understand its words. By "understand," I mean not just interpret the text and its meaning but also comprehend the place it inhabits in the world—its larger cultural, social, literary, and religious significance.

This study seeks to apply these insights to the history of a single text, the Hebrew Bible. No text in Western culture has been read and studied more closely and intensely, but until very recently its readers and students have been strangely oblivious to the book's materiality, its changing physical features, not to mention the impact of those features upon the ways the Bible has been interpreted and understood in Western culture. I hope that my study will fill part of that lacuna by tracing the Hebrew Bible's material shapes as they have changed over the last two millennia, from scroll to codex (*codex* being the term scholars use to describe what is usually called a book), from manuscript to printed book, and from print to digital text.

In addition to being influenced by the new history of the book, this study also reflects specialized developments that have taken place over the past half century in scholarship specifically about the Jewish book, and particularly the pioneering, Columbus-like work of Malachi Beit-Arié and Colette Sirat on Jewish scribal culture, and the massive charting of Jewish manuscript production that has been accomplished through the Sfardata project.[3] Sfardata is a monumental data bank of signed, dated, and localized Hebrew manuscripts produced before the year 1550 that records every codicological and paleographic fact that can be extracted from a manuscript. Although Sfardata deals exclusively with scribal culture and manuscripts, its lessons can easily be extended to the printed book. (When I use the term *book* henceforth, I refer to both scrolls and codices.)

Those lessons can be summed up in two fundamental and linked axioms of Jewish book culture that heretofore were unverifiable even if scholars grasped them in an impressionistic way. First, Sfardata has shown that Jewish book culture invariably reflects the larger (gentile) host culture in which the manuscript was produced. And second, precisely on account of these shared features, it is also possible to isolate the singular if not unique features of Jewish book culture: how Jewish scribes were in fact different from their gentile counterparts, and how manuscripts written in Hebrew script differ from non-Hebraic ones.

These axioms have two consequences. First, the tendency of the Jewish book to mirror the books of its gentile host culture has the effect of making the Jewish book into a kind of microcosm of the Western book in all its geocultural and historical varieties. Due to their worldwide dispersal, and because Jews have produced books in nearly every place they have lived, the Jewish book *in toto* reflects the entire world of the book in Western culture over the last thousand years. At the same time, the singular features of the Jewish book determine the *Jewishness* of the Jewish book, particularly in terms of its materiality. In this sense, *Jewishness* turns out to be an inscribed feature of that materiality, not an inherent quality of the texts in those books. And because that materiality changes from one geocultural center to the next, and from one historical period to another, it now becomes possible to write a history of the Jewish *book* (as opposed to the history of Jewish texts). This new history brings together the study of the text with the history of its reading and reception as shaped by the book's material form. It uses the intersection between textuality and materiality—the two sides of any book—as a window into the book's meaning in Jewish culture. And most important of all, it views the book as a whole artifact. It makes sense of all its elements—material and textual—and reads the book simultaneously as a textual constellation and as a material artifact so as to appreciate the value, the significance, that these books have possessed for the Jews who produced, owned, and held them in their hands.

In the case of the Hebrew Bible, that value is connected to, but distinct from, the Bible's function as the conveyor of the divine word. As we will see, the Jewish Bible's meaning as a book, as an artifact, has changed dramatically for Jews as they have lived in varying geographical and cultural contexts through the course of history. The history of the Jewish Bible as we will tell it is the story of those changing meanings.

Every book has a history, and this book is no different. It began as part of another project, which was supposed to be another book. In 1998, I was privileged to be invited to deliver the Sam and Althea Stroum Lectures at the University of Washington in Seattle. The series consisted of three lectures. Those I gave dealt with the material histories of the Babylonian Talmud, the prayer book (siddur and mahzor), and the Passover Haggadah. When, however, I began to revise those lectures for publication as a volume I had tentatively entitled *The Jewish Library*, I immediately realized that a book with that title had to include a chapter on the Hebrew Bible. In 1999–2000, I completed the two chapters on the siddur and the Haggadah. At that point, I decided that before I tackled the Talmud, it would be wiser for me to draft the Bible chapter, which I then began to do the following year.

The original plan for the book was to write four chapters, one per book (that is, one chapter each for the Bible, the Talmud, the prayer book, and the Haggadah) with each chapter totaling approximately one hundred typed pages (including notes). The chapters were not meant to be exhaustive treatments of their subjects but more like extended essays that would recount the material history of each book in its completeness—that is, from its beginnings in the ancient world until the present time—by focusing on watershed moments when the material shape of the book underwent dramatic changes that had a significant impact on the way Jews understood the book. The book was not intended as a work of original research; rather, my intention was to synthesize existing scholarship on both the bibliographic and textual sides of each book's history and to show how they could illuminate each other. The scholarly contribution of the study, I hoped, would lie in showing that the intersection of materiality and textuality mattered.

This plan worked well enough for the siddur and the Haggadah. But almost as soon as I began to work on the Bible chapter, I encountered challenges. According to the outline I had drawn up, I could afford to write ten to fifteen pages on the history of the Torah scroll. Yet when I completed a draft of the section that I felt was minimally acceptable, it ran to over eighty pages. The Bible as a codex was even more difficult. The problem was not only that the Bible's history was more complicated than that of any other Jewish book. If one asked a basic question—for example, "What did a Bible that a medieval Jew held in his or her hands look like?"—there was no place to find an answer. Somewhat paradoxically, I discovered, scholars had devoted less attention and work to the bibliographic and material sides of the Bible than they had to other Jewish books. As a result, I found myself forced to do primary scholarship in a way I had never intended. After some five years of research, I ended up writing a series of articles that provided the evidence for a number of fundamental claims I wished to advance in my treatment of the Bible. These three articles totaled more than a hundred and eighty pages, a virtual book in themselves, and even so, they failed to cover many significant moments in the Jewish Bible's history; in fact, they covered the Bible's history only up to the sixteenth century.

Such were the difficulties that led me to devote this study solely to the Jewish Bible. The chapters on the three other books, the Talmud, the prayer book, and the Haggadah, will appear in a complementary volume that I hope to complete in the future under the title *The Jewish Library*.

The present volume consists of four chapters, which follow the history of the Bible chronologically. The first chapter treats the Sefer Torah (the Torah scroll), the earliest material form of the Hebrew Bible; the second, the Hebrew Bible as a codex in manuscript form from its earliest appearance in the early tenth century CE through the sixteenth; the third, its history in the early age of print, from the end of the fifteenth century through the middle of the sixteenth; and the final chapter, the history of the Bible since the sixteenth century, which is essentially the story of the Hebrew Bible as a cultural book. This chapter includes a short history of Jewish translations of the Hebrew Bible and the story of the modern rediscovery of the ancient and early medieval sources.

While each chapter covers a separate period in the history of the Jewish Bible, each also recounts a somewhat different story about the Bible's meaning in the Jewish historical experience. The history of the Torah scroll is a tale of how the scroll went from being a conveyor of texts intended to be read and studied—a "book" in our parlance—to something very different, a holy artifact whose meaning lay in its role within the liturgy as a sanctified object whose significance went far beyond its role as a conveyor of divinely authored texts. In effect, this is the story of how Judaism, in its earliest phases in the ancient and early medieval periods, transformed a mundane object found nearly everywhere in the ancient world into a ritual artifact with a uniquely Jewish meaning and an entirely new religious identity.

The story of the Bible as a codex in the age of manuscript (essentially, the Middle Ages) and early print (the early modern period) explores the many ways the Jewish book nearly always reflects and transforms the books of the larger host cultures in which it is produced. In the case of the Bible, however, absorption and transformation have taken on an especially competitive, polemical edge, as the material artifact became the paradigmatic medium in Jewish culture for defining its difference from neighboring cultures. The material form of the codex came to the Jews from *without*, from the larger Islamic world within which the first Jewish codices, nearly all Bibles, came to be written. As we will see, these early Jewish Bibles distinctly mirrored Islamic books, the Qur'an in particular, partly out of cultural competition. Yet once the center of gravity for the Jewish world moved from Islamic to Christian territory, the calculus of influence and appropriation shifted dramatically. While Jewish-Christian rivalry over "ownership" of the Bible, particularly in the realm of biblical interpretation and exegesis, goes back to late antiquity, it was only in medieval Christian Europe that the material form of the Bible became a primary arena in which the contest over ownership was waged. As each religious community claimed to be the true Israel, the sole authentic heir of the biblical tradition, both used the book's material form to define the Bible as either Jewish or Christian. The story of the Hebrew Bible as a codex is the narrative of how Jews came to mark the Bible's *Jewishness* as a material object so as to differentiate it from the Bible(s) of the Christians. In doing this, the Jews simultaneously appropriated and Judaized the material features of the Christian book, or pointedly rejected them to achieve the same end. As we will see, these efforts to give a material shape to the Bible's Jewishness took different forms in the various geocultural centers where medieval and early modern Jewry lived—Sepharad, Ashkenaz, Italy, and Yemen—but in all of them, the Bible became the material text in the canon of classical Jewish literature through which Jews defined their identity as a religious tradition and community vis-à-vis rival traditions and communities.

In the book's final chapter, we will see how these efforts at defining the Bible's Jewishness continued into the modern period as the Bible became increasingly a text whose significance for many readers was cultural as much as religious, and as the Jewish Bible itself changed from a text in Hebrew (or in Hebrew letters) to a book largely known to its Jewish readers as a text translated into the many vernacular languages Jews spoke in their various diasporic homes. In becoming a text in translation, the Jewish Bible again mirrored the history of the Christian Bible since the Reformation but with a difference. That difference became more prominent with the latest development in the history of the Jewish Bible, the rediscovery in the last century of the ancient and earliest texts of the Hebrew Bible in the great treasure hoards of Qumran and the Judean Hills and the recovery of the earliest codices of the Hebrew Bible. As we shall see, these discoveries effectively created a history for the Jewish Bible, allowing us to see the different communal functions and material shapes that the Bible has taken in various moments of the Jewish historical experience. This is the history that this book seeks to trace.

CHAPTER ONE

THE TORAH SCROLL

The image on the facing page (fig. 1.1) displays what is today the oldest known complete Sefer Torah (Torah scroll), written sometime between 1155 and 1255 CE.[1] We do not know where exactly the scroll was originally written. Certain peculiar features of its orthography and atypical scribal practices point to a possible Near Eastern, perhaps Babylonian, place of origin. Our earliest trustworthy testimony about the scroll places it in Bologna, a significant Jewish community that even in the Middle Ages prided itself on its prestigious history by naming itself with the punning epithet *Bo-lan-yah*, "In it resided the Lord." How it might have come from Babylonia to Bologna is unknown, but in the early fourteenth century, again for unknown reasons, Bologna's Jewish community gave the Sefer Torah to the Dominican magister and scholar, Aimerico Giliani of Piacenza, as a gift. Even then, the scroll already had a legendary reputation. According to one source, it had been given to Charlemagne by the Byzantine emperor Constantine II sometime between 802 and 815. According to another report, the scroll

1.1 (Opposite) Torah scroll, Babylonia (?), ca. 1155–1255 (Exod. 15–16). Bologna, Biblioteca Universitaria di Bologna, Rotulo 2. Courtesy of the Biblioteca Universitaria di Bologna and Professor Mauro Perani.

had been written by Ezra the Scribe after the return of the Israelite exiles from Babylonia in 530 BCE.

Whatever its precise origins, the Sefer Torah remained for several centuries in the library of Saint Dominic's Convent in Bologna, where it was regularly seen by numerous visitors and scholars, including several figures who will reappear in the course of this book, important persons in the history of the Jewish Bible, like Benito Arias Montano (1527–1598), the editor of the Antwerp Polyglot, and Benjamin Kennicott (1718–1783), the great English Bible scholar and collector. By this time, the fame of the Torah scroll was well established. Given its legendary aura, it is not surprising that in 1796, after invading Italy, Napoleon, who prided himself on collecting valuables, confiscated and carted the scroll off to Paris with other works of art and rare books. Only in 1815, after Napoleon's fall from power, did the Sefer Torah return to Bologna, where it was housed in the Papal Library, today the University Library. Alas, in the course of its peregrinations, the scroll had become confused with another, far newer Torah scroll, and as a result, it was subsequently miscataloged as a seventeenth-century scroll. Only in 2013, while cataloging Hebrew manuscripts in the Bologna University Library, did Mauro Perani, professor of Hebrew and a distinguished codicologist, rediscover the Sefer Torah and recognize that it was the long-lost "Ezra scroll."

Such tales of legendary origins, wanderings, sometimes near destruction and miraculous salvation, or sheer survival and preservation, can be told about many Jewish books. Torah scrolls, however, are usually different. Because these scrolls cannot contain any extratextual notes or features, it is very difficult to date or localize Torah scrolls with certainty or to trace their histories. We almost never know the identities of the scribes who wrote them. Furthermore, very few Torah scrolls survive from any of the communities in which Jews lived in the Middle Ages, and the Bologna scroll is to date the earliest complete known example.[2]

Yet despite its age, the Bologna scroll is materially almost identical—albeit with some small but fascinating differences—to Torah scrolls written today, like the one pictured in fig. 1.2, a scroll I borrowed from the Hillel student organization at Harvard University and that was written about twenty years ago. Both the Bologna and the Harvard Hillel scrolls were written more or less in accordance with the same regulations determined by halacha, rabbinic law, and according to fixed requirements that have been in force for the last thousand years. In their respective illustrations, both scrolls are opened to the same sheet containing Exodus 15, the Song of the Sea, which is written in identical special stichography, or line layout, called *ariaḥ ʿal gabei leveinah* (a small brick atop a full brick). On most other sheets, the text is laid out in three columns of forty-eight lines with different types of spacing to separate one section from the next. Both scrolls are large, though the Bologna Torah is significantly larger than the Hillel scroll; it is monumental, 25 inches (64 centimeters) tall and more than 118 feet long (36 meters), written on fifty-eight sheets of leather

1.2 Torah scroll, United States, twentieth century (Exod. 15). Courtesy of Harvard Hillel.

that are now so soft they could be linen. In both scrolls, however, the sheets were dry-ruled before being inscribed, and in a practice almost unique to Jewish scribal culture, the letters in both hang from the lines rather than resting upon them. Only the consonants of the Hebrew text are written out in the text. According to rabbinic law, a Sefer Torah cannot contain vowels, cantillation, accentuation marks, or any form of punctuation.

As the identical features of the two scrolls demonstrate, scribes writing a Sefer Torah today maintain pretty much all the same regulations and practices that were observed by the unknown scribe who wrote the Bologna Torah scroll nearly a millennium ago. And most important, both scrolls are essentially ritual artifacts written to be chanted from in the synagogue as part of the formal Jewish liturgy. Neither one is truly a "book" in the conventional sense, a platform upon which to read or study a verbal text.

The Sefer Torah was not always a ritual artifact. When it first came into existence, it *was* a book—a writing platform—like other books, that is, a medium (in the form of a scroll) for conveying a text meant to be read and studied. The story of the Sefer Torah is the tale of how a book became a holy object whose holiness resides not only in the words of its text but as much in its material shape, its physical features. In this respect, the Sefer Torah differs even from other types of Jewish Bibles. As we will see in the course of this study, the vast majority of Bibles that Jews have used for the last thousand years are inscribed in the material form of the codex. A codex is a collection of sheets of some type of writing material (papyrus, parchment, paper) that is folded in the middle and sewn together, then bound with a protective cover—that is to say, more or less what we today call a *book*. In the next chapter, we will trace the history of the Jewish Bible in the form of the codex. In this chapter, our subject will be the scroll, the Sefer Torah.

We can begin to tell the story of the Sefer Torah with its name. In modern Hebrew, the word *sefer* means "book" in the contemporary sense of the term. In Biblical Hebrew, however, *sefer* refers to any written communication, ranging from a letter to a scroll.[3] As for *torah*, its root meaning is "teaching" or "instruction." The word appears frequently in the Pentateuch in reference to specific teachings and instructions, for instance, "This is the *torah* of the burnt offering" (Lev. 6:2) or "the *torah* of the nazirite" (Num. 6:13).[4] The book of Deuteronomy (29:20; 30:10; 31:26) refers to itself as "the book of this *torah*," always in the singular, suggesting that its author recognized it as a single entity, but the application of the name Torah to the Pentateuch as a whole first appears in two of the last books to become part of the Bible, Ezra (3:2; 7:6,10; 10:3) and Nehemiah (8:1–2), which were composed during the Persian period, after the return from the Babylonian exile, in the fourth century BCE.

In rabbinic literature (whose earliest documents began to be edited in the third century CE), the most common term for the Bible is *miqra*, "reading" or "what is read aloud"—a reference to the chanting of the Bible in the synagogue liturgy—but other terms are also used, including *Ha-katuv*, "scripture" (literally "what is written") and *Kitvei Qodesh* (sacred scripture or writings). In medieval Hebrew literature, the biblical corpus as a whole is often referred to as "the twenty-four" (*kaf-daled*), after the number of books in the complete Hebrew Bible.[5] Subsequently it also became known as TaNaKh, an acronym for its three main sections, *Torah* (Pentateuch), *Nevi'im* (Prophets), and *Ketuvim* (Hagiographa). Needless to say, *Old Testament* is a Christian name for the Hebrew Bible that defines its character as "old" by the fiat of the "new" Testament. The word *Bible*, from the Greek *biblia*, or "books," is also a name with no Jewish source, but it does capture the sense of the Bible as a library, a collection of originally disparate works with discrete independent histories that only later were grasped as a single entity.[6] In most biblical scholarship, the story of that process—the story of the composition of the Bible—is treated as a history of its text. What is less often recounted, however, is its material dimension—the history of the Bible as a scroll.[7]

The Early History of the Scroll

The Bible never narrates its own material history, but scholars have been able to reconstruct a rough sketch from comparative historical evidence and scattered clues that can be gleaned from the biblical text.[8] It is virtually certain that originally many of the traditions that eventually came to be written down in the Bible—songs, poems, sayings, laws—circulated orally in Israelite culture. The Bible itself reports much of its contents as having begun as speech, a large part of it divine, but on the few occasions that it refers to the inscription of the orally delivered texts, it does not tell us much. The two sets of the Ten Commandments were, of course, incised on stone tablets (*luḥot ha-even*, Exod. 24:12; 31:18; 34:1,4), but they were written by God, not Moses.[9] In later books of the Bible there are a few other references to stone inscriptions.[10] Following the Sinaitic revelation, Exodus 24:4 simply states, "Moses then wrote down all the commands of the Lord [*divrei-adonai*]," a reference to the *sefer ha-brit*, or "record of the covenant," which, three verses later (24:7), Moses reads to the children of Israel.[11] But no mention is made of what that record was written on. Deuteronomy 27:3 and Joshua 8:32 both refer to plastered stones on which the Teaching (*torah*) is to be inscribed; it is unclear whether the Teaching refers to the entire Pentateuch (*kol-divrei ha-torah ha-zot*, "all the words of this instruction," in Deut. 27:8) or to the book of Deuteronomy alone (*mishneih torat moshe*, "the repetition of the instruction of Moses," in Josh. 8:32).[12] A few verses in other books of the Bible refer to still other writing platforms, like tablets and papyrus scrolls.[13]

When the Bible (or some part of it) was first written down as a document, a scroll of some sort was the most likely medium. Later rabbinic specifications stipulate that the Torah must be written on animal skins, but some of the earliest surviving fragments containing biblical texts are written on papyrus, like the Nash Papyrus (fig. 1.3), which is inscribed in the form of a *rotulus*, a vertical scroll written in lines across its narrow width rather than in horizontally arranged columns. Some biblical narratives and references also point to the use of papyrus, a practice that fits the larger historical context of the period.[14]

From the beginning of the second millennium BCE, the land of Canaan was dominated by Egypt, and its scribal culture typically used papyrus as its preferred medium.[15] Even if it had to be imported to the land of Israel from Egypt, papyrus was far cheaper than animal

1.3
Nash papyrus, Fayyum, Egypt (?), 150–100 BCE. Courtesy of the Syndics of Cambridge University Library.

1.4
Wall painting of *capsa* with scrolls inside and writing tablets next to it, Villa dei Papiri, Herculaneum, first century CE. Naples, Museo Archeologico Nazionale inv. 4675.

skins. While papyrus rolls need not be shorter than those made from skins, it is likely that the texts on most rolls were not lengthy, certainly not as long as any existing biblical book.[16] Lengthier texts would have been inscribed on several scrolls and kept together in a single pail-like case (Gr. *kopos*; Lat. *capsa*; Heb. *kufsah*). Such containers for scrolls remained in use throughout antiquity and survived in certain Jewish communities albeit in a somewhat transformed shape. Fig. 1.4, a detail from a wall mural in the Villa dei Papiri at Herculaneum, pictures a typical *capsa* as it was used by Romans. The *capsa* remained in use throughout antiquity and survives in subsequent Jewish culture as the ancestor of the *tik* (from the Greek *thēkē*, also a case or receptacle).

The wide employment of papyrus did not preclude the use of animal skins. Even in Egypt, skins were used for especially important texts, which required a more durable medium. Among biblical texts, the first work to be inscribed on parchment may have been the book of Deuteronomy (or its earliest documentary source).[17] As Menahem Haran has noted, the fact that this text refers to itself as "this *sefer* of the *torah*" (Deut. 29:20; 30:10; 31:26) or as "this *torah*" (Deut. 1:5, 4:8; 27:3) in the singular suggests that it was probably written on a single scroll. While the Deuteronomist (Deut. 31:25–26) stipulates that the scroll is to be placed beside the ark when not being read, it may also have been publicly displayed, and then it would have made sense for it to be inscribed on a more luxurious and durable material, like animal skin, which would have visibly distinguished it from more ordinary texts written on papyrus.[18] Subsequently, the Deuteronomy scroll became the model for other texts as they attained the status of scripture, which all came to be written on animal skin as a matter of course.

As Haran has shown, a number of factors coalesced in the early Second Temple period to make skins the preferred and normative medium for writing scriptural texts.[19] For one thing, the technology for preparing skins for writing advanced substantially, making it possible for scrolls to contain lengthier texts.[20] Further, the widespread use of parchment was encouraged by the rise of the neo-Babylonian empire (and the Persian empire that succeeded it) and the subsequent spread of the Aramaic language throughout the ancient Near East, including ancient Israel. Aramaic is another northwest Semitic language akin to Hebrew and was originally written in its own Aramaic script. As Aramaic became the region's lingua franca, the entire region was "Aramaized." The scribal practices of Aramaic-writing scribes, which included the use of parchment, came to dominate the entire region, and Hebrew scribes even adopted Aramaic scribal terminology; to give one salient example, the word *megillah*, "scroll," derives from Aramaic.[21] By the time of the return from Babylonian exile (and even before Alexander conquered the Near East), it seems quite clear that animal skins had become the dominant material used for biblical scrolls.[22] Even more significantly, the Aramaic script spread throughout the region, eventually leading the Jews, after their return, to adapt its letters for Hebrew in place of the archaic Hebrew script (known in rabbinic literature as *ktav 'ivri*), which Judaeans (the inhabitants

1.5 Samaritan Torah scroll (*Aktaba Kadisha*), land of Israel, ca. 1166 CE. Reproduced by permission of the Valmadonna Trust.

of the land of Israel) had previously used. The rabbis called Aramaic script Assyrian letters (*ktav ashuri*).[23] The ancient Hebrew script was not, however, entirely abandoned. It survived in a hand today called Paleo-Hebrew, which is a self-conscious adaptation of the archaic script that Samaritans still use as their "native" script and in which they have continuously written Torah scrolls with their version of the Pentateuch.[24] The Samaritans, an ancient ethnic group, claim to be the descendants of the Judaeans who did not go into exile in Babylonia but remained in the land of Israel. Fig. 1.5 pictures a Samaritan Torah scroll (which the Samaritans call *Aktaba Kadisha*) written in Israel around the year 1166; this scroll is one of the four earliest surviving Samaritan Torah scrolls, all of which date to the twelfth century (although the Samaritans claim that their oldest scroll, known as the Abisha scroll, was written by the great-grandson of Aaron thirteen years after the Israelite conquest of biblical Canaan).[25] Paleo-Hebrew was again used in inscriptions on several Bar Kokhba coins from the second century, when the script evidently took on a symbolic nationalist charge, a reminder of a glorious past in which the Jews were an independent nation of their own.[26]

The Torah Scroll in the Second Temple Period

The evidence we have considered for the early history of biblical scrolls mainly derives from comparisons drawn with neighboring scribal cultures and scattered references to scribal practice in the Hebrew Bible. For the later Second Temple period and the centuries following the destruction of the Temple in 70 CE, several texts provide intriguing details about the production of scrolls, but the most valuable sources are *actual* scrolls, particularly those found in the caves near the Dead Sea.

Even literary documentation is valuable for offering background to the scrolls. The Hellenistic composition the Letter of Aristeas (second century BCE) relates how a delegation of Jews from Palestine arrived in Alexandria before the Ptolemaic king Demetrius bearing "fine skins on which the Law had been written in letters of gold in Jewish characters; the parchment had been excellently worked, and the joining together of the letters was imperceptible."[27] If nothing else, this brief description testifies to the importance Jews attached to the beauty of the object—and how much money some Jews were willing to spend to produce such scrolls; it is not known whether their motivation was religious or ostentatious.[28] In a different vein, the first-century historian Josephus avidly defends the accuracy of the Hebrew Bible in comparison to Greek and Roman historical texts, thereby implying the existence of a fairly standardized text. Josephus also refers several times to scrolls of the Law kept in the Temple, and relates how, after the Temple's destruction, Titus brought back to Rome a copy of the Jewish Law as a trophy.[29] This tradition reappears in later sources; one early medieval Jewish source discusses the textual variants found in a particular scroll brought to Rome from Jerusalem and deposited in the synagogue of Severus (on account of which the scroll came to be known as the Severus scroll).[30] Rabbinic texts, albeit from a later period, similarly mention model scrolls of the Law that were kept in the Temple. According to one source, there was one such scroll; according to another, three, and each one differed from the other two on a small number of particular points.[31]

These few literary references tell us something about the larger culture in the Second Temple period, but the surviving scrolls or (for the most part) fragments of scrolls provide infinitely more information. Most of this material derives either from the large corpus known as the Dead Sea Scrolls, which were found in caves near Qumran on the shores of the Dead Sea, or from scrolls found at other sites in the Judaean desert, like Masada, Wadi Murubba'at, and Naḥal Ḥever. The fragments found at Qumran and Masada all date from the period before 73 CE, and some may have been written as early as the third century BCE. Those from Wadi Murubba'at and Naḥal Ḥever come from a period about a hundred years later, around 135 CE, the culmination of the Bar Kokhba rebellion and a historical moment that appears to have signaled the emergence of the rabbinic class as a significant force in Roman Palestine.

1.6 4QDeut.[n], sheet 2 (Deuteronomy 5:1–6:1), Qumran, first century CE (?). Courtesy of the Leon Levy Dead Sea Scrolls Digital Library. IAA, Photograph by Shai Halevi.

Since their discovery less than a century ago, the testimony of the scrolls has famously revolutionized our understanding of the early textual history of the Bible. The Qumran and Masada scrolls, which represent every book in the Bible except for the two late books, Nehemiah and Esther, still display a significant degree of textual instability and show that as late as the first century CE, the biblical text remained in flux.[32] In contrast, the Wadi Murubba'at and Naḥal Ḥever fragments show much less variation, with nearly all of them pointing to the stable text that would eventually be known as the Masoretic text.[33]

In the period separating these two groups of fragments, then, the biblical text appears to have taken decisive steps toward stabilization. Only recently have scholars begun to explore the material dimensions of these scrolls to understand the key role that scribal culture must have played in the process of stabilization.[34] To date, most scholarship has focused on the Qumran fragments with the Judaean desert material still awaiting comprehensive study. Still, the research on the Qumran scrolls can lay the basis for reconstructing the historical background against which the Sefer Torah—as defined by the rabbis between the third and seventh centuries CE—emerged as a religious artifact.

The picture provided by the Dead Sea Scrolls is as complicated as it is fascinating. For one thing, it reveals a writing culture already sophisticated in the variety of its scribal practices and conventions. As Emanuel Tov has shown, the Qumran scrolls attest to the existence of multiple distinct and identifiable scribal schools. Each school followed its own conventions; some conventions were nearly universal in the ancient Mediterranean world, while others were more localized and specific to individual schools.[35] At the same time, scribes appear to have been able to utilize multiple formats and styles for writing scrolls, ranging from the relatively plain and simple to the deluxe. Most important, the scribal practices reflected in the Qumran and Judaean desert texts did *not* significantly differ, whether the texts being copied were biblical or nonbiblical. While the Bible clearly had a special, sacred status for the members of the Qumran community, its material shape did not yet reflect its uniqueness.

In most respects, the scribal culture at Qumran mirrored scribal practices found throughout the Mediterranean basin. An individual scroll generally contained a single literary work (even when that work was short and could easily have been combined with another short work in one scroll).[36] So, too, biblical scrolls typically contained a single book of the Bible. The five books of the Pentateuch were inscribed in five separate scrolls, and to that extent, each "book" still possessed an identity as its own document even if the five together were also recognized to be the Pentateuch.[37] In later rabbinic tradition, these single-book scrolls from the Pentateuch came to be known as *ḥomesh* (pl. *ḥomashim*), literally, "a fifth."[38] Fig. 1.6 pictures a fragment of one such scroll, a copy of Deuteronomy found at Qumran. These one-book scrolls were of manageable size, easy to study and to transport. As late as the third century, people seem to have traveled with Torah scrolls of this size; a Mishnaic narrative (M. Yevamot 16:7) relates how an innkeeper brought forth a certain Levite's Sefer Torah with his staff and bag as proof that he had died while his companions were away. While the dimensions of the biblical scrolls found at Qumran vary from the very small (70 mm × 2.4 m/2.7 in. × 94.5 in.) to the very large (465 mm × 29 m/18.3 in. × 1142 in.), most of the scrolls are of medium size (approximately 260 mm × 6.5 m/10.2 in. × 256 in.). These are the typical dimensions of scrolls in the Greco-Roman world. Anyone could easily hold a scroll of this size in their hands.[39]

There is almost no evidence for the existence of single scrolls containing the entirety of the Pentateuch.[40] Furthermore, a few biblical books were originally too large to be inscribed in a single scroll—the sequence of Chronicles-Ezra-Nehemiah, for example—and were therefore divided and written on multiple scrolls, and hence eventually became separate books in name as well.[41] Other Qumran biblical scrolls appear to have been produced as deluxe editions notable for their especially wide top and bottom margins, the few errors in them, and the proximity of their texts to what later became the accepted Masoretic text of the Bible. Some of these scrolls may have been intended as models, "corrected copies."[42] In fig. 1.7, showing an especially beautiful manuscript of Psalms found at Masada, one can see the large, carefully written characters, including the superscription *Mizmor l-Asaf* (A Hymn of Asaph) at the top of the Psalms with the text carefully laid out in multiple columns, and the large margins around the sheet; the size of the margins in this fragment is evident if one compares these margins to those in the Deuteronomy fragment in fig. 1.6, a much smaller and less deluxe scroll.[43] The Qumran fragments also contain scrolls that were written for more popular use. These texts were written to facilitate reading, not to preserve a specific textual tradition; as a result, these fragments often contain vowel letters (*matres lectionis*) that reflect nonstandard morphology.[44]

As this material evidence from Qumran indicates, the Bible, even if it was already believed to be a unified, divinely revealed corpus in its entirety, was treated in material practice as a library of separate works. The use of separate scrolls for individual biblical

1.7 MasPs.a (Psalm 82), Masada, first century CE. Courtesy of the Israel Exploration Society.

books, including those of the Pentateuch, remained in practice through the early rabbinic period. Only after completion of the Mishnah in the third century did the single monumental scroll containing the entire Pentateuch become prevalent, and eventually prescribed, partly due to technological advances that made it possible to produce thinner sheets of parchment.[45] Passages in the Babylonian Talmud (Bava Batra 13b–14a) record disagreements between rabbis as to whether it is permissible to "join" separate books (presumably in the Prophets and Writings) into a single scroll. A single anecdote (13b), attributed to Rabbi Judah the Prince (early third century), refers to a single scroll containing the Torah, the Prophets, and the Writings in their entirety, which was brought before the rabbis, who declared it to be kosher. Exactly how much historical weight can be given to these passages is debatable but, minimally, they suggest that well into the period of the Babylonian Talmud in the fourth and fifth centuries rabbinic authorities had to deal with a variety of divergent scribal practices. Whether or not "pandect" scrolls containing the entire Hebrew Bible actually existed—if they did, they would have been enormous—the lists in the Talmud (B. Bava Batra 14b) of sequences of books in the Prophets and Writings make sense only if the separate books in those large divisions of the Bible were being copied into single scrolls containing all the Prophets or all the Writings.[46]

A second dimension of ancient Jewish scribal practice richly documented by the Qumran fragments is the use of language and script. The languages represented in the biblical fragments are Hebrew, Aramaic, and Greek. While most of the Hebrew texts are in so-called Assyrian letters—Hebrew script based on Aramaic script—a number of biblical fragments are written in Paleo-Hebrew, which is descended from the ancient Hebrew script of the seventh and sixth centuries BCE that Israelites used before they adopted the Aramaic script in the fourth century BCE. Scholars call many of these texts proto-Samaritan, largely because the biblical text represented in these fragments often anticipates that of the later Samaritan Pentateuch.[47]

The various scripts of these fragments, not to mention their orthographic and textual peculiarities, help us appreciate the rabbis' later insistence that a Torah scroll be written exclusively in Assyrian letters. This stricture may have been intended precisely to disqualify Samaritan scrolls, and thus to consolidate the schism between the two neighboring religious communities, which both claimed to be the "true Israel."[48] Indeed, this instance may be one of the earliest examples of how the material dimension of the Bible has been deployed as a mark of self-identification in contests between competing parties (whether ethnic or religious) over "ownership" of the Bible.[49] As we will see in the next chapter, this question—"Who owns the Bible?"—becomes in the medieval and early modern periods the defining problematic in the history of the Jewish Bible as a material object. The issue of Paleo-Hebrew or Assyrian script for the Bible is an early moment in that competition.

A third area illuminated by the fragments from Qumran concerns writing material. Virtually all the biblical texts in Hebrew found at Qumran are on leather, with only a very small number on papyrus.[50] We know little about the techniques used to produce leather during this period, but preliminary investigations have determined that the leather was generally of a thick type with "moderately tanned surfaces to facilitate writing."[51] According to the scholar Mordechai Glatzer, this type of leather approximates what the rabbis later called *gvil*, namely, unsplit parchment that is processed on the outer, hair side of the skin; its natural strength makes it more suitable for writing.[52] The use of unsplit leather at Qumran for writing Torah scrolls anticipates later rabbinic practice.

In terms of specific writing practices, the Qumran scrolls display a marked sophistication, using many of the techniques that characterize subsequent Sifrei Torah written

Tetragrammaton in Paleo-Hebrew

1.8 1QpHab (Pesher Habakkuk), Qumran, first century BCE. Photo © The Israel Museum by David Harris.

according to rabbinic law.[53] The scrolls are nearly all ruled, with smaller margins on top than on the bottom, and are written in black ink in square "Assyrian" letters. A number of fragments at Qumran display special devices for marking the tetragrammaton (some of which were subsequently prohibited by the rabbis). In some scrolls, the name of God is inscribed in Paleo-Hebrew letters to set the name off from the rest of the text, which is written in Assyrian letters. Fig. 1.8 is a sheet from the famous Pesher Habakkuk scroll, a commentary on the book that understands the text as a prophecy directly about the Qumran community. In the third and fourth columns (from the right), the tetragrammaton is written in Paleo-Hebrew several times—in the third column, on the seventh line from the top and on the second line from the bottom; in the fourth column, on the next to last line of the middle paragraph.[54] In other fragments, the tetragrammaton is designated by a dicolon (with two points) or *tetrapuncta*, four dots. Dots, either below or above a word or phrase, were also used as cancellation marks. In fig. 1.9 (1QIsa^{a}1), a sheet from the single nearly complete scroll found at Qumran, the famous Isaiah scroll (here containing Isa. 40:2–28), on the eighth line, the scribe mistakenly omitted the middle section of Isaiah 40:7, which contains the divine name, and later wrote the missing section above the line using the *tetrapuncta* for the name; in addition, he wrote three cancellation dots beneath the word *devar* directly below the interpolated section to eliminate a word he had mistakenly written.[55] Whether the scribe used dots or the Paleo-Hebrew script for the divine name, the intention appears to have been to render the names *visibly* sacred to alert readers not to pronounce the divine name in vain or to erase it by accident.[56]

1.9 1QIsa^{a}1 (Isaiah 40:2–28), Qumran, ca. 125 BCE. Photo © The Israel Museum, Jerusalem, by Ardon Bar-Hama.

The layout of the biblical text at Qumran also anticipates its presentation in later rabbinic Torah scrolls. Words are separated by spaces (in contrast to many other ancient inscriptions, such as those in Greek or Latin, which display spaceless "continuous writing" [*scriptio/scriptura continua*]).[57] Different types of spacing also indicated breaks and divisions in the text. *Parashiyyot*—"chapters" in the loose sense of the term, that is, larger sections of the Bible—were indicated and set off by line spacings known as *petuḥot* ("open sections") and *setumot* ("closed sections"). The former, the *parashah petuḥah*, indicates a passage that is "thematically distinct from the section which immediately precedes it," a fact that is marked by having the passage always begin on a new line. The preceding line either is blank or ends at least nine letters from the last word in the line. The *parashah setumah* signifies a less dramatic disjunction and is more like a paragraph break; it is marked by leaving a blank space within the line.[58] In the sheet from the Isaiah scroll (fig. 1.9), open sections begin on lines 6, 12, 25, and 28, and a closed section on line 2. These types of organizational devices, as well as the use of *paragraphoi* (paragraph signs) and blank lines to separate sections, are paralleled in other ancient scribal and literary traditions (which also use them in both sacred and nonsacred texts). Where exactly to place the divisions seems to have been a fairly subjective decision on the part of the scribe; indeed, as Tov notes, the Qumran biblical manuscripts (and later Samaritan ones) are even more sectioned and subdivided than later rabbinic Masoretic texts.[59] So, too, the various poetic passages in the Bible—Exodus 15, Deuteronomy 32, Judges 5, and the entirety of Lamentations and Psalms—are inscribed using special stichography and line formatting closely resembling the layout we saw in this chapter's first image of the Bologna Torah scroll, which was opened to Exodus 15. Again, similar techniques for line management and text organization are paralleled in other ancient scribal traditions. While the Qumran scribes writing in Assyrian script generally did not try to justify the left margin—there are exceptions—they generally did not break words at the margin, or when they had to, would repeat the entire word on the next line.[60]

On the other hand, while the Qumran scrolls use section and paragraph divisions, they do not generally have marks for *verse* division.[61] The absence of the latter is an indication of the difference between the scribal or writing tradition on the one hand, and the oral reading tradition on the other. Verse divisions were part of the oral reading tradition; section divisions were part of the scribal or writing tradition, and the two appear to have pursued essentially separate existences. As Emanuel Tov has remarked, section divisions with spaces represent one of the earliest instances of explicit biblical interpretation—the other main instance being inner-biblical exegesis—inasmuch as spacing indicates the beginnings and endings of passages. These divisions were not yet codified, they can have significant exegetical consequences, and in the scrolls, they appear to reflect the decisions of scribes, not other authorities. To be sure, verse division also has exegetical consequences, but it seems that the primary motive for verse division was not so much interpretive as functional—that is, deciding upon a length appropriate (or required) for pauses in the public chanting of the Torah and for allowing the translator to interrupt the chanting to present his Aramaic translation.[62]

The final area illuminated by the Qumran material is the matter of paratextual markings (that is, marks not part of the originally inscribed text). The scrolls preserve many traces of scribal intervention—correction marks like cancellation dots, crossed-out lines, still visible erasures, and bracket signs (*antisigma* and *sigma*), as well as other markings that highlight textual peculiarities. Most of these techniques were also used by Alexandrian Greek scribes, and it is likely that the scribes who wrote the Qumran documents (whether they were part of the community or not) absorbed these practices from the larger scribal culture of the Mediterranean world. There is no reason to believe that any of these practices (except, perhaps, the use of Paleo-Hebrew for the name of God) were invented at Qumran. Later rabbinic scribal tradition maintained a number of these paratextual markings (like the famous ten *nequdot* above certain letters) even after their original function was no longer understood. Once the markings became part of the fixed inscribed text, the rabbis had to reinterpret their significance in novel, nonscribal ways.[63]

In the Rabbinic Period

This brief survey of scribal practice at Qumran shows that the rabbis' rules and prescriptions for writing Bible scrolls were not created ex nihilo. Indeed, when viewed from the perspective of Qumran, later rabbinic prescriptions take on a rather different complexion that highlights their ideological thrust.[64] Unfortunately, virtually no Torah or other biblical scrolls or even fragments of scrolls survive from between the period after Qumran, at the turn of the Common Era, and the early Middle Ages (with the exception of the Judean Desert fragments left in caves after the failure of the Bar Kokhba rebellion in the first half of the second century).[65] As a result, nearly everything we would like to know about the production of the Torah scroll must be gleaned from the various texts of rabbinic literature, which, for the most part, were edited between the third and ninth centuries. These texts in turn pose significant challenges as historical sources. Most of them are either prescriptive or homiletical in character, and therefore do not necessarily reflect actual practice. Furthermore, like rabbinic literature generally, the texts about scribal practice are all preserved unsystematically within documentary contexts that are invariably multilayered and heavily edited, and it is not always possible to separate the later from the earlier layers. Finally, many of these texts, including the Babylonian Talmud, have not yet been critically edited by modern scholars, and the available printed editions reflect textual traditions that were sometimes emended by medieval or early modern scribes or sages to reflect their own contemporaneous practice.

Because of these challenges, I will summarize the overall treatment of biblical scrolls in the relevant sources without entering into the minutiae of textual analysis. My summary will concentrate upon the main trajectories of developing attitudes over time. The primary texts to be considered are: the Mishnah, edited in the first half of the third century in the Common Era; the Tosefta, roughly contemporary or slightly later than the Mishnah; the Palestinian Talmud, first edited at the end of the fourth century; the Babylonian Talmud, whose editing began at the conclusion of the fifth century; and Masekhet Sefer

Torah, a post-Talmudic compilation whose earliest strata may go back to the third century CE—that is, the period contemporaneous with the Mishnah—but which was edited at an unknown time considerably later.[66]

We will begin with the Mishnah, the foundational document of early rabbinic Judaism, which records a number of laws concerning the writing of a proper (*kasher*) scroll and the way it is to be chanted. Virtually all the laws in the Mishnah deal specifically with reading the Scroll of Esther on Purim, the reason being simply that Esther is the only biblical text that every Jew, according to rabbinic law, is required to hear read aloud from a scroll.[67] Amazingly, there is no equivalent obligation to hear a portion of the Torah read aloud weekly in the synagogue, even though it is strongly encouraged. As a result of the latter absence and the requirement to hear the Scroll of Esther read aloud from a proper scroll, the writing of the Esther scroll, along with the writing of tefillin and mezuzot, became for the rabbis the model for the rest of scripture.[68]

A representative example of the Mishnah's scribal prescriptions is the following passage in M. Megillah 2:1–2:

> If one reads the megillah backwards, [a person] has not fulfilled his obligation. If he reads it by heart, or if he reads it in an [Aramaic] translation [*targum*], or in any language—he has not fulfilled his obligation. But it may be read in a foreign language to those who speak a foreign language [*lo'azot*]. If one who understands only a foreign language hears it in Hebrew [literally, *ashurit*, in Assyrian script], he has fulfilled his obligation. If one reads it with breaks or [hears it read] while dozing, he has fulfilled his obligation. If [one read it aloud while] writing it, explaining it, or correcting it—then, if he directed his heart [to fulfill the obligation], he fulfilled [the obligation]; and if he did not [have the intention], he did not fulfill it. If [the scroll he reads from] is written with *sam*, with *sikra*, with *kumus*, or with *kankantum*, or on papyrus [*niyar*] or on unprepared skin [*diftera*], he has not fulfilled his obligation until [he reads from a scroll] written in Assyrian letters, on parchment [*'al ha-sefer*],[69] and in ink [*deyo*].

The first part of the Mishnah's prescriptions regulate the oral performance of the *megillah*—both the proper behavior and intentions of the one who chants the scroll aloud and the requirements pertaining to the person who hears the *megillah* read aloud. None of these prescriptions relates to the scribe who writes the scroll; in fact, there is no requirement in the Mishnah that the scribe even be Jewish, let alone that the scroll be written with the proper "intention" (although in later rabbinic tradition these two criteria became critical qualifications of a "kosher" Torah scroll).[70] In the Mishnah, intentionality figures only in the performance, the act of chanting the *megillah* aloud. Even the material requirements of a kosher scroll—that the text be written on parchment, in the correct type of script, and in black ink—are treated in the Mishnah mainly in regard to its public reading to an audience.

Why is the Mishnah so reticent in regard to scribal practice? Does the Mishnah's silence reflect the fact that the rabbis themselves did not yet have fixed views on the subject? Or is it because they realized that they did not have the power to regulate the practice of scribes who were not necessarily part of the rabbinic class and may have had their own traditions with their own conventions? Does the Mishnah's focus on the reader of the *megillah* and his audience reflect a tacit acknowledgment on the rabbis' part that these were the only persons (or some of them) whom they felt they could influence through their legislation? We have no answers to these questions.

The Tosefta—the other early Tannaitic collection—does not add much to the Mishnah's prescriptions except for sporadic details, but the two Talmudim—the Palestinian Talmud and the Babylonian Talmud—paint a far richer and more textured picture of the scribal culture that emerged out of the earlier scribal world attested in the Qumran remains. The same picture is reflected in Masekhet Sefer Torah, whose earliest stratum, as noted earlier, may go back to the late Mishnaic period. In both the Palestinian and Babylonian Talmudim, scattered through many tractates, there are numerous prescriptions, references, and anecdotes relating to scribal practice and the production of Torah scrolls, but a few lengthier, more focused passages collect and anthologize the relevant laws and traditions, and thus give a better view of the state of scribal culture in the rabbinic period.[71] For example, Y. Megillah 1:71b–72a, a section of the Palestinian Talmud commenting on M. Megillah 2:1–2, quoted earlier, considers in no particular order a wide range of topics—the Assyrian script of the Torah and its "history"; the number of sheets in a scroll, as opposed to tefillin and mezuzot; writing of supralinear letters; the permissibility of damaged letters; the width of margins at the top and bottom of sheets and between columns; the number of columns on a sheet; the proper writing side of the skin; the implied prohibition against writing the divine name in Paleo-Hebrew script; the use of staves for scrolls and the methods of rolling; the writing and correcting of divine names; and the number of corrections permissible in a scroll.

As we saw earlier, many of these scribal practices are attested materially in the Qumran scrolls (which also refer to practices never mentioned in rabbinic texts).[72] The rabbis did not invent them. What this Talmudic passage exemplifies is the rabbis' effort to articulate and formalize the practices within a system of permitted and forbidden acts that determines whether or not a scroll is kosher. By setting these requirements, the rabbis "constructed" a kosher Torah scroll, and they did this by selecting from a spectrum of existing scribal practices and conventions (some of them quite subjective, the personal decisions of individual scribes), and then "freezing" or "reifying" that selection into fixed, obligatory procedures that, when performed together, produce a holy artifact, the Sefer Torah, with highly particularized and prescribed material properties.[73]

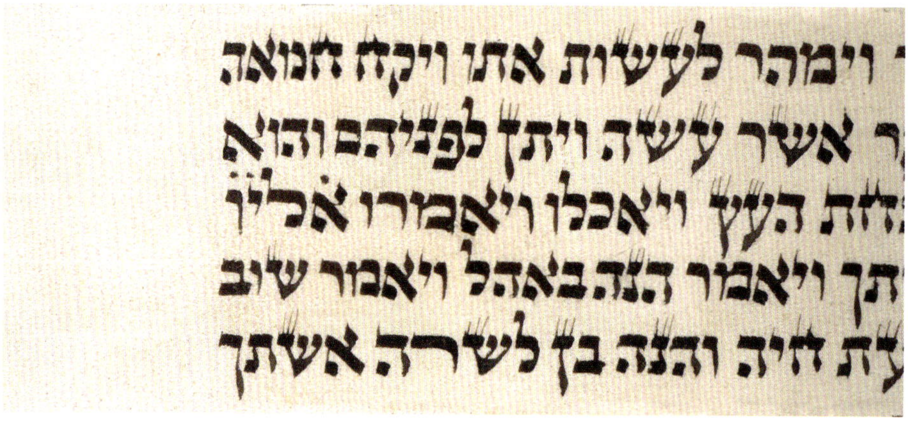

1.10 Gen. 18:9, detail. Note the three dots over the last two letters in the word *eilav*, the last word in the middle line (three lines from the top or bottom). Torah scroll, United States, twentieth century. Courtesy of Harvard Hillel.

The most prominent requirements (as stated in M. Megillah 2:2) are that the Torah scroll be written in Assyrian letters, on parchment (*'al ha-sefer*), and in ink (*deyo*). In the Talmud, these features (and others) are further elaborated and thereby regulated with much greater specificity. For example, the use of *petuḥot* and *setumot*, the spaces that mark content divisions in the text, now became a clearly demarcated system in which confusion between the two types of spacing was not tolerated (even though there is no absolute agreement on the types of spacing or where they are to be placed).[74] Similarly, certain paratextual marks used by scribes for different purposes, like cancellation dots or the brackets known otherwise as *antisigma* and *sigma* (and called by the rabbis inverted *nuns*) which often highlight misplaced passages, now became requisite features of the fixed biblical text, independent elements of its normative transmission history.[75] Thus, every rabbinically sanctioned Torah scroll contains ten *nequdot,* the points known as *puncta extraordinaria*, placed over specific words and letters in the biblical text that were once deemed questionable or incorrect; inverted *nuns* bracketing Numbers 10:35–36; and particular words with unusually shaped, suspended, enlarged, or miniaturized letters. In turn, once these paratextual elements—the *nequdot*, the *nuns*, and the orthographically marked letters—became fixed parts of the transmitted text, they also became objects of exegetical attention and subjects for rabbinic interpretation. Fig. 1.10 pictures the text of Genesis 18:9, "The [angels] said to him [*eilav*, i.e., Abraham], Where is your wife, Sarah?" As can be seen in the image, three dots are placed over the letters *aleph*, *yod*, and *vav* in the word *eilav* in the verse. Originally, these points probably indicated (in lieu of actually deleting them from the text) that the pointed letters were to be ignored and that the correct word was *lo*, "to him." Once these points were reified as part of the rabbis' Torah and their original function was forgotten, they became subjects for rabbinic exegetical comments, which, in fact, provide multiple homiletical explanations for their presence in the scroll: (1) to teach the reader that while the angels knew where Sarah was, they nonetheless asked Abraham out of politeness; (2) that the angels were the ones to ask Sarah where Abraham was (*ayo*), and thus teach the reader proper etiquette; (3) that the dotted letters teach a guest always to inquire after the health of the host's wife.[76] By offering such interpretations, the rabbis turned once unregulated scribal practices into meaningful elements of the sacred text.

The rabbis did not accept every scribal practice from previous tradition. As Tov notes, rabbinic prescriptions diverge most prominently from earlier practices in their laws about correcting scribal mistakes.[77] The rabbis were strict in prohibiting most visible modes of correction (especially drawing lines through incorrect words), and they severely limited the number of corrections permissible in a valid scroll, allowing only a small number per column and stipulating that they had to be made in specific ways. Special concern was directed to corrections involving incorrect inscription of the divine name.[78] The reasons for this were probably both aesthetic and ideological. Visible corrections marred the beauty of the scroll as well as raising suspicions that the text had been tampered with. The rabbis wished to avoid any possible indication that the Torah was less than perfect, materially or textually.

All of these tendencies—the canonization of permissible scribal techniques, the reinterpretation of anomalous paratextual features so as to make them meaningful, and the aestheticizing and theologizing of the Torah scroll into a perfect artifact—were aspects of the rabbis' overall project to turn the Torah scroll into a holy object. This project may have begun as early as the time of Ezra, in which case the rabbis were only continuing an earlier process, but its mechanics are epitomized most clearly in the way the rabbis applied the formula *halakhah le-moshe mi-sinai* (it is a law given to Moses at Sinai) to scribal practices.[79] In rabbinic literature, this formula is used widely to authorize particular legal practices whose origins cannot be traced back to biblical sources; the formula effectively attributes those practices to "private" (and unwritten) revelations given by God to Moses at Mount Sinai. Some scholars have viewed its early use as an effort on the part of the rabbis to connect the entirety of halacha to Mosaic authority. In the case of scribal prescriptions, this effort was a process, a fact supported by Martin Jaffee's observation that the instances of the formula's use in the Mishnah and the Tosefta deal with relatively minor issues within the larger corpus of rabbinic law, and that the formula is applied only sporadically and with no clear rationale, while in the two later Talmudim, the term is used "indiscriminately as a tool of jurisprudence."[80]

Thus in the Mishnah, the formula *halakhah le-moshe mi-sinai* is never applied to a single scribal practice. Beginning with the Yerushalmi, however, the formula becomes the stated source of authority for a number of obligatory practices related to writing a Torah scroll.[81] Where the Mishnah (Megillah 1:2) states that a person "has not fulfilled his obligation [to hear the Scroll of Esther] until [the text is read from a scroll] written in Assyrian letters, on parchment, and in ink," the Yerushalmi (Megillah 71d) stipulates: "It is a law given to Moses at Sinai [*halakhah le-moshe mi-sinai*] that they write [scrolls] on skins, and that they write in ink, and that they rule the lines with a reed, and that they tie [the leafs] with hair, and that they patch them with a patch, and glue [the patch] on with glue, and sew them with sinews."[82] In the Babylonian Talmud (B. Menahot 32a; B. Shabbat 79b), in turn, the Sinaitic attribution is extended to the writing of tefillin and mezuzot (though, strangely enough, not to writing a Torah scroll). In Soferim (1:1), the formula is invoked for virtually every aspect of scribal practice connected to writing sacred texts.

The expanding use of the formula *halakhah le-moshe mi-sinai* exemplifies the process by which the rabbis sought to bring scribal tradition within the bounds of their legal system. The application of the formula is not merely rhetorical. By reading these laws back to the Sinaitic revelation, the assignation effectively made the material scroll as primordial as its contents (and eliminated any possibility of understanding its material form as a product of historical development).[83] At the same time, and somewhat paradoxically, by saying that all these scribal laws were transmitted orally to Moses at Sinai as part of the Oral Torah, the attribution also made the written Torah in its material shape a *product* of the orally transmitted tradition. It thus confirmed the symbiotic complementarity of the two revelations.

The most significant change that the rabbis made to the Torah scroll was to require that a Sefer Torah be a single scroll containing the entire Pentateuch.[84] In the first place, this requirement rendered the scroll extremely difficult to use for normal reading or study, if only because of its bulkiness and size. Most early complete Torah scrolls appear to have been huge. Two fragments of Genesis (Cambridge, T-S NS 3.21 and 4.3), probably written in Palestine or Egypt in the sixth or seventh century—likely our earliest evidence for a Torah scroll from the period *after* Qumran—suggest that, if the fragments were part of a complete Pentateuch scroll (and not just a *ḥomesh* for Genesis), that scroll would have had dimensions of 585 millimeters by 38.4 meters, nearly two feet tall and 126 feet long.[85] Six scrolls, each of which is preserved in fragments as palimpsest leaves in a medical codex from thirteenth-century southern Italy (Florence, Laurenziana 74.17, fols. 73r–149r), have dimensions ranging from a little less than 2 feet in height by 62 feet in length to more than 2.5 feet tall by 46 feet long.[86] These scrolls are monumental. As Colette Sirat has remarked, by turning the Sefer Torah from something a person could easily hold in his hands and read—like any other scroll in the ancient world—into an artifact of such size, the rabbis effectively turned a "book," a text to be read, into a cult object to be revered.[87]

The Codification of the Sefer Torah in the Middle Ages

The process of transforming the Sefer Torah into a religious icon came to fruition during the Middle Ages. The transformation can be seen most clearly in two developments. The first of these was the continuing elaboration and codification of the laws governing the production and handling of a Sefer Torah. The second was the incorporation of the Torah as a material object into the synagogue liturgy and its ritualization within the public service.

The earliest medieval code-like work on the Torah scroll was the post-Talmudic treatise Masekhet Soferim (probably edited in its final form in the eighth or ninth centuries, although its first five chapters are closely based on Masekhet Sefer Torah, mentioned in the previous section, an early work that may go back to the third century, the period of the Mishnah).[88] The process of codification continued through the Middle Ages into the early modern period. The first milestone in the process was Maimonides's *Mishneh Torah*, which included an entire section titled "Hilkhot Sefer Torah" (The Laws of Torah Scrolls), whose rulings and instructions were based partly on what Maimonides had seen in an actual codex of the Hebrew Bible that he used as a model for writing his own Sefer Torah; this codex is believed today to have been the Aleppo Codex, which was then in Cairo. Throughout the later Middle Ages, many Masoretic treatises were composed that also dealt with scribal practice, with the genre culminating in Joseph Karo's sixteenth-century definitive code of Jewish law, the Shulḥan 'Arukh (*Yoreh Deah* 270–84).

Both Maimonides's and Karo's codes give the impression that their rulings were universally observed and that, by their time, the rules describing the preparation, materials, and inscription of the Torah scroll had become almost absolutely fixed, with little space left for the scribe's individuality or the variegations of changing cultural and geographical contexts. Both impressions are belied by the surviving material evidence, small as it is. As scholars have long recognized, early biblical manuscripts, including both scrolls and codices, contain numerous textual variants from the so-called Masoretic text (which, as we will see in the next chapter, emerged in its full shape only in the ninth century). It has also been demonstrated that the "correct" text of the Torah, particularly as it needed to be inscribed in Torah scrolls, remained a serious problem through the Middle Ages. As Jordan Penkower as shown, there existed four distinct text traditions of the Torah in the medieval period, each one followed in its own geocultural region—Ashkenaz, Sepharad, the Orient (Near East), and Yemen.[89] The exact shape of the square script scribes used to write the text also varied in each geocultural area (as each one developed its own distinctive hand, e.g., Ashkenazic script, Sephardic script, etc.); these developments were in turn partly determined by the type of writing instrument used in the region, a quill or a reed).[90] In addition, different regions had distinct ways of adorning the tops of certain letters with crowns (*tagin*), or writing scribal flourishes and strokes (*zaynin*).[91] There were also specific letters of certain words that in some locales were written in deliberately unusual shapes—

for example, the letter *peh*, in which its "tongue" twisted in curlicues inside the letter's "mouth."[92] Indeed, so many varying practices emerged even within a single geographical area like Ashkenaz that eventually special handbooks for scribes had to be composed. The earliest of these was a book called *Barukh She'Amar*, composed by the scribe Samson ben Eliezer (born ca. 1330); others were composed in subsequent centuries.[93] As Sid Z. Leiman has suggested, the variations from the Masoretic text found in medieval Torah scrolls may indicate that guilds of scribes had their own traditions and conventions, which differed from the codified rabbinic rules.[94] The Ashkenazic and Sephardic scripts known as STaM (an acronym standing for the three sacred textual artifacts in Judaism, the Sefer Torah, tefillin, and mezuzah), the stereotyped hand that scribes use today, did not emerge until after the sixteenth century.[95]

Aside from its text and script, other features of the material Torah scroll remained in flux during much of this period. There survive few scrolls from before the eleventh century, but those that do exist show that halachic authority did not always determine the material facts.[96] For example, in a number of early scrolls, there are dots separating verses—a paratextual addition to the consonantal text that is prohibited by halacha. In another scroll, there are catchwords at the bottom of columns.[97] Even the Bologna Torah scroll, discussed at the beginning of this chapter and written between 1155 and 1225 CE, a relatively advanced date in the history of the Sefer Torah, contains numerous anomalous, nonhalachic features. Fig. 1.11 displays a detail of the opening of the scroll shown in fig. 1.1. As one can see, the space between the columns contains final *nuns* as well as a missing word from the adjacent column's text, corrections that rabbinic halacha strictly prohibits in a kosher Torah scroll; elsewhere, there are many unusually shaped letters and various other types of prohibited paratextual markings.[98] Some scholars have suggested that the scroll was written for nonliturgical purposes (like study) but this seems unlikely. By the twelfth century, there existed numerous biblical codices in addition to Torah scrolls that could be, and *were*, used for study. In fact, the Bologna Sefer Torah was not anomalous. Its many nonhalachic features attest to the fact that rabbinic halacha was not always observed in practice, and this did not stop a congregation from using such a Sefer Torah in their services.

The most striking practice that diverged from halachic dictate involved the type of parchment used for the scrolls. Since the period of Qumran, it was conventional to write Torah scrolls on *gvil*, thick, unsplit leather that was lightly tanned on the outer hair side. In the Talmud, *gvil* is differentiated from two thinner leathers produced by splitting the skin into its different layers.[99] These two are called *klaf* and *dukhsustos* respectively. In general, *klaf* was used for tefillin and *dukhsustos* for mezuzot, although some authorities allowed *klaf* also to be used for Torah scrolls.[100] All three types underwent the same three-stage process of preparation: salting, flouring, and then tanning, namely, bringing them

1.11 Torah scroll (Exod. 15), Babylonia (?), ca. 1155–1255. Bologna, Biblioteca Universitaria di Bologna, Rotulo 2. Courtesy of the Biblioteca Universitaria di Bologna and Professor Mauro Perani.

into contact with tannin (and sometimes, dog dung).[101] All early rabbinic authorities—from the Talmud through the Geonim and Maimonides—unequivocally require that skins for writing these sacred artifacts undergo tanning.

By the High Middle Ages—the earliest period from which we have explicit documentation for the technology—very different understandings as to what constituted each layer had developed in the West (Europe) and in the East (mainly the Islamic world). Furthermore, Jews living in the two regions encountered different types of skins that were prepared and sold by their gentile neighbors in their new host cultures. In the Arabic-Islamic world, the most prevalent type was a fine parchment called *raq*, which was prepared by first salting and then soaking the hide in a water and lime solution. In Christian Europe, it was another type of parchment that was also produced by salting and soaking the skin in a lime solution.[102] Neither *raq* nor the other type of parchment underwent authentic tanning. As Haran has shown, rabbinic authorities in both the Arabic/Islamic world and Christian Europe were completely cognizant of the halachic problems posed by this predicament, and they responded to it, albeit in different ways.[103] In both communities, however, Jews eventually adapted the local technologies and writing materials used by their gentile neighbors. Jews bought and used the parchment most easily available to them. Local culture, in other words, trumped halacha.

Perhaps the most unusual case of local conditions shaping scribal practice is that of the Torah scrolls written by the Jews living in the medieval community of Kaifeng in China, one of which is pictured in fig 1.12.[104] This community, probably founded by Jewish traders on the Silk Route from Iraq or Persia in the late eighth or early ninth century, first came to the notice of early modern Western culture with the arrival in China of the Jesuit missionary Matteo Ricci in 1605. When they heard that visitors from the West who knew the Bible had come to China, representatives of the Kaifeng community approached the Jesuits under the belief that they were Jews (because who else, they asked themselves, would know the Bible?), and the Jesuits did not disabuse them of their belief. As it turned out, the missionaries were interested in the Chinese Jews for their own reasons. On the basis of the Kaifeng Jews' claim to have come to China *before* the beginnings of Christianity, the Jesuits believed that the community's Torah scrolls were uncorrupted by the alterations and falsehoods that, they claimed, the rabbis had introduced into the Masoretic text to hide the original biblical text that prophesied the coming of Christ. This belief in the rabbinic corruption of the biblical text was prevalent in the sixteenth and seventeenth centuries, and Christians believed that if they could only recover the "pristine" biblical text, they could convince the Jews to convert. Of course, once the missionaries inspected the Kaifeng Torah scrolls, they realized that these were no different than any other Torah scroll.

What they did not notice, however, were the special, indeed unique material features of these Chinese scrolls.[105] The parchment was prepared in accordance with local Chinese techniques of production, the sheets were frequently sewn together with silk threads, and—as can be seen in fig. 1.13, a detail containing the Decalogue (Exod. 20) from a scroll now owned by the Bridwell Library in Dallas, Texas—the script used in the scrolls was

1.12 Torah scroll (Exod. 20), Kaifeng, China, sixteenth century (?). Dallas, Bridwell Library Special Collections, Perkins School of Theology, Southern Methodist University. Courtesy of Bridwell Library Special Collections, Perkins School of Theology, Southern Methodist University.

written with a brush (rather than a quill or reed) in letters that look unmistakably like Chinese characters. Here, again, the impact of the local host culture upon Jewish scribal practice is obvious.

From the perspective of Jewish book history, the case of the Kaifeng Torah scrolls is not unrepresentative. Jewish book culture has always been (and continues to be) profoundly shaped by the technology and conventions of the surrounding book cultures in which the Jewish producers of the books lived. This will be seen repeatedly in the next chapter, when we come to the Bible codex. What makes the Torah scroll exceptional is the Torah's own exceptionality. Even if one takes into account the many instances in which local book culture has trumped halachic requirements, the fact remains that no other Jewish book has been more closely monitored by halacha than the Sefer Torah. We have already seen how the rabbis fixed preexisting scribal practices into prerequisites for a kosher Torah scroll, and how the attribution of Sinaitic authority to these prerequisites

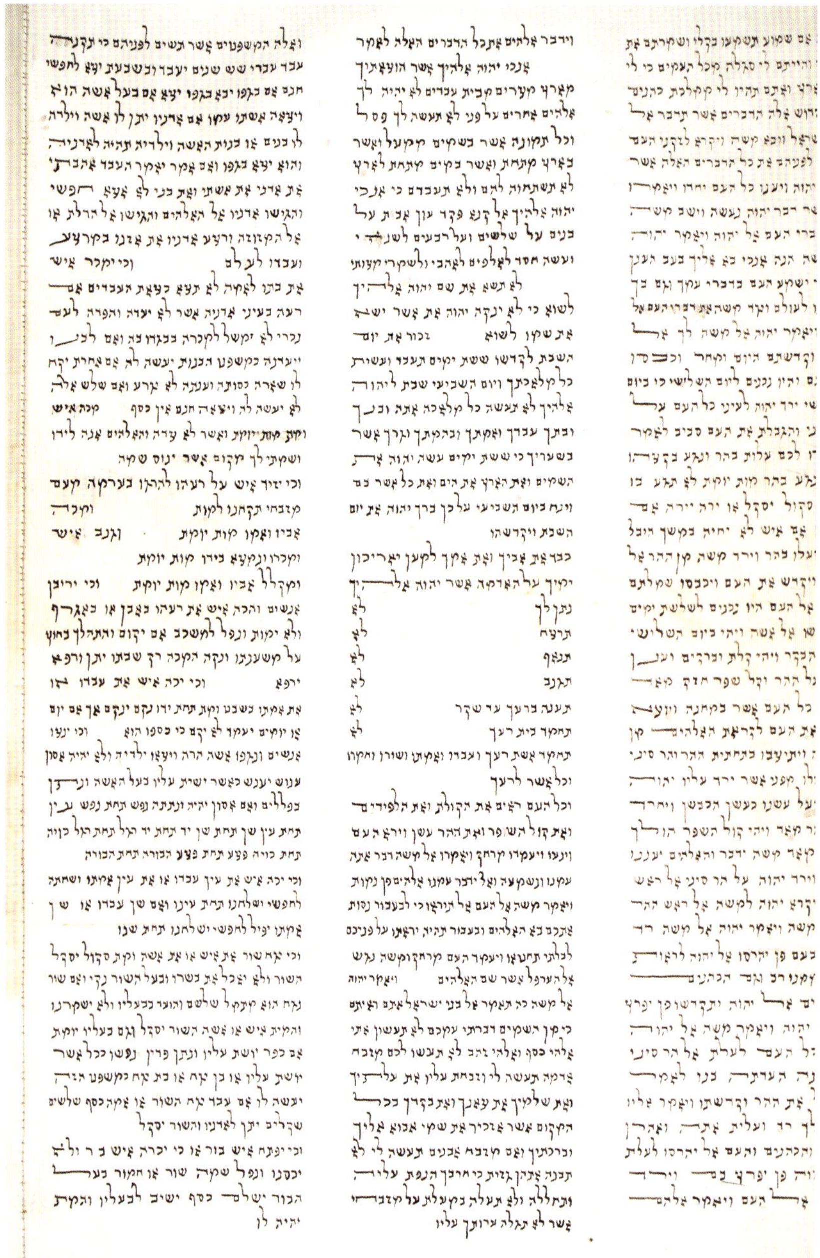

1.13 Torah scroll (Exod. 20), detail of Decalogue. Kaifeng, China, sixteenth century (?); Dallas, Bridwell Library Special Collections, Perkins School of Theology, Southern Methodist University. Courtesy of Bridwell Library Special Collections, Perkins School of Theology, Southern Methodist University.

1.14 Theodotus Inscription, Jerusalem, first century CE. Photo © The Israel Museum, Jerusalem, by David Harris.

made the material Torah scroll as primordial as the Torah's own revelation. In both ways, the Torah scroll was changed from a book into a cult object. We can now turn to the second dimension of this process by showing how the synagogue ritualized the Sefer Torah and thereby turned it into a ritual artifact.

The Liturgical Life of the Torah Scroll

As a communal institution, the synagogue predated the emergence of rabbinic Judaism, and until the third century (at the earliest) it appears not to have been under the control of the rabbis.[106] The synagogue probably emerged in the Greek-speaking Diaspora, and originally served many purposes, including use as a meeting place and a study hall. The Torah figured centrally from the beginning. The first-century CE inscription in the Theodotus synagogue found in Jerusalem (fig. 1.14) specifically mentions "reading the Law and studying the commandments" among the purposes to which the building was dedicated.[107] Exactly how the Bible was read and studied in this early period is less clear. Was "reading" the Torah the same as "studying" it? Was the Law chanted when it was publicly read? How was it taught and studied? We have virtually no knowledge about any of these matters, or whether there even existed fixed or formalized orders of readings. Our earliest source for such orders, M. Megillah 3:4–6, lists special readings for the holidays and for the Sabbaths preceding Passover (many of which pertain to special commandments to be performed during that season, like the shekel contribution to the Temple), and it may be that the earliest readings to be formalized were such seasonally relevant passages.[108]

During this period, Torah scrolls were still in the shape of smaller scrolls like *ḥomashim*, which could easily have been used for study and reading, either publicly or privately. By the early Amoraic period (the mid-third century), this situation had changed. According to halachic dictate, as we have seen, the Torah had become a single monumental scroll. As the scroll grew larger, it became less suitable for normal study. It also became much more expensive. In fact, we do not even know how many complete Torah scrolls existed or how prevalent Torah scrolls were in all communities. While individuals appear to have owned *ḥomashim*, there is little evidence to support private ownership of monumental complete Torah scrolls.[109] While the rabbis urged communities to tax themselves to buy a synagogue and a Torah scroll (T. Bava Meziah 11:23), other sources indicate that not all communities could afford their own scroll.[110] In the Babylonian Talmud, sages are queried about the permissibility of reading the Torah from *ḥomashim* rather than from a Torah scroll (B. Gittin 60a), a question that certainly suggests the community did not have a monumental Sefer Torah. Even in the Middle Ages, when there clearly existed many more Sifrei Torah, not every small community of Jews owned its own Torah scroll. In one responsum (#294), Maimonides was asked by the sages of Narbonne, hardly a tiny community, about reading the Torah from a codex Bible (*ḥumash*) if the community lacked a Sefer Torah.[111] Furthermore, even if it is not difficult to imagine students gathering around a single monumental Torah scroll to study it together as a group—as Jewish students in Yemen are reported doing—it appears, on the basis of circumstantial evidence, that study of Torah was mainly conducted from memory, with the biblical text having been memorized from hearing it repeatedly read aloud.[112] In other words, it would have been unnecessary for a physical Sefer Torah to be present for a sage to teach Torah.

As the Sefer Torah was used less for regular study, it became a ritual artifact in the synagogue service. While there is no scholarly consensus on the dating of the rituals surrounding the public reading of the Torah in the synagogue, these rituals appear to have developed in the course of the Amoraic period in both Roman Palestine and Sassanian Babylonia. In Palestine, the complete Pentateuch was read in weekly sections that followed various cycles, some taking as long as three and a half years, others as little as a single year. The Mishnah (M. Megillah 3:1) already prescribes how many readers are to be called up each time the Torah is chanted publicly—with different numbers of *ʿaliyot* (sing. *ʿaliyah*, as each reading is called) on weekdays, various holidays and festivals, and the Sabbath—but the exact divisions of the weekly readings remained in flux until the early modern period.[113] The chapters into which virtually all Bibles today are divided do not appear in Jewish Bibles until the early sixteenth century, when they were adopted from Christian Bibles.

The original purpose of the triennial reading in the synagogue was pedagogical—to teach Torah—and it may originally have involved sermons.[114] This was true in Babylonia as well, where a special holiday was instituted to celebrate the completion of the annual reading of the complete Pentateuch; the holiday is celebrated at the conclusion of Sukkot, on the "additional" day of the holiday celebrated in the Diaspora, and is known today as *Simḥat Torah*, the "rejoicing over the Torah."[115] This original pedagogical function of the Torah reading has never been completely lost; even today, rabbis (or lay members of the synagogue) deliver sermons based on the weekly reading. Although reading the Targum—the ancient translation of the Hebrew text into Aramaic, the lingua franca of Jews in the rabbinic period—is no longer practiced as part of the service, most Hebrew Bibles used in the synagogue (at least in the Diaspora) contain a translation into the local vernacular so that members of the congregation can understand the Torah reading.[116] In the final chapter of this book, we will trace the history of Jewish Bible translations; here it is sufficient to note that these translations have never replaced the Hebrew text of the Bible (as did, for example, the Septuagint and the Vulgate in early Christianity).

Over time, the pedagogical function of the Torah reading progressively diminished as its symbolic, iconic charge grew larger. The overall contours of the latter process are most visible in three distinct "para-material" elements that came to endow the Sefer Torah with the status of a cult object: first, its physical location within the synagogue; second, the liturgy of the Torah reading, specifically the rituals surrounding the procession of the Sefer Torah in the synagogue before and after its public chanting, as it is taken out of the ark and then returned to it; and third, the ways the Torah Scroll is cased and costumed.

The Home of the Torah Scroll

During the Second Temple and early Roman periods, at least until the third century, there was no permanent or fixed housing for the Torah within the synagogue building.[117] Torah scrolls were kept in a portable chest or ark, which was brought into the synagogue only when the Torah was read; some scholars believe that a special ceremony accompanied the procession carrying the Torah scroll into the synagogue building.[118] By the fourth century CE (if not earlier), a permanent Torah shrine was introduced into most synagogues; this innovation decisively changed the orientation of the synagogue service. While formerly both the synagogue structure and the recitation of prayer (*tefillah*, the classic term for what is known today as the *'amidah* or silent prayer) had been oriented toward Jerusalem and the Temple Mount (even after the Temple's destruction), the permanent Torah shrine now came to occupy the eastern wall of the synagogue facing Jerusalem, and thus became the focal point of the synagogue both architecturally and liturgically.[119]

Several types of structures for Torah shrines have been identified.[120] These include a podium, a stone platform on the wall facing Jerusalem; the *aedicula*, a freestanding shrine

1.15
Torah niche, synagogue, Dura Europos, Syria, third century CE. National Museum, Damascus, Syria.

usually built of stone and either placed on a podium or built into the wall with steps leading up to it; a niche, a more simple recess either semicircular or rectangular in form, cut into the wall and housing a container (*kufsa* or *tik*) to hold the Torah scroll; and the apse, a formal semicircular space at one end of the sanctuary for a shrine or ark (*teivah* or *arona/aron*) made either of stone or of wood. Remains of these various types of shrines and arks have been found in archaeological excavations and are also pictured in ancient sources. Possibly the best known *aedicula* is the one illustrated in the reconstructed wall mural in the famous third-century synagogue excavated at Dura Europos in present-day Syria (fig. 1.15). The elaborately decorated structure has columns on each side, a lintel with representations of the Temple façade in the center, the menorah on the left, and the binding of Isaac on the right; the interior of the space is framed by a conch or seashell, while its inside would have held a covered *kufsa* or *tik* with the Torah scroll(s) inside.

1.16 Torah ark, gold glass, Rome, fourth century CE. Photo © The Israel Museum, by David Harris.

In contrast to shrines, arks had a shape that more closely resembled a cupboard with either shelves or small pigeonhole-like cubicles in which scrolls were laid horizontally, as seen in fig. 1.16. This image was found in gold glass inside Roman catacombs from the fourth century CE; the black dots in the center of the scrolls are probably the hollows in the centers of the scrolls.

Not surprisingly, these shrines and containers all reflect the influence of Greco-Roman culture and its architectural conventions. As we have already noted, the term *kufsa* derives from the Latin *capsa*, and *tik* from the Greek *thēkē*, while the object itself is based upon the *paenula*, a case made from leather with handles to transport scrolls. The Torah ark resembles Greco-Roman cupboards used for housing scrolls, and the Torah niche and *aedicula* mirror comparable shrines found in Greco-Roman temples. The main difference between them was that the Greco-Roman shrines contained a statue of the deity while those in synagogues contained Torah scrolls.[121] While the Sefer Torah was never treated as an image of the deity, its permanent presence within the synagogue did begin to endow the physical scroll with an identity that might be considered figuratively divine.

The foundations of this identity may go back to the ancient Mesopotamian world out of which the Bible as a literary document first emerged.[122] Karel van der Toorn has argued that veneration of the Torah as a divine (or quasi-divine) object derived from the Babylonian cult of images in which local city gods were believed to actually reside within anthropomorphic statues that stood in private recesses inside city temples; on special occasions like holidays, the images were taken out of their temple shrines and publicly displayed to the inhabitants of the city, typically in formal processions.[123] Van der Toorn has speculated that such practices were prevalent in ancient Israel until the time of the Deuteronomic reform in the sixth–fifth centuries BCE, when images and cults were banned and replaced (according to van der Toorn) with a new veneration for the "book of the law" (*sefer ha-torah*). As he writes, "The ban on images and the emphasis on the Torah are complementary: the Torah was to take the place of the image."[124] Instead of placing a divine image upon the doorposts of a house or upon a person's head and body as a protective amulet, the Israelites were commanded to place selected texts from the Torah inside mezuzot and tefillin, which were placed on doorposts and worn on arms and heads (Deut. 11:18,20). So, too, the ark containing the tablets of the law became for the Israelites the equivalent of the divine statues of their gentile neighbors. Both embodied the sacred as "incarnations of God."[125] Van der Toorn's characterization is exaggerated, but it points to the similarities between belief in the primordial character and heavenly origins of the Babylonian divine image and comparable beliefs held by contemporaneous ancient Israelites regarding the heavenly and preexistent character of the Torah.[126] These beliefs continued into the rabbinic period.[127] Their influence can even be seen in the rabbis' determination to ascribe legal rules governing the writing of a Torah scroll to the Sinaitic revelation, thereby making its artifactual features divinely ordained just like its text.[128]

The Torah Procession and Its Liturgy

The most revealing signs of the figuratively divine identity of the Sefer Torah may be found in the liturgy that accompanies its double procession within the synagogue as the scroll is taken out of the ark and carried to the *bimah* (platform) and then, after the public reading, returned to the ark. The origins of this ceremony are unknown; it may go back to a very early period in the history of the synagogue when the Torah was kept outside the building and brought inside only for the public reading. The early history of the liturgy has been brilliantly reconstructed by Ruth Langer, who shows that the ritual began with a relatively unadorned rite in the rabbinic period but fully emerged in several different versions in Ashkenaz in the Middle Ages.[129] The Ashkenazic location for the rite's mature development is not surprising: as scholars have shown, the palpable, intense sense of God's presence in the synagogue was especially felt in Ashkenazi communities.[130] Even so, the strong resemblance between the versions suggests that they reflect a common practice that probably first appeared in the early post-Talmudic period, in the seventh and eighth centuries.

As Langer has reconstructed this ur-rite, it seems to have revolved around a pastiche (or florilegium) of several verses that were recited by the prayer leader and congregants: (1) "Exalt the Eternal with me, and let us extol His name together" (Ps. 34:4), which was probably recited by the prayer leader, and to which the congregation responded with the refrain of (2) "Exalt the Lord our God and bow down to His footstool" (Ps. 99:5) and (3) "Exalt the Lord our God, and bow toward His holy hill, for the Lord our God is holy" (Ps. 99:9).[131] These verses were then followed by the recitation of a line modeled upon a biblical verse but not actually found in the Bible: (4) "Let everyone ascribe greatness to our God and ascribe honor to the Torah," followed by (5) "The Torah of God is perfect, renewing life; the decrees of the Eternal are enduring, making the simple wise; the precepts of the Eternal are just, rejoicing the heart, the instruction of the Eternal is lucid, making the eyes light up" (Ps. 19:8–9); and finally, (6) "May the Lord grant strength [*'oz*] to His people, may the Lord bestow on His people well-being" (Ps. 29:11). The word "strength" (*'oz*) in the last verse was regularly interpreted in classical midrash as a reference to Torah.[132]

The rite closely associates God and the Torah. While the Torah is not explicitly mentioned until the pseudo-verse (line 4), the reader will notice that in that line God and the Torah are placed in apposition, and that apposition is then confirmed, as it were, by the series of personifications in line 5 and the citation of Psalm 19:8–9, where God's Torah is praised for doing precisely the kinds of things usually attributed to God, namely, renewing life, making the simple wise, rejoicing the heart, and so on. This apposition may also help us understand the significance of the first three verses in the rite, all of which exhort the audience to "exalt" God. This command to exalt—literally, raise up—God is elaborated in the "stage directions" that Masekhet Soferim gives for the ceremony: that the Torah scroll actually be raised on high at several points, including the first of these verses, Psalm 34:4, "Exalt the Eternal with me, and let us extol His name together." When the prayer leader opened the rite with this verse and simultaneously raised the Torah scroll for all to see, members of the congregation came as close as they ever could to seeing an icon of the deity.[133]

As Langer has shown, the Torah rite continued to develop in the Ashkenazic liturgy, with the ritual's liturgy amplified by adding verses privately spoken by each participant and interpretations of each verse in the service.[134] A parallel liturgy was developed for returning the Torah to the ark after it had been read. As in the earlier ceremony, the Sefer Torah is again associated with God through reciting Psalms 148:13–14, 29:1–11, and 24:1–11, all of which praise and exalt God and his voice. The entire Torah ceremony is bracketed, in turn, by the recitation of Numbers 10:35 (at the ceremony's very beginning) and 10:36 (at its conclusion), verses that relate what Moses said when the Ark of the Law would journey with the Israelites in the desert and when the Ark rested; both verses implicitly identify God with the Ark (or with the tablets inside it).[135] During the Torah ceremony, in turn, each person chanting the Torah or haftarah (or, in a case where another person actually did the chanting, the person called up for the reading) recited blessings before and after chanting his portion. These blessings effectively turn the chanting of the Torah or haftarah into liturgical acts.

The precise status of the Sefer Torah within this overall ceremony is difficult to pin down. The synagogue Torah ritual metonymically associates the Sefer Torah and God as he is described in the verses recited in the ritual, even though the two are never explicitly identified; on the other hand, the blessings recited before and after the public chanting clearly distinguish the two (by praising God for having given the Torah to Israel). Classical rabbinic tradition also closely associated God and the Torah, but there the relationship was figurative, with the Torah described as God's daughter or bride.[136] In medieval mystical tradition, these metaphors were literalized and taken in a much more concrete sense as religious symbols possessing a reality of their own.[137] The Torah was identified with God, and its verses were said to consist of his divine names (which could be extracted for theurgic purposes and were identified with the limbs constituting the divine body) or of his singular name, the tetragrammaton, or of his glory, the *kavod*. The synagogue Torah ritual was itself interpreted mystically, as a ritual that "has the effect of enthroning the Shekhinah" (which, in kabbalistic thought, was thought to be God's feminine presence, which dwells upon the Torah inside the ark).[138] Some contemporary scholars also have seen the synagogue ritual as a kind of reenactment of the Sinaitic revelation, in which each member of the congregation is able to feel as though he or she could "stand again at Sinai and Zion" and experience God's presence "through the very presence of the Torah scroll in the synagogue."[139] It is doubtful, however, that Jews sitting in a synagogue and listening to the Torah being chanted ever believe that they are actually hearing the *voice* of God. What is heard is the *word* of God, a divinely inspired text read aloud.[140]

To the extent that the Sefer Torah serves as an icon of divinity in the synagogue—whether literally, metaphorically, or symbolically—it is mainly figured in masculine terms, primarily as a king.[141] This figuration is not surprising. In the classical liturgy, God is regularly addressed as "king of the universe" (*melekh ha-ʿolam*); royalty has always been the most available analogy for divine power. This gendering of the Sefer Torah is not, however, universal. In both rabbinic and medieval Judaism, the Torah is also represented in feminine terms—as mother, bride, and daughter—and the commandment to love God

1.17
Maimonides, *Mishneh Torah*, Spain, 13th c.–Perugia, Italy, 14th c.; Jerusalem, National Library of Israel MS. 4.1193, fol. 32r. Courtesy of the National Library of Israel.

(particularly as spelled out in Deut. 6:4–6) was translated into an equivalent commandment to love the Torah.[142] And sometimes the gender of the Sefer Torah was less relevant than its relationship either to God or to Israel. Sarit Shalev-Eyni has pointed to a remarkable illustration of this love of Torah, which is visually pictured in a copy of Maimonides's *Mishneh Torah*, written in Spain in the thirteenth century but illustrated about a century later in Perugia, Italy (fig. 1.17). On the opening page of the Book of Ahavah ("Love")—which contains, among other laws, those concerning the writing of a Torah scroll and other sacred texts—an illustration depicts a man embracing a Torah scroll. Beneath the illustration, the word *Ahavah* is inscribed in large letters while above it is the verse from Psalm 119:97 that Maimonides chose as the epigram for the book: "How I have loved [*ahavti*] your Torah, it is my discourse all day long."[143] The embrace illustrated in the picture is not erotic but intimate and familiar; the man cradles the Torah scroll in his arms like an infant.

When the Sefer Torah is taken out of its ark and carried through the synagogue—garbed as a king—it is customary for members of the synagogue to kiss it, either directly or by touching it with their hands or with the fringes of the *tallit*, as a show of respect and honor.[144] The origins of this custom are not clear. Early Christian sources of the fifth and sixth centuries describe similar processions of gospel books through the congregation, with the book raised high over the head of the deacon, priest, or bishop, both out of respect to the book and to allow it to be seen, touched, and kissed.[145] In both cases, the kissing would seem to be the kind of "love" pictured in the illustration, a familiar and intimate gesture of attachment, the affection of a child for a parent. As Moshe Isserlis wrote in his glosses on the Shulḥan 'Arukh, citing the great thirteenth-century sage Isaac of Vienna: "And some have written that we bring the young children to kiss the Torah in order to educate them and excite them about the *mitzvot* [commandments] and such is the custom."[146]

The Sefer Torah's Garb

The most visible way the Sefer Torah in the synagogue is gendered as masculine—and by extension, made into an icon for God—is in its "dress," the coverings and costumes in which the scroll is kept in the Torah shrine and carried through the synagogue, along with the various ornamental articles that are used to decorate it. These items all underwent considerable historical development.[147]

Early rabbinic literature mentions only two types of coverings for Torah scrolls: a hard container (*kufsa* or *tik*) typically made of wood, and a cloth wrapping (*mitpaḥat*, *mapah*) made from either wool or silk, which was sometimes decorated and sometimes attached with bells.[148] In some places, both coverings were used together, with the scrolls inside the *kufsa* or *tik* wrapped in *mappot*.

As Bracha Yaniv has proposed, the later development of the Torah scroll's dress essentially followed the history of its casing in the synagogue.[149] Originally—that is, before a permanent space in the synagogue was created for the Torah, when scrolls were brought into the synagogue solely for their public reading—Torah scrolls were wrapped in a *mitpaḥat* and kept in a transportable container like the *tik*. Once permanent shrines were established in the synagogue, the type of covering varied according to the housing. In the case of an ark (*teivah* or *aron*/*arana*), which had closed doors and shelves or cubicles for the scrolls, the latter were probably placed inside with just sufficient covering to avoid the kind of disrespect decried in the Talmudic statement, "One who holds a Torah scroll naked will be buried naked" (B. Shabbat 14a). Over time, the shelves inside the ark were eliminated, and as the Torah scrolls were placed standing up, the *mitpaḥat* evolved into a full-length cloth covering, which came to be known as a *me'il*, or "dress."[150] The ark containing the Sefer Torah (and often multiple Sifrei Torah) clothed in a *me'il* eventually became standard in Europe, both in Ashkenaz and in Sepharad, as well as the latter's

1.18 Three *me'ilim* (Torah dresses): (from left to right) Italy, eighteenth century; Alsace, 1887; Morocco, early twentieth century. Gross Family Collection. Photograph by Tomer Appelbaum.

successor communities, like those in Morocco. The main difference between the two traditions is in the shape of the *me'il*; those from Ashkenaz have short side vents, while Sephardic and North African *me'ilim* have a single, nearly full-length back vent. Fig. 1.18 pictures three *me'ilim*: the flowery one on the left is Italian, eighteenth century; the middle one, an Ashkenazic *me'il* from Alsace, France, 1887, intended for the high holidays (hence its white color and the image of the shofar between two cornucopia, symbols of good luck and prosperity); on the right, a *me'il* from Morocco, beginning of the twentieth century.

In many Ashkenazi and Italian communities, the original *mitpaḥat* or *mapah*, the early cloth covering for the Torah, was also retained beneath the *me'il*; this item was known in Italy as a *yeri'ah*, and in Ashkenaz as an *avneit* (which was also used in Italy in addition to the *yeri'ah*). Both pieces of cloth took the form of bands or binders that encircled the two sections of the Torah scroll held by the separate staves and thus served as a kind of belt to keep the two halves of the scroll together. In the early sixteenth century in Ashkenaz, the *avneit* was further "ritualized." When a child was born, it became the custom for the mother to take the swaddling cloth upon which an infant boy was circumcised, cut it into four strips, and sew the strips together lengthwise to make a long band; the mother would

1.19 Five *tikkim* (Torah cases): (from left to right) Yemen, ca. 1900; Syria, 1900; Kurdistan, Iran, 1860/61; China, 1882, in Baghdadi-Iranian style; British Palestine, 1914, in Syrian style. Gross Family Collection. Photograph by Tomer Appelbaum.

then embroider and decorate the band, sometimes elaborately with scenes evoking the future life of the child, and on the occasion of the child's first visit to the synagogue, present the band, now known as a *wimpel*, to the community as a Torah binder. This practice spread from Southern Germany throughout the Ashkenazic world, and the *wimpel* become one of the best-known examples of Jewish folk art, literally tying together the two covenantal rituals, circumcision and the public chanting of the Torah.[151]

Synagogues using the *aedicula,* or niche-type housing for the Torah scroll, faced a different challenge in devising a covering for the Torah. Because these shrines were doorless and open in the front, they required a better way of protecting the scrolls. According to Yaniv, this problem was solved by retaining the ancient *tik*, which now became the standard Torah housing in Jewish communities in Yemen, Western Asia (Iraq and western Iran, and their "daughter-communities," Syria, Lebanon, India, and Egypt), and the Eastern Mediterranean (Tunisia, Libya, Asia Minor, and Greece). Even after their Torah shrines were equipped with doors, these communities continued to use the *tik* as their primary Torah case.

The *tik* underwent changes of its own.[152] To make it more convenient to use, a way was found to open the *tik* from the front, thereby allowing the Sefer Torah to be read without having to take it out of the *tik* (which was necessary so long as it opened from the top).[153] At the same time, the container developed distinctive shapes in each of the three Middle Eastern and Mediterranean communities that continued to use it. Fig. 1.19 pictures five examples from different communities: 1) Yemen (ca. 1900; wood, brass, painted); 2) Syria (1900; silver and wood); 3) Kurdistan, Iran (1860–61; brass and other metals); 4) Baghdad/India (1882, made in China; silver with gilt); 5) British Palestine/Syrian style (1914; precious metals). Of these types, the Yemenite is the simplest, and it probably most closely reflects the original shape of the ancient *tik*: a round or hexagonal box of wood with a flat top with two holes for the Torah staves (rollers). The second type, the so-called Babylonian *tik* (#3 and #5), used by Jews in Western Asia, also has a body made of bare or painted wood, which is often covered in leather, velvet, or metal, but its distinguishing feature is its spherical or onion-shaped crown-like top with diagonal finials emerging out of it. When the case is opened vertically, the insides of the crown display dedicatory plaques with verses and details about the donors. Finally, the "Mediterranean" *tik* (#2, #4) has a body similar to the Babylonian type, but its top is flat with two holes for erect staves, surrounded by a fence-like coronet called an *'atarah,* which is an integral part of the case; a dedicatory plaque divided in half is attached to the front, where the *tik* opens.

Whether the Torah scroll is dressed in a *me'il* or cased in a *tik*, two additional items traditionally adorn its top. The first of these are the *rimmonim*, the finials or stave coverings, which derive from the tops of ancient book rods used to wind scrolls in the Greco-Roman world.[154] The term in Hebrew for the book rod or roller is *'amud*, "stave," but in later tradition, once the Sefer Torah attained its monumental size and required two staves, the pair came to be known as *'etzei ḥayyim,* "trees of life" (after Prov. 3:18, "She [i.e. 'Wisdom,' interpreted by the rabbis as Torah] is a tree of life for all who grasp her"). As we know from a reference in Maimonides's *Mishneh Torah* (Sefer Torah 10:4), it was already the custom by the twelfth century to make silver or gold ornamental covers for the two staves.[155] These covers or finials had the shape of pomegranates, hence their name, which also contains an allusion to the *rimmonim* that surmounted the columns (also called *'amudim*) in Solomon's temple, as described in 1 Kings 7:18. Bells were sometimes attached to the *rimmonim* (a practice going back to the the *mitpaḥat* of the Talmudic period), and because bells were associated with bell towers, particularly among Jews living in Christian lands, *rimmonim* (despite being pomegranates by name!) began to take the form of bell towers. The earliest such *rimmonim* in the shape of towers are preserved in the Cathedral Treasure of Palma de Majorca, where, after the Jews were expelled from Spain, the *rimmonim* were plundered and taken to the cathedral to be used as verges. The very fact that

1.20 Four *rimmonim* (finials): (from left to right) Tetuan, Morrocco, 1892/93; Vienna, Austria, 1806; Afghanistan/Bukhara, 1895; Emden, Germany, 1801. Gross Family Collection. Photograph by Tomer Appelbaum.

a *rimmon* in the shape of a tower could be used as a cathedral verge is proof that the architectural form was part of a common visual vocabulary shared by Jews, Christians, and Muslims in medieval Iberia. Eventually, the tower form spread to Ashkenaz, Italy, and Eastern Europe, where the specific shape of the tower often reflected the towers built in the host communities in which the Jewish producers (or patrons) of the *rimmonim* lived.[156] (The tower shape was also appropriated for the *besamim* or spice towers used in the *havdalah* ceremony at the conclusion of the Sabbath.) Fig. 1.20 illustrates four examples of both the pomegranate and bell-tower forms: 1) Tetuan, Morocco (1892/93), an Islamic tower; silver; 2) Vienna, Austria (1806), silver, a pomegranate with the Hapsburg crown on its top, flanking the next pair; 3) Afghanistan/Bukhara (1895); silver, pomegranate shaped; 4) Emden, Germany (1801), silver, triple-level bell tower.

The second article, the Torah crown, is first mentioned in a legal responsum written by Hai ben Sherira Gaon (939–1038) of Pumbeditha in Babylonia. According to the document, the Gaon was asked whether it is permissible to use women's jewelry in preparing "a crown [*'atarah*] for the Torah, of gold or of silver or of myrtle, or of women's jewelry, such as ear-rings, rings and the like; and whether it is permissible to hang such jewelry on this crown, and then to place the crown on the Torah-scroll when it is in the

1.21 Four *ketarim* (Torah crowns): (from left to right) Hamburg, Germany, 1703–82; Vienna, ca. 1873, Turkish/Sephardic style; Rhodes, Greece, 1832–33; Galicia, Ukraine, ca. 1820. Gross Family Collection. Photograph by Tomer Appelbaum.

Torah-case [*tik*] or on top of the case, on the holiday of *Simḥat Torah*."[157] As already noted, Simḥat Torah is celebrated in the Diaspora on the ninth day of Sukkot, when the annual cycle of reading the Torah is completed.[158] In his responsum, Hai replies that there is nothing objectionable about placing the crown on the Torah, but it is forbidden, he adds, to place the crown afterward on the head of the person who reads the last portion of the Torah, "for in holy matters things are made to ascend [in holiness], not to descend."[159]

On the basis of this responsum, it thus appears that the Torah crown derived from this specific celebration and later spread to become a custom of regularly adorning the Torah with a crown. The original custom may have been to use a wreath or coronet, not necessarily a crown.[160] The term that both Hai and other early sources use to describe the crown or wreath, *'atarah*, alludes to Song of Songs 3:11, a verse spoken by the Shulamite to her companions: "O maidens of Zion, go forth and gaze upon King Solomon wearing the crown [*'atarah*] that his mother gave him on his wedding day, on his day of bliss [*u-be-yom simḥat libo*]." Some rabbinic interpretations interpret King Solomon (*ha-melekh shelomoh*) as "the king to whom peace [*shalom*] belongs," namely, God, and the *'atarah* as the Torah (*ha-torah*, with an obvious phonetic pun between the two words), while the phrase *be-yom simḥat libo* may very well have brought to mind *yom simḥat torah*, the holiday.[161] Indeed, it is possible that this midrash, with its constellation of associations, may have been the actual source for crowning the Torah scroll with an *'atarah* on Simḥat Torah.[162]

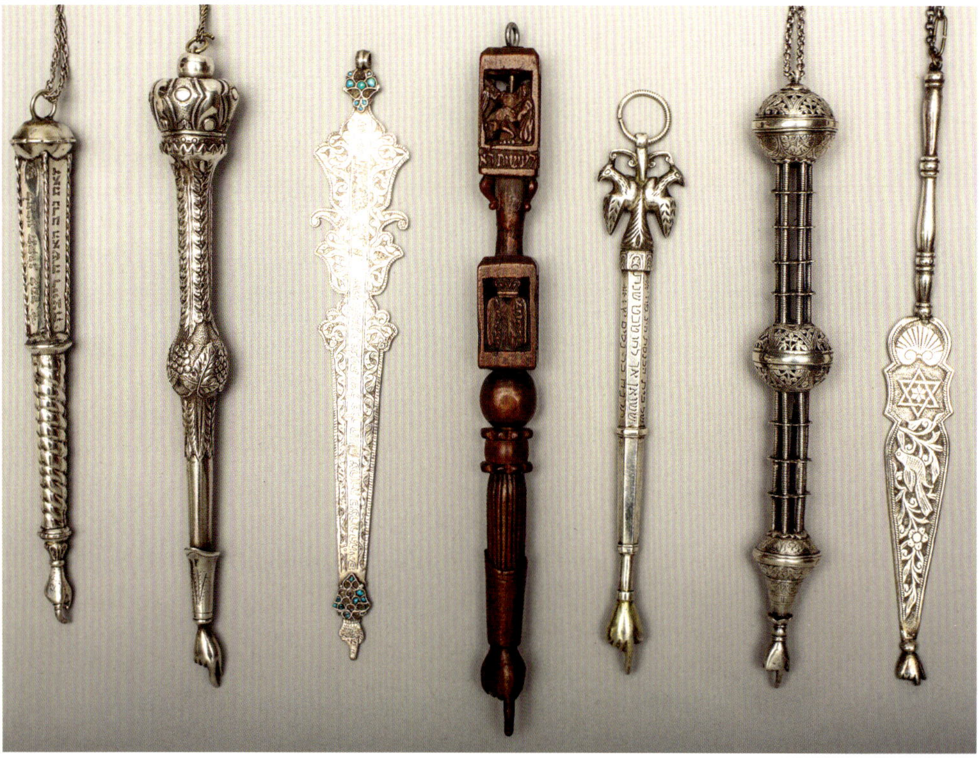

1.22 Seven *yadayim* (Torah pointers): (from left to right) Berlin, Germany, 1752–53; Vilnius, Lithuania, 1888; Balch, Afghanistan/Bukhara, 1848; Ukraine, 1872; Chechouan, Morocco, 1898; Galicia, Ukraine, ca. 1800; Tunisia, 1932. Gross Family Collection. Photograph by Tomer Appelbaum.

The word *ʿatarah* (coronet) is, however, often associated with queens rather than kings. As the Sefer Torah came to serve as an icon for God, a more regal crown fit for a king, known in Hebrew as a *keter*, became the norm, at least among European Jews (though the original wreath or *ʿatarah* is still preserved in the shape of the coronet on the Mediterranean *tik* described and pictured earlier). This masculine crown came to be known as a *keter.* Fig. 1.21 pictures four Torah crowns: 1) a *keter* from Hamburg, Germany (1703–82), silver; with two stands for the staves; 2) a Turkish/Sephardic *keter* (ca. 1875), made in Vienna, Austria, from precious metals; 3) an *ʿatarah* from Rhodes, Greece (1832/33, silver); and 4) another, especially beautiful *keter* from Galicia, Ukraine (ca. 1820, silver, with lions and antlered deer climbing up the treelike top).[163]

The regal element epitomized by the crown eventually came to imbue the overall appearance of the Sefer Torah. A crown became a standard feature of the *tas* or shield worn over the *me'il*, a dedicatory plaque that was regularly used by the late fifteenth and sixteenth centuries.[164] Still later, the image of a crown above the words *keter torah* (or their abbreviation, *khav-tav*) came frequently to adorn both the *me'il* and the *parokhet*, the curtain covering the front of the Torah ark.[165] And finally, even the most recent ritual article to be associated with the Torah scroll came to assume a regal shape under the force of the crown. This is the *yad* (literally, "hand"), or Torah pointer, a stick of either metal or wood with a hand culminating in an outstretched finger. The earliest dated *yad* is from Ferrara, Italy, 1487–88, but most early pointers come from the very late sixteenth and early seventeenth centuries.[166] In North African and Arabic-speaking lands, the *yad* frequently has the shape of a *hamsa*. In European countries, by contrast, the *yad* typically took a scepter-like shape. Fig. 1.22 pictures seven *yad*s and the variety of shapes they can take: 1) Berlin, Germany (1752/3), silver; 2) Vilnius, Lithuania (1888), silver; 3) Balch, Afghanistan/Bukhara (1848), silver; 4) Ukraine (1872), wood; 5) Chechoun, Morocco (1898), silver; 6) Galicia, Ukraine (ca. 1800), silver; 7) Tunisia (1932), silver.

The full dress of the Torah scroll in the synagogue—whether with a crowned *me'il* or a *tik* with a built-in crown—thus represents the Torah scroll as *melekh ha-'olam*, "king of the universe." So, too, is God addressed in the classical liturgy.

The Artifactual Power of the Torah Scroll

The iconic features of the Torah scroll endowed it with an aura of sanctity that extended far beyond its status as the conveyor of a divinely inspired text. According to one Babylonian sage (B. Sotah 39b), it is forbidden to leave a synagogue before the Sefer Torah has been taken out of the building, a prohibition he bases on the verse, "After the Lord your God you should walk" (Deut. 13:5). Similarly, the Talmud (B. Makkot 22b; B. Kiddushin 33b) requires every person to stand in the Torah's presence as though a king—or God—were present. It was forbidden to touch the bare parchment of a scroll, a taboo that may help explain the origins of the enigmatic Mishnaic phrase *sefarim ha-metam'im et ha-yadayim* (books that impurify the hands).[167] This phrase has traditionally been understood as denoting the canonical books of scripture (books *in* the canon impurify, those *outside* don't), but its original meaning has still not been satisfactorily explained. At the very least, the prescription that books of the Bible "defile the hands" discouraged physical contact with those books, either to protect the parchment or because it was considered disrespectful.[168]

To be sure, the Sefer Torah's aura of sanctity is also reflected in more mundane statements and practices, some of them legally normative, others popular customs. For example, there is a hierarchy according to which scrolls containing different sections of the Bible (e.g., Torah, Prophets, Writings) are permitted to be placed upon one another: the Torah must always be on the top.[169] Similarly, rabbinic halacha prohibits the selling of Torah scrolls except under special circumstances (e.g., providing a dowry and ransoming captives) and recommends that worn-out scrolls be buried in graves alongside sages.[170] But its "godliness" could also endow the Torah scroll with virtually magical powers.[171] When the rabbis (B. Sanhedrin 21b) discuss the commandment to the future king of Israel to have "a copy of this teaching [*mishneh ha-torah ha-zot*] written for him in a scroll" (Deut. 17:18), they interpreted the phrase *mishneh ha-torah* as meaning two Torah scrolls (*shtei torot*)—one for the king to leave in his palace; the other, to carry with him and to "make into an amulet [*qamea*ʿ] for himself and to tie to his arm."[172] Actual amulets have been found in Palestinian synagogues near Torah shrines, possibly because, as some modern scholars have suggested, the amulets were believed to derive their power from the ark and its scrolls (a belief that might also explain why biblical phrases are used so commonly in magical formulas).[173]

The artifactual powers attributed to the Torah scroll were familiar to gentiles in the ancient world.[174] In a remarkable passage in his *Orations against the Jews* (*Adversus Judaeos*), Oration 1, the fourth-century Syrian Christian father, John Chrysostom (349–407 CE), fulminated against the synagogue and the claims made for its holiness on account of the Torah scrolls housed inside it. "Let nobody venerate the synagogue because of its books," he writes, "but let them hate and turn their back on it because the Jews maltreat the holy ones [i.e., the prophets], because they refuse to believe their own words, because they accuse them of the ultimate impiety [that is, the Jews falsely claim that the prophets do not know of Christ and his coming]." John's point—which is unexceptionable if not for its specific polemical content—is that mere possession of a holy scroll does not impart holiness to its owners unless they understand its correct interpretation and believe in its truth. "The books don't make a place holy but . . . [it is] the intention of those who come together [in a place] that makes it pure."[175] John's vehemence reflects the fact that not only Jews but also Christians (some of whom were probably in John's audience when he delivered the sermon) believed in the supernatural efficacy of the Torah scroll. Nor was it only Christians who condemned Jews for "Torah idolatry." The eleventh-century Karaite Daniel al-Kumisi (1088) similarly accused rabbinite Jews (as he called rabbinic Jews) of prostrating themselves idolatrously before the Torah when they removed it from its ark.[176]

In the Middle Ages, belief in the Sefer Torah's artifactual power became even more widespread. Fig. 1.23, a miniature from the famous fourteenth-century Spanish Haggadah, today known as the Sarajevo Haggadah, shows a group of Jews on Passover eve leaving the synagogue to go home to their seder. Behind them is an open Torah ark with three Torah scrolls standing upright, and a figure—it is not clear if it is male or female—is reaching up to touch the scrolls and probably kiss them. The art historian Shalom Sabar has connected this illustration to a folkloric custom originally practiced by Jews living in the Islamic world (and which continued to be practiced by Jews living in the Near East and North Africa) to leave the Torah ark open after the conclusion of services so that women could approach it and address the Torah scrolls with special petitions and prayers

1.23
Sarajevo Haggadah, ca. 1350, Spain, fol. 34r: Synagogue; Library of the National Museum of Bosnia and Herzegovina. Courtesy of the National Museum of Bosnia and Herzegovina, Sarajevo.

for healing, fertility, livelihood, matchmaking, and the like.[177] Whether or not this illustration testifies to that custom, the amuletic powers attributed to the Torah scroll were frequently invoked in cases of difficult childbirth, even as late as the early modern period. An engraving in an eighteenth-century ethnographic study, P. C. Kirchner's *Jüdisches Ceremonien* (Nürenberg, 1724) (fig. 1.24) illustrates a widely practiced custom among Germanic Jews of bringing a Torah scroll into the birthing room; in the detail reproduced here, one can see the scroll open on the table on the left side of the room behind its upright "dress" while the pregnant mother is on the birthing stool to the right. This practice, it should be noted, was criticized by some rabbinic authorities but to little avail.[178] In Russia, there was an unusual custom of running a string tied to the doors of the Torah ark in the synagogue through the streets of the town to the home of the pregnant woman and giving

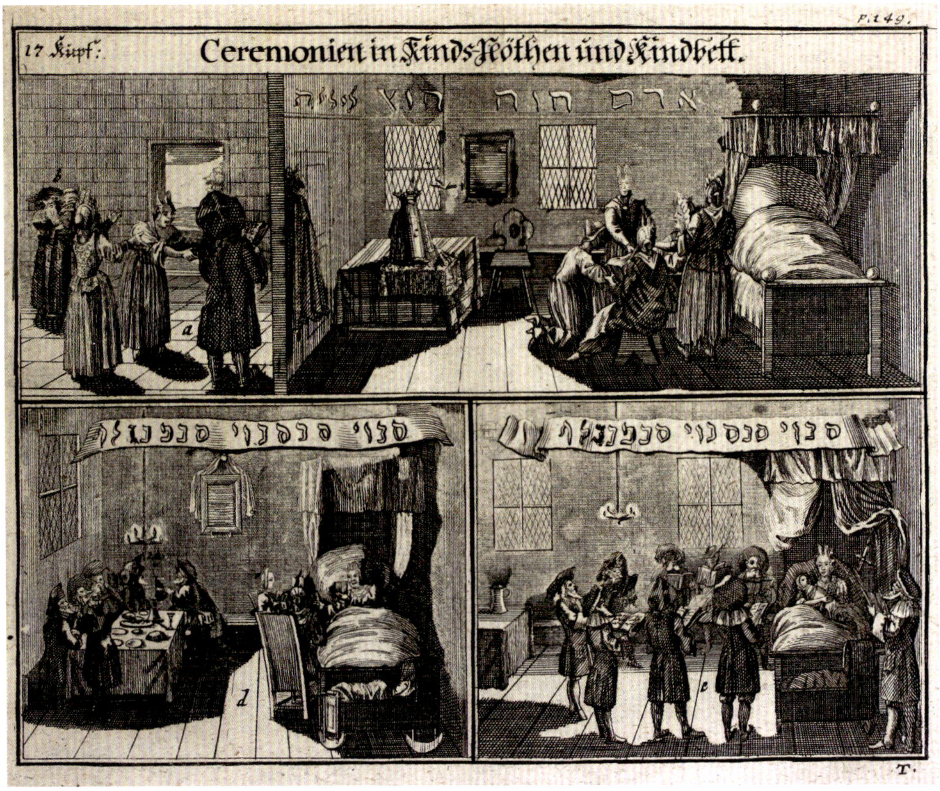

1.24 P. C. Kirchner, *Jüdisches Ceremonien*, Nürnberg: Peter Conrad Monath, 1724. Gross Family Collection. Photograph by Tomer Appelbaum.

the end of the string to the woman in labor to pull so that she could literally open the doors of the Torah ark; this act of sympathetic magic was believed to have the power to hasten the opening of the woman's womb.[179]

The Torah Scroll as a Symbol of Judaism

Jews in the late antique and medieval periods were not the sole parties to attribute symbolic meaning to the Torah scroll. Among Christians, the Torah scroll became a symbol for Judaism itself.

This is not surprising. As we have seen, during the late antique period gentiles were familiar with the Torah scroll. Its public use in the synagogue was known and denounced by Christian preachers like John Chrysostom. Later, in the Middle Ages, gentile authorities made Jews swear oaths before their Torah scrolls just as Christians took oaths on their Bibles.[180] For medieval Christians, however, the Torah scroll took on an additional symbolic meaning that went far beyond the meaning of the text inscribed in the scroll. The material shape of the Jews' Hebrew Bible came to possess the symbolic significance of religious identity. Christians differentiated themselves from Jews by identifying their religion with the codex, in opposition to Judaism, which they associated with the scroll. Just as the codex had replaced the scroll, they argued, so too Christianity had superseded Judaism.

This dual opposition—between Jew and Christian on one hand, and scroll and codex on the other—informs the following passage, written in the thirteenth century by Durandus, bishop of Mende (in Egypt). In the course of describing a certain painting in a church, Durandus remarks:

> And note that the patriarchs and prophets are painted with scrolls in their hands. Some of the apostles [are] with books and some with scrolls: namely, because before the advent of Christ the faith was set forth under figures, and many things were not made clear; to represent this, the patriarchs and prophets are painted with scrolls to signify that imperfect knowledge. But because the apostles were perfectly taught of Christ, therefore the books [that is, codices], which are the emblems of this perfect knowledge, are open.[181]

The patriarchs and prophets about whom Durandus speaks are Old Testament figures, but it is not always easy in medieval Christian art to distinguish between figures from the Bible and their later Jewish descendants. As Sara Lipton has argued, because of the Augustinian doctrine that "Judaism was a static and sterile relic, unchanged and unchangeable," biblical "Jews" could equally characterize the contemporary Jews of the illustrator's day. Thus the "scrolls" held by the biblical figures in the illustrations could symbolize and refer to a Judaism practiced by contemporary Jews.[182]

The same opposition is represented in illustrations found in copies of the *Bible moralisée*, lavishly illustrated Bibles specially commissioned by the royal family of France in the thirteenth century for their education and edification. Fig. 1.25 reproduces two roundels from a famous *Bible moralisée*. The illustrations accompany Exodus 32:19, a verse that describes Moses's return to the camp of the Israelites upon descending from Mount Sinai; the picture specifically illustrates the verse that describes how Moses, when he saw the Golden Calf, "hurled the tablets from his hands, and shattered them at the foot of the mountain." The commentary accompanying the verse explains, "Moses who destroyed the tablets signifies Jesus Christ who destroyed the Old Law. The people sought forgiveness, and then Moses retrieved new tablets, thus signifying Jesus Christ who reforms the Holy Church so that She might do his will."[183] This lesson is illustrated in the two roundels. In the upper picture, Moses hurls several broken tablets to the ground before the shocked Israelites. In the lower roundel, Jesus throws scrolls on the ground before several obviously

1.25 *Bible moralisée*, France, thirteenth century; Vienna, Österreichische Nationalbibliothek, Cod. 1179, fol. 37v. Courtesy of Öesterreichishe National Bibliothek, Vienna.

distressed Jews (who can be identified as Jews by the pointed *Judenhutte* they wear). In the latter illustration, the inscription on the scroll reads, "Here Synagoga is broken by the Son of God." As Lipton notes, there is some ambiguity in the pictures: it is not clear whether the Jews in the lower roundel are meant to represent Jews who at the time of Jesus refused to abandon their faith and follow his teaching, or medieval Jews contemporary with the author and illustrator of this Bible. The scroll in the picture more closely resembles a *rotulus*, the typically smaller scroll written vertically (like the Nash papyrus, pictured in fig. 1.3), which is the kind of scroll that medieval Christians would have most easily recognized, and so one is inclined to follow the more contemporary reference. In either case, Judaism is symbolized by a scroll, and that image is overwhelmingly negative.

For Christians, then, the binary of scroll versus codex had become a visual code to designate the opposition between Judaism and Christianity. Somewhat ironically, Christians turned the material New Testament codex, particularly the gospel book, into an icon for God's physical presence within the church in ways strikingly parallel to the way Jews made the Torah scroll into an icon for God's presence in the synagogue.[184] But the conceptual development of the scroll/codex binary signals a dramatic change in the fundamental status of the Bible that had taken place by the Middle Ages. Scripture had become a *contested* text. Judaism and Christianity—and to a lesser but still significant extent, Islam—both claimed exclusive possession of the Bible and fought over its ownership.

This competition became arguably the defining crux of the history of the Bible in Western culture in the medieval and early modern periods. The battle over ownership was fought most famously on exegetical and theological fronts, but it extended to the material shape of the Bible. Early on, Christians adapted the new writing platform of the codex for inscribing the books of the New Testament, while for centuries Jews continued to use the scroll as the sole writing medium for the Hebrew Bible. Yet once Jews also began to write their texts in codices, they had to give that medium a distinctive shape to define its "Jewishness." Each religious community came to possess a somewhat different material Bible in the shape of the codex, and each side in the conflict used the materiality of the Bible as a medium for expressing religious identity and difference.

In the course of this struggle over ownership, it is nonetheless noteworthy that Jews, unlike Christians, never adopted the Torah scroll as a symbol of their identity.[185] They had other symbols—in the ancient world, for example, the menorah; in the medieval and early modern periods, the Tablets of the Decalogue, and still later, the Magen David (or Seal of Solomon).[186] But the Torah scroll never became a symbol of their national or religious identity for Jews. For all its symbolic meaning within the synagogue—its charge as an icon of divinity—the Sefer Torah's materiality, its physical presence, remained its irreducible defining feature.

ומשארתך׃ ארור פרי בטנך
ופרי אדמתך שגר אלפיך
ועשתרת צאנך׃ ארור אתה
בבאך וארור אתה בצאתך׃
ישלח יהוה בך את המארה
את המהומה ואת המגערת
בכל משלח ידך אשר תעשה
עד השמדך ועד אבדך
מהר מפני רע מעלליך
אשר עזבתני׃ ידבק יהוה
בך את הדבר עד כלתו אתך
מעל האדמה אשר אתה
בא שמה לרשתה׃ יככה
יהוה בשחפת ובקדחת
ובדלקת ובחרחר ובחרב
ובשדפון ובירקון ורדפוך
עד אבדך׃ והיו שמיך אשר
על ראשך נחשת והארץ
אשר תחתיך ברזל׃ יתן
יהוה את מטר ארצך אבק
ועפר מן השמים ירד עליך
עד השמדך׃ יתנך יהוה
נגף לפני איביך בדרך אחד
תצא אליו ובשבעה דרכים
תנוס לפניו והיית לזעוה
לכל ממלכות הארץ׃ והיתה
נבלתך למאכל לכל עוף
השמים ולבהמת הארץ

ואין מחריד׃ יככה יהוה
בשחין מצרים ובעפלים
ובגרב ובחרס אשר לא
תוכל להרפא׃ יככה יהוה
בשגעון ובעורון ובתמהון
לבב׃ והיית ממשש בצהרים
כאשר ימשש העור
באפלה ולא תצליח את
דרכיך והיית אך עשוק
וגזול כל הימים ואין מושיע
אשה תארש ואיש אחר
ישגלנה בית תבנה ולא
תשב בו כרם תטע ולא
תחללנו׃ שורך טבוח
לעיניך ולא תאכל ממנו
חמרך גזול מלפניך ולא
ישוב לך צאנך נתנות
לאיביך ואין לך מושיע׃
בניך ובנתיך נתנים לעם
אחר ועיניך ראות וכלות
אליהם כל היום ואין לאל
ידך׃ פרי אדמתך וכל יגיעך
יאכל עם אשר לא ידעת
והיית רק עשוק ורצוץ
כל הימים׃ והיית משגע
ממראה עיניך אשר תראה׃
יככה יהוה בשחין רע על
הברכים ועל השקים

אשר לא תוכל להרפא
מכף רגלך ועד קדקדך׃
יולך יהוה אתך ואת
מלכך אשר תקים עליך
אל גוי אשר לא ידעת
אתה ואבתיך ועבדת שם
אלהים אחרים עץ ואבן׃
והיית לשמה למשל
ולשנינה בכל העמים
אשר ינהגך יהוה שמה׃
זרע רב תוציא השדה
ומעט תאסף כי יחסלנו
הארבה׃ כרמים תטע
ועבדת ויין לא תשתה ולא
תאגר כי תאכלנו התלעת׃
זיתים יהיו לך בכל גבולך
ושמן לא תסוך כי ישל
זיתך׃ בנים ובנות תוליד
ולא יהיו לך כי ילכו בשבי׃
כל עצך ופרי אדמתך
יירש הצלצל׃ הגר אשר
בקרבך יעלה עליך מעלה
מעלה ואתה תרד מטה
מטה׃ הוא ילוך ואתה
לא תלונו הוא יהיה לראש
ואתה תהיה לזנב׃ ובאו
עליך כל הקללות האלה
ורדפוך והשיגוך עד השמדך

CHAPTER TWO

THE HEBREW BIBLE IN THE AGE OF THE MANUSCRIPT

The illustration opposite this page (fig. 2.1) is the recto of a folio from the *Keter Aram Tzova*, the fabled Aleppo Codex. This manuscript was written by the scribe Shlomo ben Boya'a around 930 CE in the land of Israel, possibly in the city of Tiberias. The many annotations on the page (written in a miniscule script on the upper and lower lines and in the markings between the text columns) are known as the Masorah and were added by another sage-scribe, Aaron ben Asher, who is believed to have been the greatest expert on the biblical text in his time.[1] Although the name of the original patron and owner of the volume is not known, the Bible was eventually acquired by a certain Yisrael ben Simḥah of Basra, who dedicated it to the Karaite synagogue of Jerusalem, where it was used for public reading and study. Karaism was the most significant sectarian movement in medieval Judaism; it occupies a position of signal importance in the history of the Hebrew Bible, as we shall see in the course of this chapter.

2.1 (Opposite) *Keter Aram Tzova* (Aleppo Codex) (Deut. 28:18–45), Tiberias (?), land of Israel, 920 CE. Courtesy of the Ben-Zvi Institute, Jerusalem. Photograph by Ardon Bar Hama.

At the very end of the eleventh century, in 1099, following the sack of Jerusalem, Crusaders stole the Bible from the Karaite synagogue. Eventually it was ransomed from captivity and taken to the synagogue of the Jerusalemite community, then living in Fustat, Old Cairo, in Egypt, where, as most scholars today agree, the great sage Maimonides (1135–1204) consulted and used the book as the model for the Torah scroll he wrote for himself. In his famous code, the *Mishneh Torah* (*Hilkhot Sefer Torah*, chap. 8), Maimonides based the laws for writing a Torah scroll on the text in the volume.

We do not know what happened to the Bible over the next three hundred years, but by the mid-fifteenth century, the book had landed in Aleppo, Syria, where it was kept in the city's Old Synagogue in a locked chest inside a cave behind the building in which, the Jews of Aleppo believed, the prophet Elijah had once hid. The Aleppo Jews also believed that the Bible possessed virtually amuletic powers that protected their community from harm, and they jealously guarded it, allowing the book to be displayed publicly only on rare occasions.

On December 2, 1947, everything changed. Following the establishment of the state of Israel, riots against Jews broke out throughout Syria. The Old Synagogue in Aleppo was vandalized and torched; initially, it was believed that the Bible had also been lost, either in the flames or by looting. Happily, the volume had been safely removed from the synagogue before the looting and entrusted to a Christian Arab, who hid it in his house for the next ten years. In 1958, after lengthy secret negotiations, the Bible was smuggled out of Syria and brought to Israel, where it was delivered to the president of Israel, Yitzhak Ben-Zvi. Ben-Zvi in turn entrusted it to the Ben-Zvi Institute, a research center dedicated to the study of Jewish communities of the Near East. Today, the Aleppo Codex is displayed in the Shrine of the Book at the Israel Museum in Jerusalem, together with the Dead Sea Scrolls.[2]

Tragically, however, at some point after being taken out of Syria, the volume was vandalized, with the result that today most of the Pentateuch (up to the last word of Deut. 28:17) is missing, as well as a good part of the Song of Songs (from 3:13 on), and all of Ecclesiastes, Lamentations, Esther, Daniel, and Ezra-Nehemiah. As of this writing, the missing sections have still not been recovered. The page pictured in fig. 2.1 is the first of the surviving folios in the codex.

Yet even in its diminished state, the Aleppo Codex is an extraordinarily important manuscript. For one thing, in the view of most scholars today, the codex preserves the most accurate text of the Hebrew Bible. In addition, the Bible is also one of the earliest Jewish texts written in the form of a codex. *Codex* is the scholarly term for what we call a book—that is, a collection of groupings or gatherings (or quires) of folded sheets of writing material (papyrus, animal skin, paper, etc.) that are sewn together at their middle fold and encased within a protective binding. (Most, but not all, "books" are codices; many contemporary paperbacks are simply single sheets of paper glued together at the spine.)

Nearly all the extant early Jewish codices contain, like the Aleppo Codex, texts of the

Bible. All of them were written in the Near East—Syria, Palestine, Egypt, Tunisia, and Iraq—between the early tenth and mid-eleventh centuries.[3] Exactly how many full codices with the Masorah were produced during this period is not known, but there must have been many more than have survived. In addition to *Keter Aram Tzova*, a single complete text of the Hebrew Bible (known as the Leningrad Codex because it is kept in the State Library of Russia in Saint Petersburg, formerly Leningrad) exists, as well as several codices containing either the Pentateuch or large sections of the Prophets and the Hagiographa. There are also hundreds of leaves representing lost codices, many of them preserved in the Saint Petersburg collections.[4]

In addition to these large deluxe and intact codices and the scattered leaves, an enormous number of fragments of biblical books dating from before the thirteenth century have been preserved in the Cairo Genizah; according to one scholar's estimate, there are at least ten thousand biblical fragments.[5] Some of these fragments derive from codices similar to the Aleppo Codex and contain the full Masorah (probably 10–15 percent of the total). Many others lack Masoretic notes but are vocalized (and often accentuated) and written on parchment with sufficient care to have served as study texts (roughly one-third of the surviving fragments), while an enormous number of fragments written in smaller formats on either cheaper parchment or paper appear to have been transcribed unprofessionally, without the care and exactitude found in the two other types. This last group constitutes roughly 50 percent of the Genizah's biblical fragments and was probably written for popular use by individuals, perhaps with the purpose of allowing laypersons in the synagogue to follow the public reading of the Torah with their own private copies.

This evidence from the Cairo Genizah indicates the wide variety of Bibles in codex form that were produced and used by Jews in the early Middle Ages (between the eighth and thirteenth centuries). If the evidence is representative, it suggests the relative proportions of the different types of Bibles Jews utilized during this period. This would mean that the vast number of Bibles were the popular ones produced for use by ordinary Jews; the evidence also suggests that they were used intensively, because they survive only in fragments. Deluxe and intact Bibles like the Aleppo Codex were the most expensive to produce, and the most carefully protected, and they must have been owned mainly by wealthy Jews or communal institutions like synagogues (which received them as donations from wealthy individuals). Nonetheless, these deluxe Bibles—precisely because of their high quality—provide us with the richest evidence for the material history of the Jewish Bible in the early Middle Ages. That history must have begun at least a century or two prior to the production of the surviving codices. Even though they are the earliest Jewish codices, these deluxe codices were not the work of beginners. Among the most beautiful Hebrew manuscripts ever composed, they display such extraordinary scribal sophistication that they must have been products of a tradition of codex production that probably began in the late seventh or early eighth century.

These early biblical codices are known as Masoretic Bibles on account of the Masorah, the vast system of annotations and enumerations of various lexical, phonetic, and syntactic phenomena in the biblical text, which appear on the Aleppo Codex page in the upper and lower margins and, in abbreviated form, in the space between the columns. Aside from the biblical text, the Masorah is the most important element in a medieval Jewish Bible codex.[6] There are several reasons for its importance, and its presence on the page eventually became the primary mark of the "Jewishness" of a Bible. Indeed, it would not be inaccurate to say that the story of the Jewish Bible from the early Middle Ages down to the present day is in large part the story of the Masorah.

The First Hebrew Bible Codices

As a writing platform, the codex first made its appearance in Western culture around the turn of the Common Era. According to current scholarly opinion, the form of the codex derived from the ancient tablet, which was typically made of wax inside a wooden frame, sometimes with multiple frames attached to each other in an accordion-like fashion.[7] Rabbinic literature contains numerous references to such tablets. Known as *pinkasim* (sing. *pinkas*, from the Greek *pinax*), the tablets were used for record-keeping, for private notes, and probably for legal and homiletical traditions which the rabbis did not want to write down in a parchment scroll, possibly out of fear that the texts might be mistaken for parts of the Bible.[8] One rabbinic passage even refers to a *pinkas* of papyrus.[9] None of these *pinkasim* have survived. The earliest surviving ancient codices (or fragments of codices) are from Egypt (mainly from the third, fourth, and later centuries), and consist of sheets of papyrus containing both classical Greek texts as well as numerous fragments of the Greek translation of the Bible.[10] In the next chapter we will briefly describe one fragment from a papyrus codex containing a text of the Septuagint that may have been written by a Greek-speaking Jew. Even so, it is clear that early Christians were heavy consumers of the codex form, and more than any other ancient group, they showed a marked preference for recording their religious texts, the Pauline epistles and the gospels in particular, in such books.[11]

By the fifth century, the relationship between scroll and codex had changed. The codex had effectively overtaken the scroll and become the preferred book form for nearly every population in the late antique world, with one exception: the Jews.[12] The earliest surviving Hebrew codices come from the early tenth century, and even if the use of the codex by Jews predates these codices by a century or two, it is clear that it took Jews at least four hundred years longer to adopt the new writing platform than most everyone else in the Mediterranean world. Why? In part, it may have been a reaction on the part of the rabbis to Christians' early appropriation of the codex; the rabbis insisted that Jews write the Torah solely in a scroll (and in accordance with the many laws relating to its inscription) as a way of maintaining its inviolability, and at least in the first centuries in the common era, they seem to have resisted writing down their nonbiblical traditions in any formal way. Early Christians, in turn, may initially have seized upon the codex precisely to distinguish their scriptural texts from the rabbis' Sefer Torah. Alternatively, they may have used the codex precisely because it was still considered a less important writing platform than the scroll and therefore more appropriate for texts (like the gospels or the Pauline epistles) that were not yet considered fully authoritative or canonical.[13] Medieval Christians eventually seized upon the codex's supersession of the scroll to express Christianity's supersession of Judaism, but Jews themselves never took up the scroll as an icon of self-identification in the way Christians employed the codex.[14] Although Jews may not have used codices, there is no evidence to suggest that the reason for this was because they considered the codex a non-Jewish writing platform or a Christian one.

Whatever the ancient rabbis' reason for not taking up the codex, it was not until centuries later that Jews finally adopted the book form (while, of course, maintaining exclusive use of the Sefer Torah in the synagogue). Wide use of the codex throughout the Mediterranean world was probably the major reason for this shift, but the transition could only have been bolstered by the fact that, by the eighth century, Jews were living primarily under Islamic dominion, not Christian, and so any earlier rationale connected to Christianity for avoiding the codex had lost its force. Nonetheless, the fact that nearly all surviving early codices are Bibles—precisely the text that the rabbis would have had the strongest reasons *not* to write in a codex—suggests the profound change in sensibility that must have taken place in Jewish culture.[15] It is worth noting that Muslims too, roughly at the same time, began to write their sacred text, the Qur'an, in codex form.[16] The impact of Islamic book culture on its Jewish counterpart at the time is evident in the Hebrew term used to designate a codex, *miṣḥaf*, a word borrowed from the Arabic *muṣḥaf*. The very fact that Jews had to go to Arabic for a name indicates the foreignness and novelty of the book form in Jewish culture as well as the importance of the Islamic context for understanding the Jews' adaptation of the form.[17]

For Jews, however, the codex was not merely a new book form or writing platform. For one thing, because it was not a Sefer Torah and therefore not regulated by all the halacha governing its material sacrality, scribes were now able to inscribe elements (like vocalization marks and paratexts) in a codex Bible that they were forbidden to write in Torah scrolls. In this respect, the codex represented a genuinely new discursive space in Jewish literary culture. This new space is epitomized in the page format of the early Masoretic Bible, the page from the Aleppo Codex pictured in fig. 2.1. The format of this page displays features that simultaneously look back to the ancient scroll and forward to the medieval codex.[18] On the one hand, the three columns on the page roughly replicate the appearance of a parchment sheet of a Torah scroll with the text written in the same prominent, square Assyrian letters and in the same dark ink (albeit in slightly narrower columns in the codex than in a Torah scroll). On the other hand, the codex page contains elements that, according to rabbinic halacha, could not be written in a Sefer Torah: the vocalization/vowelization marks (*niqud*), the cantillation notes (*te'amim*), and above all, the many Masoretic notations in the margins. This page, with its three elements accompanying the biblical text, was an entirely new discursive presence in Jewish literary history.

The Masorah on the page is recorded in two distinct fashions. The intercolumn annotations, which typically consist of abbreviations in the form of single letters, are known as the *masorah parva* or *masorah qetanah* (short or minor masorah). Those in the two (sometimes three or four) line notes on the very top and very bottom of the page are called the *masorah magna* or *masorah gedolah* (lengthy or major masorah). Both types of Masoretic notes annotate the same kinds of textual phenomena, one in abbreviations, the other more expansively. The latter often include collations of different types of textual idiosyncracies.

What Is the Masorah?

The word *Masorah* is usually translated as "tradition" (like the similar-sounding word *masoret*), but it is likely that the term derives from a less frequent meaning of the root *m-s-r*, "to count," thus making the Masorah "an enumeration."[19] And indeed, much (though not all) of the Masorah is enumerative, and those enumerations are closely associated with the two additional elements found on the codex page: the *niqud* and the *te'amim*. Although neither the *niqud* nor the *te'amim* is formally part of the Masorah, much of the Masorah is about them, and it is therefore impossible to talk about the Masorah without taking them into account. The Masoretes—as the authors of the Masorah are known—did not invent the vocalization or cantillation systems but inherited them from earlier tradition. Unhappily, we know almost nothing about the Masoretes (or about the Masorah) before these Masoretic codices. The Masoretes were, however, the first to inscribe vocalization and cantillation directions on the page. Part of the reason for this was tactical and polemical. The various Masoretic centers and their respective schools differed on the proper way to write and pronounce many words. Moreover, each school had its own procedures for inscribing vocalization and cantillation marks, that is, for writing vowels and notes.

The subject matter recorded in the Masorah can be divided into two categories. The first includes annotations concerning the differences between the writing and reading traditions of the Bible, specifically those pertaining to the correct inscription of the biblical text, particularly when the two traditions differ. *Qeri u-ketiv* annotations indicate where the text is to be read differently from the way it is written (which is to say, where the scribal tradition differed from oral reading practice); *ketiv ve-lo qeri* are cases where words in the text are not to be read; *tikkunei soferim*, words added to the text by scribes; and *'iturrei soferim*, words omitted by scribes.[20] Some 1,350 *qeri u-ketiv* notes are found in the Masorah, and together with the other scribal annotations just listed, these notes amount to about 5 percent of the total number of Masoretic annotations. Despite their relative paucity, these notes are clear evidence of one function the Masorah served, which was to ensure the accuracy of the written text of the Torah according to scribal tradition as well as the correct reading tradition for that text.

The other 95 percent of the data recorded in the Masorah—the vast majority of its notes—are enumerations of every conceivable textual, syntactic, and orthographic peculiarity in the biblical text. These notes are recorded either in the *masorah parva* found in the side margins and between the text columns, or in the *masorah magna* on the top and bottom of the page. The *masorah parva*'s notes are nearly all single-letter abbreviations. The most common of these is the letter *lamed*, which stands for the Aramaic term *leit*, literally, "there is none," meaning that the form of the word being annotated is unique, a hapax legomenon.[21] Most of the notes, however, record recurring phenomena and list the number of times a given word or phrase appears in the Bible; the number is signified by the alphabetic letter with the appropriate numerical value: for example, a *daled* (the fourth letter in the alphabet, hence the number "four") denotes that the word or phrase appears four times.[22] These enumerations pay special attention to instances of exceptional orthography, in particular defective and *plene* spellings (where words are written with or without the *matres lectionis*, consonants that function as vowels).[23] The Masorah also includes contrastive and comparative notes, which annotate the minute differences between parallel but not identical words, phrases, and verses.

The *masorah magna*, found on the two upper and lower micrographic lines of the page, is essentially an expanded version of the *masorah parva*. Thus, where *masorah parva* might simply note that a given word appears four times in the Bible, *masorah magna* lists the verses (usually by their initial words, since chapter and verse numbering did not yet exist). Most often, it lists exceptions. Where they became too lengthy to fit on the page, these lists of extraordinary textual occurences were sometimes appended at the end of the codex. Still later, in the Geonic period (eighth to tenth centuries, named after the Geonim, as the leaders of the great Talmudic academies were known), independent collections of singular Masoretic annotations were also compiled. The best known of these works is *Okhlah Va-okhlah*, which takes its title from two cases of hapax legomena relating to the word *okhlah*, which is written once in the Bible without a *vav* (1 Sam. 1:9), and once with it (Gen. 27:19).[24] *Okhlah Va-okhlah* also includes various mnemonic aids (*simanim*) for remembering famously confusing exceptions. For example, to remind the reader that in Ezekiel's prophecy concerning the man who "has *not eaten* upon the mountains" (Ezek. 18:6), the verb *has (not) eaten* (*ākhāl*) is written with a long *a* (Hebrew *qamets*, a word whose root also means "to shut"), in contrast to Ezekiel 18:11, where in the prophecy about the man "who has eaten upon the mountains," the verb for *has eaten* (*ākhal*) is spelled with a short *a* (Hebrew *pataḥ*, a word whose root means "to open"), the Masorete made up the epigram, "He who had eaten [i.e., Ezek. 18:11] opened [*pataḥ*] his mouth, while he who had *not* eaten [Ezek. 18:6] shut [*qamats*] his mouth."[25]

These codices were typically produced by multiple individuals who are often named in the colophons—a scribe (*sofer*) who wrote the unpointed consonantal text of the Torah; a punctuator (*nakdan*) who added the vocalization, punctuation, and accentuation marks; and a Masorete (*masran*) who added the Masoretic notes and often checked the Hebrew text for mistakes and corrections. In some cases the punctuator and the Masorete were the same person, but usually not the scribe and Masorete.[26]

This fact is significant for several reasons. First, it shows that early on the production of Hebrew codices was a collaborative effort, not the work of a single person. The fact that multiple figures wrote, punctuated, and masoreted the text also helps explain why in nearly all the earliest surviving codices—the only near exception is the Aleppo Codex—the Masorah does not entirely agree with the biblical text that it accompanies. In fact, no two Masorahs in different codices are entirely identical, and each one implicitly dictates a slightly different biblical text! While the Masorah is often considered to be the final stage in the stabilization of the biblical text, this last fact reminds us that the process has never been truly brought to completion.

As a visible feature of the material Jewish Bible, the Masoretic apparatus first appears in these earliest Hebrew Bible codices of the tenth and eleventh centuries. One assumes that the Masorah initially began before Jews adopted the codex, when the Bible was still being written exclusively in a scroll, but no early Torah scrolls with Masoretic notes survive, nor do we have fragments of Masoretic annotations written on separate sheets or leafs, either from a scroll or a codex.[27] We can only speculate about the prehistory of the Masorah before the early codices.

The Invention of the Masorah

In most traditional and modern scholarly accounts, the Masorah is traced back to the classical rabbinic period.[28] This claim is not without basis: the roots of the Masoretic project certainly date to very early in Jewish tradition. The word *masoret/masorot* appears in the Talmud in a context that suggests that it may refer to specific items of the Masorah.[29] Many midrashim build upon lexical or orthographic oddities in the biblical text, and numerous passages testify to the early sages' fascination with every eccentricity—oral, orthographic, syntactic—in the text. According to rabbinic tradition, the *soferim*, the scribes of the early Second Temple period (third or fourth century BCE), already knew that the *vav* of the word *gaḥon* ("belly," Lev. 11:42) stands in the middle of all the letters in the Torah; that the words *darosh darash* ("diligently understood," Lev. 10:16) marked the midpoint of its words; and that Leviticus 13:33 was the midverse in the Torah (B. Kiddushin 30a).

Indeed, according to the Talmud, the reason a scribe was called a *sofer* was because a scribe counted (*safar*) words and verses in the Bible (B. Kiddushin 30a). The rabbis themselves counted 5,845 verses in the five books of the Torah.

Nonetheless, the elaborate and fully developed system documented in the early biblical codices was truly unprecedented. Nothing in earlier Jewish tradition approaches the Masorah's exhaustive, virtually obsessive accounting of every scriptural detail. But the precise function of this project is not clear. The traditional view is that the primary aim of the Masorah "was clearly and undoubtedly the precise preservation of the holy text."[30] This is certainly true for part of the Masorah—the *ketiv-qeri* notes, *tikkunei* and *'itturei soferim*, and similar annotations—but this rationale does not satisfactorily account for the vast number of Masoretic annotations, particularly those enumerating exceptional textual phenomena. The massive effort that must have been expended in creating these elaborate lists and cross-references was simply excessive for the annotations to have been merely an instrument of stabilization. A vocalized, punctuated "perfect" copy of the biblical text alone—in a scroll or in a codex—would have been more effficient.

What other functions or purposes could these annotations have served? Some scholars have suggested that the Masorah, specifically the *te'amim*, "represents an early exegetical commentary on the Bible."[31] Others have proposed that the notes may have served as a tool for grammatical or exegetical study, or even as a kind of data bank of examples to help exegetes or grammarians.[32] Some parts of the Masorah and its effort to produce a definitive text of the Bible have parallels in projects undertaken in the Islamic world, albeit a century or two earlier, specifically in the initiatives undertaken at the behest of the caliph Uthman (ruled 644–56) to produce an official edition of the Qur'an; both the Islamic and the Masoretic projects appear to have been motivated by similar tensions between the writing and reading traditions.[33] The invention of *niqud* and the *te'amim* clearly parallels the inscription of vowel signs in Qur'an codices, a development that probably took place in both religious communities between the late seventh and ninth centuries.[34] Some scholars have also pointed to precedents in the emergence of early Qur'anic grammatical writing, and to Alexandrian scholia of the Hellenistic period and the canon tables of early Christian Bibles, as well as Syriac marginalia dealing with textual questions.[35] None of these cases, however, resembles the Masorah closely enough to adequately explain its emergence.

The obscurity surrounding the Masorah's beginnings also relates to the fact that we have little knowledge about its authors, the Masoretes or *ba'alei ha-masorah*. Again, we do not know when the earliest Masoretes lived, but by the beginning of the eighth century, there appear to have developed several distinct Masoretic schools, each with its own mode of inscription and tradition of vocalization, cantillation, and pronunciation. These schools were known after their locations: Babylonia, Palestine, and Tiberias. Tiberias eventually established itself as the authoritative school; it is also the only school for which we possess

2.2 Fragment of Bible codex with Palestinian vocalization (Ezekiel 31:4–36:7), Cairo Genizah. Cambridge, T-S 249.5. Syndics of Cambridge University Library.

substantial explicit evidence. All extant codices and substantial fragments of codices follow the Tiberian tradition, although single leaves and smaller fragments of both the Babylonian and Palestinian schools have been identified in the Cairo Genizah. The differences among the schools are visible in the fragments pictured in figs. 2.02 and 2.03, in contrast to the page fron the Aleppo Codex (fig. 2.1). Fig. 2.2 is a leaf from a Palestinian codex written *serugin*, in a kind of shorthand, with the first word of each verse inscribed in full, while subsequent words are indicated only by their accented syllables; such texts were probably meant to facilitate memorization.[36] Fig. 2.3 is from a famous Bible known as Codex Babylonicus, containing the Latter Prophets, probably written in the tenth or eleventh century; the Masoretic notes in the margin follow the Tiberian school and were probably added at a later point.[37]

As these illustrations demonstrate, the most visible difference between the Tiberian school on the one hand and the Babylonian and Palestinian schools on the other is that the latter inscribed the vocalization (*niqud*) and cantillation signs (*te'amim*) supralinearly—*above* the consonantal text—while the Tiberian school wrote the *niqud* beneath the line, and the *te'amim* both above and beneath it. The Masoretic notes of the two other

Jes. 1,1 — 1,13 1b

חזון ישעיהו בן אמוץ
אשר חזה על יהודה
וירושלם בימי עזיהו יותם
אחז יחזקיהו מלכי יהודה
שמעו שמים והאזיני ארץ
כי יהוה דבר בנים גדלתי
ורוממתי והם פשעו בי
ידע שור קנהו וחמור
אבוס בעליו ישראל לא
ידע עמי לא התבונן הוי
גוי חטא עם כבד עון
זרע מרעים בנים משחיתים
עזבו את יהוה נאצו את
קדוש ישראל נזרו אחור
על מה תכו עוד תוסיפו
סרה כל ראש לחלי וכל
לבב דוי מכף רגל ועד
ראש אין בו מתם פצע
וחבורה ומכה טריה לא
זרו ולא חבשו ולא רככה
בשמן ארצכם שממה

עריכם שרפות אש
אדמתכם לנגדכם זרים
אכלים אתה ושממה
כמהפכת זרים ונותרה
בת ציון כסכה בכרם
כמלונה במקשה כעיר
נצורה לולי יהוה צבאות
הותיר לנו שריד כמעט
כסדם היינו לעמרה דמינו

שמעו דבר יהוה קציני
סדם האזינו תורת אלהינו
עם עמרה למה לי רב
זבחיכם יאמר יהוה
שבעתי עלות אילים וחלב
מריאים ודם פרים וכבשים
ועתודים לא חפצתי כי
תבאו לראות פני מי בקש
זאת מידכם רמס חצרי
לא תוסיפו הביא מנחת
שוא קטרת תועבה היא

2.3 Codex Babylonicus with Babylonian vocalization (Isa. 1:1–1:15), folio 1b. Babylonia, 915 CE. Reproduced from *The Hebrew Bible—Latter Prophets, the Babylonian Codex of Petrograd*, ed. Hermann L. Strack (Saint Petersburg, 1876). Widener Library, Harvard University.

schools were also far less extensive than those of the Tiberian Masoretes, and they were generally recorded in separate books.[38] This is important because it demonstrates that the page layout of the Masoretic codex as we know it (as represented in the Aleppo Codex, for example), and as it continued to be copied throughout the Middle Ages, was the creation of the Tiberian school.

Why so little survives of the Babylonian and Palestinian schools is something of a mystery, as well as the reason why the Tiberian school eventually became the authoritative school.[39] Certainly once the Tiberian school had asserted its dominance, scribes stopped copying the Babylonian and Palestinian Masorah. As a number of examples testify, biblical texts with Babylonian and Palestinian Masorah were "corrected" to conform with the Tiberian tradition. In the first half of the tenth century, the Karaite sage Ya'qub al-Qirqisani noted that the Babylonian Masorah had once "filled the world," but in his own time the Tiberian school was becoming increasingly prevalent.[40] A likely reason that the Babylonian school once enjoyed such wide acceptance is its association with the Geonic rabbinic establishment in Babylonia.[41] Qirqisani and others (including contemporary Muslim authors) attributed the decline of the Babylonian school to the fact—or belief—that the Hebrew of the Babylonians had been corrupted by Aramaic, the lingua franca of Babylonian Jewry (and by and large the language of the Babylonian Talmud).[42] In contrast, the inhabitants of Tiberias were believed to have preserved the purest traditions of native Hebrew pronunciation and Bible reading—a claim, as scholars have noted, analogous to that made about pre-Islamic Arabic poetry, which was also idealized in early Islamic culture.[43] In fact, it may be that the Tiberian Masoretes succeeded in dominating later Masoretic tradition not because of their school's inherent superiority but because they alone learned how to use the new (to the Jews) form of the codex. The fact that so little remains of the Palestinian or Babylonian schools, compared to the many codices from the Tiberian tradition, may be due neither to an accident of history nor to the unhappy fact that history belongs to the victorious, but simply to the fact that the Tiberians figured out how best to exploit the codex to disseminate their traditions.[44]

The earliest known named figure associated with the Tiberian school is Pinḥas Rosh Ha-yeshiva, who lived no later than the first half of the ninth century, and possibly a century earlier.[45] Another early figure, Asher Ha-Zaken Ha-Gadol, was the founder of the Ben Asher family, which eventually became the dominant dynasty in the Tiberian tradition. The Ben Ashers' rivals were the Ben Naftali family, but only second-hand knowledge of their traditions survives, possibly for the same reason that so little remains of the Babylonian and Palestinian schools. Asher's great-grandson Moses ben Asher was a fabled Masorete—he is named in the colophon of the Cairo Prophets Codex (which was actually copied from an earlier codex in order to associate Moses with the later codex)—and his son, Aaron, who lived in the first half of the tenth century, was considered the most reliable and authoritative Masorete in history.[46] The most famous of his achievements was the complete Bible that Maimonides cited in the *Mishneh Torah* as the model codex from which he copied his own Torah scroll, a codex most scholars today believe was the Aleppo Codex.[47] According to the scholar Moshe Goshen-Gottstein, the creation of this codex was unprecedented. It was "a perfect copy," and Aaron ben Asher oversaw its production so as to make it "the first codex of the complete Bible with full Masoretic annotation . . . , the final achievement of the continued work of generations of *the* dynasty of Masoretes, the descendants of 'the old Asher' and 'the crowning undertaking' of the Masoretic tradition."[48] And we might add, of the Tiberian Masoretic tradition. The perfection of the Aleppo Codex—the exemplar for all subsequent Masoretic codices—guaranteed the victory of the Tiberian school over its rivals.

The few biographical facts we know about the early Masoretes may be less important than the question of their religious identity: specifically, whether or not the Masoretes (and the ben Ashers in particular) were Karaites.[49] Karaism, the most significant schismatic movement in early medieval Judaism, derived its name from the Hebrew root *q-r-aleph*, "to read," which is also the root of *miqra* (literally, "what is read [aloud]"), one of the rabbis' most common names for the Bible. Karaites called themselves as *bnei miqra*, "sons of miqra," or *ba'alei miqra*, "masters of miqra." (The name Karaite [*qara'i*] was originally a somewhat derisive cognomen applied to them by their rabbinic opponents, whom the Karaites in turn called "Rabbanites.")

The reason Karaites called themselves by this name, *bnei* or *ba'alei miqra*, was not only because of their expertise in the Bible but mainly because they trumpeted scripture as the sole authoritative, divinely inspired text and rejected the authority of rabbinic tradition, specifically the Oral Torah, as the rabbis called the extrabiblical corpus of legal and nonlegal traditions that they claimed God had revealed orally to Israel at Mount Sinai along with the "written" Torah. The Oral Torah was eventually committed to writing in a succession of texts and compilations, the last of which, the Babylonian Talmud, reached its edited final shape roughly around the time Karaism emerged. The Karaites' reliance on scriptural authority alone is summed up in the slogan attributed to the movement's legendary founder, Anan ben David (ca. 715–ca. 795 or 811?), who reputedly told a follower who had asked him about a certain practice, "Ḥapisu be oreita shapir ve-'al tish'anu 'al da'ati" (Search deeply in the Torah for yourself, and don't rely on my opinion).[50]

According to the most recent scholarly consensus, Karaism crystallized in Iraq as a movement between the eighth and early tenth centuries, eventually emerging out of a number of smaller sectarian groups that were united in their opposition to the rabbinic establishment in Baghdad.[51] The same period—the eighth and ninth centuries—also witnessed widespread sectarian ferment throughout the Islamic realm, and Jewish sectarian movements, including Karaism, probably developed as part of that larger upheaval.[52] Precisely because of its marginal position on the periphery of established Jewish society in Babylonia, Karaism appears to have been more porous and susceptible to external influences, and in this way it absorbed features of Islamic belief and culture earlier and more readily than did rabbinic Judaism. This is evident in early Karaite theology, which emphasized reason and rationalism as absolute values, as well as in the movement's ascetic predilections and exegetical traditions. Many of these ideas and practices were subsequently taken up—some might say, co-opted—by the Rabbanites, and in this way, they eventually permeated all sectors of medieval Judaism.[53]

The precise relationship between Karaism and the Masoretic movement is disputed. Some later Masoretes may have been actual Karaites or affiliated with their circles, but the Masoretic movement itself predated the origins of Karaism proper.[54] Some of the early Masoretic Bibles were eventually donated and dedicated to Karaite synagogues, a fact certainly attesting to the respect and authority that Karaites felt for the Masoretic project, but there is no evidence that these codices were originally produced for Karaite patrons.[55] On the other hand, we do know that Karaites permitted the use in the synagogue of a vocalized codex with cantillation marks in place of a Torah scroll for liturgical reading.[56] (Karaites believed that the vowels and cantillation marks had been inscribed in the Torah that Moses received from God at Mount Sinai; this was a necessary corollary of their rejection of the Oral Torah, for if they had not believed that those paratextual marks were originally written in the Torah, they would have had to accept the fact that they had been transmitted through oral tradition—for them, an impossibility.)

While this circumstantial evidence points to some kind of positive connection between the Masoretes and Karaism, it is also the case that some Karaites treated the Masorah derisively.[57] The Masorah's interminable lists and enumerations may even have seemed somewhat primitive to some Karaites, particularly members of its intellectual elite. Sophisticated Karaites were more interested in the use of the Bible as a source for the sciences of grammar, philosophy, and theology.[58] Furthermore, the Karaites were generally more concerned with the proper reading tradition of the Torah than with its writing tradition, which the Masorah clearly privileges.[59]

These reservations militate against a simple identification of the Masoretes as Karaites. As Marina Rustow has observed, Karaism "grew out of the Masoretic focus on Scripture—not the other way around."[60] Whatever their precise relationship, Karaism and the Masoretic project were both products of a stream in early medieval Judaism in the Islamic Near East that we might call Biblicism. Whether or not the Masoretes agreed with the Karaites in rejecting the Oral Torah, both groups represent an alternative route in early medieval Jewish culture—a path not taken—that drew upon biblical study and devotion to scripture as its lifeline, rather than Talmudic tradition and allegiance to the Oral Law—that is to say, to religious traditions that were not scripturally based.[61] In this respect, Karaism and the Masorah can be viewed as two halves of an early chapter in the lengthy history of rivalry within Judaism between scripture and the Oral Law, particularly as the latter was embodied in the Babylonian Talmud. While this contest was eventually won by the

Talmud, it is possible to look upon the Masorah, with its intensive preoccupation with the biblical text, as the Biblicists' equivalent of the Rabbanites' Talmudism. The Masoretes immersed themselves in the words of the Bible and invested as much intellectual energy in its study as the rabbis devoted to the innumerable traditions of the Oral Law. And just as the Babylonian rabbinic sages stressed the inviolable orality of the Oral Torah, insisting it be taught in public orally from memory, the Masoretes insisted upon the perfect inscription of scripture. The creation of the Masorah, the emergence of Karaism, and Jews' adoption of the codex (and its concurrent replacement of the scroll as the privileged writing platform) were all part of a single larger cultural epiphenomenon.

If this was the case—that the Masorah came out of a more pervasive stream of Biblicism in late antique and early medieval Jewish culture, and not from either a sectarian or orthodox brand of Judaism—it is also more easily understandable how and why, as the Tiberian Masorah came to be accepted as authoritative, both Rabbanites and Karaites sought to appropriate the Masoretic tradition as part of their respective invented pasts.[62] For both communities, the Masorah signaled the emergence of a new kind of Bible study. The Masorah is our first evidence for a class of professional Jewish readers of the Bible, namely, the Masoretes themselves. The monumental Torah scroll that rabbinic law fixed as the only permissible type of Torah was ill suited if not almost impossible to use as a tool for study. The Sefer Torah was a religious artifact, a sacred liturgical object whose text was chanted aloud in the synagogue, but it was not a book that anyone read as one ordinarily reads a book—that is, for acquiring knowledge of its contents. During the classic rabbinic period (second to sixth centuries), that kind of knowledge was acquired—"learned"—largely through the ears, aurally, as a text the sages and their students memorized from having heard it read aloud repeatedly in the synagogue, in study circles, and perhaps elsewhere. Indeed, a few statements in rabbinic literature mention sages who knew the entire Torah by heart.[63]

The most compelling, albeit circumstantial, evidence for the rabbis' aurally derived knowledge of Torah comes from midrash, the rabbinic name for Bible study. Midrash abounds in oral/aural puns and in exegeses based on phonetic links between otherwise unrelated verses and passages, all of which point to a knowledge of the biblical text based upon auditory acquisition. Indeed, the twin tendencies of midrash to focus upon single verses and phrases that are usually taken out of context and to solve exegetical problems through phonetically related solutions (like similar sounding words in completely unrelated verses) indicate an aural environment in which the rabbis studied and learned the Bible, and in which they heard scripture.[64]

In comparison, the type of textual knowledge informing the Masorah could only have been acquired by actual readers of the biblical text, individuals whose knowledge of scripture was acquired visually, through seeing and reading it on a page. This is obvious from the Masorah's constant attention to orthography, as epitomized in *plene* and defective readings, which have to be seen to be recognized. While it is always a mistake to underestimate the powers of memory (and the human capacity for memorization), it is hard to imagine the enumerative lists of the Masorah—even those not based on orthography—being composed by persons who knew the text solely from having heard it read aloud.

To be sure, the Masorah represents a strange type of reading. With its obsessive inspection of every minute detail in the Bible, it is a cross between bookkeeping and connoisseurship, both an inventory of the Bible's contents and a collection of its gems. Even so, the emergence of the Masorah points to an innovative, unprecedented reading practice in Jewish literary culture. Through the Middle Ages, that reading practice would revolutionize Jewish biblical exegesis, particularly in the development of *peshat* exegesis, as the various types of medieval Jewish "plain-sense" interpretation came to be called. If midrash as a mode of study and interpretation is best appreciated within an aural environment, *peshat* is truly conceivable only within a visual reading environment, one that was in fact created by the early Masoretic Bible.

The Visual Dimension of the Early Masoretic Bible

The evidence the Masorah provides for the history of Jewish reading is not the only noteworthy feature of the early Masoretic codex's visual dimension. The page layout in the codex is equally significant. As we noted earlier, the format of the Aleppo Codex page (fig. 2.1) partly imitates the columns of a Torah scroll, but its most original feature is the inscription of the *masorah parva*'s abbreviated notations in the spaces between the columns and the more expansive *masorah magna* in micrography on the upper and lower margins. This design has no clear precedent in either Jewish or Islamic book production. To be sure, the margin is the obvious location for notes, but the micrography is actually part of the page's writing grid, not its margins. Indeed, the Masoretic notes most resemble a kind of frame or wall surrounding the biblical text (even if it is frequently interrupted).[65] Such a fence or wall (or possibly brickwork) around the Torah is depicted in the striking border design found fig. 2.4, a page from a Bible possibly written in the land of Israel around 1020–21 CE that contains the Song of the Sea (Exod. 15).[66] The biblical text is laid out in the special stichography known as "a half-brick over a whole-brick" (*ariaḥ ʿal gabei leveinah*) (B. Megillah 16b).[67] That special layout was adapted to the codex Bible from the Torah scroll, as we saw in the Bologna Sefer Torah (fig. 2.1), and is already attested in the Dead Sea Scrolls.

A wall of annotations or a chainlike border around the stichography could not, however, be written in a Torah scroll. As can be seen in fig. 2.4, lines of the Masorah written in micrography fill and delineate the white spaces of the alternating *x* and diamond designs within the border, in a format that might be viewed as a kind of visual exemplification of the saying attributed to Akiba in Mishnah Avot 3:13, *masoret seyag la-torah* (the *masoret* is a fence around the Torah).[68] While it is not clear what the word *masoret* in its original

2.4 Bible (Exod. 15), land of Israel, 1020–21. Saint Petersburg, National Library of Russia, EBP II B8, fols. 56v–57r. Courtesy of the National Library of Russia.

context actually meant—it almost certainly did *not* refer to the Masorah—some medieval commentators on the Mishnah did understand the phrase in that way, and it is possible that the Masoretes themselves understood it as a description of their own project. Indeed, an early Masoretic poem describes the Masoretes as having "erected as a fence [*hikifu gader*] around the Torah of our God / Well-arranged Masoras to instruct the ignorant."[69] How aptly these lines of verse capture the visual appearance of the Masorah and suggest at least one of its functions.[70]

In other early codices, including the Prophets Codex from the Karaite synagogue Moussa Dar'i in Cairo (probably written in Tiberias, ca. 1000),[71] the Masorah is inscribed around the text columns in designs of varying abstraction. As David Lyons has shown, many of these designs are used to set off a distinct type of Masorah, *masorah metsarefet*, "cumulative" or "collative Masorah," which lists groups of unrelated words, phrases, or verses that share a common exceptional lexical feature. Fig. 2.5, a page from the Cairo Prophets Codex (Cairo, Karaite Synagogue, Moussa Dar'i, fol. 174) containing 2 Samuel 21:20, records a Masoretic list of twenty-four hapax legomena, all of which begin with the letters *vav* and *mem*; the list itself is inscribed in a micrographic design that resembles a broken belt with tiny pyramids or triangles at each of the double-line breaks.[72] Designs in other codices display architectural motifs, like the stacked pyramids crowning the Masorah in fig. 2.6, a page from the Leningrad Codex. These designs resemble those in

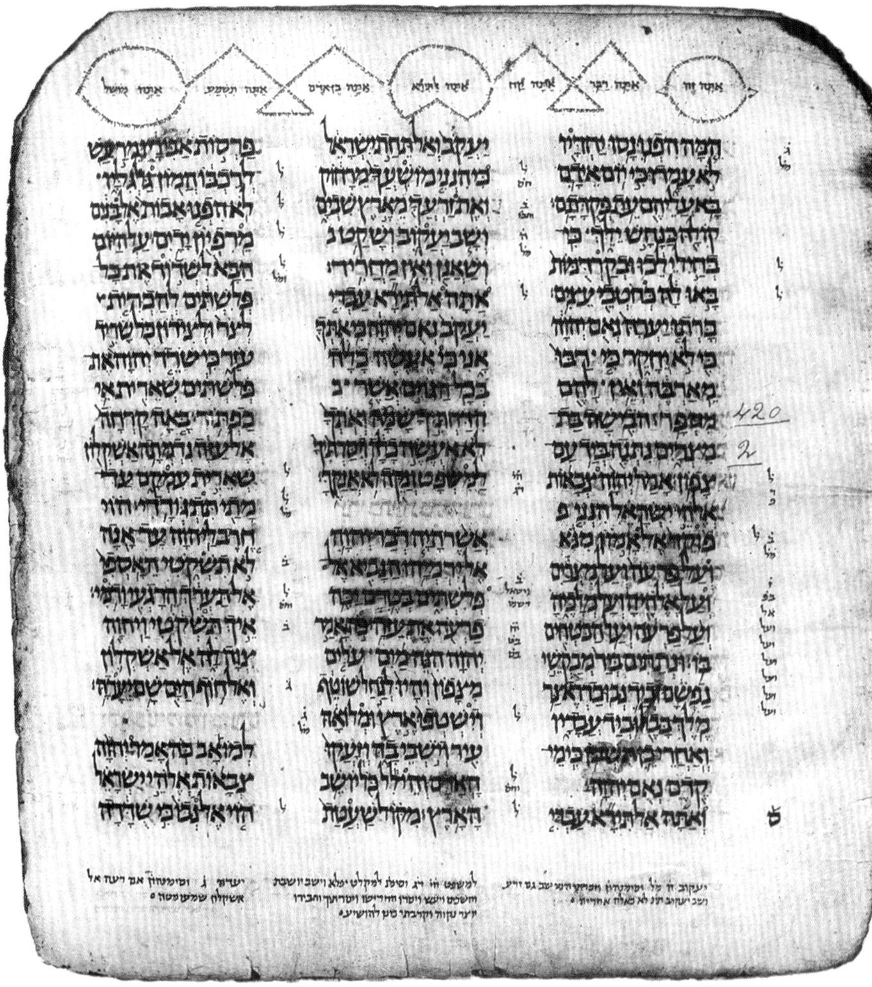

2.5 Cairo Prophets Codex (2 Sam. 21.20), land of Israel, 1129–30. Formerly belonged to the Karaite Synagogue [or Community] of Cairo; current location unknown.

very early Qur'ans (like the ones discovered in the Great Mosque of Sana'a, Yemen). These early micrographic designs anticipate the much more complex architectural and geometric designs used in later medieval Spanish Jewish Bibles.[73] Still other early designs imitate floral or vegetal patterns, which also become far more sophisticated and complex in later medieval Bibles.[74] This use of micrography as a medium of design is one of the distinctive (if not unique) features of Jewish book art.[75]

The purpose behind recording the Masorah in these micrographic designs remains unclear. Some of them may have been intended to serve as mnemonic devices, visual

2.6 Leningrad Codex, Cairo, 1008 CE. Saint Petersburg, National Library of Russia, EBP IB 19A. fol. 40v. Courtesy of the National Library of Russia.

spurs to aid students in memorization of the Masorah.[76] Certainly they were occasions for scribal virtuosity, ways scribes could give expression to their own personalities by adding a creative dimension to the acting of copying.[77] They may also have been intended to evoke in the reader—or more precisely, the viewer—a certain feeling or attitude. Their function was evocative and affective, not representational. As Oleg Grabar has observed about the similar designs and decorations in the eighth-century Qur'ans found in Sana'a,

2.7 Leningrad Codex, Cairo, 1008 CE. Saint Petersburg, National Library of Russia, EBP IB 19A. fol. 474r. Courtesy of the National Library of Russia.

they signaled the importance and uniqueness of the codex either "by physically and visually separating it from its surroundings or by inciting in the user a sentiment of awe, perhaps of holiness, certainly of anticipatory and sensory pleasure, as he opened the book."[78] In this respect, the fencelike borders literally frame the text for the viewer/reader, elaborately enhancing and focusing attention on the beauty and preciousness of the words within.[79]

2.8 Qur'an, Iraq, ca. 1000, Dublin, Chester Beatty Library Ms. 1406. © The Trustees of the Chester Beatty Library, Dublin.

The parallels in design between these Bibles and contemporaneous Islamic books, particularly Qur'ans, suggest that they may have been produced in workshops that employed both Jewish and Muslim scribes and artisans.[80] Wherever the codices were produced, the parallels between the Jewish and Islamic books are most vividly displayed in the carpet pages—so-called because their designs resemble those woven into Oriental carpets—which are found at the beginning and the end of both Qur'ans and Bibles of the period.[81] Fig. 2.7 is a carpet page from the famous Leningrad Codex. This page's striking design consists of two overlapping squares forming a series of triangles that border a hexagon formed by the two squares inside; within the hexagon, there is a large six-pointed star (which, in turn, is set against a brownish background with floral designs resembling Moroccan leather). The star will be familiar to Jewish viewers as the Magen David, or Shield of David, a symbol found in many cultures throughout the Near East and usually called the Seal of Solomon; the original function of the design was probably quasi-magical—as an amulet to ward off demons—and there is no reason to assume that its meaning on this page is necessarily Jewish or nationalistic.[82] The inside of the star contains the colophon of the scribe, Shmuel ben Ya'akov. The indebtedness of this page to Islamic book art can be seen by comparing it to fig. 2.8, a page from a Qur'an written in Iraq around the year 1000 that employs the same design of a circle enclosing interlocking squares. Admittedly, the biblical page is more ornate—in place of the star, the Qur'an has a simple rosette in the middle, and it lacks the small decorative rosettes with flowers

2.9 Leningrad Codex, Cairo, 1008 CE. Saint Petersburg, National Library of Russia, EBP IB 19A. fol. 476r. Courtesy of the National Library of Russia.

inside them within the triangles and spaces between the squares. But the most striking difference between the Bible and the Qur'an is that the design of the biblical page consists of micrography—in this case, verses in praise of the Torah.

These decorated carpet pages with their micrographic designs are among the most complex in the history of the Jewish book. In the Leningrad Codex there are two groupings of these pages, both at the conclusion of the codex and separated by some ten folios

2.10 Leningrad Codex, Cairo, 1008 CE. Saint Petersburg, National Library of Russia, EBP IB 19A. fol. 476v. Courtesy of the National Library of Russia.

of Masoretic rules; the first grouping consists of twelve carpet pages, the second, of four.[83] Figs. 2.9 and 2.10 are two sides of a single folio from the first group, and along with the folio in fig. 2.7, they demonstrate the variety of shapes that these pages take. The complex visual experience they elicit from viewers is obvious. Like their Islamic counterparts, these pages are essentially ornamental—that is, they consist of the regular repetition of one or two forms or motifs that are organized into an ordered whole, but with subtle variations, irregularities, and shifting perspectives inserted so as to mutually reinforce each other and make the form of the page harmonious yet not entirely predictable.[84]

The overall shape of fig. 2.9 is an abstract design of alternating diamonds and triangles symmetrically organized around a single large diamond with four triangular arrowheads meeting to form an emblem-like design. Fig. 2.10 is a gate, an arch resting upon two large foundations with what may be an abstract lamp hanging from its center, all composed in alternating tear-shaped and triangular designs. In both pages, the size of the micrography varies, but in both cases the writing is subordinated to the dominant pattern, and its verbal meaning—the words written in micrography—is subordinated to the pattern's ornamental function. The micrography, however, is not impossible to read; in fact, in some cases—for example, in the large lines across the arch in fig. 2.10—it is very clear. In others, the viewer is forced to read it from different directions—as in the diamonds in fig. 2.9—sometimes on a slant from bottom to top, at other times from top to bottom or around bends and curves; this clearly requires a dedicated effort on the part of the reader. But whether or not the writing is actually read, the undulating shapes of the letters in each line endow a kind of perspectival depth to the overall image, imbuing it with liveliness, movement, and dynamism. As with the Islamic carpet pages, the "physical and optical play with spatial forms creates an inner tension that counteracts what would otherwise be a static composition."[85] In the Hebrew Bible codices, the recognizable graphic element contributes further complexity and tension while the irregularities inherent in script make the borders of the designs even more dynamic. The viewer is invited both to read the page and to view it solely as an image.

As with the micrographic designs found on the text pages of these same Bibles, the carpet pages must have had multiple purposes: as testimony to religious piety, as showpieces of conspicuous wealth, and as symbols of religious significance.[86] The intricate, sometimes labyrinthine designs with their abstracted geometrical shapes (as in fig. 2.9) would have been fitting sites for meditation, and architectural pages (like fig. 2.10) may have served as figurative points of access or entry to the sacred codex. Both pages would have prepared the book's reader as he or she approached the text, whether for study or worship. The micrography on the page constantly instilled in the reader a consciousness of the *writing* as a material presence, an awareness that the words in the codex were not simply conveyors of a text but objects in their own right. Whatever their purpose, these pages were meant to be *seen*. As such, they further highlight the visual experience of reading the Bible.

A visual dimension of such complexity was new to the history of Jewish book culture in the ancient world. As we have seen, both this material dimension and the new type of reading that accompanied it were manifestly influenced by the books and reading practices of early medieval Islamic culture in the Near East, the gentile host culture in which these books were produced and their Jewish producers lived. This is not unusual: the material

Jewish book almost invariably mirrors the books of the surrounding gentile culture, and where it does not, the reason for deviation from the general rule must be sought. The mere fact that these early Jewish Bibles reflect contemporaneous Islamic books, Qur'ans in particular, is therefore not surprising in itself. What is unusual is that, in most other cases, Jewish appropriation of gentile book culture is ambivalent, wracked by anxieties about influence and feelings of competitive rivalry and ideological conflict. In these early Masoretic codices, in contrast, the appropriations are not visibly worried. To all appearances, Jews adopted the decorative motifs and material features of the Islamic book because they believed that if these features were appropriate for an Islamic book like the Qur'an, they certainly belonged in a codex of the Hebrew Bible.

In the centuries that followed, this feeling changed. The dynamics of cultural exchange and influence that shaped the Hebrew Bible's material history became increasingly problematic, especially insofar as they touched upon the Jewishness of the Bible as a book. Masoretic micrography came to play a prominent role in articulating and giving expression to that Jewishness. And through the micrography, the Hebrew Bible and the Masorah came to possess a significance that went far beyond the content and meaning of either text.

The Hebrew Bible in the Later Middle Ages

The early Masoretic codex bequeathed to medieval Jews one model for the Bible. Over the centuries, however, the form of the Masoretic Bible underwent material changes while additional types or genres of Bibles developed with different functions and material features. The physical shapes of these Bibles track the history of all the geographical and cultural centers Jews inhabited in the Middle Ages and often directly reflect their varying and distinct book cultures.

The differences among Bibles produced in various regions begin with the text. As Jordan Penkower has shown, there developed in the Middle Ages four distinct text-type traditions for the Hebrew Bible, which diverged (albeit usually in minor details) in orthography, spacing, accentuation, and vocalization. These distinct text traditions corresponded to the main geocultural areas of Jewish settlement in the medieval period: the Orient (the countries of the Near East, Egypt, and North Africa), Sepharad (the Iberian Peninsula and its environs, including southern France), Ashkenaz (northern France and Germany), and Yemen.[87] In the later Middle Ages, the Orient fell increasingly out of the picture, while Italy developed into a major center of Jewish book culture. Each of these geocultural areas—most visibly, Sepharad, Ashkenaz, Italy, and Yemen—lent the Bibles produced in their realms material features sufficiently distinctive as to make them immediately recognizable.[88]

The early Masoretic Bible appropriated the features of the Islamic book, the Qur'an in particular, and simultaneously "Judaized" the Islamic influence by making Hebrew micrography the instrument for appropriating Islamic design and decoration. This double process of appropriation and Judaization continued through the Middle Ages, as Jews came to live increasingly under Christian domination, but the matter of influence and appropriation became far more vexed, fraught by anxieties on both sides. In the heated rivalries and often hostile (and violent) competitions between Jews and Christians, both religious communities laid claim to "ownership" of the Bible. These battles over ownership were waged on various fronts, most famously through interpretation and exegesis, but also through the material shapes of Bibles. The history of the Hebrew Bible from the Middle Ages until today is, in a very real sense, the story of how Jews have laid claim to its ownership by marking and defining the Bible's Jewishness in material terms through giving it a distinct physical shape. As a consequence, more than any other Jewish book, the biblical codex as material artifact became a virtual register of the different stances that medieval Jews took toward the Christian cultures in which they lived.

One important caveat is in order before we begin to tell this story. The surviving codices are only a fraction of the Hebrew Bibles that once existed, and we do not know how representative they truly are. As Michelle Dukan has noted, the picture that emerges from studying these volumes is inevitably skewed, since the surviving codices are by and large the more luxurious and valuable books (which is why they were preserved).[89] As noted earlier, the fragments from both Qumran and the Cairo Genizah enable us to see the variety of Bibles in use in the ancient world and in the early Middle Ages (at least in the Mediterranean world from the eighth century through the eleventh), particularly the more popular types owned and used by private individuals. For the later Middle Ages, no such genizah survives, and we have little evidence for what an ordinary Bible—those that were regularly and intensively used by most Jews—looked like.[90] The existing corpus of medieval Hebrew Bibles is thus virtually guaranteed to be unrepresentative, inevitably tilted toward the Bibles that were *less* ordinary. While we assume that the more ordinary Bibles shared the basic structures and shapes of the more extraordinary volumes, it is also the case that the deluxe books, precisely because their material detail is so rich, offer us more (and more valuable) evidence for what the Bible *meant* (and could mean) as a book to its owners and readers than do the more popular books.

The Main Genres of the Medieval Hebrew Bible

In the Middle Ages, three distinct generic types of Hebrew Bible developed: the Masoretic Bible, the liturgical Pentateuch, and the study Bible. These three types are represented in all the medieval Jewish centers, but each assumed a somewhat different shape in medieval Sepharad and Ashkenaz, and later in Italy and Yemen.[91]

The first of these types, the Masoretic Bible, was the direct heir of the early Near Eastern Masoretic codex. Like their ancestor, these Bibles usually comprise a complete TaNaKh, in which case they are often called *ha-'esrim ve-arba* (the twenty-four [books]), but volumes containing only one or two of the TaNaKh's three main sections (Torah, Nevi'im, Ketuvim) are not uncommon. For the most part, the biblical books are ordered in these volumes in the sequence first set out in the Talmud (B. Bava Batra 14b), but throughout the Middle Ages, there were differences in the sequence of the Writings, and particularly the Five Scrolls (Ecclesiastes, Esther, Song of Songs, Lamentations, and Ruth).[92]

The genre of the Masoretic Bible is defined by its contents—on the one hand, the vocalized and accentuated biblical text with cantillation marks, typically presented in either two or three columns, and on the other, the Masoretic annotations, usually both the *masora parva* and *masora magna* written in micrography, both laid out in the same way they were inscribed in the early codices. While the medieval codices sometimes contain other works (like grammatical and Masoretic treatises at the beginning and end of the volumes), the Bible text pages usually do not contain any text other than the Bible and the Masorah.[93] It seems likely that, in some cases, a Masoretic Bible served as a model for scribes (*sefer mugah* or *tikkun soferim*) to be used as an exemplar for writing a Sefer Torah or another biblical codex. In any event, the Masoretic Bible was the standard form for a complete Bible.

The second type of Bible used by medieval Jews was the *ḥumash*, or liturgical Pentateuch, namely, a Pentateuch accompanied by the haftarot (sing. haftarah, the reading from the Prophets that is chanted following the weekly Torah reading in the synagogue) and the Five Scrolls. In addition, many *ḥumashim* contain the Aramaic Targum, typically Onkelos, though in a few cases other Aramaic Targumim are used, while in Arabic-speaking locales (like al-Andalus and Yemen), the *Tafsir* (Arabic translation) of the great Geonic sage Saadiah Gaon (882/892–942) sometimes replaces the Targum. In some codices, the commentary of the celebrated eleventh-century exegete Rashi (Solomon ben Isaac, d. ca. 1105) is also included on the page, at times as a substitute for the Targum, at other times in addition to it. I have called this type of Bible "liturgical" because its organization corresponds to the sections of the Torah that were chanted in the synagogue on the Sabbath and on holidays as part of the prayer service. On occasion, these books also include the Sifrei EMeT (Job, Proverbs, and Psalms), as well as Megillat Antiochus (Antiochus Scroll), a medieval account of the Maccabean Revolt that was read aloud in the synagogue on the festival of Ḥanukkah, and chapters from the prophet Jeremiah that were read on the fast day of *Tish'ah Be-'av* (Ninth of Av). The name *ḥumash* sometimes appears in the colophons of these Bibles.

The liturgical Pentateuch's structure has no precedent in the early Near Eastern tradition represented by the Masoretic codices. While we do not know precisely how or where the *ḥumash* first developed—there are some indications that it might have arisen in Babylonia (where the practice of reading through the Torah in annual cycles first became normative)[94]—the genre is paralleled in different types of Bible books that were developed in the Latin West for biblical readings during the Mass.[95] There is, however, no indication that either the Jewish or Christian books gave birth to each other, and it is hardly surprising that both Christian and Jewish scribes would have come up with similar types of Bibles, because they were so convenient for their respective liturgies.

The third type of Bible Jews used in the Middle Ages was the study Bible. These are Bibles that appear to have been composed intentionally for the purpose of Bible study. To be sure, both Masoretic Bibles and liturgical Pentateuchs were undoubtedly also used for study—what Bible have Jews not used for study?—but study Bibles are distinguished by the visual prominence of their function. Either they include two or more commentaries on the same page, often in addition to the Targum or *Tafsir*, or the commentary occupies a place (and space) on the page so prominent as to make it the page's primary focus, even more important than the biblical text itself. Like the *ḥumash*, the study Bible has no precedent in earlier tradition. In the Middle Ages, Jewish Bible commentaries were generally inscribed in separate books or booklets called *quntresim* (sing. *quntres*, from the Latin *quinterion*, a quire of five sheets). The study Bible marks a departure from this practice. With the biblical text and its commentary (or commentaries) on the same page, the study Bible was obviously much more convenient for study, but it was also much more difficult for scribes to copy because they had to forecast the precise proportion of commentary to text to make the format work successfully.

In addition to these three main types of Bibles, there were several subtypes: Psalters; separate codices containing the haftarot alone or the Five Scrolls, or both; and (particularly in parts of the Near East), booklets with separate weekly Torah readings.[96] Depending on the region in which it was produced, each of the three distinct types of Bibles assumed a different material form. These differences are especially clear for Masoretic Bibles and liturgical Pentateuchs that were produced in the two main centers of Sepharad and Ashkenaz.

The Bible in Sepharad

Extensive Jewish settlement in the Iberian Peninsula began in the Islamic era, and it is not surprising that the medieval Sephardic Hebrew Bible codex was the direct successor to the early Masoretic Bibles from the Near East and North Africa. Whether the latter codices came to Iberia directly from the Near East or through North Africa, routes of transport between these regions were facilitated by their common location in the greater Islamic empire that spanned almost the entirety of the area through southern Europe.[97]

The Masoretic Bible was the most common type produced in Sepharad, and its producers early on followed the early Near Eastern codices in adopting the material features of the Islamic book: aversion to figurative representation and pervasive use of geometric, floral, and architectural decoration. Unhappily, not a single Bible produced during the Islamic period of Sephardic history survives, but the Islamicizing nature of Sephardic

Bibles continued into the Christian period. (In the conventional historiography of Sepharad, the Islamic period is usually said to begin in 711, with the Muslim conquest of the Visigoths, and to end in 1212, with the battle of Las Navas de Tolosa and the Christian reconquest of much of Spain, even though some important centers like Toledo were conquered by Christians as early as 1085, while others, the Kingdom of Granada in particular, remained under Muslim rule until 1492. The Christian period conventionally is said to begin in 1212 and to end with the Expulsion of the Jews in 1492.) The earliest dated Bible from Spain—part of a Masoretic Pentateuch (Toronto, Friedberg MS 9-005)—was written in 1188 by the scribe Meshulam ben Todros in Girona.[98]

Sephardic scribes were known for their skill as copyists, and the Bibles they produced were famous for their accuracy.[99] Their excellence was recognized even in Ashkenaz. The eminent German sage Meir of Rottenberg (end of thirteenth century) refers to "the superior and exact books of Spain."[100] Another Talmudist of the period, Menahem Meiri (Perpignan, 1249–1316), describes a rabbi from Germany who journeyed to Toledo to acquire a Pentateuch copied from the scroll of the Masoretic expert R. Meir Halevi Abulafia in order to use the Sephardic codex to write Torah scrolls in Ashkenaz![101]

Probably the most famous of all such Sephardic codices was a model codex known as the Sefer Hilleli, or Hilleli Codex, reputed to have been written around the year 600 CE, but more probably completed around the year 1000 in the city of Leon. In 1197 CE, the Almohades, an Islamic caliphate from North Africa, attacked the Jewish communities of Castile and Aragon and carried away at least part of the complete codex; the rest subsequently disappeared. Before its disappearance, however, the codex was widely consulted and copied, including the copy pictured in fig. 2.11, which was completed in Toledo in 1241 (nearly two hundred years after Toledo came under Christian rule). Among its singular features, this copy records the extraordinary *tagin* (crownlets or ornamental strokes atop letters) as well as certain peculiarly shaped letters (*otiyyot meshunot*). The presence of both features in the codex is a likely sign that it was used by scribes as an exemplar.

In its page format and other material features, this copy of the original Hilleli Codex closely resembles the early Near Eastern Masoretic codices and, one assumes, Bibles produced in Sepharad in the eleventh and twelfth centuries, the Andalusian Golden Age, when much of Iberia was still under Islamic rule. Yet even *after* the Islamic period, from the early thirteenth century when those parts of Iberia not already under Christian rule were Christianized until the expulsion of the Jews from the peninsula at the end of the fifteenth, the vast number of Hebrew Bibles in Sepharad retained these Islamically derived features.[102] This is especially true of Bibles produced in Castile. In the north, in the Crown of Aragon, which had always been Christian, there are notable exceptions, among them some of the most famous Bibles produced in Spain, like the Cervera and Kennicott Bibles; these Bibles contain representational and decorative features more characteristic of Christian books, particularly influences deriving from Italy and France.[103]

2.11 Hilleli Codex (Exod. 32:17–27), Toledo, 1241. New York, Jewish Theological Seminary of America, MS L44a, 100v. Courtesy of the Jewish Theological Seminary of America.

It is important to add, too, that the Islamicizing tendency, particularly its aniconism, is not characteristic of other Sephardic books; Spanish Haggadoth, many of which were produced in Catalonia, are replete with figurative representations.[104] But the Islamicizing tendency is especially characteristic of the Sephardic Bible; indeed, this is arguably the most exceptional fact about its history as a material artifact. This exceptionality is especially noteworthy because it violates one of the general rules of Jewish book culture,

2.12 Bible, Toledo, 1232. Paris, BnF héb. 25, fol. 31v. Bibliothèque Nationale de France.

namely, the tendency of Jewish books to mirror the books of their gentile host culture. Jewish Bibles produced in Christian Spain should all look like the Christian Bibles of their contemporaries, but most don't. The fact that they do not requires an explanation.

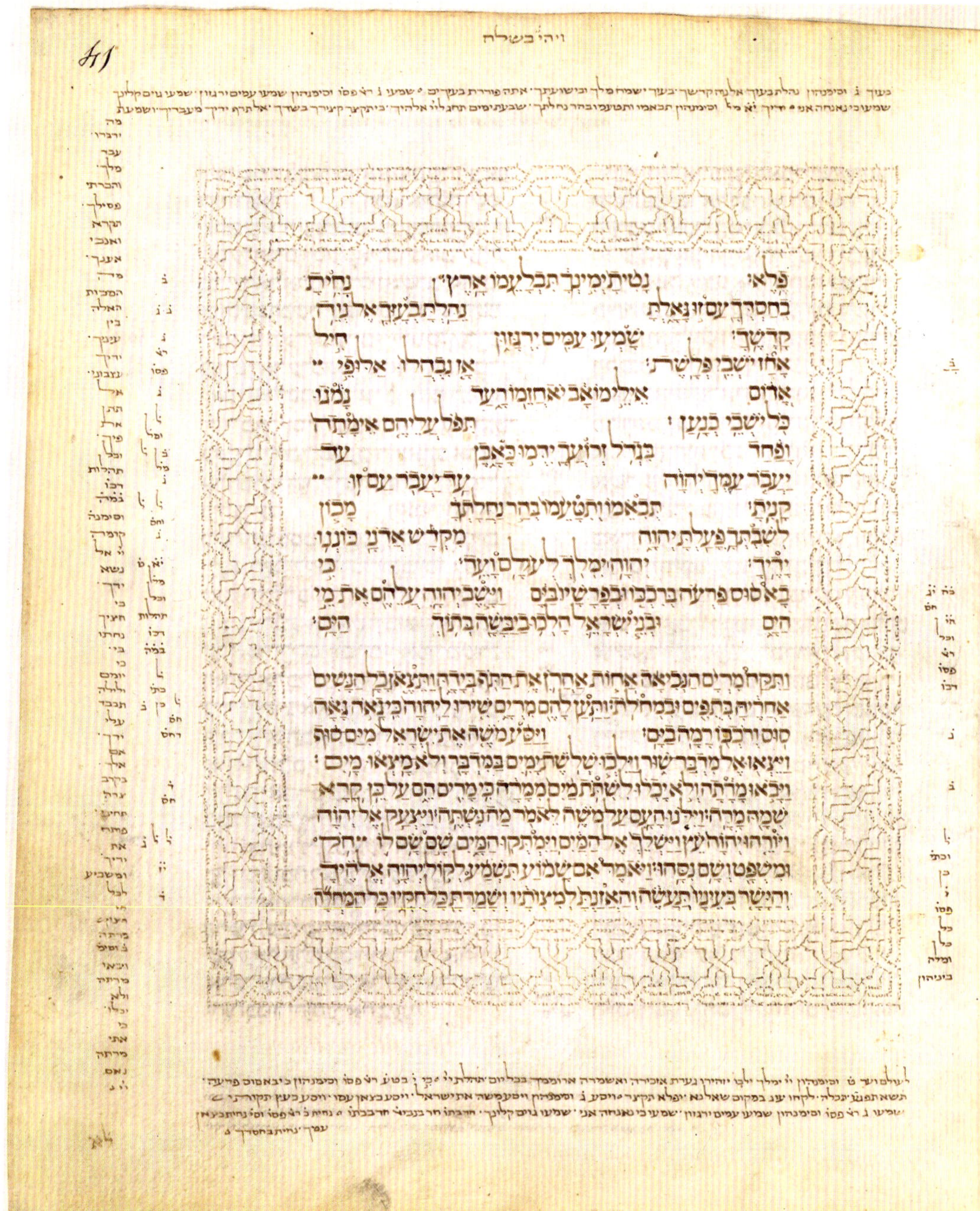

41

פלא נטית ימינך תבלעמו ארץ נחית
בחסדך עם זו גאלת נהלת בעזך אל נוה
קדשך שמעו עמים ירגזון חיל
אחז ישבי פלשת אז נבהלו אלופי
אדום אילי מואב יאחזמו רעד נמגו
כל ישבי כנען תפל עליהם אימתה
ופחד בגדל זרועך ידמו כאבן עד
יעבר עמך יהוה עד יעבר עם זו
קנית תבאמו ותטעמו בהר נחלתך מכון
לשבתך פעלת יהוה מקדש אדני כוננו
ידיך יהוה ימלך לעלם ועד כי
בא סוס פרעה ברכבו ובפרשיו בים וישב יהוה עלהם את מי
הים ובני ישראל הלכו ביבשה בתוך הים

ותקח מרים הנביאה אחות אהרן את התף בידה ותצאן כל הנשים
אחריה בתפים ובמחלת ותען להם מרים שירו ליהוה כי גאה גאה
סוס ורכבו רמה בים ויסע משה את ישראל מים סוף
ויצאו אל מדבר שור וילכו שלשת ימים במדבר ולא מצאו מים
ויבאו מרתה ולא יכלו לשתת מים ממרה כי מרים הם על כן קרא
שמה מרה וילנו העם על משה לאמר מה נשתה ויצעק אל יהוה
ויורהו יהוה עץ וישלך אל המים וימתקו המים שם שם לו חק
ומשפט ושם נסהו ויאמר אם שמוע תשמע לקול יהוה אלהיך
והישר בעיניו תעשה והאזנת למצותיו ושמרת כל חקיו כל המחלה

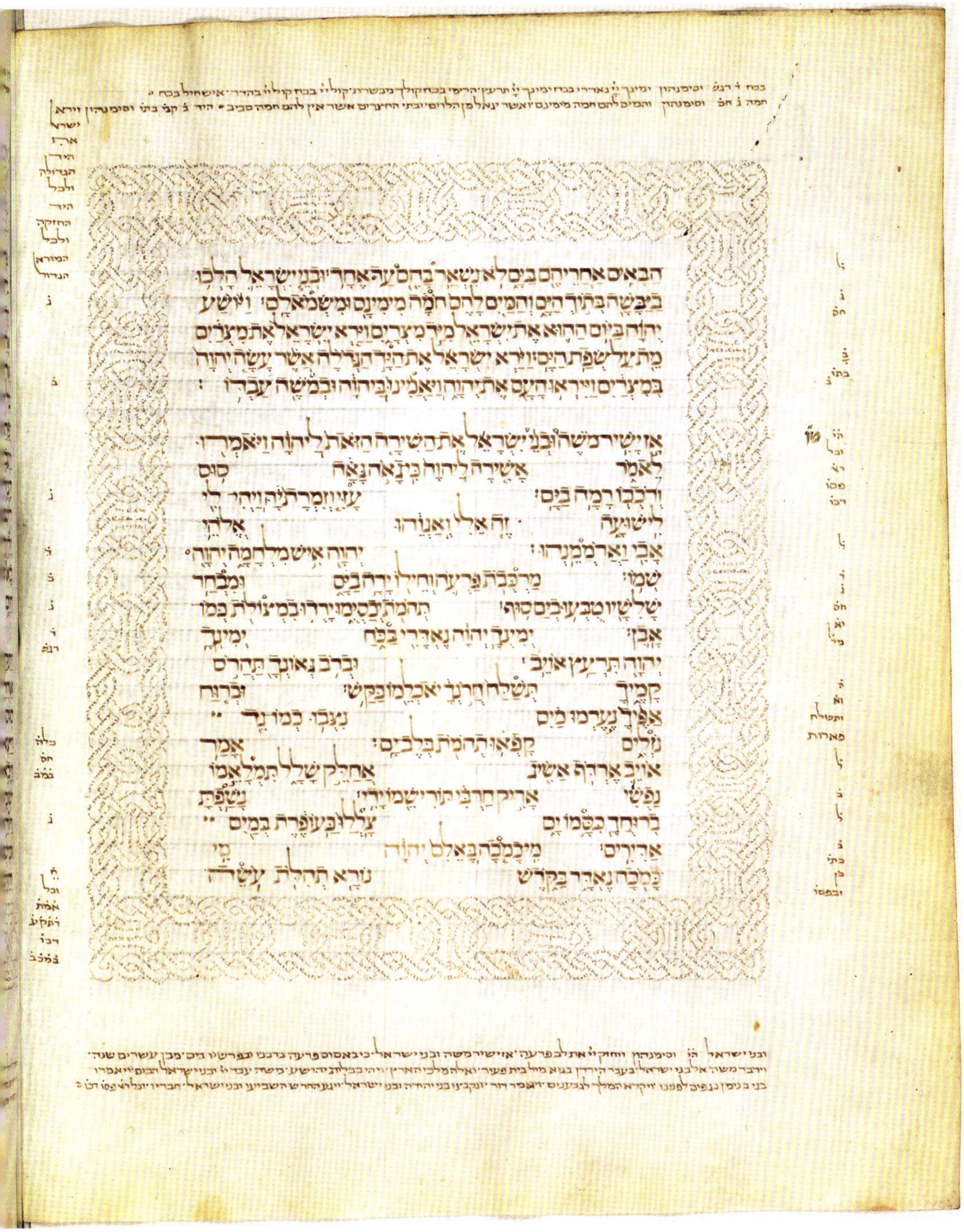

2.13 Bible, Toledo, 1232. Paris, BnF héb. 25, fol. 40v–41r. Bibliothèque Nationale de France.

To be sure, the Islamicizing character of Sephardic Bibles is most visible in the luxurious decorated codices. These volumes maintain the aniconism and carpet pages, as well as many less prominent features characteristic of Islamic book culture. The close resemblance of early Sephardic Bibles to early Masoretic codices can be seen in the page reproduced in fig. 2.12, the earliest dated decorated Masoretic Bible from Sepharad, a relatively small book (185 × 220 cm) written in Toledo in 1232, with the biblical text in double columns. On this page, the *masorah magna* appears on double lines at the top and bottom of the folio, while the *masorah parva* is in the right and middle margins. On the lower left-hand margin, the *seder* (weekly synagogue reading in the triennial cycle; pl. *sedarim*) is marked by a floral-like decorative medallion above the letter *samekh* (for *seder*); this device resembles the *ansa* used in Qur'ans to mark *suras*. This custom of marking both the triennial *sedarim* as well as the weekly *parshiyyot* (sing. *parashah*; the weekly Torah reading in the annual cycle) derives from the early Masoretic codices, but its persistence in Christian Spain is even more noteworthy inasmuch as by this time probably no one in the world still used the triennial cycle.

The other noteworthy decoration in this manuscript is found on the magnificent page opening displayed in fig. 2.13, which contains the Song of the Sea (Exod. 15). The text on the page is laid out in special stichography (dictated by halacha) called *ariaḥ ʿal gabei leveinah* (a small brick atop a full brick), and it is framed by an intricate interlaced border created of micrography; the frame extends over the opening of two pages. As demonstrated by fig. 2.4, a page from the early eleventh-century Bible discussed earlier, the interlaced border design used for the elaborate micrographic wall or frame for Exodus 15 was already conventional two hundred years earlier. By the early thirteenth century, it appears to have become a staple of Sephardic scribal tradition.[105]

The earliest dated surviving Sephardic *ḥumash* (liturgical Pentateuch) was composed in 1318 (Oxford, Bodleian Library, MS Kennicott 4), but most examples of the genre in Sepharad come from the late fourteenth and fifteenth centuries. There is good reason to believe that this genre initially flourished in Ashkenaz and later spread to Sepharad. While the basic contents of Ashkenazic and Sephardic *ḥumashim*—the weekly *parashiyyot* of the Torah, the haftarot, and the Five Scrolls—are identical, and while both share the identical structural organization, many of the Sephardic Pentateuchs contain the Masorah, reflecting its prominent position in Sepharad. It is inscribed in these codices in the same kind of micrographic geometrical designs as those in contemporaneous Sephardic Masoretic Bibles. An especially elaborate example is the page pictured in fig. 2.14, the late fourteenth-century London Catalan Pentateuch. This page again contains Exodus 15, and as in the Toledo 1232 Masoretic Bible pictured in fig. 2.13, the Masorah is written in a double wall around the text with wavelike semicircles filling the space between the two walls.

2.14 Pentateuch, Catalonia, late fourteenth century. London, British Library MS Harley 5773, fol.56r. © The British Library Board.

A number of very elaborate decorated liturgical Pentateuchs were also produced in Lisbon in what scholars have identified as a workshop active in the 1480s and 1490s.[106] The many remarkable Bibles produced in that workshop include one truly exceptional codex, the Duke of Sussex's Portuguese Pentateuch, a page of which is reproduced in fig. 2.15. With the exception of the heading *Vayiqra* (the first word of Leviticus, which this page opens), the biblical text is written in an elegant semicursive North African hand rather than the square script typically used in Sephardic Bibles.[107] The scribe's use of the semicursive appears to have been a concession to his patron, who was probably more comfortable reading that script.[108]

The Aramaic Targum was less frequently copied in Spanish *ḥumashim* than it was in Ashkenazic ones, a fact that may be partly explained by a preference in Spanish communities for studying the Bible with the Judeo-Arabic translation, or *Tafsir*, of Saadiah Gaon.[109] This practice is famously attested in the ethical will that the great translator Judah Ibn Tibbon (1120–ca. 1190) wrote to his son Samuel (who grew up to become an even greater translator than his father), in which he admonished, "Read every week the Pentateuchal section in Arabic. This will improve thine Arabic vocabulary, and will be of use in translating, if thou should feel inclined to translate."[110] A century later, however, Spanish sages began to encourage their communities to read Rashi along with the weekly Torah reading in place of the Targum.[111] Not surprisingly, this substitution was first introduced into Sepharad by Ashkenazi emigrants led by the Tosafist R. Asher ben Yehiel (ca. 1250–1327), who moved from Germany to Spain in 1303. Asher's son, Jacob, the author of the important early legal code *Arba' Turim*, explicitly ruled that reading Rashi was equivalent to reading the Targum because it, too, "explained" the meaning of the Torah.[112] The preeminence assigned to Rashi was possibly owed less to his contextual (*peshat*) interpretations than to the fact that he presented rabbinic tradition in an accessible, carefully abridged, reader-friendly style.[113] The adaption of his commentary in Sephardic Bibles is clear testimony to how Ashkenazic conventions penetrated Sepharad; the same phenomenon also took place in the opposite direction.

The history of the decorated Hebrew Bible in Sepharad between the mid-thirteenth and late fifteenth centuries has been studied extensively by Jewish art historians.[114] Two features emerge from those studies that are critical to understanding the meaning of the Hebrew Bible for Jews in the Iberian Peninsula. The first is the remarkable fact that Sephardic Bibles retain Islamic design as their overall stylistic form (whether the designs be classical Islamic or Mudejar) despite the fact that they were produced in Hispanic Christian kingdoms. (The term *Mudejar* refers to the Islamic minority population under Christian rule and the stylistic culture developed by that population and later adapted by both Christians and Jews, often as a sign of wealth and luxury.)[115] The second striking feature noted by scholars is the presence of full-page illustrations, usually found (like carpet pages) at the beginning of codices, depicting the holy implements from the

2.15 Duke of Sussex's Portuguese Pentateuch, Lisbon, 1480–90. London, British Library MS. Add. 15283, fol. 88r. © The British Library Board.

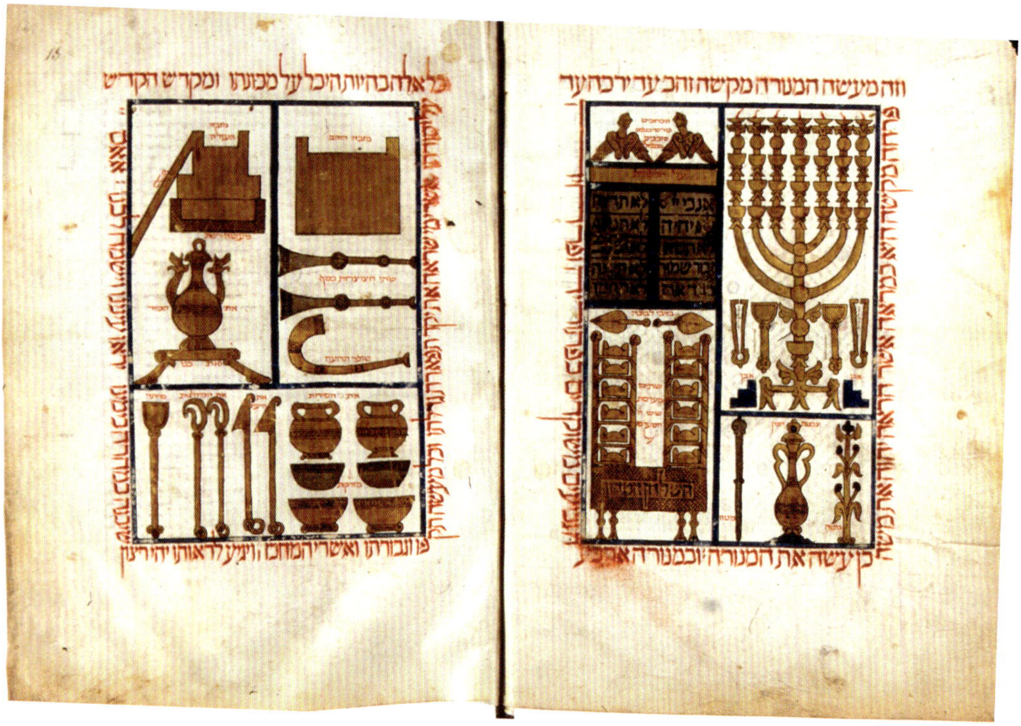

2.16 Bible, Perpignan, 1299. Paris, BnF héb. 7, fols. 7v–8r. Bibliothèque Nationale de France.

destroyed Jerusalem Temple—the menorah, the altar, the show-table, and the various tools that priests used in offering sacrifices. These Temple implement illustrations are found in a group of approximately twenty-five Bibles produced in the Kingdom of Aragon and in Roussillon mainly in the first half of the fourteenth century. Fig. 2.16 is a typical example of a Temple implement page as it appears in one of the earliest of these Bibles, composed in Perpignan in 1299.[116]

Both the Islamicizing tendencies of Sephardic Bibles and their use of Temple implement pages offer keys to understanding the significance that these Bibles as material artifacts held for their owners and users. We can begin with the Islamicizing tendency. As we noted, this tendency appears to violate the general rule that Jewish books mirror the books produced by the gentile host society in which they are produced. Admittedly, there are exceptions to this tendency among Sephardic Hebrew Bibles, for example the Cervera and Kennicott Bibles mentioned earlier. Furthermore, contemporary Christians in Spain as well as Jews adapted the Mudejar style, particularly in architecture and textile design.[117] Still, the simple fact is that most Sephardic Bibles do not look at all like contemporary Christian Bibles, and deliberately so.[118] Why did the Jews of Sepharad cling to the models set by the Islamic past and avoid the Christian books of their own time? Some have suggested that it was a reflex of the cultural conservatism of Sephardic Jewry, or that it represented a nostalgia felt by Jews in Christian Spain toward the so-called Golden Age of Spanish Jewish history, centered in al-Andalus, in the mid-tenth to mid-twelfth centuries, when Sephardic Hebrew culture reached the apogee of its achievements.[119] Indeed, Jews in Christian Spain carried on other features of Arabo-Islamic society as late as the Expulsion, like writing poetry in Arabic quantitative meters.[120] These explanations may all be true, but there may have been an additional layer of significance to the choice of decoration. Islamicizing tendencies—in book decoration and architecture, perhaps even in continuing to write poetry in Arabic meters—may have served a more contemporary, politicized purpose.[121]

By associating their books with those of the Mudejar minority culture and rejecting models and conventions perceived as Christian, Iberian Jews may have sought to use the material shape of their Bibles as a mode of resistance to the dominant Christian culture, as a means to identify not only their books but themselves as a separate and distinct, albeit minority, culture. Adhering to these Islamicizing tendencies would have held special meaning in the thirteenth century, which witnessed the violent dislocations of the Christian conquest of the south.

This strategy became even more valuable after the 1391 persecutions of the Jews and the forced conversions that followed them, and after the failure of the apocalyptic expectations predicted for the beginning of the fifteenth century and the disappointment that must have followed once those hopes failed to materialize. The Sephardic Jews' Mudejar neighbors posed little threat to their identity, and by materially identifying their books (and synagogue buildings) with Mudejar tradition, the Jews were able to resist Christian hegemony and to define themselves as a distinct, uncompromised minority culture.[122] We know from other cases that the material shape of a canonical text can shape religious identity. Here the material shape of the Hebrew Bible served as a medium of cultural self-definition and resistance.

A similar explanation may lie behind the Temple implement illustrations in the Roussillon and Catalan Bibles of the fourteenth century. These illustrations should be read not in visual isolation or as mere pictorial images but together with the texts inscribed in monumental frames around them (at least where there are such verses). These texts are: (1) biblical verses like Exodus 25:34 and Numbers 8:4, which relate directly to the Temple implements, the menorah in particular (as in fig. 2.16, from the Perpignan Bible); (2) verses that pray for the rebuilding of the Temple; and (3) others that praise Torah and wisdom, usually through a mélange of verses from Proverbs (e.g., 2:3–11; 3:1–3; 6:23) and Job (18:16), which often use metaphors and similes that liken the commandments to a *ner* (lamp) and Torah to *or* (light) (see Prov. 6:23 in particular) or that compare the value of wisdom, Torah, and the commandments to silver, gold, onyx, sapphires, and so on. The overall effect of these inscribed verses is to Judaize the implements illustrated within their frames by surrounding them with Hebrew texts inscribed in the same square Assyrian script used to write the Bible.

This Judaizing effort was especially necessary because the Temple implements—the treasured spoils of the destroyed Jerusalem Temple—were fiercely contested objects, with both Jews and Christians vying for ownership because they believed that in the messianic age these lost objects would be restored to them as part of their respective scenarios of redemption. In the late antique and early medieval periods, both religious traditions used their books to picture the Temple implements in this eschatological light. In Hebrew Bibles, depictions of the Mount of Olives are typically part of implement illustrations; this image was a conventional sign for messianic hope, and its meaning would have been understood by any Jew. In Christian tradition, illustrations of the implements were found in Latin Bibles going back to the seventh-century Codex Amiatinus, which itself derived from the sixth-century Codex Grandior of Cassiodorus, as well as in Iberian Bibles from the tenth through the thirteenth century; the implements also appeared in a fourteenth-century Iberian manuscript of the *Historia Scholastica* of Peter Comestor (d. 1178–80).[123] In the early fourteenth century, implement pages begin to appear in Sephardic Bibles, and their simultaneous appearance in Jewish and Christian Bibles was not coincidental. In conjunction with the messianic expectations current among Catalan and other Sephardic Jews following the Barcelona Disputation of 1263—which largely revolved around the messianic doctrines of Christianity and Judaism and their respective veracity—and the widespread longings around 1358 and 1403 for "end dates" for the arrival of the messianic period, the Temple implements took on an especially powerful symbolic charge.

This symbolism also informs Jewish biblical exegesis of the period.[124] In his popularizing quasi-kabbalistic commentary, the exegete Baḥya ben Asher (Saragossa, d. 1340), a student of Naḥmanides, comments on Exodus 25:9: "It is known that the Tabernacle and its implements were all *ṣiyyurim gufaniyyim* [material images] [that were intended] to make comprehensible the *elyoniyyim* [divine images] for which they were a model."[125] Baḥya then explicates the spiritual meanings of each implement and concludes, "And it is important to say that even though . . . the holy material Temple implements were fated to be destroyed in the *golah* [diaspora], you should not imagine that . . . their forms and models ceased to exist *le-ma'alah* [in the higher world]. *They continue to exist and will exist forever* [my italics]."[126] What Baḥya seems to be indicating is specifically the image of these implements, almost in a Platonic sense, as though it were a Form or Idea in the Intelligible world. For the same reason—because they were believed to possess timeless spiritual power—the pictures of these implements were placed in the Bibles at the very beginning of the codices, where they also marked the Jewishness of these Bibles. They were not "illustrative" illustrations intended to show the reader what the implements looked like.[127] They were icons of identity.

A similar symbolic meaning lies behind a term that became a popular cognomen for Masoretic Bible codices in fourteenth-century Sepharad.[128] This term is *miqdashyah*, literally, "the sanctuary of the Lord."[129] Some of the codices with this name, though not all, also contain Temple implement illustrations and are thus truly self-reflexive books illustrating their sanctuary-likeness through their pictures of the Temple implements. The use of the term as a designation for Bibles was not, however, a fourteenth-century invention, nor did it derive from the presence of Temple implement illustrations in the codex. The connection between the Tabernacle and the Torah can be traced back to Qumran and later appears in Karaite literature.[130] In his *Sefer Dikdukei Ha-teʿamim*, the Masorete Aaron ben Asher analogized the three courtyards of the Temple to the three divisions of the Bible (with the Pentateuch equaling the Holy of Holies, the Prophets the Inner Courtyard or Holy Place, and the Hagiographa the Outer Courtyard). Medieval sages like Abraham Ibn Ezra also employed the term *miqdash* as a metaphor/symbol of scripture: the Temple was the site in which God revealed himself, and the Torah is the record of that revelation.[131]

The most extensive explication of the term is found in the introduction to the grammatical treatise *Maʿaseh Efod* (The Making of the Efod), which was composed in 1403 by the Catalonian polemicist and grammarian Isaac ben Moses Ha-Levi, better known in Jewish tradition as Profiat Duran (1360–1412).[132] In this work, Duran attributes to Bible study an inherent merit, indeed a virtual "artifactual power," in the phrase coined by Kalman Bland. Duran describes Bible study as the true *ʿavodah* (worship) of God.[133] Torah, he writes, possesses a *segulah*. This term refers in the Bible to something "highly treasured" but by the course of the Middle Ages had come to mean "an occult virtue," as one scholar has recently written—that is, a virtually amuletic source of special power.[134] Internalization of the Torah through memorization of its words and contemplation of its inner meanings is the true worship of God, the path to "the ultimate, eternal felicity."[135] But Duran goes even further, writing that "even *esek* (engagement), *hagiyah* (recitation), and *qeriʾah* (reading) alone [without comprehension] are part of *ʿavodah* and are able to help draw down the divine influence and providence through the *segulah* that adheres in them, because this too is God's will."[136] Indeed, he argues, God intentionally prepared the Torah for Israel in its time of exile, after the destruction of the Temple, precisely so that it could serve as a *miqdash meʿat* (small sanctuary), within whose pages God's presence might be found just as his presence formerly dwelled within the Temple's four walls. Along the same lines, Duran claims, study of Torah atones for sins just as sacrifices once did.[137] In actuality, the study of Torah is so implicated in the fate of Israel that its neglect by the Jews of Ashkenaz—because of their lamentable concentration upon Talmud study—led to their persecutions and travails in the fourteenth century. So too, he writes, the Jews of Aragon were saved from destruction only because of their *shimush tehillim* (recitation of Psalms), a kind of devotional reading with its own theurgic powers.[138] In the years between

1391 and 1415, when the Church in Spain embarked upon an especially virulous mission against the Jewish population within its realm, Torah study would have taken on an especially urgent meaning as a source of artifactual power.

Maude Kozodoy has persuasively argued that Duran wrote *Ma'aseh Efod* secretly while living publicly as a Christian under the name of *magister* Honoratus de Bonafide (and working as a physician and astrologer in the court of King John I of Aragon), all the while continuing to observe Judaism in private.[139] In addition, he also wrote several anti-Christian polemical works while posing as a *converso*. How Duran was able to write such books in Hebrew for Sephardic Jews and other *conversos* without being discovered is amazing. Nonetheless, Kozodoy's provocative claim about Duran's *converso* identity casts his emphasis on the occult power of study and recitation of the Bible—that is, on internalization and memorization of its words—in a striking new light. For the community of *conversos* like Duran, *Ma'aseh Efod*'s argument that Torah study could serve as a focus for the intellectual worship of God offered, as Kozodoy writes, "a powerful message of hope, a message that a life without observance, or with minimal observance, was not without religious value."[140] And for Jews who had not succumbed to conversion, the message of *Ma'aseh Efod* was equally powerful. Duran was offering these contemporaries an avenue of salvation that was immediately available to them, a sacred shelter where they could occupy themselves in Torah study and thereby defend themselves against the hostile world outside—in other words, the Bible as a refuge. This was the real force of the Temple analogy as Duran used it. It is not difficult to imagine how a fourteenth- or fifteenth-century Sephardic Jew, looking at the carpet pages with the Temple implement illustrations, might have felt the palpable connection between the divine presence dwelling in the Temple and the material Bible containing those images.[141] The pages of these Bibles provided their owners and readers with a sense of the comforting presence of God, no matter how beleaguered their historical situation actually was.

Because the principal goal of Bible study for Duran was memorization of the text, he also paid special attention to the material features of the Bible codex, an attention that is virtually unique among medieval Jewish writers. Thus, he argues, the student should write out *simanim* (mnemonic signs), presumably in the margins of the text; he should always read from the same book; the text studied should be written in square, Assyrian letters inscribed in bold and heavy strokes, "for because of its beauty the impression of this script remains in the common sense and in the imagination"; and most significant of all, "one should always study from beautifully made books that have elegant script and pages and ornate adornments and bindings, and the places of study—I mean, the *batei ha-midrash* (study houses)—should be beautifully constructed and handsome, for this enhances the love of study and the desire for it."[142]

To justify these recommendations, Duran drew again upon the Temple analogy, saying that it is only fitting to decorate and beautify "this sanctified book which is a *miqdashyah*" because it is God's will that the sanctuary be decorated and ornamented with silver and gold and fine gems. And for this reason, he added, it has always been helpful for learned scholars to be wealthy so as to be able to own their own books and not have to borrow them. To this observation, however, he added the following derisive caveat: the wealthy patrons of his day, he wrote, believe that merely "possessing these books is sufficient as self-glorification, and they think that storing them in their treasure-chests is the same as preserving them in their minds."[143] Duran clearly did not share this belief, but because he was unable to ignore the social and political power of these aristocrats, he conceded that there is still "merit for their actions, since in some way they cause the Torah to be magnified and exalted; and even if they are not worthy of it, they bequeath a blessing to their children and those who come after them."[144] Therein lies the Bible's real artifactual power. It can even help those who are not worthy of its assistance!

Duran clearly knew that the luxurious Bibles owned by these rich aristocrats—the only persons in Iberian Jewish society of the time with the financial means to pay for such Temple-like Bibles—were "trophy books," commissioned by their owners to display their wealth. Yet for better or for worse, these wealthy patrons also constituted the community's leadership. As Eva Frojmovich has suggested, the ornamental designs used in the books are reminiscent of precious Andalusian textiles, themselves signs of nobility and aristocracy for Christians as well as Muslims; by using them in their Hebrew Bibles, Jewish owners advertised their social status as equivalent to that of their gentile neighbors.[145] And yet, the books were not solely advertisements. As Frojmovich writes, "The Hebrew Bible pages create images of religious contemplation, analogous to the complicated patterns of Islamic textiles that were to be savored slowly in a contemplative fashion."[146] The spiritual rewards of ostentation should not be overlooked. No matter how complex the motives of their owners may have been, these Bibles possessed a nexus of overdetermined meaning that can help us understand the privileged position occupied by the Bible in Sephardic culture.

The Bible in Ashkenaz

The Hebrew Bible in Ashkenaz in its two main regions (northern France and England on the one hand, Germany on the other) possessed for Jews a somewhat different cultural meaning than it did in Sepharad. For one thing, throughout Ashkenaz, the *ḥumash*, the liturgical Pentateuch, was the dominant type of Bible, not the Masoretic Bible (as was the case in Sepharad). Roughly two-thirds of the surviving Hebrew Bibles written in Germany, northern France, and England in the thirteenth and fourteenth centuries are *ḥumashim*; on the Iberian Peninsula, roughly the same percentage were Masoretic Bibles. While the textual contents and overall structure of both Masoretic Bibles and *ḥumashim* were similar in Sepharad and Ashkenaz, their material features, especially their decoration and art, differed in the two realms, so much so that their Bibles look almost unrelated. As material

2.17 Pentateuch, England, 1189. London, Valmadonna Trust, Ms. 1, fol. 59b–60a (Exod. 40– Lev. 1). Reproduced by the kind permission of the Valmadonna Trust.

artifacts, the Bibles of Sepharad and Ashkenaz represent two distinct responses to the Christian host cultures in which they were produced.

These differences are reflected in both the Masoretic Bibles and liturgical Pentateuchs produced in the various regions of Ashkenaz. The Ashkenazic Masoretic Bible resembles its Sephardic counterpart in generally replicating the early Near Eastern Masoretic codices of the tenth and eleventh centuries, with the biblical text laid out in columns (although Ashkenazic Bibles usually have three columns, while in Sepharad two increasingly became the norm) and with the *masorah magna* and *parva* written in micrography, the former in two lines in the top margin and three in the bottom, and the latter in the space to the right of each column. Unlike Sephardic codices, however, Ashkenazic codices rarely contain at the beginning and end Masoretic treatises like Aaron ben Asher's *Sefer Dikdukei Te'amim*. On the other hand, the Pentateuchal text in Ashkenazic Masoretic Bibles is often accompanied by the Aramaic Targum Onkelos, which is frequently written interverse: each biblical verse is immediately followed by its Aramaic translation, verse by verse, in each text column. This practice is attested in some of the earliest surviving Ashkenazic Masoretic Bibles, as well as in many Ashkenazic *ḥumashim*, but almost never in Sephardic Bibles.[147]

The origin of the interverse Targum is not known. The earliest testimony to the practice is to be found in fragments of Palestinian Targumim from the Cairo Genizah, in which each verse of the biblical text is followed by the Targum; usually, the texts are written in three columns, and there is no distinction in size or script between Bible and Targum.[148] The specific Palestinian Targumim represented in these fragments were almost never copied in the Middle Ages but were replaced by the Targum of Onkelos, also Palestinian in origin but less expansive than the others, and probably for that reason favored in Babylonia, where it became the canonical Targum. One of the earliest manuscripts to contain Targum Onkelos (as well as the Masorah), a fragmentary Pentateuch (Ms. Vatican ebr. 448), probably dates from the late eleventh century and may have been Babylonian in origin.[149] The interverse Targum is found in the earliest dated *ḥumash* from an Ashkenazic land, a Pentateuch (fig. 2.17) written in England in 1189 (also making it the earliest datable and localizable Hebrew manuscript to be written in England).[150] To be sure, not all Ashkenazic liturgical Pentateuchs have the interverse Targum. Some French *ḥumashim* either omit the Targum altogether or, more tellingly, substitute Rashi for the Targum. In those cases, Rashi is sometimes written in a second column next to the scriptural text and at other times interverse.[151] The De Castro Pentateuch (formerly Sassoon 506, now Jerusalem, Israel Museum 180/94), completed in 1344, has both Targum and Rashi, each verse followed by Targum, followed in turn by Rashi. The scriptural text is in a darker square Ashkenazic hand, the Targum and Rashi in a slightly less dark and smaller semicursive script. One can see this layout in fig. 2.18, the codex's first page, the opening of Genesis. As the reader will note, there are also illustrations inside and outside the roundels above the initial word *Bereishit* (in super-large letters). In these paintings, Adam and Eve are portrayed twice; once (outside the roundels) as they are about to eat from the tree of knowledge (pictured in the center of the images), with Eve proferring the fruit to Adam; and second (inside the roundels) as they are about to be expelled from the Garden of Eden, with Adam pointing an accusing finger at his wife.[152]

The presence of the Targum in these Bibles raises the larger question as to how these books were actually used in the synagogue.[153] Did Ashkenazi Jews substitute a *ḥumash* (or, for that matter, a Masoretic Bible) for a Torah scroll to chant from liturgically as part of the synagogue service? As we noted earlier, Karaites may have read the Torah in their synagogues from biblical codices rather than from Torah scrolls. We also know that some rabbinic authorities, beginning with the Geonim of Babylonia and continuing with their successors in the Iberian Peninsula, Provence, and even northern France, initially permitted communities that did not own a Torah scroll to use a codex.[154] Rabbis in Palestine, Germany, and Italy, however, categorically forbade the practice, and by the end of the thirteenth century, the prohibition was obeyed universally.

Yet even if most codices were not employed to substitute for a Sefer Torah, it is very likely that sages and individuals wealthy enough to own their own liturgical Pentateuchs

2.18 De Castro Pentateuch, Germany, 1344. Jerusalem, Israel Museum 180/94, fol. 1v. Photo © The Israel Museum, Jerusalem, by Ardon Bar-Hama.

used them in the synagogue to follow along with the public reader as he chanted the weekly Torah reading from the scroll. A well-known Talmudic injunction attributed to the fourth-century Amora R. Huna bar Judah (who repeated it in the name of his predecessor, R. Ammi) states, "Every person is obligated to complete the weekly lectionary readings [*parshiyyotav*] with the congregation [by reciting] Hebrew Scripture [*miqra*] twice and the Targum once" (B. Berakhot 8a–b).[155] We have no idea how extensively this injunction was observed during the Talmudic period, but the profusion of liturgical Pentateuchs with Targum written interverse produced in Ashkenaz in the thirteenth and especially fourteenth centuries points to its wider practice during this period. R. Meir of Rothenburg (ca. 1215–93), citing an earlier responsum of Provençal sages, writes that if a practiced Aramaic translator is present in the synagogue, he should read the Targum along with the Torah; if not, a person should fulfill the Talmudic injunction privately at home.[156] In contrast, Isaac bar Moses of Vienna (1189–1250), the author of the influential *Sefer Or Zaru'a*, describes personally seeing his teachers, R. Judah He-Ḥasid and R. Abraham ben R. Moshe, reading the weekly parashah in synagogue in precisely this way—twice in Hebrew, once in Targum—while listening to the Torah reader publicly chant the portion.[157] This kind of private reading must have satisfied a religious need that was not being fulfilled by passively listening to the Torah chanted aloud by another person.

The fact that Isaac mentioned his teacher's practice suggests that it was unusual, if not novel. In fact, private reading by individuals in a communal setting was a developing trend in the literate culture of western Europe during the thirteenth century.[158] In 1259, students at the University of Paris were formally required to bring their own copies to the public lectures in which the texts were explicated and taught. Around the same time, Humbert of Romans (ca. 1194–1277) is quoted as saying that collective prayer was "enriched by individuals gazing on the text of a written prayer as it was collectively pronounced."[159] Liturgical Pentateuchs would have served the same purpose of enrichment for Jews by enabling individuals to become active participants in communal reading events like the synagogue Torah service.

This last observation leads in turn to the additional question of the relationship between Jewish Bibles in Ashkenaz and the Christian Bibles of Latin Europe during this period. The size, format, and mode of decoration of Bibles in the two religious communities point to a connection of some sort.[160] In respect to size, as scholars have shown, the twelfth century witnessed, first in Italy and later through the rest of Europe, the production of a great number of multivolume Bibles, many of enormous dimensions. Then, in the thirteenth century, first around Paris and later throughout Europe, the dimensions of the Latin Bible began to shrink, and the large multivolume sets were replaced by single volumes containing the entirety of scripture, written on thin parchment (itself the product of new technologies) and copied in tiny but clear handwriting. These portable Bibles—frequently referred to as Paris Bibles—were a product of the commercial book trade in and around Paris and served a large audience: students and masters, members of the court and the church hierarchy, wealthy collectors, and especially mendicant friars, who carried them as they traveled to preach and teach scripture. As these Bibles proliferated throughout Europe, they became available to the entire literate public and were also acquired by laypersons for private study.[161]

Jewish Bibles in Ashkenaz did not follow the same neat chronological development as their Latin counterparts, but the range of their sizes roughly mirrors that attested in Christian book culture.[162] In Ashkenaz, between the mid-thirteenth and mid-fourteenth centuries, one finds both "giant" Hebrew Bibles and smaller portable ones.[163] Many thirteenth-century Ashkenazic Bibles are large codices, although none of them comes close to Erfurt 1 (Berlin; Staatsbibliothek, Ms. Or fol. 1210–11), completed in 1343, the single largest Hebrew Bible in existence, with dimensions of 629 × 470 millimeters (= 24.7 × 18.5 in.).[164] Exactly what purpose these huge Hebrew Bibles served for their Jewish readers is unclear.[165] Christian "giant" Bibles appear to have been produced in connection with the monastic reforms of the late eleventh and twelfth centuries, which insisted upon the renewal of communal reading in monasteries; the size of these books certainly would have facilitated public reading.[166] Gigantic, lavishly decorated Bibles also made excellent gifts from powerful and wealthy individuals to rulers and religious institutions (like monasteries), where they were donated to strengthen strategic political relationships. In this case, size enlarged value.[167]

These motivations and purposes, however, are less relevant to Jewish Bibles. There were no Jewish monasteries, and in the thirteenth century, no one in Ashkenaz used a codex for communal reading of the Torah in the synagogue. Moreover, virtually all Hebrew manuscripts in the Middle Ages were commissioned by and for individual owners, not institutions (even if some individuals later dedicated and donated the codices to synagogues to serve as communal property), so it is unlikely that they were produced intentionally as gifts.[168] As Malachi Beit-Arié has suggested, it may be that the enormous dimensions of these codices simply embodied "the wish of the patron to produce and own an unprecedented book."[169] It may also have been the case that Jews saw Latin giant Bibles owned by Christians and then thought that they too should have such books, if only out of cultural competition.

Beginning around 1300, however, the dimensions of the Hebrew Bible began to shrink, albeit gradually. A number of portable Hebrew Bibles with much smaller dimensions were produced around 1300, especially in the Lake Constance region in southern Germany, among them the famous Schocken Bible and the Duke of Sussex German Pentateuch, a *ḥumash*.[170] There is an even more remarkable codex, a complete Hebrew Bible, undated but apparently composed around the same time as the Schocken Bible, with 408 folios of such thin and fine parchment that the codex is little more than three-quarters of an inch thick while the folios measure a mere 100 × 75 millimeters (3.9 × 2.95 in.).[171] In the later fourteenth and fifteenth centuries, particularly in Italy, which absorbed many Jewish scribes

2.19
Bible, Lorraine, Franche Comté, 1286. Paris, BnF, Héb. 4, fol. 249v. Bibliothèque Nationale de France.

expelled from Ashkenaz, complete Bibles in single volumes regularly possessed dimensions of this order. Although these relatively small Hebrew Bibles developed around a century after the Paris Bibles, they doubtless provided their owners with the same portability.

It is, however, in its decorations and illustrations that the Ashkenazic Bible most closely mirrors its Latin counterpart and contrasts most dramatically with Sephardic Bibles. The Islamically derived features of the Sephardic Masoretic Bible—aniconism, carpet pages, and the colonnaded Masoretic pages with lists at the beginning and end of the book—are naturally absent from the Ashkenazic codices, which instead tend to have representational drawings and paintings. (There are some Ashkenazic liturgical Pentateuchs with pictures of the menorah, but unlike their Sephardic counterparts, these typically contain narrative illustrations of biblical scenes surrounding the menorah, and only rarely include other Temple implements.)[172] While decoration had a functional purpose in both Sephardic and Ashkenazic Bibles, the specific devices they used for this purpose were typically very different. For example, as Dalia-Ruth Halperin has recently shown, scribes in both Ashkenaz and Sepharad used Masoretic micrography at the bottoms of pages to mark quire beginnings and ends (possibly to assist gentile bookbinders in ordering the quires correctly), but in Ashkenaz the micrography often consists of representational drawings while in Sepharad it is always aniconic.[173] In Sephardic Bibles, *ansa*-like signs drawn in the margins mark the beginnings of *parashiyyot* (and *sedarim*). In contrast, Ashkenazic Bibles use enlarged initial words and, in more deluxe codices, initials enclosed in decorated panels to highlight for the reader the beginnings of biblical books and sometimes *parashiyyot*.[174] This, too, parallels developments in thirteenth-century Paris Bibles, where initials (usually letters, however, not words) began to serve as the primary spaces for decoration and illustration.[175] An especially lavish initial-word panel is found in a French Hebrew Bible (BnF Héb. 4, fol. 249v) composed in Lorraine, Franche-Comté, in 1286, pictured in fig. 2.19. This page, the beginning of 1 Kings, has its initial word *Ve-ha-melekh* (And King [David was now old]), empanelled against a blue and red checkered background and enclosed in a colonnade complete with watchtowers and a howling gargoyle on its right side, while the two columns rest on figures of jousting knights labeled in the text, respectively, "This is David" and "This is Adoniyahu." The scene alludes to the coup attempted by Adoniyahu, David's son, against his father as narrated in 1 Kings 1. (The spears held by the knights meet in two shields in the space between the columns, from which rises the tail of a dragon whose head reaches up to the initial word panel.) While the identification of the two figures is keyed to the biblical text, iconography depicting jousting knights has many parallels in contemporary Latin manuscripts. It was clearly part of the wider visual vocabulary.[176]

Still more common in Ashkenazic Bibles than painted historiated illustrations are initial word panels and other decorations inscribed in ink by pen in micrography containing the Masorah.[177] Fig. 2.20, from the famous giant Bible known as Erfurt 2, is an especially ornate example of a page with such decoration. The initial word of the book of Genesis, *Bereishit*, is written in large Gothic-like Ashkenazic square letters and enclosed within an arch whose tympanum is filled with various grotesques—dragons, griffins, and camel-like hybrids. Still other mythical beasts populate the roundels at the bottom of the page. These grotesques mirror marginal drawings in contemporary Latin codices, liturgical books as well as Bibles.[178] In the case of this Hebrew Bible, it is not clear whether the grotesques were meant to be mainly decorative or whether they were intended to signal to the reader a kind of *tohu va-vohu* lying beyond the edges of the orderly universe whose creation begins to be narrated on that page. Whatever their specific purpose or meaning, they impart to the page a distinctive presence.

2.20 Bible, Erfurt, Germany, late thirteenth century. Berlin, Staatsbibliothek zu Berlin: Preussischer Kulturbesitz, Ms or. Fol. 1212 [Erfurt 2], 1v. Courtesy of bpk, Berlin / Staatsbibliothek/Art Resource, New York.

2.21 Berlin, Erfurt, Germany, late thirteenth century. Berlin, Staatsbibliothek zu Berlin: Preussischer Kulturbesitz, Ms or. Fol. 1212 [Erfurt 2], fol. 146v detail. Courtesy of bpk, Berlin /Staatsbibliothek/Art Resource, New York.

Not all micrographic illustrations in Ashkenazic Bibles are of such monstrous creatures. Sometimes the pictures relate directly to the contents of the page.[179] Even so, the vast number of micrographic figures are grotesques: invariably eye-catching, occasionally charming, and to a modern eye, incongruously bizarre. Fig. 2.21, a detail from the same giant Bible, Erfurt 2, shows two rather harried-looking hybrids, one of them either swallowing or spewing forth a one-eyed snakelike creature, probably a stuck-out tongue with an arrowheadlike tip. There is no clear connection I can discover between the image and the text on the page, Leviticus 35, a chapter dealing with the laws of the sabbatical and jubilee years. Indeed, within this literary context, the two hybrids look like aliens who have just landed on the folio from outer space.

These micrographic illustrations did not pass unnoticed by rabbinic authorities of the period. In the influential pietistic manual *Sefer Hasidim* (Book of the Righteous), ascribed to Rabbi Judah He-Ḥasid (d. 1217), the author instructs his reader that "one who hires a scribe to write the Masorah for the Twenty-Four Books [i.e., the Bible] should make a condition with the scribe that he should not make the Masorah into drawings of birds or beasts or a tree, or into any other illustration . . . for how will he be able to see [and read the Masorah]?"[180] This injunction predates any surviving Ashkenazic Bible, so it is clear that the practice of writing the Masorah in designs was a longtime practice in Ashkenazic book culture. Whether or not Judah was the first to oppose the practice, the ubiquity of these micrographic drawings in Ashkenazic manuscripts makes it clear that his objections and those of other rabbinic authorities were ignored by Ashkenazi scribes and Masoretes.

Still, the question posed in *Sefer Hasidim* is telling. How *will* the reader be able to read the Masorah if it is recorded in the shape of these designs? If the Masorah inscribed in these designs was indeed meant to be read, the task would have required enormous effort from the reader. Indeed, this may have been part of the purpose of the designs. Perhaps the concentration necessary to decipher the text, along with the unusual shapes of the designs, was intended to facilitate memorization.[181] Another scholar has suggested, less convincingly, that the Sephardic designs had mystical meanings and kabbalistic significance.[182] But the purpose of the decorative Masorah may not even have been reading per se. The micrographic designs may have been ornamental in the sense that Oleg Grabar has used this term to describe the geometric and floral designs in early Qur'ans: affective in purpose, intended to imbue the reader with feelings of awe and respect for the text in the book.[183] We have already applied Grabar's insight to the carpet pages in the early Near Eastern codices and to the Sephardic Bibles with their own geometric and floral designs, and it is equally applicable to these Ashkenazic Bibles. Just as the Masoretic annotations safeguarded the correct transmission of the biblical text, these intricate designs with their fierce dragons and hybrids may have been intended to protect the pages of these books from hostile invaders of another sort.[184] And possibly, the Masorah recorded in these Bibles—in the intricate aniconic designs in Sephardic Bibles and the grotesques and hybrids of Ashkenazic codices—may not even have been intended to be read or studied. The Masorah may have been inscribed in these Bibles specifically because it had become, by this time in the Middle Ages, a necessary presence in a Jewish Bible. It had to be on the page because it had become a mark of the Jewishness of the Bible.

To be sure, some scribes doubtless used these intricate and unusual designs to express their virtuosity. But scribal virtuosity alone would not have justified their presence in Bibles, nor does it explain the ambiguous and often enigmatic nature of the images. Here again, comparison with contemporary Latin manuscripts of the period may be helpful. Recent art historical scholarship has focused extensively on marginal art, particularly as found in Psalters and, somewhat later, in Books of Hours, and on the ways these marginal images in Christian books challenge and undermine the structured order embodied in the hegemonic, hierarchical texts on the page.[185]

These Christian images can be truly outrageous, even obscene—pictures of "lascivious apes, autophagic dragons, pot-bellied heads, harp-playing asses, arse-kissing priests, and somersaulting jongleurs," as Michael Camille has described them.[186] In comparison, the marginal images in Jewish books are models of restraint and modesty. Nonetheless, in their own way, the Jewish images similarly confront, if not challenge, the textual space they surround. Like the grotesques in Christian manuscripts, the micrographic Masoretic figures in Hebrew Bibles are literally marginal (and even in the initial panels the grotesques frequently inhabit the panel's margins).[187] The biblical text that these images surround is the most controlled, regulated, and hierarchical verbal entity in all Jewish literary culture, and by inhabiting the margins of these pages, the images inherently possess a discordant relationship to the text; they inject incongruity onto the page. It is worth remembering that, of all types of Jewish scribal activity, copying a Bible, either in a scroll or a codex, is the one that most requires the scribe to be a pure copyist, leaving almost no room for innovation or personal creativity, precisely because the whole point of copying a Torah is to reproduce the original as accurately as possible. And as we know, one purpose of the Masoretic notes was to guarantee the Bible's textual accuracy, to ensure the exact reproduction of the original. By turning these same annotations into fanciful, hybrid, Masorah-eating (or spewing) creatures, might the scribe have been using them—very playfully—as small rebellious figures, challenges to his own prescribed existence as a mere scribe? Or, at the very least, to show the reader that he was more than a copyist?

In whatever way we interpret the meaning of these images, there is no question that they mirror Christian book art of the period. Rather than viewing them as mere borrowings, however, it might be more correct to characterize them, along with the other material features of the Ashkenazic Bible, as deliberate appropriations of the Christian host culture, aggressive efforts to Judaize the visual imagery of the surrounding Christian culture. While the iconography of the marginal illustrations may have derived from gentile sources, the scribes or Masoretes who designed these illustrations imbued them with an indelible Jewishness by literally making the iconography out of Masorah, the very stuff of Jewish biblical traditionality. These Masoretic decorations are a perfect example of what Ivan Marcus has called "inward acculturation": the process through which Jews adapted Christian themes and reworked and fused them with native Jewish traditions, and then, having absorbed them in this reconstituted fashion, "understood them to be part and parcel of their Judaism."[188]

In the past, medieval Ashkenazic culture has frequently been portrayed as existing in relative isolation from, if not active hostility toward, its Christian surroundings. Recent scholarship has revised that picture by showing that encounters between the two communities—fraught as they could be with theological conflict and physical violence, and despite the fact that Jews and Christians continued to live separate lives—were still intensely productive, with demonstrable borrowings and appropriations in both directions.[189] The appropriative stance toward Christian culture embodied in these Ashkenazic Bibles stands in sharp contrast to the very different strategy that scribes in Sepharad adapted by Islamicizing their Bibles as a path of resistance to the Christian host culture and a mode of asserting their identity as a minority culture within the majority population.[190] Ashkenazi scribes did not so much resist Christian hegemony as exploit it by remaking these Christian designs in their own image to express their identity as Jews.

The difference between these two responses is profound, but it is significant that both were articulated in the material medium of Masoretic micrography. The corpus of annotations that began as a textual apparatus now became, in the hands of scribes, a creative tool for negotiating religious identity and cultural difference between the Jews of a particular community and their gentile neighbors. By the end of the medieval period and the beginning of the age of print, the Masorah would become the mark of the Jewishness of a Jewish Bible in still other ways.

The Study Bible in Ashkenaz and Sepharad

The third type of Jewish Bible found in the Middle Ages is the study Bible. To be sure, all the Bibles we have discussed thus far could have been—and probably were—used for study, but by this I mean those Bibles that appear to have been intentionally written for the purpose of study. As noted earlier, the main indications of this purpose are either the presence of multiple commentaries on the page or the prominence of the commentary's place; both signs suggest that the Bible was produced specifically as a book for study.

Even so, the lines separating the different subgenres of the medieval Jewish Bible are blurred, and different types of Bibles in the Middle Ages clearly overlapped in their purposes and roles. One of the earliest examples of a study Bible, the manuscript known as Leipzig 1, which contains what some scholars believe to be the earliest evidence for the original text of Rashi's commentary, is a liturgical Pentateuch with the haftarot and Scrolls composed in France, probably in the early thirteenth century. Fig. 2.22 shows a typical page in this codex. In its various columns and windows, the page also records the Masoretic notes of earlier Ashkenazi sages as well as many comments upon and additions to Rashi's commentary.[191] The presence of these layered texts on the page seems to testify to the scribe or patron's original intention that the codex be used for study, not simply for synagogue use as a *ḥumash*, and its numerous annotations attest that the book was indeed studied actively and intensely.

The history of the study Bible is closely intertwined with the history of medieval Jewish biblical exegesis. As we have seen, Jews' initial adaptation of the codex, along with the creation of the Masoretic Bible in the ninth and tenth centuries, had a revolutionary impact on Jewish reading practice and how the Bible subsequently came to be studied and interpreted.[192] The various material shapes taken by the Hebrew Bible in the later Middle Ages also influenced those different types of exegesis and were in part their products.

Even a short history of medieval biblical exegesis is beyond the scope of this book, but what is most important for our concerns is the difference in attitude toward Bible study between Sepharad and Ashkenaz. These differences have sometimes been exaggerated in past scholarship, but they were still significant.[193]

We can begin with Sepharad. Throughout its history, its exegetes were continuously enriched by the grammatical tradition pioneered by the Masoretes and the developing sciences of philology and philosophy, which came to Jews through exposure to the intellectual culture of the Islamic world. These influences first appeared in the Geonic period

2.22
Pentateuch with Rashi and other commentaries, France, early thirteenth century (?). Leipzig, Universitätsbibliothek Ms. B.H.1, fol. 203v. Courtesy of the Leipzig University Library.

in Babylonia and continued in the Christian kingdoms in Iberia and adjacent areas like Provence, where they influenced the work of such biblical exegetes as Abraham Ibn Ezra (1089–1167), David Kimḥi (ca. 1160–ca. 1235), and Naḥmanides (1194–1270). Despite the complaints of figures like Profiat Duran over the waning of Bible study, there existed a more or less continuous history of biblical commentary in Sepharad until the Expulsion of the Jews. Not surprisingly, the Pentateuch was the primary focus of the educational curriculum, while the Prophets and the Writings were subjects for more advanced levels.[194] Fig. 2.23 is from a volume of First Prophets, copied in Segovia in 1487, that contains on its pages the Targum and the commentaries of Rashi, David Kimḥi, and Levi b. Gershon. The books of Proverbs, Job, and Ecclesiastes were studied especially intensively as ethical tracts; a good number of manuscripts of these books with commentaries on their pages survive.[195]

2.23 First Prophets with commentaries of Rashi, David Kimḥi, and Levi b. Gershon, Segovia, 1487. Oxford, Bodleian Libraries, Kennicott 5, fol. 46v. The Bodleian Libraries, University of Oxford.

In Ashkenaz, the attitude toward study of the Bible developed along a different path. In northern France, from the eleventh through the twelfth centuries, there existed a distinguished line of biblical exegetes, which began with the eleventh-century sage Jacob b. Yakar (990–1064), "a teacher of gemarah and Scripture," and continued with his disciple, the legendary Rashi (Shlomo Yitzḥaki, 1040–1105), and then Rashi's disciples and followers, among them Joseph Kara (ca. 1065–ca. 1135), Joseph Bekhor Shor (twelfth century), Samuel ben Meir (ca. 1085–1158), and Eliezer of Beaugency (twelfth century). These exegetes drew on the late midrashic tradition even though they famously eschewed midrash for what they called *peshat*. This term is difficult to translate, and it clearly meant different things to different exegetes, but it is probably best understood (at least in Ashkenaz) as the (more or less) literary-contextual sense of scripture. After the Crusader period, however, the independent study of scripture waned in Ashkenaz and was overshadowed by the study of Talmud (even though the Talmudists denied that they had forsaken the study of scripture because, they claimed, the Talmudic corpus contained an enormous amount of biblical exegesis).[196] Nonetheless, Bible study remained a staple of elementary education in Ashkenaz and maintained its ardent supporters. German pietists (*ḥasidei Ashkenaz*) in particular stressed its importance as part of their critique of the dialectical study of the Talmud as championed by the Tosafists.[197]

These differences in attitude toward Bible study influenced the literary forms that Bible commentary took in the Arabic-speaking Jewish community on the one hand, and Christian Europe on the other. Following the path first set by the tenth-century Babylonian Gaon Saadia in his commentary on the Bible, many later Sephardic commentators self-consciously composed *ḥibburim*, literary treatises. While these commentaries typically proceeded line by line (or phrase by phrase), they regularly included programmatic introductions and sometimes lengthy digressions that are almost essayistic explorations of problems raised by verses. In contrast, Ashkenazic commentaries tended to be purely lemmatic, that is, brief comments on specific words or phrases. In fact, we do not know how the Ashkenazic commentaries were originally written—whether they were composed as actual commentaries, or whether (as some scholars have suggested) they originated as notes in the margins of biblical codices, sometimes in response to remarks of earlier commentators (like Rashi), and were later collected by disciples and then copied by scribes into separate books to create continuous commentaries.[198] The case of Rashi is especially complicated because it is clear that Rashi's commentary was edited, added to, and glossed by his students (and perhaps by Rashi himself) as well as by later scribes—indeed, so much so that it may be impossible today to determine exactly what Rashi's commentary originally looked like.[199]

Whether they originated as independent works or as marginalia, most Jewish biblical commentaries in both Sepharad and Ashkenaz ended up circulating and being studied in separate books called *kuntresim* (sing. *kuntres*, from the Latin *quinterion*, a quire of five sheets). Fig. 2.24 is a page from a remarkable example of a *kuntres* written in France in the early thirteenth century. The page contains Rashi's commentary on Exodus 25, the biblical passage describing the Temple implements, and incorporates within its page design an illustration of the menorah. The fact that the illustration in the Rashi *kuntres*

2.24
Rashi Commentary (*kuntres*), France, early thirteenth century. Oxford, Bodleian Libraries MS. Opp. Add. Fol. 69, fol. 40r. The Bodleian Libraries, University of Oxford.

is so clearly integrated into the page's format strongly suggests that it was part of the original commentary and at least conceptually part of Rashi's interpretation.[200] Like this example, most *kuntresim* were typically written in semicursive rabbinic script, with the comments separated by a lemma, the word or short phrase from the Bible that keyed the reader to the comment's scriptural occasion.

A *kuntres* could also be a deluxe codex. The earliest illustrations in any medieval Hebrew book are found in a folio-sized *kuntres* containing the commentaries of Rashi and other French exegetes from his school that was written in the vicinity of the German town of Würzburg in 1232–33. The illustrations that serve as initial panels for the different biblical books were drawn by a Christian artist who received instructions from the Jewish scribe as to what to draw; we know the artist was Christian because a recent study of the manuscript has revealed the Latin directions to the artist as well as outlines in the margin

2.25
Compendium of School of Rashi Commentaries (*kuntres*), Würzburg, Germany, 1232/33. Munich, BSB Heb. Cod. 5, 1, fol. 29v. Courtesy of the Bayerische Staatsbibliothek. [Above: detail. Left: in context]

for the Hebrew letters the artist was supposed to draw in the panels.[201] Fig. 2.25 is the beginning of the section *Vayishlaḥ* (beginning with Gen. 32:4); the historiated initial depicts the reconciliation of the brothers Jacob and Esau (almost an objective correlative for the Jewish-Christian collaboration that produced the book!).

As with *ḥumashim*, we do not know exactly how these *kuntresim* were used. While it seems most likely that they were studied alongside biblical codices, some readers may have used them alone, the Bible presumably being known by heart and the lemmas serving merely as verse reminders. The problem with studying this way—that is, without a Bible at hand to consult in cases of confusion—was sufficiently well known that the twelfth-century exegete from Narbonne, Joseph ibn Kimḥi, the father of David (RaDaK), had to warn his reader always to have a Torah in front of him, "and then everything will be in the right place."[202]

At some point, scribes began to copy Bibles with commentaries on the same page, and thus the study Bible was born. Leipzig Ms. B.H.1 (fig. 2.22), discussed earlier, is an example of this genre, although it is also a liturgical Pentateuch in its overall structure. Unfortunately, the manuscript has no colophon, and scholars have debated its dating, some arguing that it was produced in the first half of the thirteenth century (that is, within a little more than a century after Rashi's death), others pushing its date into the fourteenth century.

The page from Leipzig B.H.1 is laid out in a format that is best known today as the format of the Talmudic page, with the core text—in this case, the Bible—written in the middle of the page in larger square script and the commentaries around it in a smaller, semicursive hand. This page format was initially developed by Christian scribes in northern France in the twelfth century for writing the Bible with the Glossa Ordinaria, the classic digest of patristic exegesis. Fig. 2.26 is an example of the format as it appears in a glossed Pentateuch, probably from the late twelfth century.[203] As Chrisopher de Hamel has shown, the format first appeared in northern France earlier in that century. By the thirteenth century, it had spread to the rest of Europe; it took Christian scribes roughly a century to perfect the form and make it both aesthetically pleasing and legible.[204] Jewish scribes became familiar with the format, possibly (as Colette Sirat has suggested) through Latin codices with glosses that were taken as collateral from Christians by Jewish moneylenders who, even if they could not read the Latin, could see the format.[205] This glossed layout first appears in Hebrew books in France in the early thirteenth century. By the late fourteenth and fifteenth centuries, it had spread to Jewish communities in Germany, Spain, and Italy. Eventually—after Daniel Bomberg employed it in his edition of the complete Talmud (1519/20–23) and in the Second Rabbinic Bible (1524–25)—the format became the iconic Jewish page, particularly for any text with commentaries.[206]

Fig. 2.27 is a page from a study Bible written in 1327, probably in Italy. The codex contains the Five Scrolls with the Targum and the commentaries of Rashi and Abraham Ibn Ezra; the page in the illustration has the text of Song of Songs 4:4–8. While the biblical

2.26 Pentateuch with gloss, France, late twelfth century (?). Oxford, Bodleian Libraries, Auct. E.inf.7, fol. 128r. The Bodleian Libraries, University of Oxford.

2.27
Five scrolls with Targum and commentaries of Rashi and A. Ibn Ezra (Song of Songs 4:4–8), Italy (?), 1327. Oxford, Bodleian Libraries, MS. Digby Or. 34, fol. 17v. The Bodleian Libraries, University of Oxford.

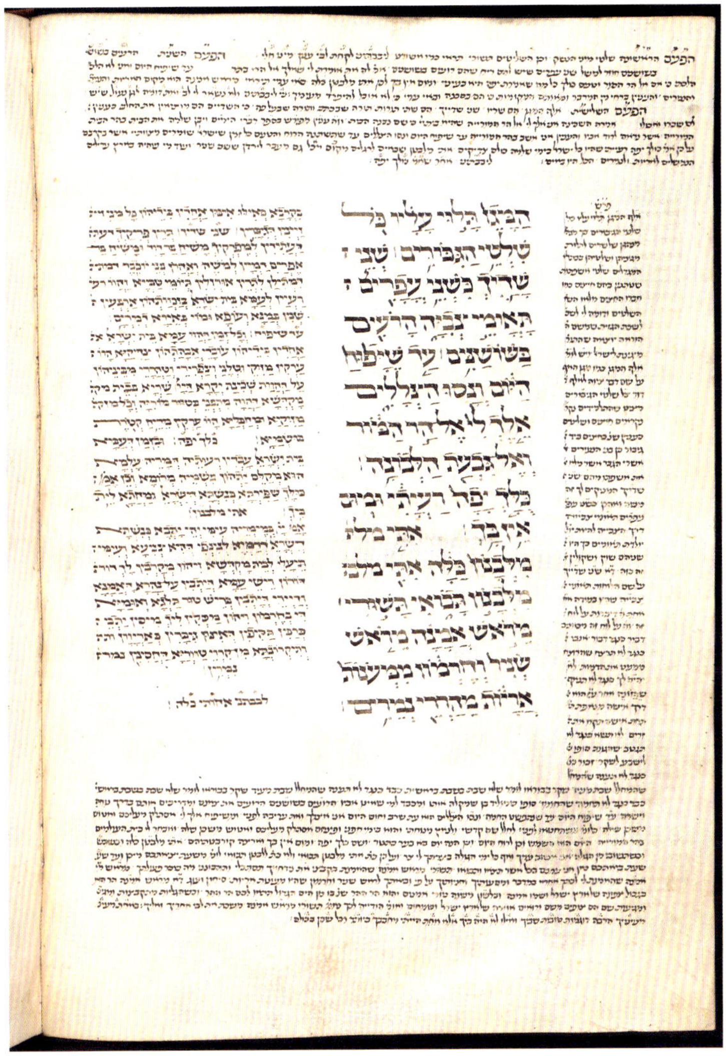

text and the Targum are written respectively in larger and smaller Ashkenazic scripts, the commentaries are in an Italian semicursive hand, making this codex a visible example of how the format of the study Bible traveled (with scribes) from one country to another.[207]

The glossed format with the biblical text and commentaries on the same page was obviously more convenient for a student to use for study. But more than being convenient, it was transformative. It changed the very nature of Bible study. Placing the Bible with its commentary on the same page made studying Bible with commentary a normative practice. Second, it changed the nature of reading the Bible. With the commentary on the page, the student was less likely to read the biblical text sequentially; rather, he or she now read it verse by verse with the commentary intervening wherever it existed. The biblical text was thus atomized into smaller lexical and semantic units that combined verse and exegesis. To be sure, atomization had also occurred in the case of midrash, where, as I suggested, the Bible was studied as an aurally acquired text concentrated on smaller units that effectively served as sound bites. In the case of the codex, however, the atomized text was one that was read on a spatial surface. Because text and commentary occupied the same space, the glossed page, as Colette Sirat has noted, forced the reader to confront the two simultaneously, going back and forth between text and comment, and out of that repeated confrontation, the habit of reading the Bible with commentary became a regularized dialogical act.[208] Multiple commentaries on the same page encouraged comparative study of biblical commentaries. Furthermore, the regularization of reading Bible with commentary eventually led to the composition of super-commentaries—commentaries that commented upon and explicated earlier commentaries—and even to glossed commentary pages, with a "core" commentary like Ibn Ezra's in the center of the page (that is, where the biblical text would otherwise have been) surrounded in the margins by a super-commentary on Ibn Ezra's commentary.[209] Such super-commentaries regularly compare one commentator to another.

For all its utility and convenience, this glossed format was not easy for scribes to produce. To make the page work, the scribe virtually had to prophesy how much core text (i.e., Bible) he could write in the center of the page and have a sufficient amount of commentary to fill the remainder of the folio; if he had too little, he wasted parchment, and if he had too much, he had to run the commentary onto the next page or write it in the margins. The difficulties and challenges a scribe faced in producing such a page help explain why the number of manuscripts with this format are small compared to other types. After print, the format became widespread and, over time, virtually canonical.[210]

The Bible in Italy

As the site of the earliest dated European Jewish manuscript, Italian Jewish book culture exhibited a distinctive character from its beginnings.[211] Southern Italy in the Byzantine period was one of the original founts of early Ashkenaz, and Italian Hebrew book culture in its early phases exhibited strong affinities with its French and German counterparts.[212] Beginning in the mid-fourteenth century, Italy became a haven for refugees, at first for Jews expelled from Ashkenaz, and then, after 1391, for émigrés from Sepharad.[213] Both groups of immigrants included scribes who continued to write manuscripts in their native scripts in addition to adopting the distinctive script and formats of Italian Jewish book culture at the behest of patrons.

Scribes working in Italy—Ashenazis, Sephardis, and native Italians—produced a vast number of Hebrew manuscripts. Indeed, nearly one-third of all surviving dated Hebrew manuscripts were written in Italy between 1350 and 1550. In the late fifteenth and sixteenth

2.28
Duke of Sussex's Italian Pentateuch, Italy, fourteenth or fifteenth century. London, British Library Ms. Add. 15423, fol. 117r. © The British Library Board.

centuries, Italy also became the major center for Jewish printing. As a result, the influence of late handwritten Italian Hebrew Bibles on early printed Bibles was immense, and the latter books in turn exerted an enormous impact upon the material shape of all subsequent printed Bibles.

Hebrew Bibles written in Italy included all three types of Bibles surveyed thus far—the Masoretic Bible, the liturgical Pentateuch, and the study Bible—but the Italian versions had distinctive features. The most significant is the gradual disappearance from the page of the "paratexts" that previously had nearly always accompanied the biblical text—either the Masorah, the Targum, or commentaries—and a corresponding increased attention to the biblical text as the exclusive subject of the page. From 1375 on, a significant number of Bibles are produced in Italy in which the Bible text is written in a single page-wide column, without the Masorah or texts like the Targum or commentaries.[214] The page-wide, single-column format is not unique to Italy—specimens are to be found in Ashkenaz and Sepharad, as well as in early Oriental (Near Eastern) codices and particularly in Yemenite Bibles—but in proportion to all the biblical manuscripts produced in each geocultural area, the number of page-wide single-column Bibles written in Italy (including those in Ashkenazic and Sephardic script, which were most likely written by émigré scribes) is the highest.

A number of these "plain" Bibles are also beautifully illustrated. One of the more striking examples is the Duke of Sussex's Italian Pentateuch, written in the fourteenth or fifteenth century. Fig. 2.28, a page containing the beginning of the book of Deuteronomy, displays typical Italian floral decorations and initial letter panels, the latter a relative rarity in Hebrew manuscripts, which tend to have initial word panels. Initial letter panels, in contrast, were typical of Christian Latin manuscripts from the Carolingian period on, and in manuscripts of the late Middle Ages those letter initials became the most frequent sites for illustrations in Latin books.

Both features of these Bibles—their concentrated attention on the biblical text and the use of initial letter panels—are significant for what they suggest about the place of Italian Jewish book culture within its larger cultural context. The "plain" Hebrew Bibles—of course, decorated manuscripts like the Duke of Sussex's Italian Pentateuch are plain only inasmuch as they lack paratexts—reflect the humanist interests of Renaissance Italy, a rich cultural sensibility shared by contemporary Christians and Jews alike. As scholars of the period have noted, humanist Latin Bibles of the fifteenth and early sixteenth centuries frequently contain the biblical text alone without commentaries or other accompanying mediators between text and reader.[215] For humanists, these volumes represented a kind of return *ad fontes*. The reader, Christian or Jew, is seen as returning directly to the original fount of wisdom to enjoy its bounty for and by himself or herself, without the intervention of commentaries or translations. The same motivation appears to lie behind the Hebrew "plain" Bibles written in Italy.[216]

The page from the Duke of Sussex's Italian Pentateuch (fig. 2.28) also illustrates another distinctive trait of Italian Bibles, namely, their use of semicursive rather than the square letters that had been used for writing the biblical text since the creation of the rabbinic Sefer Torah.[217] The difference between the two scripts is especially evident on this page because the initial letter *aleph* is written in the more typical square script.

These fifteenth-century "plain Bibles" were not the first to use semicursive; there were a few earlier examples, and in the late medieval period one can see a growing preference for semicursive script in Ashkenazic and Sephardic manuscripts as well.[218] In the second half of the fifteenth century, however, the practice became far more common in liturgical Pentateuchs copied in glossed formats in northern Italy, and later it spread to other biblical manuscripts. Given the traditional mandate to write the biblical text exclusively in square letters, the shift to semicursive is both dramatic and enigmatic. There does not appear to have been any economic reason for the switch, nor does it seem to have been motivated by factors like legibility. Rather, as Malachi Beit-Arié has suggested, the most likely reason was aesthetic, with semicursive being "regarded by medieval scribes and owners of books as more beautiful and elegant than the various square modes."[219] This preference for beauty over halachic tradition suggests the enormous sea change taking place in late medieval and early modern Jewish cultural sensibility, a sea change that was especially dramatic in Italy.

The third and final distinctive feature of Italian Hebrew Bibles is their small size. Many are of quarto and octavo-like dimensions, and some are virtual miniatures, as small as 8.5 × 5.8 centimeters (3.4 × 2.3 in.).[220] Both the use of the semicursive script and the tiny size of these Bibles, as well as the growing preponderance of "plain" Bibles, albeit sometimes lavishly illustrated ones, point to the increasing popularity of the Bible as a book sought out by nonscholarly lay patrons and owners. The Bible is not the only book to gain such popularity among Jews in Renaissance Italy; prayer books also became more common. The increased number of these books indicates, as Robert Calkins has written (in regard to Christian books of the period), "profound changes in the role of books in society and in the nature of religious worship," namely, "the pervasive need for more immediate, personal, and meaningful religious experience through private devotions."[221] This need was probably fueled by the growth in literacy, which in turn increased demand for books not only among the intellectual elite but also among the growing mercantile classes.

The impact of these changes can also be seen in the increased popularity in Renaissance Italy of two "parabiblical" books, the Psalter and what are called Sifrei EMeT, codices consisting of the three poetic texts, Job, Proverbs, and Psalms.[222] While both types of books have antecedents in earlier Sephardic and especially Ashkenazic book traditions, where the codices are generally large in format, the Italian codices are distinguished (again) by their numbers, their use of semicursive script, and their small size.[223] Furthermore, both Psalters and Sifrei EMeT cross genres by combining features of the prayer book and the Bible. The Psalter was used as a book of private prayer and an object of study; numerous commentaries were written on it, some polemical, others more philosophical, and they were sometimes inscribed with the biblical text in a glossed format. The Sifrei EMeT were objects of scholarly discussion and intellectual exchange between Jewish and Christian humanists in Renaissance Italy.[224] The book of Job in particular was interpreted by both circles of *eruditi* as a source of the *prisca theologia*, the original, pristine truth from which all later theological traditions and philosophical systems—neo-Platonism, Judaism, Christianity—were believed to have devolved. Job, Solomon, even David, were all seen as types of the *priscus philosophus*, the "ancient wise man who, after attaining universal knowledge, transcended human reason in order to reach the ultimate happiness of the religious philosopher who finds in God all responses to his intellectual curiosity."[225]

The same culture of Renaissance humanism that cultivated *prisca theologia* as an ideal encouraged other kinds of intellectual exchange between Jews and Christians. Foremost among these was the emergence of Christian Hebraism with its new interest in classical Jewish texts. Christian Hebraists played a critical role in the early history of the printed Hebrew Bible. The sixteenth-century print shop, as students of early printing have observed, was a meeting place for figures of all sorts, Christian, Jews, Muslims, and philosophical *eruditi*, who all worked in collaboration, fostering a virtually unprecedented exchange of labor and ideas.[226] Within this syncretistic environment, the sharp lines between separate religious identities could easily blur, even if a limited number of Jews were involved. It is not surprising that a number of Jews who worked in the early printing houses converted to Christianity.

This was the other, darker side of Jewish-Christian exchange, and the work of one exceptionally talented Jewish scribe who converted to Christianity epitomizes the complexity of the historical moment and the many questions it raises. Isaac ben Ovadiah of Forli, a prolific scribe working mainly in Florence in the mid-fifteenth century, produced at least twenty-five extant manuscripts between 1427 and 1467, a remarkable number of codices even for Christian humanist scribes of the period. The quality of Isaac's scribal work was even more remarkable than its quantity. As Nurit Pasternak has noted, Isaac was "a paragon of the Florentine '*bel-libro*' among Jewish scribes of his day."[227] His work was characterized both by the high quality of its materials and its level of execution, which drew upon both the traditions of Hebrew book manufacturing and the new technology of the day. Isaac appears to have worked closely with local book traders, and his manuscripts were decorated and illuminated in Christian ateliers by some of the best local artists, including Fra Angelico. A number of Isaac's manuscripts were commissioned by Christians, including a Sefer EMeT (MS Jerusalem, Israel Museum 180/55) that bears the device of Lorenzo il Magnifico di Medici.

Exactly when Isaac converted to Christianity is not known, but on the final folio of a Bible (MS Firenze, Biblioteca Medicea Laurenziana, Plut. 1, 31) commissioned by Lorenzo il Magnifico de Medici in the mid-fifteenth century, he proclaimed his faith in Christ in no uncertain terms by writing: "For the honour and glory of Joshua Nazarenus our Lord King of the Jews."[228] We do not know what motivated Isaac to convert, whether it was the climate of syncretism encouraged by the culture of *prisca theologia* or the outcome of a sincere religious experience of his own, or whether he was driven by reasons of convenience to advance his career. Whatever led him to Christianity, his conversion effectively produced some of the oddest Hebrew Bible manuscripts in the Middle Ages.[229]

Fig. 2.29 is the opening of Genesis in another of Isaac's Bibles. The beautifully inscribed Hebrew script testifies to the fact that its scribe was a Jew by birth and upbringing. Its two columns, written in an Italian semicursive hand, replicate what we have seen is a typical Italian Hebrew biblical format. The colorful floral design framing the page is reminiscent of other Italian biblical manuscripts, even if its scrolling vines are especially elaborate. What transports the page to another realm, however, is the large initial letter *bet* (of *bereishit*) in gold leaf, which occupies nearly half the folio and frames a scene of the crucifixion with Saint Dominic and Saint Thomas kneeling before Christ's feet, while Mary Magdalene and Mary the mother of James stand behind them.[230] At the very bottom of the page, another roundel displays Jesus being baptized.

One cannot imagine a more shocking picture to capture and convey the incongruity and hybridity that had come to characterize the Jewish Bible.

2.29
Bible. Scribe: Isaac ben Ovadiah of Forli, Florence, Italy, 1427–67. Firenze, Biblioteca Medicea Laurenziana, Conv. Soppr. 268, fol. 1r. Courtesy of the Biblioteca Medicea Laurenziana.

The Bible in Yemen

Until now, virtually all the medieval Bibles we have looked at were produced in countries under Christian rule. (As we noted earlier, no Bibles from Muslim Spain survive, although even those produced in Christian Spain continued to use Islamic or Islamicizing features.) In concluding this chapter, and before turning to the early printed Hebrew Bible in the next chapter, we will take a short geographical detour to look at Hebrew Bible manuscripts produced in Yemen. These Bibles point to a road not taken—what the Hebrew Bible might have looked like if the brunt of its history had not taken place in Christian contexts.

The Jewish community of Yemen had one of the lengthiest continuous histories of any Diaspora community, lasting a good millennium and a half, from antiquity until 1949–50, when, in the fabled Operation Magic Carpet, much of the Jewish population was spirited out of the country and airlifted to the state of Israel. The Yemenite community's origins are not known.[231] According to native popular legends, Jews first came to Yemen before the destruction of the First Temple, after Jeremiah prophesied Jerusalem's doom; according to other legends, they arrived even earlier, at the time of Solomon. The third-century catacombs of Beth She'arim in the Galilee contain sarcophagi for Jews from Yemen whose bodies were brought to the Holy Land for burial, and a Hebrew inscription from the fourth century is preserved on a pillar that is now found in a mosque near Sana'a. During the Byzantine period, Jews are mentioned as active in military attacks against the eastern empire. The later Himyarite kings of Arabia are said to have converted to Judaism, and one chieftain, known as Dhu Nuwas (ca. 520), was famous for his exploits against the Ethiopian Christians after they invaded Yemen.[232]

Exactly what religious practices these early Jewish inhabitants of Arabia observed is far from clear, but by the sixth century, rabbinic Judaism had penetrated the region. Following the Muslim conquest in the seventh century, and particularly in the eighth through tenth centuries, Yemenite Jewry became closely attached to the Babylonian center of rabbinic Judaism and its academies. Indeed, linguistic research over the last half century has shown that the traditional Hebrew (and Aramaic) pronunciation of Yemenite Jews—particularly as they recite and orally study classical texts like the Bible, the Targum, the Mishnah, and the Talmud—is probably the surviving oral tradition closest to that spoken by Jews in the Babylonian Geonic period (as attested in medieval accounts of peculiarities of Babylonian pronunciation of Hebrew).[233]

Yemen's singular loyalty to Babylonian traditions is the only explanation for the fact that the Yemenite community—alone among all other Jewish communities in the entire late ancient and early medieval worlds—is the only one to have adhered to the Babylonian Masorah and its modes of (supralinear) transcription of vocalization marks (*simanei niqud*), long after the rest of the Jewish world had accepted the Tiberian school of Masorah (along with its system of sublinear transcription). Not until the twelfth century did the Yemenite community change, and then only because of the influence of Maimonides, with whom the community had already established a strong connection on account of the counsel and consolation the great sage had offered them in his Epistle to Yemen, written in 1172 CE, after the appearance of a messianic pretender in the Yemenite community. The absolute authority Maimonides subsequently enjoyed in Yemen was so great it eventually led them to adapt the Tiberian system after the arrival in Yemen of the *Mishneh Torah*, Maimonides's code of law, in which the Spanish sage explicitly declares (in Hilkhot Sefer Torah 8:4) that he copied his own Sefer Torah using as his model the codex in Egypt whose Masorah had been written by the great Tiberian Masorite Aaron ben Moshe ben Asher (which, as we have already noted, most scholars today believe was the Aleppo Codex, *Keter Aram Tzova*). Even so, vestiges of the Babylonian Masoretic system and its supralinear transcription (as well as those of pre-Babylonian native Yemenite traditions) remained in Yemenite reading and scribal traditions.[234] Thus, even after the Tiberian Masorah was accepted by scribes, supralinear Babylonian transcription of the vocalization of the Targum continued to be practiced in Yemen.

The singular stance that Yemenite scribal culture takes toward the Masorah characterizes other practices as well.[235] Early on, Yemenite Jews developed their own distinctive script, whose letters are shorter and wider than those in other Jewish hands, partly because of a specially cut flat calamus devised by Yemenite scribes.[236] Because no books were printed in southern Arabia until the late nineteenth century, and even then only in Aden, and the only available printed books were those brought there by foreign emissaries and visitors, handwritten books remained more prominent in Yemen, and its scribal culture developed singular features, including the distinction of scribal dynasties, the most famous of which was that of Benayah (active mainly in Sana'a between 1460 and 1483) and his three sons and one daughter (who was also a scribe), and two grandchildren. So far as we can tell from their surviving manuscripts, Benayah and his descendants specialized in Bibles and grammatical texts.[237] Along with the adaptation of the Tiberian Masorah, Yemenite scribes followed virtually all the halachic strictures set by Maimonides in the *Mishneh Torah*, and those were in turn based upon the text of the Aleppo Codex, including specific rules about the orthography of the text, its layout (with open and closed sections), and stichography (as in the Song of the Sea).[238] As a result, Yemenite Bibles are among our best witnesses to the Tiberian tradition (even if these manuscripts also maintained Babylonian supralinear transcription of the Targum).

Yemenite Bibles include both Masoretic Bibles and *ḥumashim*, as in the Sephardic and Ashkenazic worlds, but each genre has its own name in Yemen. The Masoretic Bible is called a *Taj*, the Arabic equivalent to the Hebrew *Keter*, "crown," a term that in the Arabic-speaking Jewish world was used to designate a deluxe Bible, like the famous *Keter Dameshek* (Damascus), written in Burgos in 1260. The use of the Arabic *Taj* (which was the original term, not the Hebrew *keter*) in Yemen almost certainly derives from the fact that the book known today as *Keter Aram Tzova*, the Aleppo Codex, was originally called

2.30 Pentateuch (Taj). Scribe: Benayah ben Saadiah ben Zechariah, Yemen, 1470. London, Valmadonna Trust Library, MS 11, pp. 452–53. Reproduced by the kind permission of the Valmadonna Trust.

"al-Taj," and Bibles copied from it (or from exact copies) were therefore given that name.[239] Like the Masoretic Bible in Sepharad and Ashkenaz, the Yemenite *Taj* contained only the vocalized biblical text with the *te'amim* and Masorah; however, Yemenite scribes were inconsistent in transcribing the *te'amim,* which vary according to local traditions, and the Masorah, sometimes recording both the *masorah magna* and *parva* and at other times only the *parva* or selections from it.[240] In many cases, the *Taj* is written in a single page-wide column. Because these books were sometimes used as model books for scribes writing Sifrei Torah, which generally has fifty-one lines per column, Yemenite scribes often wrote twenty-five lines of a given column on the recto of a folio, and the other twenty-six on the verso. There are, however, *Taj* Bibles that use the double- and triple-column format typically used in Sepharad and Ashkenaz.[241]

The *ḥumash* or liturgical Pentateuch also had its own name in Yemen: *parashah* (after the term for the weekly Torah readings). Yemenite *parashot* generally included, in addition to the haftarot and *megillot*, Targum Onkelos (sometimes, as noted above, with supralinear vocalization), and Saadiah's Judeo-Arabic *Tafsir*.[242] In the course of time, Rashi and other commentators from European Jewish communities were added to the page, and from the nineteenth century on, Yemenite *parashot* also included a work on Yemenite vocalization and Masoretic tradition entitled *ḥelek Ha-Dikduk*, written by the foremost early modern Yemenite sage, Rabbi Yaḥya Ṣaliḥ, known as the MaHaRiTZ (d. 1805).[243]

After printed editions of *ḥumashim* from Europe reached Yemen in the late seventeenth and eighteenth centuries, scribes also began to copy by hand the page format of the printed books, specifically the glossed, Talmudic-page-like form that had developed in the Christian West. Such is the power of the printed book!

Perhaps more than anything else, the singularity of Yemenite book culture is reflected in the decorations found in their Bibles, particularly in *Tajim*. As one would expect with any work produced within the Islamic orbit, the decoration is almost entirely aniconic with mainly geometric and floral designs, including elaborate, sometimes painted carpet pages and the frequent use of *ansa*s, palmettes, and other medallion-like decorations on the text pages. This decoration draws on both Islamic and Ethiopic (Christian) designs.[244] What is most distinctive about these biblical designs, however, is their use of the Masorah. As in both Ashkenazic and Sephardic Bibles, the Masorah is always written in micrography, but in the Yemenite *Taj* Bible, it tends to appear in designs that repeat throughout the volume—zigzag lines, intertwined cables, or diamond shapes around the borders of the page. Fig. 2.30 is an opening from a Pentateuch written by Benayah ben Saadiah ben Zechariah, the founder of the famous scribal dynasty, sometime in the second half of the fifteenth century. Although the page design is simple, the zigzag lines of the Masoretic border on the sides of each page in the opening have an energy and playfulness that enliven the entire textual space.

The history of the Bible in Yemen represents an unusual chapter in the history of the Jewish Bible. The surviving manuscripts—a few as early as the thirteenth century, although most are later—are, along with the early Masoretic codices, among the few examples of Bibles produced in lands under continuous Islamic rule. The situation of the Yemenite community was not easy or prosperous. Particularly after the early fifteenth century, the Jewish community lived in extreme poverty and underwent numerous tribulations and persecutions at the hands of the native Yemenite rulers and later the Ottoman Turks. Internally, the community was wracked by repeated appearances of various false messiahs. Yet because of its isolated position in Arabia, Yemenite Judaism does not appear to have been significantly shaped by the sectarian and religious conflicts that dominated early and high medieval Judaism elsewhere—neither the struggle between Karaites and Rabbanites nor that between Judaism and Christianity. The development of the Jewish Bible in Yemen thus represents a path that almost no other Jewish community in the world was able to pursue. This path was mainly determined by internal Jewish dynamics, including Babylonian versus Tiberian orthodoxy, the impact of the Maimonidean heritage on the native Yemenite tradition, and the relatively untroubled opportunity for adapting Islamic and Ethiopic designs without having to assume a polemical or subversive stance toward them. For all the travails of its unhappy history over the last five centuries, Yemen suggests what the Jewish Bible might have looked like if not for the struggle over "ownership" that characterized its development throughout the Christian West.

CHAPTER THREE

THE JEWISH BIBLE IN THE EARLY AGE OF PRINT

Around the year 1455, Johannes Gutenberg printed his famous Bible with movable type in the German city of Mainz, and thereby inaugurated the age of print in the West. Our earliest dated printed Hebrew book—an edition of Rashi's Bible commentary—is from 1475, but it is certain that Jews were printing books before that time, probably even a decade earlier. By the year 1500—the conventional date for the end of the incunable (cradle-age) period of printing—the printed Hebrew book had become an established presence in Jewish culture. Copies of approximately 140–150 different editions of books printed in Hebrew type—from Italy, Spain, Portugal, and Turkey—survive from this period.[1]

By now it is a commonplace that the introduction of print in the West was the most transformative event in the history of the book since the invention and adaptation of the codex in the first five centuries of the common era. The invention of print touched every aspect of Western culture, and the printed Jewish book had an impact on every facet of Jewish existence. Historians, however, continue to debate whether the invention of print constituted a true revolution.[2] Did print in fact initiate an unprecedented era and radically change the nature of book production and distribution and reading practices in ways that

3.1 Pentateuch (Num. 31:32–33:53), Spain, thirteenth century (left); Pentateuch (Num. 33:11–53), Hijar, Spain (right). Eliezer Alatansi, 1486–89. Courtesy of the Library at the Herbert D. Katz Center for Advanced Judaic Studies, Kislak Center for Special Collections, Rare Books and Manuscripts, University of Pennsylvania.

manuscript culture never approached? Or was the invention of print actually the culmination of a series of processes and developments that had already begun in the late Middle Ages with gradual changes in the way manuscripts were copied, sold, bought, and read, and did the invention of print only intensify, quicken, and expand those changes?

The printed Hebrew Bible almost perfectly exemplifies the difficulty in answering this question simply. For one thing, early Hebrew printed Bibles—like most early printed books—did not seek to look new. To the contrary: early printers tried to make their books appear as much like manuscripts as possible—precisely because these were the books that readers recognized—and they borrowed the features of manuscripts to give shape to their printed books.[3] Fig. 3.1 is a page-opening from a thirteenth-century Spanish Masoretic Bible. The left-hand page of the opening is formatted in double columns like a typical Sephardic Masoretic Bible. At some point, however, the middle quire of the codex fell out and was lost, and a later owner substituted for the missing folios the roughly equivalent pages from a Bible printed by Eliezer ben Abraham Alantansi in Hijar in the Kingdom of Aragon sometime between 1486 and 1489. The right-hand page is from Alatansi's edition.

As can be seen, the overall double-column format of the two pages is identical, and the printed font of Alatansi's Bible closely imitates the beautiful Spanish square script of the handwritten codex. To be sure, there are visible differences: the printed page has more lines of text, and it lacks both the vocalization (*niqud*) and the Masorah. Viewed side by side, these two pages exemplify the difficulties in demarcating the precise transition from manuscript to print. The two pages are different, but they are also very similar.

This same combination of difference and similarity informs the printed book's other features. As it developed into the sixteenth century, the printed Hebrew Bible came to differ significantly from the Bible in the manuscript age. Yet no single feature of the printed book was entirely new, and even the combination of features that it displayed was to some extent anticipated in earlier handwritten Bibles.

So, too, in the case of readership. To what extent printing actually expanded the audience of readers of the Hebrew Bible is a difficult question to answer. Jews read and studied the Bible as intensively and actively before print as after it, and there is no reason to believe that it dramatically expanded the Jewish readership of the Bible. On the other hand, as we shall see, it is clear that print vastly expanded the number of Christian readers of the Hebrew Bible (and the Jewish commentators on the Bible page). This last assertion leads, however, to a larger challenge in assessing the revolutionary impact of print on the Hebrew book. Print did not occur in a vacuum. It was one of a number of momentous changes that touched traditional Jewish culture in the early modern period. Among these, perhaps the most significant for the Jewish book was the growth of Christian Hebraism, a term modern scholars have invented to describe Christians in the late Middle Ages and especially in the early modern period who became interested in the study of classical Jewish sources, the Bible and Kabbalah in particular, in their original languages.[4] The motives of these Hebraists varied: some wished to study the original texts to refute Jewish "superstitions" and reveal their calumnies against Christians; others wished to use the Jewish texts to understand early Christianity; and still others believed that rabbinic texts hid the secrets of Christian truth and that once these truths were demonstrated to Jews, they would lead to conversions. Hebraists played a decisive role in the history of the printed Jewish Bible in the sixteenth century and later.

The Jewish Bible in the Incunable Period

The two earliest dated Hebrew books—the first published in Italy in 1475, the second in Spain in 1476—were editions of Rashi's commentary on the Torah, but neither included the biblical text; in other words, they were printed *kuntresim*.[5] As Herbert Zafren first noted, early Jewish printers printed more biblical commentaries than Bibles.[6] Exactly why is not clear, but the most plausible reason is that the number of Bibles in manuscript still in circulation may have seemed to them sufficient to satisfy market demand.[7] In addition,

3.2 Pentateuch, Bologna: Abraham ben Hayyim dei Tintori, 1482. Philadelphia, Rosenbach Museum and Library. Courtesy of the Rosenbach of the Free Library of Philadelphia.

the technological challenges involved in printing a vocalized and accented Hebrew text—the way Hebrew Bibles had always been written—were immense and, in the early stages of printing, possibly too difficult for printers to overcome.[8] The very first biblical book to be printed was a Psalms with Kimḥi's commentary (Bologna, 1477). Each verse was followed by commentary (like an interverse Targum), and initially the printers intended to vocalize the entire text, but after a portion of the first quire they gave up.[9] As the page from Eliezer Alatansi's Bible illustrated in fig. 3.1 shows, many of the earliest Bibles were unvocalized. Fig. 3.2 is an opening from the first Bible to be successfully vocalized, a Pentateuch with Targum and Rashi. This *ḥumash*, printed by Abraham ben Hayyim dei Tintori in Bologna in 1482, adopted the traditional medieval format of the glossed page with the text in a larger square font, the Targum next to it in a small square font, and Rashi in an elegantly cast Sephardic semicursive font. This printed font would eventually become known as "Rashi script."

3.3
Pentateuch (Joshua 1), Prophets, and Hagiographa, Soncino: Joshua Solomon b. Israel Nathan Soncino, 1488. The Bodleian Libraries, University of Oxford.

In 1488, Joshua Solomon ben Israel Nathan Soncino published the *editio princeps* of the complete Bible, with vowels and accents. Fig. 3.3 is the opening page of Joshua and is framed with a magnificent woodcut border picturing putti with bows and arrows cavorting in the page's margins. The frame, "one of the loveliest specimens of fifteenth-century Italian book production," had originally been commissioned by the Neapolitan printer Francesco del Tuppo for an edition of Aesop's *Fables* (Naples, 1485); once he finished his edition, del Tuppo sold the frame to Soncino, who used it in several books.[10] The rest of Soncino's Bible was printed in double columns that copied the format of Masoretic Bibles, although they lacked the Masorah. The absence of the Masorah may have been due to the technical difficulties of printing in miniscule type; on the other hand, it may reflect the general disregard for the Masorah in the late Middle Ages, particularly in Italy, a disregard that stemmed at least partly from awareness of how corrupt its text had become.

During the incunable period, approximately fifty editions of the complete Bible or sections thereof (Former and Latter Prophets, or Hagiographa alone) were printed.[11] In the 1490s Gershom Soncino published "pared-down" editions of the Bible that mirrored the Italian manuscript tradition of small, portable Bibles with a single, page-wide column and no other text on the page; as we noted earlier, this format resembled the typical humanist book with its emphasis on the core text. The second of the two editions of the complete Bible printed by Gershom Soncino in several volumes in Brescia, between 1492 and 1494, is in octavo, in a single column on the page. As Soncino wrote in the colophon, the edition was intentionally designed to be a portable Bible.

The one type of Bible that was poorly represented in the incunable period was the study Bible. While numerous editions of individual biblical books or sections like the Prophets or Hagiographa were printed with a single commentary and many commentaries were published as stand-alone books (like *kuntresim*), only two Bible editions featured two commentaries, both of them printed by Don Samuel D'Ortas in Leiria, Portugal.[12] This changed in the sixteenth century.

The First Rabbinic Bible

In the first half of the sixteenth century, the nature of Hebrew printing—and of the Jewishness of the Hebrew book—underwent massive changes. Before the sixteenth century, whether in the age of manuscripts or in the fifty-year incunable period of early printing, the Jewish book was, for all practical purposes, a text by a Jewish author written in Hebrew script and produced by a Jewish scribe or printer for a Jewish reader. Beginning in the sixteenth century, none of these verities could any longer be taken for granted. Gentiles regularly owned the publishing houses that printed Hebrew books; Christians (who were sometimes former Jews) wrote books in Hebrew; Christian Hebraists were avid readers of Hebrew texts; and not all Jewish readers could be assumed to know Hebrew (for instance, Spanish *conversos* who had returned to Judaism). As a result, books for Jews were now produced in languages other than Hebrew or one of the Jewish languages (e.g., Yiddish or Judeo-Arabic or Ladino, a Spanish vernacular written in Hebrew script). Because of these changed circumstances, the very definition of a Jewish book was called into question. The Jewishness of a book in Hebrew script could no longer be assumed as natural. It now had to be asserted and demonstrated.[13]

No book illustrates this crisis of identity more dramatically than the Jewish Bible and the creation of what eventually became known as the Rabbinic Bible (*Biblia Rabbinica*, henceforth referred to as RB) or, in Jewish circles, the *Miqraot Gedolot* ("The Large Scriptures," probably a reference to its folio size). This book appeared in two editions in Venice, the first in 1517 and the more famous second edition in 1524–25.[14] The story behind these two editions provides by itself a revealing illustration of the sea change that the Jewish book underwent during this period.[15]

That story begins sometime before 1515, when the scion of a wealthy family of Christian merchants from Antwerp named Daniel Bomberg (b. 1483) arrived in Venice.[16] At the time, Venice, one of the flourishing capitals of Europe and a booming financial and commercial center, was in the process of becoming the center of printing in Italy, partly because of its increasingly strict copyright laws.[17] The young Bomberg initially came to Italy probably to represent his family's hugely successful export-import business, but shortly after arriving in Venice, he set up a publishing house with the intention of printing Hebrew books. His partner, a Jew who had converted to Christianity and become an Augustinian monk, is known today only by his Christian name, Fra Felice de Prato (Brother Felix of Prato), or Felix Pratensis. We know little about Felix except that he was both exceptionally learned in classical Jewish sources and truly gifted as a textual scholar.[18]

The first book that Bomberg and Pratensis produced (in the printing house of Peter [Pierro] Lichtenstein) was a *Psalterium*, a Latin translation of the Psalms by Pratensis, which appeared in September 1515. The very next month, Bomberg, Pratensis, and Lichtenstein jointly applied to the Venetian Senate for a privilege, or exclusive right, to publish three additional Latin translations of Hebrew books—a grammar with a dictionary and two kabbalistic treatises—as well as "a Hebrew Bible, in Hebrew letters, both with and without the Aramaic Targum, and with Hebrew commentaries."[19] As Jordan Penkower has shown, the latter request was for the book that eventually became the Hebrew Bible that Bomberg and Pratensis (by this time Lichtenstein had dropped out of the partnership) published in Bomberg's publishing house in Venice in 1517.[20] This edition appeared in two formats. The first was folio-size and included both the Targum and a commentary on the text (Rashi on the Pentateuch, Kimḥi and others on the rest of the Bible). This book eventually came to be known as the First Rabbinic Bible. The second format was a Hebrew Bible in quarto, without Targum or commentary, which was printed sheet by sheet on the press immediately after the folio's sheets had been printed and the type was rearranged for the quarto's smaller size.

Shortly after receiving the Venetian privilege, Bomberg applied for an exclusive patent for the use of Hebrew printing type (a request he justified by citing the great expense he had incurred in having the Hebrew type cast specially for his press). When his petition was granted, Bomberg effectively had a monopoly on all Hebrew printing in Venice.[21] Bomberg doubtless owed his success in gaining the privilege and patent to his being both a Christian and a wealthy businessman with capital to spend in Venice. Even more important for marketing the book was the support he received from Pope Leo X and the papal imprimatur that went along with it. Leo was a humanist deeply sympathetic to Christian Hebraist interests and had openly vouched for the importance of Jewish books to Christianity.

3.4 Arba'ah Ve-'Esrim (First Rabbinic Bible), Venice: title page by Daniel Bomberg, 1517. From the collection of Dr. David and Jemima Jeselsohn, Zurich.

Receiving the pope's approbation was not a minor accomplishment. The First Rabbinic Bible was published in 1517 in two separate editions, one intended for Jewish readers, the other for Christians. The Christian edition had the same title page as the Jewish one, but its verso contained a dedication in Latin to Leo X in which Pratensis wrote that, in addition to the Hebrew biblical text, he had included the "Chaldee scholia, to wit the common Targum and that of Jerusalem [which] contain many obscure and recondite mysteries [*ultra . . . arcana et recondita mysteria*], not only useful, but necessary to the devout Christian."[22]

Apart from this Latin dedication, the Christian edition was essentially identical to the Jewish one. Both had the same title page (fig. 3.4), the first title page in a Jewish printed book to use the architectural image of a gate, itself a visual pun, because the Hebrew word for a title page, *sha'ar*, actually means "gate" or "entranceway." The Hebrew text in both the Jewish and Christian versions of the book was the same. Pratensis did not simply copy a single manuscript or previous edition of the Bible, but with Bomberg's financial assistance, he collected manuscripts (mainly Sephardi but some Ashkenazi as well) and produced, in good humanist fashion, what he believed was the most accurate text of the Bible. Indeed, in his Latin prologue to the Bible, Pratensis announced to the pope that all previous manuscripts in circulation have "almost as many errors as words in them" and that "no one has attempted [an edition comparable to his] before."[23] As Penkower has remarked, the First Rabbinic Bible was in fact the first genuine *edition*—based upon a critical examination of manuscripts—of the Hebrew Bible.[24]

The page format (fig. 3.5) that Pratensis used for the Bible was somewhat different from earlier formats used in Jewish Bibles; the Hebrew text was in the inner column at the top of the page, with the Aramaic Targum next to it in a parallel column printed in a font that was only slightly smaller. In fact, the 1517 Rabbinic Bible was the first complete edition to contain an Aramaic Targum on nearly all the books of the Bible (with the exception of Daniel, Ezra-Nehemiah, and Chronicles). It was also the first edition to have a medieval Jewish commentary on every book (Rashi on the Pentateuch, David Kimḥi on the Prophets, and various others on the Hagiographa).[25] As can be seen, the commentary, printed in a smaller rabbinic font, occupies the vast majority of the page's space beneath the two columns of Bible and Targum. For the first time in a printed Bible, Felix noted variants (including plene-defective spellings) in the margins and marked the *qeri* (while keeping the *ketiv* in the text), unlike earlier editions, which had printed the *ketiv* with the pronunciation of the *qeri* in the text itself. The First Rabbinic Bible was also the first Hebrew Bible to use chapter numbers, which were based on Christian Bibles, as well as to divide the books of Samuel, Kings, and Chronicles into two books each, with marginal notes at the points of division stating, for example, "Here non-Jews [*ha-lo-'azim*] begin the second book of Samuel, which is the second book of Kings to them."[26]

3.5 Arba'ah Ve-'Esrim (First Rabbinic Bible) (Gen. 1), Venice: page 1 by Daniel Bomberg, 1517. From the collection of Dr. David and Jemima Jeselsohn, Zurich.

As these directions to the reader indicate, the First Rabbinic Bible was the first printed Hebrew Bible to intentionally address itself to both Jews and Christians (albeit in separate editions). We do not know how commercially successful these editions were. The average print run of an edition of a complicated folio-size book like RB 1517—in which Bomberg had invested considerable sums in gathering manuscripts, commissioning Hebrew type, and production work—was probably around one thousand copies.[27] If Felix's apostasy was widely known, that awareness may have diminished its marketability among Jews (and perhaps increased it among Christians). What is known is that the 1517 quarto edition, which may have originally been intended primarily for a Christian audience unable to read the Hebrew commentaries, was so successful that Bomberg reprinted it in 1521.[28]

The Second Rabbinic Bible

Barely eight years after publishing the First Rabbinic Bible, Bomberg published another edition of the Rabbinic Bible. This edition, known today as the Second Rabbinic Bible of 1524–25, was a truly new book and advertised itself as such, sometimes even by referring back to its predecessor. Thus, where the 1517 Rabbinic Bible was the first Hebrew book to use an architectural gate on its title page, the title page of the Second Rabbinic Bible of 1524–25 (fig. 3.6) signaled its newness to the reader by again using a gate but adding a panel in the tympanum with the inscription *Sha'ar Adonai He-ḥadash*, "the New Gate of the Lord." Nor was the claim to newness merely an advertisement. In the first place, this edition's editor, Jacob ben Ḥayyim ibn Adoniyahu, was a Jewish scholar with a reputation for wide learning and deep expertise in the full range of classical Jewish literature from Bible and rabbinics to kabbalah.[29] Ibn Adoniyahu had come to Venice from Tunis, and prior to working on the Second Rabbinic Bible, he had edited several other books for Bomberg, including two kabbalistic biblical commentaries and, most probably, *Meir Nativ* (Venice, 1523), the biblical concordance compiled by the fourteenth- to fifteenth-century polemicist Isaac Nathan b. Kalonymus. This book would prove indispensable to Ibn Adoniyahu in editing the Rabbinic Bible.[30]

Fig. 3.7 is the opening text page of the Second Rabbinic Bible, and aside from its elaborate initial word panel for *Bereishit* (In the beginning), its format is typical for the book. Unlike Pratensis's First Rabbinic Bible, which had forgone the typical text layout of a study Bible, Ibn Adoniyahu's edition returned to the traditional format—a strategic decision obviously intended to make the book appear familiar to its readers—albeit more complex than nearly any of its predecessors, with five distinct units on the page: the biblical text (on this page, a single line beneath the initial word panel, with the text in larger square letters), the Targum (in the line to the left of the biblical text); the Masorah (directly beneath the biblical text and Targum in a semicursive font); and two commentaries (Rashi in the block on the right, Ibn Ezra in the block to the left). In editing the biblical text, Ibn

3.6 Torah, Nevi'im, Ketuvim (Second Rabbinic Bible), Venice: title page by Daniel Bomberg, 1524–25. Courtesy of the Library at the Herbert D. Katz Center for Advanced Judaic Studies, Kislak Center for Special Collections, Rare Books and Manuscripts, University of Pennsylvania.

3.7 Torah, Nevi'im, Ketuvim (Second Rabbinic Bible) (Gen.1), Venice: page 1 by Daniel Bomberg, 1524–25. Courtesy of the Library at the Herbert D. Katz Center for Advanced Judaic Studies, Kislak Center for Special Collections, Rare Books and Manuscripts, University of Pennsylvania.

Adoniyahu followed Pratensis in producing a critical text, but he was more consistent and improved upon the First Rabbinic Bible by relying almost exclusively on Sephardic manuscripts, which were closest to the Tiberian tradition (in contrast to Pratensis, who had also used Ashkenazic sources).[31] Also unprecedented was the inclusion of a second commentary on the page for every biblical book, in addition to the Targum and Rashi: Abraham Ibn Ezra on the Pentateuch, Isaiah, the Minor Prophets, Psalms, Daniel, and the Five Scrolls, and various other commentators on the remaining books of the Prophets and Hagiographa. Most important, Ibn Adoniyahu, for the first time ever, edited the Masorah from manuscripts and, in a revised form, published it on the page with the Targum and the two commentaries. Those sections of the expanded Masorah that did not fit onto the biblical text page—an even vaster corpus consisting of all the lists and annotations preserved in different manuscripts—were placed at the end of the final volume, in what has come to be known as the *masorah finalis*. These annotations were arranged alphabetically so that a reader could easily find the corresponding entries in the *masorah magna* on the biblical text page. In this way, as Penkower has noted, the *masorah finalis* effectively functioned as a kind of Masoretic lexicon or concordance.[32] Finally, Ibn Adoniyahu also wrote a lengthy introduction to the Bible that includes a brief autobiography, a history of the book's composition and publication, and a defense of the Masorah and its importance. This introduction was the first printed treatise on the Masorah.

The Second Rabbinic Bible was published in 1524–25 and reprinted by Bomberg in 1546–48. For most students of the Bible, Jews and Christians alike, Ibn Adoniyahu's biblical text became the undisputed *textus receptus*; indeed, it took nearly four hundred years to shake Ibn Adoniyahu's text from its pedestal.[33] And for Jews, the 1524–25 edition, with its multiple commentaries and supplementary texts, quickly established itself as the exemplary model for a study Bible.

Why did Bomberg publish this new edition of the Rabbinic Bible barely eight years after publishing the First Rabbinic Bible in 1517? Possibly he feared that he would not get another *privilegio* and wanted to take advantage of the one he had before its ten-year validity ran out. Perhaps he believed that a new edition produced by a recognized Jewish scholar like Ibn Adoniyahu would be more commercially successful than the 1517 edition, which had been edited by a known apostate.[34] The most plausible rationale for Bomberg's decision, however, has nothing to do with marketability or other publishing factors. Penkower has proposed that Ibn Adoniyahu persuaded Bomberg to print the new edition for three reasons that appear to have struck a personal chord for the Christian publisher. First, he argued that Pratensis's 1517 Bible had not, in fact, succeeded in its stated goal of restoring the biblical text to its "true and genuine purity." Second, he convinced Bomberg that the only way to establish a truly accurate biblical text was to do it according to the Masorah, and to accomplish that, it was necessary for him to edit the Masorah (which had become corrupted in the course of the centuries). And most important, he argued, the Masorah contained its own teachings, and these were kabbalistic *sodot*, mystical secrets.[35] Adoniyahu knew that Bomberg was a Christian Hebraist interested in kabbalah, and both men knew there was a demand among Christian Hebraists for Jewish books containing kabbalistic mysteries. Furthermore, as Penkower has shown, Ibn Adoniyahu was a kabbalist himself, and was interested in the Masorah for precisely these reasons.

Ibn Adoniyahu never explicitly acknowledges this last motivation, but Penkower's argument is persuasive. The Masorah was clearly the raison d'être for the new edition. At the end of his introductory treatise, Ibn Adoniyahu gave the following account of how he persuaded Bomberg to publish the new edition:

> And when I saw the great benefit which is to be derived from the Masorah magna, the Masorah parva, and the Masorah finalis, I informed Seignior Daniel Bomberg, may his Rock and Redeemer protect him, and showed him the benefit to be derived from it. Whereupon he did all in his power to send into all the countries in order to search after whatever may be found of the Masorah; and praised be the Lord, we obtained as many of the Masoretic books as could possibly be got. The previously mentioned Seignior [Bomberg] never proved indolent, his hand was not closed, nor did he draw back his right hand from producing gold out of his purse to pay the expenses of buying the books and those of the messengers who were engaged to search for them in the most remote corners and in every other place they might possibly be.[36]

It is worth noting that Ibn Adoniyahu's praise of Bomberg's generosity and native piety is echoed in statements by other contemporaneous Jews who worked for Bomberg or were beneficiaries of his largesse.[37]

At the introduction's very beginning, however, Ibn Adoniyahu gave a somewhat different version of his earliest encounters with Bomberg in rhymed prose, almost as though it were an intriguing, romance-like narrative; in fact, in the original Hebrew it reads very much like one of the rhymed narratives in Immanuel of Rome's *Maḥberot*, among the most popular works of Hebrew belles-lettres in the late medieval and early modern periods. Ibn Adoniyahu's autobiographical narrative begins while he was still living in Tunis, "flourishing in my abode, diligently pursuing my studies," when he was suddenly forced by unspecified misfortunes to flee his homeland for Italy. After making his way to Venice, he subsisted in beleaguered, impoverished conditions until one day, as he was wandering through the city's market and streets, he suddenly encountered—"for God summoned him before me"— "one of the righteous Christians, a highly distinguished person, by the name of Seignior Daniel Bomberg, may his Rock and redeemer protect him." And then, he continues:

> [Bomberg] brought me to his printing house, and showed me his entire house of treasures, and said, "Turn in, abide with me, for here you shall find rest for your soul, and balm for your wound, as I want you to correct [*she-tagiha*] the books which I print, remove the stumbling-blocks of error, purify and refine them in the furnace of examination, and weigh them on the scales of correctness, until they emerge fine as refined silver and pure as purified gold.
>
> Although I saw that his desire was greater than my ability, yet I thought to myself: One should not refuse a superior. . . . And it came to pass, after I had remained there for some time, doing my work, the work of heaven, the Lord, may He be blessed, roused the spirit of the noble man [*heiᶜir ruaḥ ha-sar*] for whom I worked, and enthused him with the courage to publish the Twenty-Four [books of the Hebrew Bible]. He said to me, "Now gird your loins like a man, for it is my desire to publish the Twenty-Four accompanied by the commentaries, the Targum, the Masorah Magna and the Masorah Parva, . . . and following all this [at the end of the volume], the Masorah Magna according to the alphabetical order of the Arukh,[38] so that the reader can speedily consult it to find what he wants."

In this narrative, Bomberg, the righteous Christian, literally provides salvation for the hapless Jew Ibn Adoniyahu by taking him into his house and putting him to work in his printing press, where he eventually produces the Rabbinic Bible with the complete Masorah. Behind Bomberg, however, stands the figure of God, who both "summoned" the righteous gentile to save the Jew and who later "roused the spirit of the noble man . . . and enthused him with the courage to publish the Twenty-Four" with its full array of accompanying texts. The phrase "roused the spirit of the noble man" (*heiᶜir ruaḥ ha-sar*) is a direct allusion to the first verse in the book of Ezra, which recounts how "the Lord roused the spirit" of King Cyrus of Persia to issue the proclamation that allowed the Israelites to return to Jerusalem and rebuild the Temple. Both Cyrus and Bomberg are gentile figures of power who are manipulated by God and commissioned by him to execute projects of restoration: the first to restore Israel to its homeland, the second to restore the Hebrew Bible to its original glory. In this narrative construction, Ibn Adoniyahu stands in the same relationship to Bomberg as did the scribe Ezra to Artaxerxes, Cyrus's successor. Ezra and Ibn Adoniyahu are both Jewish servants of gentile masters, and both, in Ibn Adoniyahu's words, eventually "show the nations and princes the beauty and excellence of our holy Torah."[39]

This remarkable narrative captures the complexity of the cultural and religious context in which the Rabbinic Bible was created, an environment characterized by fluid interaction between social groups otherwise often impervious to each other and usually not in direct, let alone friendly, contact. As is now known almost for certain, Ibn Adoniyahu eventually—sometime after 1538—converted to Christianity.[40] There is, however, no indication in his introduction or elsewhere in the Second Rabbinic Bible that thoughts of conversion were in his mind at the time, nor is there anywhere so much as a hint that he had theological or religious sympathies toward Christianity at the time of his work on the Bible edition. Nonetheless, Ibn Adoniyahu's narrative of salvation maps the routes by which an intellectual figure could move from one religion to another. Ibn Adoniyahu was not the only one of Bomberg's editors and printers to apostatize (nor was Bomberg the only gentile Venetian printer of Hebrew books to employ Jewish converts). Some scholars have speculated that Bomberg's Hebrew publishing endeavors were motivated by missionary impulses, but there is no hint of this in the Second Rabbinic Bible.[41] Nor does Ibn Adoniyahu's introduction cast any light on Bomberg's motivations, although it certainly points to a new reality of connections and relationships between Jews and Christians.[42]

The exceptionality of Ibn Adoniyahu's narrative is paralleled by the singularity of the Second Rabbinic Bible as a book. In its comprehensive scope, this Bible brought together on each page all the features of the separate genres that had existed from the medieval period on: the Masoretic Bible (with the biblical text and Masorah), the liturgical Pentateuch (with the Targum and Rashi); and the study Bible (with the additional second commentary of Abraham Ibn Ezra on the Pentateuch and other commentators on other biblical books).[43] The only thing it lacked was the haftarot after each weekly reading of the Torah. In all other respects, it was a kind of "compleat" Bible, which could fulfill every possible use that a Bible could serve for a Jew. But more than being "compleat," it also aimed to appeal to all Jews, that is to say, to different populations of Jews.

That ambition is visible in Ibn Adoniyahu's specific choices for the second commentary in the different volumes of the Second Rabbinic Bible. By the early sixteenth century, Rashi's commentary on the Pentateuch had become a kind of universal presence in the Jewish Bible—in Sepharad as much as in Ashkenaz—so it is no surprise to find it in Ibn Adoniyahu's edition.[44] This is not the case in regard to the second commentaries in the 1524–25 edition: Ibn Ezra on the Pentateuch, and Ibn Ezra, David Kimḥi, and Gersonides, all classical commentators from the Sephardic tradition (in the latter's larger sense, including, that is, figures from Provence, like David Kimḥi, or from Languedoc, like Gersonides). Ibn Adoniyahu's decision to include these commentaries clearly targeted a Sephardic audience, either in Italy or in other post-Expulsion Sephardic communities in places like Salonica and Constantinople in the Ottoman Empire. At the same time, it accomplished something even more significant. By having both an Ashkenazic and a Sephardic commentary on the page, the Rabbinic Bible joined readers of both communities into a single audience and effectively produced a new canon of classical Jewish exegesis. Even if this was not Ibn Adoniyahu's conscious intention, his inclusion of the more grammatically and philosophically oriented Sephardic commentators had perceptible repercussions in contemporary Ashkenaz. As the historian Elhanan Reiner has argued, the presence of

Sephardic commentaries in the Second Rabbinic Bible posed a serious challenge to the traditional Ashkenazic curriculum and aroused the ire and opposition of some Polish Ashkenazic rabbinic authorities who were not inclined to approve of rationalist, philosophically inclined Spanish exegetes, let alone admit them to the canon of permitted works for study.[45] And for the later history of Jewish reading, the presence of multiple commentaries on the page was consequential in still another way. It not only invited but almost demanded comparative exegetical study and thereby made study of the Bible with multiple interpretations virtually normative for Jews. In doing this, the Rabbinic Bible page format restored to Jewish biblical exegesis a certain midrash-like spirit: a motivating desire to use Bible study to discover the text's richness and multiplicity, its capacity to sustain different, sometimes conflicting meanings, rather than the single universal sense that had been the object of medieval *peshat* interpretation.

All these features directly related to the edition's Jewish audience. For Christian readers, the book had other, albeit related, attractions. One reason Ibn Adoniyahu included Ibn Ezra and other Sephardic commentators may have been to attract Christian readers with an interest in Hebrew grammar and philology. The first half of the sixteenth century witnessed a dramatic increase in Hebraic literacy among Christians, largely due to the flourishing of Christian Hebraism in all its varieties.[46] Recent scholarship has documented much more significant and wider use of both editions of the Rabbinic Bible among Christian Hebraists in the sixteenth century than had been previously known.[47] Even if most Hebraists' control of Hebrew was limited, a select few—figures like Sanctes Pagninus (1470–1541), Conrad Pellican (1478–1556), and Sebastian Muenster (1488–1552)—read Hebrew with enough facility to handle rabbinic biblical exegetes like Rashi, Kimḥi, and Ibn Ezra.[48] In the general introduction to his bilingual edition of the Pentateuch, *Miqdash Adonai* (Basel, 1534–35), with the original Hebrew and his own Latin translation, Muenster not only cited the three Jewish commentators (and still others) but even quoted verbatim (in the original Hebrew and in Latin translation) from Ibn Adoniyahu's introduction to the 1524–25 Rabbinic Bible regarding the origins of the Masorah.[49] It is likely that Bomberg was aware of readers like Muenster. Further, as noted earlier, the kabbalistic secrets imputed to the Masorah would have been an additional attraction for Christian readers. Even if Bomberg understood that the book's principal audience was going to be Jewish, he would have wished to target any Christian reader he could.[50]

The Second Rabbinic Bible, then, had multiple readerships, and for each one it served a somewhat distinct purpose. For Jews, the edition combined in a single volume the features of what had previously been—in the manuscript age and incunable period—distinct types of Bibles, and it recorded the Masorah, something no previous printed Hebrew Bible had provided. For Christian Hebraists, it offered a definitive Hebrew text and a representative selection of classical Jewish commentary. And for Ibn Adoniyahu, the work's greatest achievement was certainly the corrected edition of the Masorah. This edition not only rehabilitated the Masorah and restored it from the corrupt and neglected state into which it had deteriorated in the course of the Middle Ages, but it also elevated the Masorah to a new level of importance. For one thing, Ibn Adoniyahu argued in his introduction for the Masorah's Sinaitic origin, a claim that had never been explicitly made.[51] With the edited Masorah as its foundation and rationale, Ibn Adoniyahu's edition justified its claim to being the authoritative text of the Hebrew Bible. By the early seventeenth century, this claim was recognized and accepted by Christians as well as Jews.[52] Indeed, the virtually undisputed stature that Ibn Adoniyahu's text eventually assumed for all students of the Bible was such that when Rudolf Kittel (1853–1929) decided in 1901 to edit the *Biblia Hebraica* (Leipzig, 1906), the first truly modern attempt to produce a scholarly critical edition of the Bible, the text he chose for the edition was that of the Second Rabbinic Bible.

It is obvious but nonetheless worth repeating that only a printed book of this kind could have attained standard acceptance and wide circulation. In the age of the manuscript, the Bible had circulated in numerous copies, each slightly different. Now there existed a single universal text that could circulate in numerous editions—and with an equally definitively edited apparatus like the Masorah, which also had previously circulated in manuscript with numerous variants, many of them corrupted.[53] As we will see in the next chapter, the greatest impact of the Second Rabbinic Bible's presentation of the Masorah came some two centuries later, when it became the target of the Christian assault upon the Rabbinic Bible. The Jewish response to that assault was a culminating moment in the lengthy process that made the Masorah the defining mark of the Jewishness of the Jewish Bible.

As a publishing venture, Ibn Adoniyahu's Rabbinic Bible was very successful. Bomberg reprinted the edition in 1546–48. In 1568–69, Giovanni di Gara, Bomberg's successor as the leading publisher of Hebrew books in Venice, published a third edition, and this was in turn followed in 1617–18 by a fourth edition printed by Alvise Bragadin, di Gara's rival and eventual successor. A year later, Ludwig König published an edition in Basel edited by the eminent Christian Hebraist, Johann Buxtorf.

Since then, numerous editions have appeared with varying numbers of commentaries.[54] Fig. 3.8 is a facing page opening from the most elaborate of these editions, *Qehillot Moshe*, the seventh, so-called Amsterdam Rabbinic Bible, published in 1724–28 by Moshe Frankfurter (1672–1772). This edition contained eight commentaries, a record exceeded only by *Torat Ḥayyim* (Jerusalem, 1986–93), which has ten commentaries (but lacks the Masorah, thereby disqualifying it from being considered an authentic Rabbinic Bible).[55] All these editions have used variants of the glossed page format employed in Bomberg's edition but without any single standardized or fixed page layout and pagination.[56] (Since

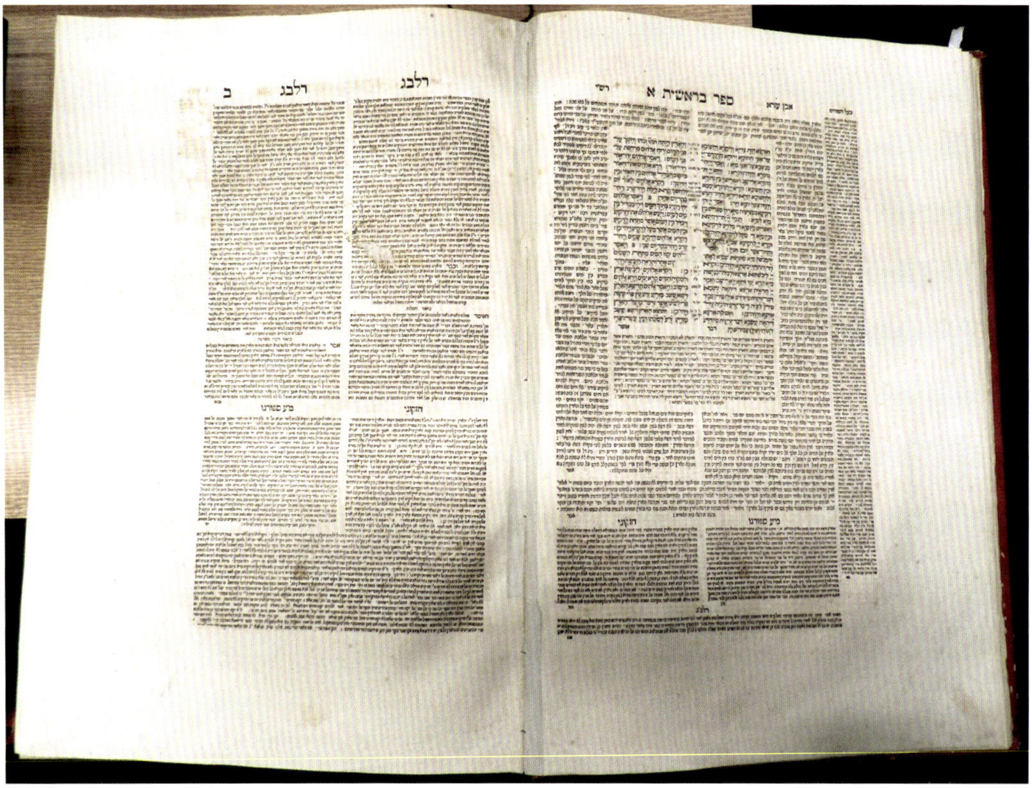

3.8 Qehillot Moshe, Amsterdam: pages 2–3 by Moses Frankfurter, 1724–28. Courtesy of the Mendel Gottesman Library, Yeshiva University.

biblical texts are always referred to by chapter and verse, there was no inherent need for standard pagination.) At the same time, commentaries in addition to Rashi and the Targum were also added to *ḥumashim*, liturgical Pentateuchs, and the differences between these distinct types of Bibles blurred. Fig. 3.9 reproduces a page opening from a *ḥumash* printed by the famous Vilna publishing house of the Widow of Romm and His Brothers, in which the glossed layout expanded to the recto of the facing page to accommodate all the commentaries on the text. The size of volumes like these has also varied considerably, from large folios to portable quarto sizes. There have even been miniature Bibles.[57] And of course it is now possible to read the Bible on a computer screen or on your phone (although, to the best of my knowledge, there is no *Miqraot Gedolot* app as yet).

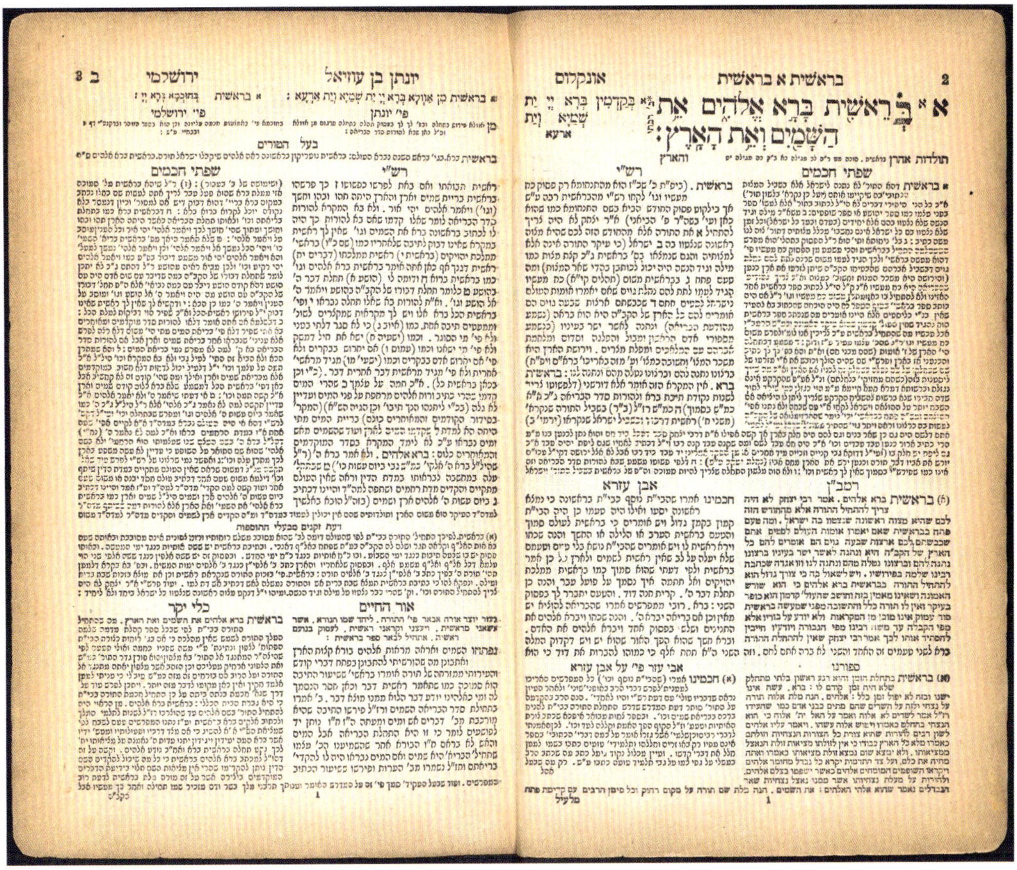

3.9 Pentateuch (Gen. 1), Vilna: pages 2–3 by the Widow of Romm and His Brothers, 1912. Widener Library, Harvard University.

To be sure, many editions with just the biblical text were continuously printed throughout this lengthy period. Yet aside from these (relatively minor) changes in format and technology, the material history of the Jewish Bible in Hebrew has undergone no radical innovations or transformations since Bomberg's 1525 Second Rabbinic Bible. At least so far, the digital revolution has not led to any truly revolutionary changes in the Bible's materiality, as it has, for example, in the Talmud and the Jewish prayer book. This fact alone is another proof of the outsize place occupied by the Second Rabbinic Bible of 1524–25 in the history of the Jewish book.

CHAPTER FOUR

THE JEWISH BIBLE SINCE THE SIXTEENTH CENTURY

The history of the Jewish Bible since the sixteenth century is largely the story of the transformation of the Hebrew Bible into a new type of Bible, a cultural Bible, that is, a Bible whose authority had less to do with its theological truth or liturgical function than with its constitutive character as a foundational document of Jewish culture.[1] This does not mean that the earlier forms of the Hebrew Bible ceased to exist or to enact their traditional roles in Jewish life. The Sefer Torah continued to be chanted in the synagogue much as it had in the previous fifteen centuries. When the classical Masoretic Bible, with its two or three columns of text surrounded by the *masorah magna* and *parva*, essentially stopped being produced as an independent biblical book, its place was taken by the Rabbinic Bible, which, as we saw in the last chapter, collapsed into one book all the earlier types of Bibles: the Masoretic Bible with the Masorah, the liturgical Pentateuch, and the study Bible. The printed *ḥumash*, the liturgical Pentateuch, itself became a conventional venue for printing new commentaries written in a traditional mode, and new editions appeared with these commentaries, often either produced or initiated by the authors of the commentaries. The material form of these volumes tended to follow the glossed page format of the Rabbinic Bible.

All of these developments, however, were essentially more of the same. The truly innovative and radical changes in the Jewish Bible's history in the modern period, as both a text and a material object, came with its transformation into a "worldly" document—the term *secular* carries too many associations—divorced from traditional liturgical and theological contexts. This transformation partly mirrors a similar change that the Christian Bible underwent during this period, as it too became a cultural Bible, as Jonathan Sheehan has written. But there were important differences between them. In the case of the Jewish Bible, the features of the new Jewish cultural Bible appear most dramatically in four distinct developments: the emergence of the Bible as an aesthetic object, specifically in the form of the illustrated Esther scroll; the widespread shift that the Jewish Bible underwent from being a text in Hebrew to a text in translation; the invention of a political Bible in the shape of Zionist ideology; and the birth of the Jewish critical Bible, a development instigated by the rediscovery and recovery of the ancient and medieval manuscripts of the Hebrew Bible.

The Illustrated Esther Scroll

Of all the material forms of the Hebrew Bible, the Torah scroll was the most traditional. It was also the most stable of the Jewish Bible's material forms, and it was the exemplar that set the hierarchy for the other scrolls chanted in the synagogue: *Megillat Ester*, the Esther scroll, most famously; those for the other books chanted in the synagogue on festivals and fast days (Song of Songs, Ecclesiastes, Ruth, and Lamentations) as well as haftarot and *navi* scrolls. As we have seen, halacha prohibits the inscription of anything but the consonantal Hebrew text in a kosher Sefer Torah, and there has never existed an illustrated or decorated Torah scroll. This had nothing to do with any prohibition against representational art, popularly associated with the Second Commandment. The Second Commandment prohibits the worship of images—at most, it might apply to the making of engravings or three-dimensional images suitable for worship.[2] As we saw, decorated and illustrated Bible codices were frequent if not common in the Middle Ages, and they sometimes included representational paintings with human figures.[3]

These considerations must be borne in mind to appreciate the radical novelty of the illustrated Esther scroll when it first emerged in the early modern period. Following the rise of print, illustrations and decorations (except for some ornamental initial word panels) effectively disappeared from printed books of the Jewish Bible. Unlike the Luther Bible, for example, Hebrew Bibles in print were not illustrated. To be sure, illustrations did not disappear from all printed Jewish books. Haggadot for Passover continued to appear in illustrated editions, and there are a few illustrations in some printed prayer books, but Jewish Bibles were rarely hand colored or decorated with marginal ornamentation even after being printed, as were many Latin texts (like the Gutenberg Bible) in the age of early printing.[4]

Almost in response to this dearth of illustrated printed books, two new genres of illustrated Hebrew texts written and illustrated by hand emerged in their full shape in Italy in the middle of the sixteenth century and the early seventeenth century: the ketubah, or marriage contract, and the illustrated *Megillat Ester*, or Esther scroll. The earliest surviving illustrated ketubot come from Italy in the early seventeenth century, although there are references to such works existing in Sephardic communities already in the late fourteenth century.[5] The earliest known decorated Esther scroll was written by a woman scribe, Estellina, the daughter of Menachem, in Venice in 1564, but most surviving scrolls, like ketubot, date from the mid-seventeenth century, again in Italy.[6] The fact that both genres developed almost simultaneously and in the same geographical locale was not an accident. Both owed their development to the growth of a new class of wealthy Italian Jewish families of bankers, merchants, and doctors. The members of these families, living in sophisticated and worldly urban centers, aspired to the opulent lifestyle of their gentile neighbors. This opulence included the ostentatious display of treasured possessions that showed off the family's or individual's wealth, an ambition easily satisfied by handwritten, decorated literary texts, each of which could be said to be, by definition, uniquely special (because every manuscript is unique), and therefore something no one else possessed. The illustrated ketubah and Esther scroll fit the bill exactly. Not surprisingly, both share similar artistic programs, including the display of family emblems (mimicking the coats of arms that noble Christian families had inherited from their feudal past). While both the ketubah and the *Megillat Ester* serve religious needs and functions within the Jewish calendar, their iconography—putti, architectural frames with sculpted figures, the twelve signs of the zodiac, the four seasons—was decidedly secular, with images often drawn from early engravings and printed books of the period.[7]

The illustrated Esther scroll was not without a special irony. As we noted in the first chapter, the book of Esther is, in fact, the only biblical text that, according to biblical and later rabbinic mandate, must be heard chanted aloud from a scroll. While the Sefer Torah became the exemplary scroll in Jewish religious tradition, the original source of the rules governing inscription was the Esther scroll. Still, already by the Talmudic period, there existed a hierarchy among scrolls in terms of halachic strictness, and Esther scrolls were treated significantly more laxly than were Torah scrolls.[8] Before the sixteenth century, however, there is absolutely no evidence for the practice of decorating or painting actual scrolls (although images relating to the book of Esther are found in codices).[9] Given the unqualified prohibition against adding anything, let alone pictures, to a kosher Torah scroll used for liturgical chanting in the synagogue, the sheer existence of illustrated Esther scrolls that could have been used for public reading must be regarded as a startling innovation in the history of the Bible scroll.

The development of the illustrated Esther scroll proceeded quickly. Already by the seventeenth century in Italy, several distinct fashions in illustrating and decorating these

4.1 Esther scroll, Ferrara, Italy: 1615–18. Scribe: Moshe Poscarel (Pescarolo). Gross Family Collection. Photograph by Tomer Appelbaum.

scrolls had developed. On some, scrolls, columns, arches, and other architectural motifs reminiscent of those found on title pages in books frame a space dedicated to the handwritten text, with small vignettes above and below these spaces illustrating episodes in the narrative, often with midrashic elaborations on the story. On others, decorative patterns separate text columns. Fig. 4.1 reproduces the beginning of a *Megillat Ester* signed by a Moshe Poscarel (Pescarolo) and written in Ferrara sometime between 1615 and 1618.

4.2 Esther scroll, Amsterdam: Salom D'Italia, 1640. Gross Family Collection. Photograph by Tomer Appelbaum.

The text blocks are framed in borders decorated with vases, flowers, vines, and birds, while above them, panels illustrate moments in the Esther narrative: on the right, Ahasuerus seated on his throne with his courtiers, on the left, the famous banquet at which (according to a midrash) the king ordered his wife Vashti to appear naked. Still other *megillot* had elaborate geometric and floral patterns actually cut out of the parchment to form a kind of lacework frame around the text.

From Italy, the practice of decorating *megillot* quickly spread throughout Europe and reached even the Ottoman Empire. In the mid-seventeenth century, printers in Italy and then in Holland (and after 1700, in Germany) began to use copper plates to print illustrations onto parchment scrolls, while dedicated spaces between the printed engravings were left to be filled in with the traditional text written by hand, as Jewish law mandates it must be. Fig. 4.2 pictures such a *megillah*, designed and engraved after 1641 by the most famous Jewish artist to work in Amsterdam, Salom d'Italia (1618/19–ca. 1664).[10] The triangular opening sheet depicts two angels holding up a shield containing the coat of arms of the patron's family while beneath them a cartouche contains the blessings to be recited over the *megillah* (which suggests that this scroll may have been intended for synagogue use by the public reader). The handwritten text blocks are enclosed in elaborate architectural gates atop which two reclining women rest on the gates' arches. Between the large entrance gates, figures from the Esther narrative stand in smaller arches, while beneath them are depicted framed episodes from the story. Engraved scrolls like these were loosely modeled on hand-decorated *megillot*, and in response to their popularity, scribes and illustrators, in central Europe especially, began to produce hand-decorated scrolls that imitated the engravings down to the cross-hatched shading typical of this printing method. The history of the decorated Esther scroll had thus moved near full circle in less than two hundred

years: from handwritten to hand-decorated scrolls to printed illustrations to hand-copied imitations of print.

Like all illustrations accompanying texts, the illustrations on the Esther scrolls offered "interpretations" of the biblical narrative, some drawn from classical rabbinic literature, others contemporizing the story; these illustrations could be studied by the *megillah*'s owners and users, and they added to the scroll's value.[11] Still, these scrolls were primarily aesthetic objects, works of art, prized and valued for their beauty. A milestone in the material history of the Jewish Bible, the illustrated Esther scroll represents not only a further aestheticization of the Hebrew biblical book but a genuine transformation of the original artifact—a liturgical scroll—into an object whose main meaning consisted in its aesthetic dimensions.

The Jewish Bible in Translation

The most striking feature of the history of the Jewish Bible from the sixteenth century on has been its transformation from a Bible almost exclusively written in Hebrew into a Bible known and used primarily through its translations into the numerous vernacular languages that Jews have spoken wherever they have lived over the last five hundred years. In this, the Jewish Bible has mirrored the material history of the Christian Bible since the sixteenth century.[12] But the histories of Jewish and Christian Bible translations over this period are not identical. In the case of Christian Bibles, the explosion of Bible translations in the early sixteenth century had much to do with the Reformation and the insistence of the various Protestant churches upon direct access to the biblical text for the individual believer. There was a serious theological dimension to translation. With the rejection of the Latin Vulgate, which since antiquity had been the authorized Bible of the Catholic Church, the post-Reformation Christian Bible primarily became a Bible translated into the vernacular languages of Europe—actually, a translation of a translation, that is, of the Septuagint or the Vulgate. As Jonathan Sheehan has shown, the linguistic transformation of the biblical text quickly led to the construction of a new kind of Bible, a cultural Bible, and that Bible was, in fact, multiple Bibles—a poetic Bible, a pedagogical Bible, a philologist's textual Bible, and a historian's historicized Bible. The last two were particularly significant because, absent theology, the main way to justify the accuracy of the translation and its fidelity to the original (whatever the "original" may have been) was through the new scholarly disciplines of philology and archival research in ancient primary sources. A critical, historical approach to the biblical text and the activity of biblical translation thus became intimately linked in early modern European scholarly culture almost from its beginnings.

For the Jewish Bible, the shift to vernacular translations was partly a response to the Reformation. But Judaism has never seen direct access to the Bible as a theological necessity in the way that Christianity, or certain streams of Christianity, have. Jewish Bible translation was primarily driven by the radical changes in Hebraic literacy that were forced upon European Jewry by the tumultuous history of the Jews in Europe in early and later modernity. These changes in Hebraic literacy not only made translations necessary but also made the very Jewishness of the Bible—and especially the identifying marks of its Jewishness, like the Masorah—contested and hence complicated features of the Jewish Bible's character.

Translation is part of the material history of a book. Language is a material fact, a matter not only of sound but of script. When a text moves from one language to another, it changes its material form. And in the case of the Jewish Bible, the identity of its language has occupied a uniquely critical, literally defining position, given that, at least until the early modern period, the very identity of the Bible as a Jewish book hinged upon its language. By definition, the Jewish Bible was the Bible in Hebrew (whereas the Christian Bible was a Bible in translation, either in Greek or in Latin). Beginning with the late fifteenth century, however, this defining feature became less absolute and more contingent. In the century following the Expulsion from Spain in 1492, a significant number of Jews, who either themselves or whose parents had converted to Christianity under compulsion, escaped the clutches of the Inquisition and returned to the Jewish faith but found themselves unable to read the classical Jewish texts in their original language. These *conversos* required translations to be able to participate as full members in the Jewish community, particularly in the synagogue. At roughly the same time, the growing number of Christian Hebraists—Christians who believed that the truths of Christianity lay buried in classical Jewish texts and learned Hebrew to gain access to them—radically changed both the readership and the production of Jewish books. The most striking representative of this class in the history of the Jewish book is Daniel Bomberg, who was only one of many important Christian publishers of Hebrew books (including Bibles); the publishing houses of these Christian Hebraists dominated Hebrew printing from the beginning of the sixteenth century. As a result, it was no longer possible to take for granted that a Jewish book was a Hebrew text (or one written in a Jewish language, such as Yiddish, in Hebrew script) that was composed by a Jew and later produced as a book by a Jewish scribe or printer and intended for a Jewish readership. Some of the Hebrew texts found in Christian Hebraists' works were even originally written by Christians![13]

Yet despite these changes in Hebraic literacy, and for all the proliferation of Jewish Bible translations, the Bible in translation never supplanted the Hebrew Bible in Jewish tradition. The Hebrew text continued to be chanted from the Torah scroll in the synagogue liturgy. Even as an object of study, the Hebrew text of the Bible remained the primary focus, with translations serving mainly as instruments of explication and interpretation, as complements to the Hebrew, not its replacement. With the exception of a few cases—like that of the *conversos* in the sixteenth and seventeenth centuries—most Jews had some access to the Bible in Hebrew (even if only to pronounce its words) and never considered discarding it for a translation.

This distinguishing feature of Jewish Bible translations—at least until very recent times—is perhaps the biggest difference between the Jewish Bible in translation and the Christian Bible, which has always been a Bible in translation. And this difference has been most important in the modern period. In order, however, fully to appreciate this modern difference, it is necessary to review in capsule form the premodern history of Jewish Bible translations from the ancient period onward.

Jewish Translations from Antiquity to Early Modernity

The earliest known Bible translation—and the very first Jewish Bible translation—is the translation into Old Greek eventually known as the Septuagint. The translation of the Pentateuch (the earliest part of the Septuagint) probably took place in the third century BCE, very possibly on the basis of oral translations that accompanied the reading of the Law in Hebrew in early Greek-speaking synagogues or other institutions. Scholars have conventionally attributed the impetus for the translation to the Hebraic illiteracy of the Alexandrian Jewish community, a result of both its geographical distance from Israel and its progressive Hellenization.[14] The legend that gave the Septuagint its name—that it was produced at the behest of the emperor Ptolemy by seventy sages—is attested in the Letter of Aristeas, a text that claims to be contemporaneous with the translation but was probably composed in the second century BCE, probably for apologetic purposes and to show that even a pagan emperor recognized the Hebrew Bible's importance. The Jewish Alexandrian philosopher Philo (ca. 25 BCE–ca. 50 CE) already refers to the divine inspiration under which the translators worked (*On Moses*, 2:25–44), and this legend continued to be elaborated in Jewish tradition as late as the Babylonian Talmud.[15] In its most extensive version (B. Megillah 9a–b), the seventy sages are depicted as seated in seventy cubicles, where they are all said to have translated independently and to have made the identical fifteen changes to the text because "God put wisdom in their hearts."[16]

There is, in any case, no question as to the Jewish origins of the Septuagint. Even some of its earliest surviving fragments may have been written by Greek-speaking Jews. Fig. 4.3 reproduces a small fragment of a papyrus codex, probably written in the second or third centuries CE, which was found in an ancient rubbish dump in Oxyrhynchus in Egypt as part of a trove of ancient Latin and Greek documents, including many texts from both the Septuagint Old Testament and the New Testament. The entire surviving codex contains sections from Genesis 14–27; this fragment preserves Genesis 24:31–42. Scholars have argued that the fragment, if not the entire codex, was written by a Jewish scribe, on the basis of the fact that spaces in the Greek text appear to have been left blank so that they could be filled in with the tetragrammaton written in Hebrew script. At some later

4.3 Septuagint (fragment, Gen. 24:31–42), Egypt, 2nd–3rd century CE. Oxford, Bodleian Library, P. Oxyrhynchus 656. The Bodleian Libraries, University of Oxford.

point, however, the spaces were filled in by a scribe who did not know Hebrew with the Greek word *kurios* (Lord); it is clear from its script that the word *kurios* was written by a different hand that the main scribe's. Because only a Jew would have wanted to write the tetragrammaton in Hebrew, it is therefore surmised that the original scribe was Jewish.[17] The scribe's identity is especially significant because it is often claimed that early Christians, not Jews, used the codex as a writing platform for their scriptures, and they did so to distinguish themselves from Jews, who, it is said, exclusively used the scroll as a writing platform. If the scribe of this fragmentary codex was Jewish, it would argue for the opposite reasoning: early Christians may have written in codices not to differentiate themselves from Jews but precisely because the codex was a scribal practice of the Greek-speaking Jewish culture from which Christianity emerged.

No early source about the Septuagint indicates that there was any opposition in the Jewish community to the translation. And while Hebraic illiteracy among Alexandrian Jews may have been one motive for producing it, it may not have been the only or original reason. If the translation originated in the early synagogue as part of scriptural study, its purpose may have been explicatory and interpretive rather than purely translational. As we now know, Jewish missionizing in the Greek-speaking Diaspora continued well into the Christian period, and the translation into Greek would certainly have facilitated Jewish proselytizing, as well as paving the way for future use by Christian missions to the Jews and gentiles in the Hellenistic and Roman periods. Indeed, the very fact of its Jewish authorship and the Jews' own legend of its divinely inspired production endowed the Septuagint with a special authority that held great meaning for Christians. As a result, the Septuagint became the basis for most early Christian translations, including the Old Latin, which eventually supplanted the Septuagint in the Western Church. To be sure, the Church's wholesale adoption of the Septuagint eventually led to its disavowal by rabbinic Jews; a famous statement in the post-Talmudic tractate Soferim compares the day the Bible was translated into Greek to the day the Israelites worshipped the Golden Calf, "for the Torah could not be properly translated."[18] The need for a Greek translation did not vanish, however, and the Septuagint was soon replaced by the more literal translation of Aquila of Sinope (ca. 150 CE). Unhappily, only a few fragments of Aquila's translation survive, but it is quoted approvingly by the rabbis.[19] In addition to Aquila, Jewish translations into Greek were produced by Theodotion (Ephesus?, d. ca. 200 CE) and Symmachus (Palestine?, second century CE, cited in the Mishnah as Sumkhus), both of which survive only in fragments and citations, mainly in Christian literature.[20] Throughout the Middle Ages, a translation evidently continued to be a felt need of Jews living in the Greek-speaking Diaspora, and there are fragmentary indications of additional translations (many written in Judeo-Greek, that is, Greek in Hebrew characters).[21] Mention should also be made of the possibility that there existed early translations into Latin by Jews in Italy, even though no texts of these translations survive.[22]

Jews living in the Greek- and Latin-speaking worlds were not the only ones to produce translations. In Hellenistic and Roman Palestine, evidence for Targumim, as Aramaic translations of the Bible come to be known, for either liturgical or study purposes, goes back to the Second Temple period; among the Qumran documents, there are fragments from Targumim on Leviticus and Job. From the second century on, as Aramaic increasingly became the lingua franca of Palestinian Jews, the weekly chanting of the Torah reading in the synagogue came to be accompanied by an orally recited Targum. Originally, neither the synagogue nor communal liturgical prayer was the province of the rabbis, but from the late third century on, as both institutions gradually came under rabbinic control, the rabbis sought (to the best of their power, and not always successfully) to regulate the performance and contents of the Targum with strict rules, the most stringent of which was the requirement that the Targum be recited orally and not from a written text (so as to avoid any confusion between the Targum and the biblical text).[23] At least through the rabbinic period, the Targum was a "tradition" rather than a fixed text, and while there may have been written texts, these functioned as notations to be memorized for oral performance. Eventually the orally transmitted Targumim were committed to writing in several versions: Targum Pseudo-Jonathan and Onkelos are the best known of these versions. While these extant texts of the Targumim certainly preserve very old elements, they should not be thought identical to the versions that were recited in the ancient synagogue.[24] Fig. 4.4 pictures the first page of the single codex containing Targum Neophyti, the longest and most complete of all the Palestinian Targumim; the name of the Targum, Neophyti, derives from the fact that the codex, which was copied in the early sixteenth century, originally belonged to the College of the Neophytes (that is, "newly made" persons), an educational institution in Rome for young men who had converted from Judaism and Islam to Catholicism and were trained to become missionaries. At a later point in time, the codex was transferred to the Vatican, where it was miscataloged as Targum Onkelos. It was only in 1949 that two Spanish professors recognized that it was not Onkelos but an entirely different Palestinian Targum.[25]

There is a widely held misconception that the Targum came into existence because Hebrew was no longer comprehensible to most Jews in Palestine and the Aramaic translation was a substitute for the original language. As Steven Fraade and Willem Smelik have independently demonstrated, there is no evidence to support this claim. The Aramaic Targumim nearly all point to concurrent use of the Hebrew original with the translations, with the latter serving as counterpoints to the former, as explicatory commentaries as much as translations in the modern, strict sense of the term.[26] (Obviously, every translation is an interpretation, but some translations are more openly interpretive and expansive than others.) Ancient Jewry, whether in Roman Palestine or in Babylonia, was bilingual (in Hebrew and Aramaic) if not multilingual, and the Targumim were products of that linguistic environment if not active exploiters of its potentialities. The so-called Palestinian

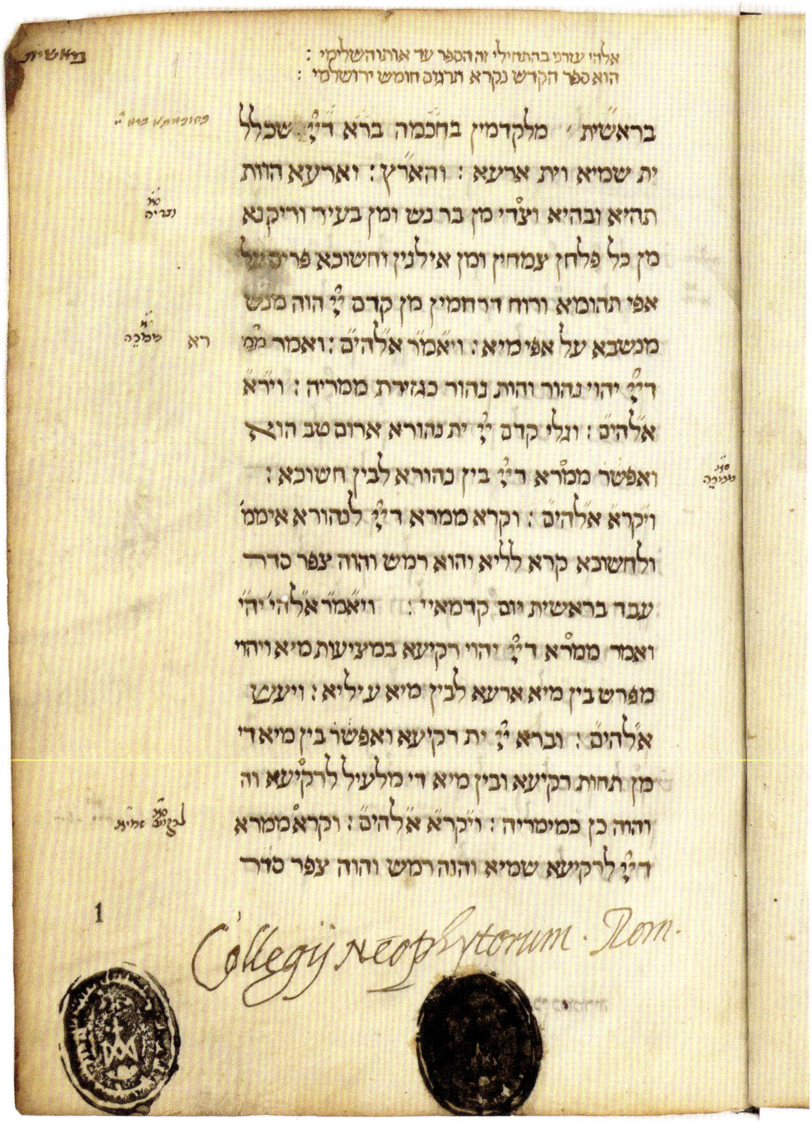

4.4 Targum Neophyti, Rome, 1504 (?). Biblioteca Apostolica Vaticana, Codex Neofiti 1, p. 1. © 2016 Biblioteca Apostolica Vaticana.

Targumim of the Pentateuch—the texts known today as Targum Pseudo-Jonathan, Targum Neophyti, and the fragmentary Targum (or Targum Yerushalmi)—are highly paraphrastic, so filled with homiletical and other exegetical additions that they sometimes border on being rewritten versions of the Bible, rather than translations in the more literal sense of the term to which we are accustomed. In contrast, the more succinct (and literal) Targum Onkelos and its companion on the Prophets, Targum Jonathan, were composed in Palestine but later revised and edited in Babylonia, where they eventually became the canonical Targumim, replete with their own Masorah (at least for Onkelos). As we have already seen, the Babylonian Talmud (B. Berakhot 8a–b) mandates the reading of Targum, presumably Onkelos, along with the doubled reading of the Hebrew text of the weekly Torah portion. This prescription was eventually realized on the pages of the medieval liturgical Pentateuch, with the Targum inscribed either interverse, as a separate column on the page, or as its own unit on a glossed page format.[27]

The Septuagint and the Targum are both anonymous (despite their supposed attributions). The first Jewish Bible translation with a known author is the *Tafsir* by Saadiah Gaon (882–942), a translation into Judeo-Arabic (Arabic written in Hebrew script, although there is some evidence that Saadiah may have originally written it in Arabic script).[28] Saadiah's translation was not the first translation into Arabic. In the period after the Islamic conquest in the seventh century, as Arabic came to replace Aramaic as the lingua franca of the Near East, there is evidence of widespread translation activity among Jews living in the Arabic-speaking world, including Hebrew-Arabic glossaries, probably written between the eighth and early ninth centuries, that explained the meaning of difficult words in the biblical text. There are also early translations of the Pentateuch into Arabic, which have been dated to the ninth century (because they use a Hebrew script reflecting a phonetic system for spelling Arabic rather than the classical Arabic spelling that Saadiah employed, which would later become standard.)[29] The Karaite translations into Arabic by known authors like Salmon ben Yeroḥam and Yefet ben Eli—which are written in Arabic script—all date from the tenth and eleventh centuries.[30] These translations were extremely literal; because they sought to reproduce the structure of the original Hebrew, they sometimes border "upon the unreadable," as one scholar has written.[31] Indeed, the Karaites' devotion to the literal text even led them to transliterate the Masoretic Hebrew text of the Bible into Arabic script to preserve the text's correct pronunciation and reading tradition.[32] These transliterated Bibles are preserved in several fragments from codices that were found in the Cairo Genizah. Fig. 4.5, containing Leviticus 7:4–13, is a leaf from one such codex. The rationale behind these transliterations was neither the Karaites' ignorance of Hebrew nor their assimilation into Muslim society but rather, as Geoffrey Khan has written, the Karaites' desire to establish a distinct sectarian identity, along with their wish to defy Rabbanite authority, in this case the Talmudic prohibition against writing the Torah in any script other than Assyrian letters.[33] In creating this new type of Bible for themselves, Karaite scribes even adapted the scribal and codicological practices with which their Muslim counterparts wrote Qur'ans, including monumental script and red ink for transcribing the vowels (to distinguish the humanly determined vowels from the divinely revealed consonantal text).[34]

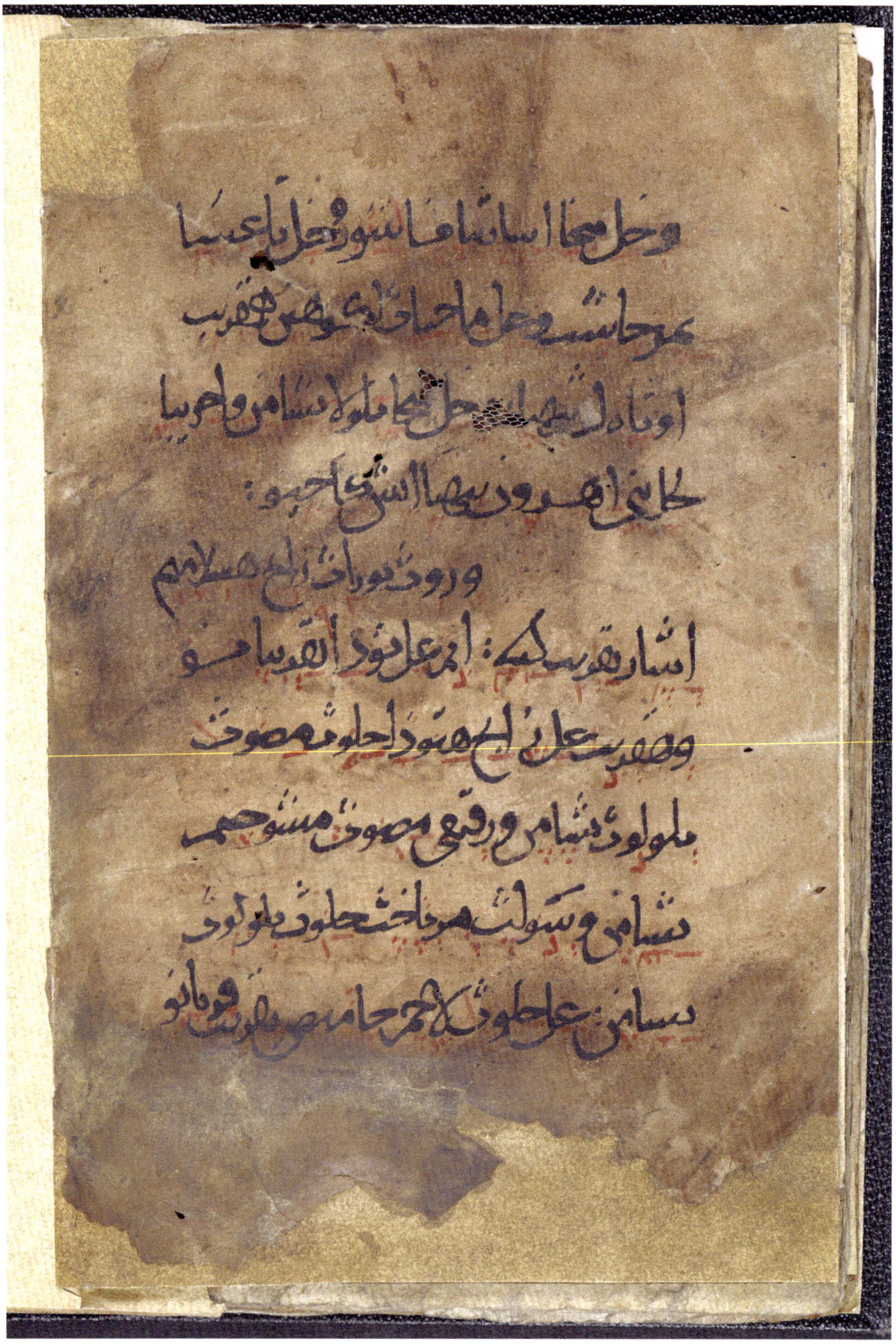

4.5 Hebrew Bible in Arabic transliteration (Lev. 7:4–13), Near East, ninth to tenth century. London, British Library Or.5563S, 40r. © The British Library Board.

These early Karaite translations help us appreciate the significance of Saadiah's *Tafsir*. In a recently discovered fragment of a hitherto unknown "long introduction" to the original translation, Saadiah left documentation of his motives.[35] As he tells us, he began the work that eventually became the *Tafsir* when he was around twenty years old, shortly after he had left his birthplace in Egypt and settled in Tiberias to pursue his studies there: "For a long time, in my hometown, I dwelled constantly on my desire, which was to have a translation of the Torah composed by me in use among the people of the true religion that would not be refuted by speculative knowledge or rebutted by tradition; but I refrained from taking that on . . . because I thought that in the lands far from my hometown there were translations that were clear and formulated precisely."[36] Once in Tiberias, however, Saadiah discovered that there were no satisfactory translations, so he began his own. This original translation was annotated with brief comments explaining specific translation decisions.[37] Later, sometime after 928, when he had settled in Iraq and was appointed as a *Gaon*, the head of the Talmudic academy at Sura, Saadiah expanded these annotations into a full-fledged commentary in which he embedded his original translation. Only many years later, at a student's request, did he finally disembed the translation and publish it in a revised form as a separate work without notes. This is the work that became known as the *Tafsir*.

For all its convoluted history, Saadiah's motivation in producing the translation remained consistent: to create a work that, as he wrote in his introduction, "would not be refuted by speculative knowledge or rebutted by tradition." The two threats to which this statement refers derive from accusations that were leveled against existing translations of the Bible, such as those made by contemporaneous Muslim theologians or Karaites. The former group criticized rationally and theologically untenable locutions, like biblical anthropomorphisms, as well as stylistic deficiencies, such as the too literal translation of repetitions in the biblical text and other infelicities of language, and used them to denigrate biblical style (particularly in comparison to the classicist perfection of the Qur'an) and thus prove the inferiority of Judaism to Islam. Karaites, in contrast, sought to use their literal translations and polemical commentaries to delegitimize traditional rabbinic interpretations of the Torah (which often involved substantive expansion of the text's meaning). To counter both attacks, Saadiah used translation as a tool to promote his own ideology. The *Tafsir* is a comparatively free translation (which avoids anthropomorphisms and needless repetition) with a masterly control of Arabic literary diction that rivals the classical Arabic of the Qur'an.[38] It thus "proves" that the rabbinic tradition possessed a Torah that was as philosophically tenable and beautiful as the Qur'an.

Among Jews, Saadiah's translation was not accepted without criticism. In some quarters, it met outright opposition. Eventually, however, it came to be accepted in the Arabic-speaking Jewish world as an authoritative translation and continued to be copied well into the Middle Ages, even after Judeo-Arabic ceased to be the lingua franca of Jews living in the post-Islamic realm.[39] In Sepharad, as we have seen, it was still being transcribed on the pages of liturgical Pentateuchs along with the Targum as late as the thirteenth century (although eventually it was supplanted by Rashi). To this day, the *Tafsir* is printed in Yemenite Pentateuchs. In the history of Jewish Bible translation, however, its openly ideological features make it something of an anomaly with few parallels before the early modern period. Even so, the story of its genesis—from translation to commentary, and back to translation—is a perfect illustration of the intimate connection between the two activities, translation and commentary, in Jewish Bible translation. While we usually think of a commentary on a translation, here the translation emerged out of the commentary.

Jews continued to produce new translations of the Bible throughout the Middle Ages. Indeed, Jews translated the Bible into virtually every vernacular they spoke. In the Sephardic world, Saadiah's *Tafsir* remained the standard translation through the period of Islamic rule of the Iberian Peninsula. Beginning in the twelfth and thirteenth centuries, translations rendered the Hebrew text into Castilian. Most of these translations were commissioned by Christians, either out of intellectual interest or as trophy books designed to display their owner's wealth and status, but it is possible that some were commissioned and used by *conversos* who were either unable to read the Hebrew original or afraid to do so lest they be accused of Judaizing. In most cases, the translations were completed with the assistance of Jews, some of whom were *conversos*.[40]

The most remarkable of all these translations is known as the Arragel or Alba Bible (after either its translator-author or a later owner).[41] In 1422, Don Luis de Guzmán, Grand Master of the Order of the Calatrava, invited Rabbi Mosé Arragel of Guadalajara to produce a new translation of the Bible from the Hebrew that would be free of the errors in earlier translations, along with a commentary that would collect and synthesize classical Jewish interpretation (from the rabbinic through the medieval period) as well as Christian interpretations of the same passages where they differed from the Jewish tradition. To ensure the orthodoxy of the final product, Don Luis also appointed several clergymen, including two friars, a Dominican and a Franciscan, to check the translation and commentary. Initially, Arragel resisted the invitation—he did not see how the Jewish and Christian traditions could be juxtaposed without acrimony and recriminations—but eventually he agreed to participate, and then spent eight years writing the translation and the accompanying commentary. The final manuscript was lavishly decorated with miniatures painted by several different workshops of Christian artists; Arragel is believed to have supervised the artists, and the miniatures sometimes allude to motifs known only from midrash.

Fig. 4.6 displays a characteristic page from the single extremely lavish codex in which Arragel's translation survives. The page is a translation of Genesis 27–28, which includes both the story of Jacob's deception of his father Isaac to receive the blessing of the firstborn and the story of Jacob's dream at Beth-El where God appears to the patriarch and he

4.6 Arragel Bible, Maqueda, Spain, 1422–30. La Casa Ducal de Alba (Palacio de Liria, Madrid), Biblia de Arragel, fol. 43v. The Library of the House of Alba, Fundación Amigos de Sefarad and Houghton Library, Harvard University.

famously sees the angels ascending and descending on a ladder stretching from earth to heaven. The text of the translation is in the two columns in the center of the page. Arragel's commentary surrounds it on three sides, and on the bottom of the page (and in the lower right margin) carefully painted illustrations realistically depict, on the left side, the blind Isaac feeling the arms of Jacob (which he has covered with animal skins to disguise himself as the hairy Esau, while the latter sits forlornly with his bow and arrow behind Isaac's bed). On the right side, Jacob is seen dreaming as he sleeps with his head resting on three stones; next to him, the angels ascend and descend the ladder to heaven. It is worth noting that in his commentary Arragel cites the various rabbinic traditions regarding the number of stones Jacob took, which range from twelve (one for each future tribe) to three (one for each patriarch) to two (the minimum number that the plural *stones* can refer to).[42] There is little question, however, that the original meaning of the illustration of the three stones, which was painted by a Christian artist, related to the Christian interpretation of the stones as figures for the Trinity.[43] Arragel then tried to Judaize the Christian interpretation. This small detail is a good illustration of the complex and dialectical religious syncretism that informs the codex as a whole.

Arragel sought to make his commentary as unpolemical as possible. To the extent that we can tell from the single surviving text, the Alba Bible manuscript, he succeeded.[44] Without compromising his own beliefs, he managed to present the Jewish tradition of interpretation without offending Christian sensibilities. Unhappily, the complete story of the Bible is not known, and it is unclear whether the completed translation reached Don Luis de Guzmán before his death. Even so, the entire project, beginning with its commissioning, should be understood as an ambitious effort to facilitate interreligious communication and understanding between Jews and Christians. This use of translation as a tool for social change has few parallels in the Middle Ages in either Christian or Jewish culture, and it is especially remarkable given the intensely combative religious context of the time, with Vincent Ferrer's fervid missionizing and the Disputation of Tortosa in 1413–14. At the same time, the translation also raises all the questions of deciding what a book's Jewish identity consists of. Jews and Christians were both involved in its production from the moment of its commission to its final approval, if such a moment ever took place. Arragel's translation and commentary derive directly from a Jewish understanding of the Bible. Its codicology displays certain features otherwise unique to Hebrew manuscripts.[45] Yet there is no Hebrew script in the codex, and the patron was a Christian who hardly intended to produce a Jewish book.

The question of the work's Jewish identity also touches upon a practical question: to what extent did Jewish *conversos* in the fifteenth and early sixteenth centuries truly need a Spanish translation of the Bible? At least in the first half of the fifteenth century, there were many *conversos* in Iberia who had grown up as Jews and were sufficiently literate in Hebrew so as not to need translations. Indeed, several very learned *conversos* were involved

4.7 Complutensian Polyglot (Gen. 1:1–13), Alcala de Henares: Arnaldi Giullelmi de Brocario, 1514–1517. Houghton Library, Harvard University.

in the production of Christian editions of the Old Testament in Hebrew, in particular the multilingual Complutensian Polyglot Bible sponsored by the archbishop of Toledo and Grand Inquisitor, Cardinal Francisco Ximénes de Cisneros (1436–1517), and published in 1514–17 in Alcalá de Henares.[46]

Inspired by Origen's *Hexapla*, Cisneros published the Old Testament in three parallel columns, the Latin Vulgate in the center, the Greek text on the right, and the Hebrew on the left, just as, so Cisneros wrote in the general preface, Christ on the Cross was flanked by the two thieves crucified at his sides. The outside margin contains the roots of difficult Hebrew words; the bottom half of the page, the Aramaic Targum and its Latin translation. The purpose of this massive undertaking—one of the great projects of early humanism—was to defend the Catholic faith and combat heresies by providing recourse to the original texts of the Bible; that recourse, it was believed, would correct errors of understanding. The Hebrew text in the Complutensian, as well as the text of the Targum and its translation, was edited and produced by the *converso* Alfonso de Zamora (ca. 1474–1544) assisted by a second *converso*. As recent scholarship has demonstrated, however, Zamora frequently "corrected" the Hebrew Masoretic text to make it conform to the Vulgate.[47] Somewhat ironically, in the Biblia Regia, a second, even more ambitious polyglot Bible that was produced and printed by Christopher Plantin in Antwerp some fifty years later, between 1568 and 1573, its editor, Benito Arias Montano, an exceptionally learned Christian Hebraist who did not have a drop of Jewish blood, deliberately restored the Hebrew text to its Masoretic accuracy—so extensively, in fact, that he was accused of Judaizing.

Neither the Complutensian nor the Antwerp Polyglot was by any definition a Jewish Bible, but it is worth comparing the two Christian editions with the almost contemporary Second Rabbinic Bible.[48] A polyglot intentionally juxtaposed versions of the Bible in multiple languages to produce an authoritative Catholic text. In contrast, Ibn Adoniyahu's Rabbinic Bible presented multiple commentaries on its pages to offer its reader the multiplicity of meanings that classical Jewish tradition saw in the biblical text (along with, of course, the Masoretic apparatus that guaranteed the accuracy of the traditional text upon which all the commentators based themselves).[49] In other words, the two Bibles had distinctly different purposes and meanings for their producers and readers. And not surprisingly, the two used very different page formats: the Polyglot's vertical synoptic columns, in the one case; the Rabbinic Bible's glossed (Talmud-like) layout, on the other.

Eventually these two page layouts became virtual emblems for the Bibles of the two religious faiths. The proof can be seen vividly in a multilingual Jewish Bible produced in Constantinople in 1546 by Eliezer ben Gershom Soncino. Possibly inspired by the Complutensian, the first edition of Soncino's polyglot consisted of a Pentateuch with the Targum, Rashi, Saadiah's Judeo-Arabic *Tafsir,* and a translation into Judeo-Persian (in Hebrew script). The following year, Soncino published a second edition that replaced the Judeo-Arabic and Judeo-Persian texts with Spanish and Greek translations (in Hebrew

4.8 *Torat Adonai Temimah* [Polyglot Torah with Rashi, Onkelos, Saadia's *Tafsir,* and a Judeo–Persian translation), Constantinople: Eliezer Soncino, 1546. Courtesy of the National Library of Israel.

script), this one obviously meant for a different group of immigrants.[50] The clear purpose of this polyglot was to provide the different vernacular translations for Jewish readers who needed them, not to enable comparative study so as to arrive at the Bible's true meaning. Even so, the real sign of this polyglot's Jewishness was its page format, as illustrated in fig. 4.8. The page pictured here is the beginning of Deuteronomy from the original edition. The biblical text is in the center of the page in a typical larger square font; the Aramaic Targum is in the inner (right-hand) column, and Rashi's commentary fills the entire bottom of the page, while the Judeo-Arabic stretches across the top and the Judeo-Persian is in the outer (left-hand) margin. Layout here has literally become an identity. Despite its multilingual contents, both editions of the polyglot used the "Jewish" glossed page format rather than the "Christian" synoptic columns format (which might have proven more convenient for Soncino's readers). The glossed page format had become a virtual emblem of Jewishness.

Soncino's polyglots targeted the various communities into which post-Expulsion Sephardic Jewry had splintered. The first translation of the Bible into Spanish specifically targeted for Spanish-speaking Jews—that is, *conversos* who had remained in Spain and then escaped—appeared in 1553 under the title *Biblia en lengua española traducida palabra por palabra de la verdad hebrayca por muy excelentes letrados, vista y examinada por el officio de la Inquisicion. Con privilegio del yllustrissimo Señor Duque de Ferrara* (The Bible in the Spanish Language, Translated Word for Word from the True Hebrew by Very Excellent Literati, Viewed and Examined by the Office of the Inquisition. With the Privilege of the Illustrious Master Duke of Ferrara). This Bible is known popularly as the Ferrara Bible, after the place of its publication.[51]

The history of this Bible is a virtual parable of post-Expulsion Sephardic Jewish history. Sometime before 1550, Abraham Usque, a *converso* living in Portugal under the Christian name of Duarte Pinhel, fled to Italy, where he resumed life as a Jew. With a fellow ex-*converso*, Yom Tov Attias (formerly Jeronimo de Vargas), a typographer by profession, Usque established a print shop in Ferrara in which he and Attias published some twenty-eight books principally directed to a market of other former *conversos* like themselves, including the Ferrara Bible. This book became the first printed translation of the Bible into Spanish for any audience of readers.

Because he had to submit the book to the Inquisition, Usque issued the Bible in two slightly different versions, one for Christians, the other for Jews. The Christian edition was dedicated to Ercole d'Este, the Duke of Ferrara, and its title page was signed as published by Duarte Pinhel and Jeronimo de Vargas. The edition intended for the Jewish market, Usque's primary audience, was dedicated to Dona Gracia, the head of the wealthy Nasi family from Portugal, *conversos* who had escaped to Ottoman Turkey and are believed to have helped subsidize the publication. This edition was signed by its publishers under their Jewish names, Abraham Usque and Yom Tov Attias. The text of the translation in the two editions, which was based upon earlier translations, is essentially the same, but there are several small and significant variants between them. For example, the messianically charged verse Isaiah 7:14, "The *ʿalmah* will conceive and give birth to a son whom I will name Immanuel," appeared in three different versions: one translating the word *ʿalmah* as *moça*, the vernacular for "a young woman"; a second translating it as *virgo* (virgin); and a third that simply transliterated the word as *la* ALMA. Along the same lines, the Jewish version of the Ferrara Bible regularly replaces the Hebrew *Adonai*, "Lord," with a capital A.[52]

Of all its features, however, the most revealing is its title page, reproduced in fig. 4.9. Beneath the large title, the cartouche depicts a storm-tossed galleon with one mast shattered but the other intact, and on its top an astrolabe, a nautical instrument used to guide a ship. Not coincidentally, the astrolabe was also Usque's printer's mark. This iconic image, as scholars have recognized, carried a deeply Jewish allegorical meaning in which Usque portrayed his sense of his own mission as a printer and translator.[53] The ship represents the Jewish people, tossed in the turbulent storms of the Inquisition but still afloat and

4.9 *Biblia en Lengua Española* (Ferrara Bible), Ferrara: title page by Abraham Usque (Duarte Pinhel) and Yom Tov Attias (Jeronimo de Vargas), 1553. Widener Library, Harvard University.

being guided toward safety by a printer of Jewish books, Usque himself. The coded meaning of this title page was, in other words, emblematic of its producers' sense of their own mission. The Ferrara Bible was not simply a translation for Jews who could not read the Hebrew text. It was a vehicle for survival. In the entire history of the Jewish book, there is no more compelling representation of the self-conception of a Jewish book producer and his role in Jewish culture.

Vernacular translations in Western and later Eastern Europe, the world of Ashkenaz, followed a different path. From the medieval period, there are no surviving Bible translations into Judeo-French, but there are many *le'azim* (sing. *le'az*), transliterations into Hebrew script of words from a Judeo-Romance language close to a Judeo-French vernacular that are preserved in medieval Old French-Hebrew glossaries and in the biblical commentary of Rashi.[54] These *le'azim* have led scholars to believe that there was an orally transmitted tradition of translation into the Judeo-French vernacular in northern France as early as the eleventh century.[55] Scholars have proposed a comparable history for a tradition of Judeo-Italian Bible translation (for which actual literary evidence does not appear until the sixteenth century).[56]

Translations into Yiddish—first as it was spoken in the Rhineland, and later when it became the lingua franca of Eastern European Jewry—appears to have followed a similar trajectory.[57] There developed early on an oral tradition of word-for-word translation of the Hebrew Bible for use in the *ḥeder*, the elementary school. This type of literal translation was, however, only the first stage of elementary education; it was followed by a second stage, in which the student learned how to connect words and phrases and verses and then, in a final stage, to understand a verse's meaning through the commentaries of Rashi and other medieval commentators. Possibly as early as the fourteenth century, the initial part of this three-stage process, the word-for-word translation, began to be transcribed into writing, and eventually became known as *Taytsch-ḥumash* (German Pentateuch). These texts, however, were never meant to be used as standalone translations in place of the Hebrew Bible, but merely as aids to help young students follow the weekly Torah portions as read in Hebrew.[58] This fact was already noted by late medieval writers. As they pointed out with derision, these overly literal translations so abjectly followed the Hebrew text's word order and syntax that they were basically impossible to understand.[59]

In 1544, the *Taytsch-ḥumash* was printed for the first time in two separate editions, one in Augsburg, the other in Constance. The primary audience for both editions was, as their title pages explained, Jewish "women and girls . . . and [male] householders who would like to study . . . but are ashamed to study the portion and the commentary with a teacher."[60] (The Constance edition, published by the Christian Hebraist Paulus Fagius, included a preface in which Fagius explained that he had printed the book for Christians as well as Jews in order to demonstrate to his co-religionists the Jews' "misunderstanding" of the Pentateuch.)[61] Both editions were printed in an attractive font called *vaybertaytsh* (women's German) which is actually based on the Ashkenazic semicursive; eventually, this font became the typical one used in most subsequent Yiddish Bible-related books. *Vaybertaytsh* is the Ashkenazic equivalent of Rashi script (so-called because early printers used it in Bibles to print Rashi), which is actually based on a Sephardic semicursive!

Neither the Augsburg nor the Constance edition (nor the reprintings of the Augsburg edition) was particularly successful commercially, and none rivaled the popularity of the biblical epics in rhymed verse (like the famous *Shmuel-bukh*, which retold the Book of Samuel) or other Bible-like books that offered free translations of the biblical text interspersed with generous samplings of classical midrashim and legends (a Jewish literary tradition that can be traced back to expansive Palestinian Targumim, like Pseudo-Jonathan, which offer many free elaborations as part of their "translation").[62] The most successful book of this kind was the *Tse'ena Ure'enah*, its title taken from Song of Songs 3:11, "Go forth and behold [O daughters of Zion]," a phrase quoted on its title page as an invitation "to come and behold" this marvelous book, "the like of which had never been seen before!" This work retells the biblical narrative by weaving it together with traditional legends, rabbinic and medieval commentaries, selections of popular mysticism, and ethical homilies.[63] Composed at the end of the sixteenth century by Jacob ben Isaac Ashkenazi (1550–1625), its purpose was "to enable men and women . . . to understand the word of God," as its earliest extant copy (Basel, 1622) states. Eventually, the *Tse'ena Ure'enah* came to be known primarily as a book for women (who typically read it at home in place of the weekly Torah reading in the synagogue), but its original purpose was to supplement the Torah reading in the synagogue, not to substitute for it.

Reprinted numerous times, the *Tse'ena Ure'enah* became one of the great best sellers in Jewish book history. Especially popular were its many illustrated editions, one page of which, taken from the very fine 1796 Sultzbach edition, is reproduced in fig. 4.10.[64] The font used for the text is the *vaybertaytsh* mentioned above, while the woodcut on the page depicts Moses at the burning bush (Exod. 3:1–5), having shorn his sandals, kneeling before the triangular image of God within the circular flames surrounding the bush. Moses's position in prayer is distinctly Christian, an observation that should not come as a surprise since virtually all illustrations in early Jewish printed books through the eighteenth century were based upon Christian models. Many of these were taken from Matthaeus Merian's *Icones Biblicae* (1625–27), which themselves were based on earlier prints by Hans Holbein and others.[65] While the Christian models were sometimes altered—particularly when they displayed too blatant Christological imagery—in most cases, as here, they were retained much as they had been. The *Tse'ena Ure'enah*'s use of Christian models for its illustrations recalls the ways medieval Ashkenazi Jewish scribes and artists utilized Christian models for their Bible illustrations. Both cases demonstrate how deeply these books, for all their Jewish contents and traditionality, were embedded in the larger cultural context in which their producers lived.

The success of the *Tse'ena Ure'enah* epitomizes the tendency among Yiddish-speaking Eastern European Jews to privilege expansive retellings of the Bible linked to legends and homilies over more literal or restricted translations of the text. One reason for their preference was certainly a greater interest among these audiences in what the Bible means (or could mean) than in what it actually says.[66] The same preference helps to explain the nearly complete commercial failure of two publishing projects undertaken at the end of

פרשת שמות

4.10 *Tse'ena Ure'enah*, Sultzbach: Aharon and Son Zeckel, 1796, fol. 66a. Gross Family Collection.

the seventeenth century in Amsterdam to issue sophisticated Bible translations that would convey its plain meaning without the intervention of all the *Tse'ena Ure'enah*'s exegetical and homiletical expansions taken from postbiblical Jewish tradition.[67] The first of these projects, undertaken by an Amsterdam printer named Uri Fayvesh Halevi in the mid-1670s, was initially inspired by the success of the Ferrara Bible among Spanish-speaking Jews in Amsterdam and the popularity of contemporary Protestant translations. (The city possessed both Ashkenazi and Sephardi communities.) Ashkenazi Yiddish-speaking Jews felt a certain shame that their ability to understand the Bible was inferior to that of their Sephardic peers. To that end, Uri Fayvesh hired Yekuthiel ben Isaac Blitz to produce a translation; unhappily, Blitz's translation was decidedly inadequate, based more on borrowings from German translations (including Luther's Bible) than on the original Hebrew, with the result that the translation read more like German than Yiddish. Taking note of the shortcomings in Blitz's translation, the Sephardic publisher Joseph Attias (who had been one of Fayvesh's original backers) hired Joseph ben Alexander Witzenhausen to do another translation (which did indeed turn out to be better than Blitz's). The two publishers eventually went to war, with each seeking to ban the other's translation. It hardly needs mentioning that both publishers expected to make a financial killing on their editions, but the two editions, both published in 1679, failed to find audiences or to sell copies. As the two publishers learned the hard way, Yiddish-speaking Jews still preferred either the overly literal (to the point of incomprehensibility) *Taytsch-ḥumash* or the explicitly homiletical *Tse'ena Ure'enah*, which taught the traditional Jewish understanding of the Bible, over a more modern translation like those of their Christian neighbors.[68]

Modern Translations

Jewish Bible translations in Western Europe from the Enlightenment in the eighteenth century onward followed a distinctly different trajectory than those into Yiddish. The impetus for translation came from multiple sources: internal Jewish needs like Hebraic illiteracy (for whatever social or historical reason) and the inadequacy of existing translations, as well as the impact of external forces, particularly those that followed from the Protestant Reformation and the new importance that Luther's emphasis on unmediated access to the Bible as the basis of Christian faith gave to vernacular translation. The emergence of the new critical scholarship dealing with the Bible (a development for which Protestantism should be given a major share of credit) raised for Jews (as it did for Christians) a plethora of fresh challenges to the traditional conception of scripture with its assumptions about the Bible's literary unity as a document, belief in Mosaic authorship of the Pentateuch, and faith in the prophetic inspiration behind the Bible as a whole. Yet while all these ambitious intellectual assaults on the traditional Jewish Bible undoubtedly served as background for the development of modern Bible translations by Jews in Western Europe, the immediate instigation for the first translation came from a seemingly minor issue: the orthography and pointing of the Masoretic text and its vocalization.

The history of this challenge is too lengthy and complex to relate in full.[69] As part of its attack on the Catholic Church, Protestantism rejected Jerome's Vulgate as the authoritative

Bible text and urged a return to the original Hebrew and Greek texts as the bases for new vernacular translations. (Luther himself owned a copy of Gershom Soncino's octavo edition, published in Brescia in 1494, and as the annotations in the margins of its pages indicate, he used its text extensively in his own German translation.)[70] Catholics responded to the Protestant challenge by attacking the Masoretic text of the Bible—the term *Masoretic text* is itself a creation of this period—which, they argued, was less authentic than the Latin Vulgate because the fourth-century church father Jerome had done his translation from a Hebrew text as yet uncorrupted by the changes that the tenth-century Masoretes had wrought upon the original Hebrew text; through these deliberately deceptive changes, Catholic scholars contended, Jews had altered the Bible's true meaning, specifically its Christological references. The primary technique that Masoretes had used, Catholics argued, was to change the vocalization and pointing of the consonantal text to fit their own purposes. As noted earlier, the consonantal text can be vocalized and therefore understood differently depending on the vowels placed beneath the consonants.

Protestants responded to this accusation by defending the originality and authority of the Masoretic text's vocalization. In response, Catholic critique of the Masoretic text became even more fierce and rigorous, thereby encouraging an increasingly suspicious approach to the biblical text. In this they were helped by Pietro della Valle's discovery and publication in 1616 of the Samaritan Pentateuch, which they claimed was earlier and therefore more original than the Jews' Masoretic Bible. Eventually, Protestants split into two camps—one (mainly in Germany and other German-speaking realms) maintaining the originality of the vowel points and the "perfection" of the Masoretic text; the other (in France and England) willing to concede the "imperfection" of the presently existing text (and the superiority of the Samaritan text) but still believing in the possibility of reconstructing the original "perfect" Hebrew Bible. This move worked to encourage Protestant critical study of the Bible. In either case, the result was that both Protestant and Catholic scholars adapted a critical philological and historicist text-focused approach aiming to recover the biblical urtext within an academic, less theologically inflected context.

In England, the new scholarship took a practical turn by applying its insights to producing new translations of the Bible based on the supposedly more accurate texts of the Hebrew Bible. As Jonathan Sheehan has argued, translation thereby became one of the primary mediums for early modern Bible scholarship.[71] The story of this development begins with Benjamin Kennicott (1718–1783), an Oxford theologian, Bible scholar, and collector of Hebrew books who, in 1753, issued a call for an unprecedented project: to collate and compare every available manuscript and early printed copy of the Hebrew Bible in order to reconstruct the best possible text and its variants.[72] After studying more than six hundred manuscripts and fifty early printings, Kennicott finally published his *Vetus Testamentum Hebraicum cum Variis Lectionibus* (1776–80), in two massive volumes presenting in parallel columns the unpointed consonantal text of the Hebrew Bible alongside the Samaritan Pentateuch with every variant he could find. While Kennicott's project received both applause and criticism, it had a significant impact in confirming the unreliability of the Masoretic text. Even before it had been fully published, Kennicott's work inspired Robert Lowth in 1779 to undertake a new translation of the book of Isaiah based on its methods. In Germany, where Kennicott was even more influential than in England, the celebrated biblical scholar Johann David Michaelis (1717–1791), in the years between 1769 and 1789, produced a popular translation of the Hebrew Bible in the spirit of Kennicott's work that was based on many emendations of the "corrupted" Masoretic text and other corrections that yielded a more "rational sense."[73]

By this time, the German *Haskalah*, the Jewish Enlightenment, was underway. As part of its project to reinvigorate Jewish culture within European society, the early leaders of the movement, Moses Mendelssohn (1729–1786) and Naftali Hirz Wessely (1725–1805), sought to re-create Jewish Bible study by joining the literary and textual sophistication of contemporary European scholarship with the richness and creativity of traditional Jewish biblical commentary. At the same time, they endorsed Bible translation—that is, into what they considered proper and correct German, not into Yiddish—as a valuable resource for restoring Bible study to its role at the center of a reformed Jewish educational curriculum.[74] The problem they faced, however, was that the available translations into proper German were all done by Christians like Michaelis, and those translations, as Mendelssohn wrote, were "full of snares and stumbling blocks" to traditional Jewish belief and practice.[75] And the most troubling features of the Christian translations were the often capricious and willful emendations that underlay their translations of the biblical text.

To remedy this unfortunate situation, in 1778 Mendelssohn and a fellow *maskil*, Solomon Dubno (1738–1813), announced a plan to publish a new edition of the Pentateuch. This edition would include a German translation into *Hochdeutsch*, High German, albeit transliterated in Hebrew letters; a commentary, the *Be'ur* (Elucidation), as a complement to the translation that would summarize and discuss traditional Jewish exegesis (including both rabbinic midrash and medieval *peshat* interpretation); and a set of annotations (eventually called *tikkun soferim*) that would discuss the proper Masoretic text and correct errors in other editions. As it was finally published between 1780 and 1783 under the title *Sefer Netivot Ha-Shalom* (The Book of the Paths of Peace), Mendelssohn's German translation and commentary presented the Bible to its Jewish audience in a suitably contemporary fashion—for example, Mendelssohn adopted Robert Lowth's ideas about biblical poetry—while providing at the same time a strong, unyielding defense of the Masoretic text and classical Jewish commentary.

In short, *Sefer Netivot Ha-Shalom* was both an innovative and traditional Bible, as can be seen in fig. 4.11, the first page, containing Genesis 1:1–2. The page layout makes both sides visible simultaneously by adopting the traditional format of the Rabbinic Bible with its multiple text blocks and then substituting new texts for the traditional ones: the *hochdeutsch* translation for the Targum, the *tikkun soferim* for Rashi, and Mendelssohn's *Be'ur* in place of a second commentary.[76] Each of these text blocks was printed in the conventional font for its traditional counterpart: the Hebrew biblical text in the familiar square font in a somewhat larger size, the translation in a smaller square font, the *Be'ur* in Rashi script, and *tikkun soferim* in a tinier Rashi-script font. This page format served to make the elements on the page appear and feel familiar to its Jewish readers even if they were not traditional features. And thus, though not for the first time, page format—the look of the page—again became a defining feature of the Jewishness of the Jewish Bible.

With Mendelssohn's defense of the Masorah, the story comes nearly full circle. The original Masoretic project, as it reached its culmination in the tenth and eleventh centuries, sought to establish the correct and accurate biblical text. The Second Rabbinic Bible edition fixed in print a standard, universal Hebrew text according to the determinations of the Masorah. By the time of Mendelssohn's Bible, this so-called Masoretic text had become, for Christians, essentially a veil to see through in order to discover behind it what they believed was the "original" and "true" biblical text, that is, the Bible before the Jews had falsified it through the corrections and emendations of the Masorah. And for Jews like Mendelssohn, in responding to the Christian challenge, the Masorah became the very essence of the Bible's Jewishness, the site of its proper identity. The physical appearance of Mendelssohn's Bible—the very fact that it looked like a typical volume of a *Miqraot Gedolot* or a *ḥumash*—was a representation of traditional Jewish identity even if the contents of the page reflected the new and changed exigencies of Jewish existence in eighteenth-century Germany.

Sefer Netivot Ha-Shalom was reprinted multiple times between 1783 and 1870 and spawned an unprecedented flood of new Jewish translations of the Bible. Between 1780 and 1923, some sixteen complete German translations of the Bible by Jews were published. These translations were all printed in Latin characters, not transliterated into Hebrew letters, and were clearly intended for Jews who not only had insufficient access to the Hebrew Bible but also no longer felt comfortable even reading Hebrew script. The most popular of these translations was the multiauthored "Zunzbible" (1837), edited by Leopold Zunz (1794–1886), the cofounder of Die Wissenschaft des Judentums, and the first Jewish translation to advertise itself as reflecting the most current philological and historical advances of contemporary scholarship. Others included denominational Bibles, like the Reform Bible translation of Ludwig Philippson (1849) and the neo-Orthodox translation and commentary of Samson Raphael Hirsch (1867). The latter translations were targeted for specific religious sectors of the Jewish population, and anticipate the many denominational translations later produced in America.[77]

The last of the German-Jewish translations of the Hebrew Bible was, arguably, the most radical Bible translation ever attempted. Between 1925 and 1929, Franz Rosenzweig (1886–1929) and Martin Buber (1878–1965) translated and published the five volumes of

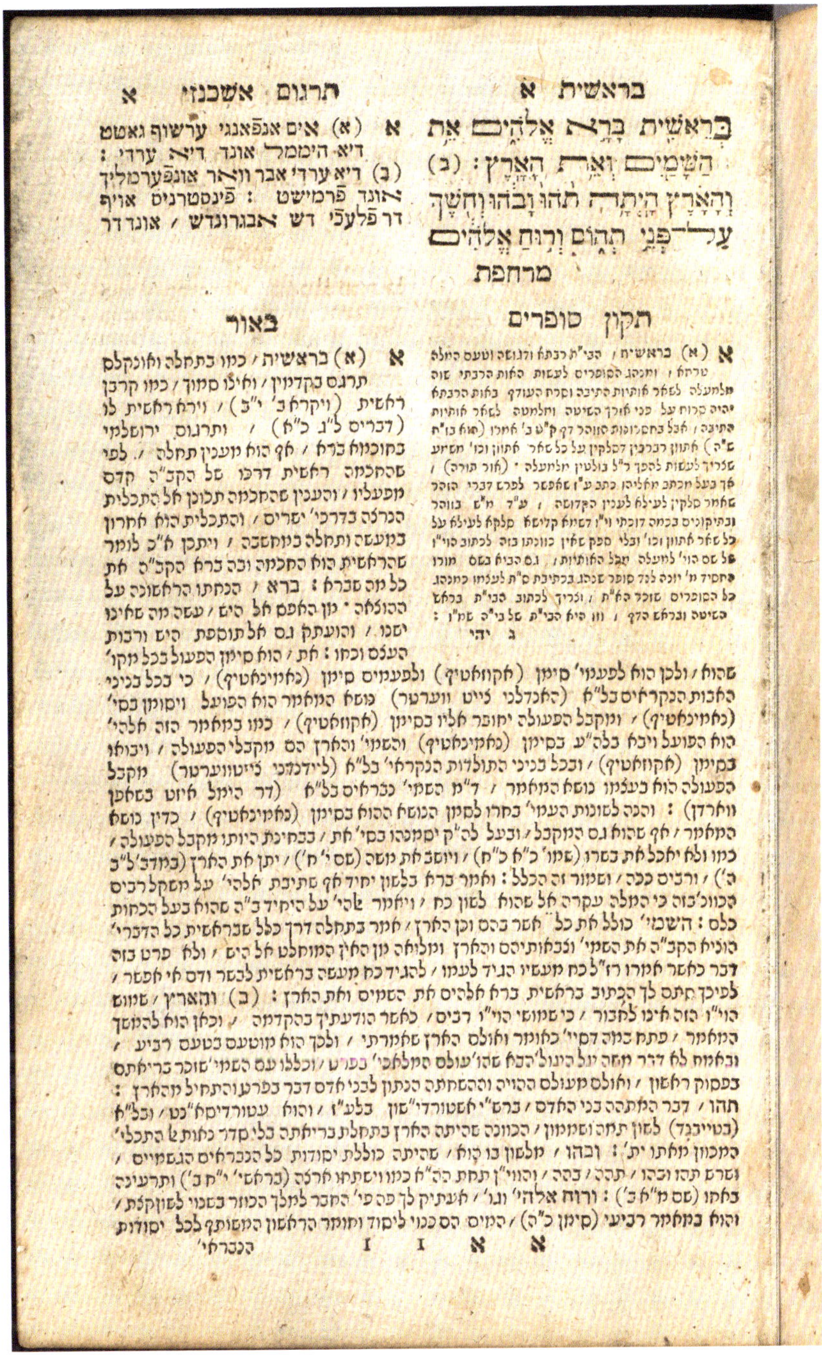

4.11 Moses Mendelssohn, *Sefer Netivot Ha-Shalom* (Berlin: n.p., 1780–83), p. 1 (Gen. 1:1–2). Widener Library, Harvard University.

the Pentateuch under the title *Die Schrift*, literally "the Writing." After Rosenzweig's death in 1929, Buber continued the translation alone, even after he emigrated to British Palestine in 1938. The last volume of the final revised edition of the entire Bible appeared in 1962.[78] Thus the translation appeared after the Holocaust, after the main centers of German-speaking Jewry had been destroyed and their residents exterminated, and after the collapse of the German-Jewish cultural symbiosis that had created the environment for the translation in the first place.

From its inception, the explicit goal of *Die Schrift* was to recover the Bible as a spoken text (despite its title!) so that the Bible could again address and speak to people as the sacred Word of God. Where previous German-Jewish translations had sought to render the Bible into a vernacular to which its readers could respond with familiarity, the Buber-Rosenzweig translation aimed to shock its readers by the strangeness of its language, a kind of invented Hebraic-German, a language no one had ever spoken, so as to force the reader to hear the text anew.[79] To this end, the translators focused upon *Leitwörter*, literally, "theme-words," by which they meant "the repeating of word-stems in the German translation where identical roots of words appear in the original Hebrew."[80] These repeating sounds—the translation was meant to be read aloud—would replicate the rhythmic spokenness of the original text, and these auditory repetitions pointed to its underlying meaning. At the same time, the translators also tried to retain the primal meanings of root words; thus, *mizbeiaḥ* (from the root *z-b-ḥ*, "to slaughter"), though usually translated as "altar," became *Schlachtstatt*, "slaughter-site."[81] All these translational practices were meant to "de-familiarize" the text—a strategy that, as scholars have noted, epitomized the work's essentially "modernist" character.[82]

The modernism of the Buber-Rosenzweig translation is reflected in its material shape, here seen on the opening page of the Genesis volume (fig. 4.12). The text is printed in a clear modern font, not in the *Fraktur* type used in earlier German Bibles, with wide, clean margins and no chapter or verse markings. The absence of paratexts and commentaries signified both the Bible's explicit disengagement from any exegetical tradition (although Buber and Rosenzweig did consult Jewish commentaries as they translated, albeit unsystematically), and the translators' desire that the reader directly engage and hear the text without mediation.[83] To emphasize the Bible's spokenness, Buber and Rosenzweig laid out the text in "cola," lines of irregular length that look like free verse but are in fact approximations of the length of a breath.[84]

The sight alone of this page—unlike that of any other Bible—was meant to jolt the reader into engaging with its presence. Where Mendelssohn had used page layout to convey the image of tradition and thereby make familiar new and unfamiliar contents, Buber and Rosenzweig made material shape serve the exact opposite function: to estrange its reader from the Bible as the book they had always known, to shock them into reading the text anew, and thus turn that moment of reading into an occasion for a revelatory experience.

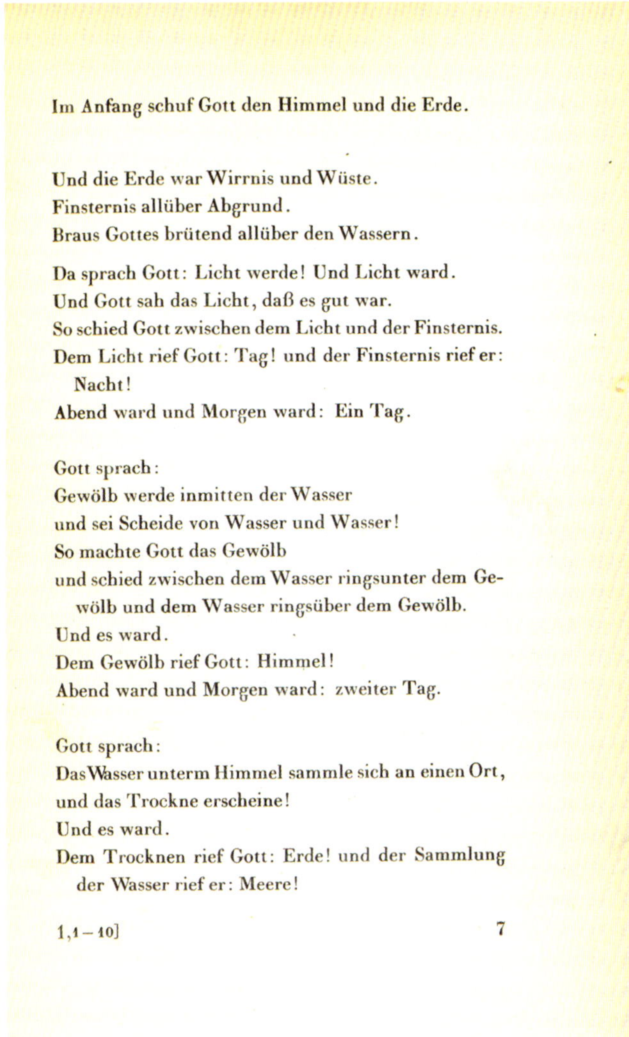
Im Anfang schuf Gott den Himmel und die Erde.

Und die Erde war Wirrnis und Wüste.
Finsternis allüber Abgrund.
Braus Gottes brütend allüber den Wassern.

Da sprach Gott: Licht werde! Und Licht ward.
Und Gott sah das Licht, daß es gut war.
So schied Gott zwischen dem Licht und der Finsternis.
Dem Licht rief Gott: Tag! und der Finsternis rief er:
Nacht!
Abend ward und Morgen ward: Ein Tag.

Gott sprach:
Gewölb werde inmitten der Wasser
und sei Scheide von Wasser und Wasser!
So machte Gott das Gewölb
und schied zwischen dem Wasser ringsunter dem Gewölb und dem Wasser ringsüber dem Gewölb.
Und es ward.
Dem Gewölb rief Gott: Himmel!
Abend ward und Morgen ward: zweiter Tag.

Gott sprach:
Das Wasser unterm Himmel sammle sich an einen Ort,
und das Trockne erscheine!
Und es ward.
Dem Trocknen rief Gott: Erde! und der Sammlung der Wasser rief er: Meere!

1,1–10] 7

4.12
Martin Buber with Franz Rosenzweig, *Das Buch Im Anfang* (*Die Schrift* I) (Berlin: Verlag Lambert Schneider, n.d.), p. 1. Courtesy of the Stern-Hellerstein Family Collection.

The radical course that translation took in Germany was unparalleled in other European countries, but the Mendelssohn translation did spawn translations into other European vernaculars, including both Italian and French.[85] The most interesting of the post-Mendelssohn translations were those into English, both those done in England itself and in the United States. In England, David Levi (1742–1801) launched an especially courageous and spirited attack on Kennicott, Lowth, and what he called the "superficial tinsel" of their emended translations, and eventually issued his own edition of the Pentateuch. In fact, Levi's translation was really the Authorized English Version (also known as the King James Bible) with Levi's corrections and notes explaining how he had removed the most egregious Christian elements in the translation.[86] Still, as one scholar has pointed out, the willingness on the part of staunch English Jews like Levi to use the Authorized Version despite its Christian provenance offers a striking contrast to the case of German Jewry.[87] For all their desire to effect the acculturation of Jews within enlightened German society, Jewish figures like Mendelssohn rejected the existing German translations by Christians as unfit for Jews and insisted upon producing their own Jewish translations. In contrast, the Anglo-Jewish community appeared to have felt that the Authorized Version was "the common property of Jews and Christians alike," and that an "improved version"—namely, one that removed the offending elements—was not only acceptable but in the interest of all English society, Jews and Christians alike. Indeed, this comfort level with the Bible of their host culture persisted into the twentieth century, when Chief Rabbi of the British Empire Joseph H. Hertz (1872–1946) produced his *Pentateuch and Haftorahs* (1937), an edition that for much of the twentieth century was "*the* Jewish lens for viewing the Biblical heritage of the Israel [*sic*] people in the English-language world."[88] In his commentary, Hertz adamantly defended traditional Jewish beliefs and vociferously polemicized against modern biblical criticism as "a perversion of history and a desecration of religion."[89] Even so, in the first edition of his Pentateuch, Hertz had no problem reprinting the Revised Authorized Version as the basis for his commentary.[90]

The attitude of American Jewry toward the kind of Bible translations they thought appropriate for themselves was very different. In the preface to the second edition of his *Twenty-Four Books of the Holy Scriptures* (1856), Isaac Leeser (1806–1868) boldly declared that "it would be a species of mental slavery to rely forever upon the arbitrary decree of a deceased King of England, who certainly was no prophet for the correct understanding of Scripture."[91] Leeser, the leading Jewish religious and intellectual leader in the United States during the antebellum period, published the first vocalized Hebrew Bible in America (1845) and, some nine years later, virtually single-handedly, the first translation of the complete Bible by an American Jew. Using the Zunz Bible as his self-proclaimed model, Leeser's translation was openly apologetic and polemical.[92] It drew heavily upon classical Jewish sources, especially Rashi; it admitted being "Orthodox" in its understanding of the Bible and sought to refute Christian interpretations that Leeser believed erroneous.[93] The translation quickly attained almost canonical status among Jews in America and was doubtless one of the major cultural accomplishments of nineteenth-century American Jewish culture.

Even so, Leeser's translation was marred by many textual inaccuracies and literary infelicities. By the end of the century, there was a widespread recognition of the need for a new modern translation that would respond to the upsurge of interest in the Bible that infused American culture at the time among both Christians and Jews. The call for a new Jewish translation also intensified after the appearance in England in 1881 of the Revised Version of the King James Bible; this version was produced by many of the most important

Christian Bible scholars of the day, and it made the Leeser Bible look especially outdated. After a number of false starts, the Jewish Publication Society of America finally agreed to undertake full sponsorship of the project, and a leading American Jewish Bible scholar, Max L. Margolis, was hired to be the general editor.[94] The original plan was for Margolis to revise the new Anglo-Protestant Revised Version for Jewish readers—no one believed that a single scholar, even someone as competent as Margolis, could compete with a committee of the world's greatest Bible scholars—but Margolis single-handedly introduced more than forty thousand changes into the text and for all practical purposes produced an original translation, which was finally published in 1917 as *The Holy Scriptures, according to the Masoretic Text: A New Translation with the Aid of Previous Versions and with Constant Consultation of Jewish Sources*. As its preface stated, the new translation aimed "to combine the spirit of Jewish tradition with the results of biblical scholarship, ancient, medieval, and modern . . . and gives to the Jewish world a translation of the Scriptures done by men imbued with the Jewish consciousness."[95] This edition was indeed the first modern scholarly Jewish translation of the Bible.

Alas, the more modern the translation, the briefer its shelf life. Less than forty years later, in 1955, the Jewish Publication Society (JPS) appointed a committee chaired by Harry M. Orlinsky, an eminent Bible scholar (who had experience in Bible translation from working on the recently completed American Protestant Revised Standard Version) to produce a new translation that would be both stylistically "intelligible" to contemporary readers and "intrinsically" Jewish, and that would reflect the massive advances in biblical scholarship that had taken place in the years since 1917.[96] In 1962, the Torah volume appeared, and in 1985, the entire Bible in a single volume. Its title—*TANAKH: A New Translation of the Holy Scriptures according to the Traditional Hebrew Text*—bore witness to its identity as a Jewish translation.

The JPS translation is, at least for the present, the most widely used translation in the English-speaking world. Even so, it has not realized its ambition to become the universal Bible of English-speaking Jewry, either in America or abroad, at least for synagogue use, which is where most Jews today are likely to encounter the Bible. In fact, it probably does not equal the universality of either the Leeser or the 1917 JPS translations. Since 1962, the JPS Torah translation has been appropriated and revised by the Reform and Conservative movements, each of which has produced denominational volumes for synagogue use with commentaries appropriate to their theologies. The Orthodox community, in turn, has largely rejected the JPS *TANAKH* in favor of its own translations, which claim to be entirely based upon classical Jewish commentaries.[97] At the same time, a number of sophisticated translations of the Hebrew Bible by individual American Jews have sought to appeal to the unaffiliated population, to secular and cultural Jews, as well as to non-Jewish readers with a literary, not religious, interest in the Bible.[98] The almost sectarian variety

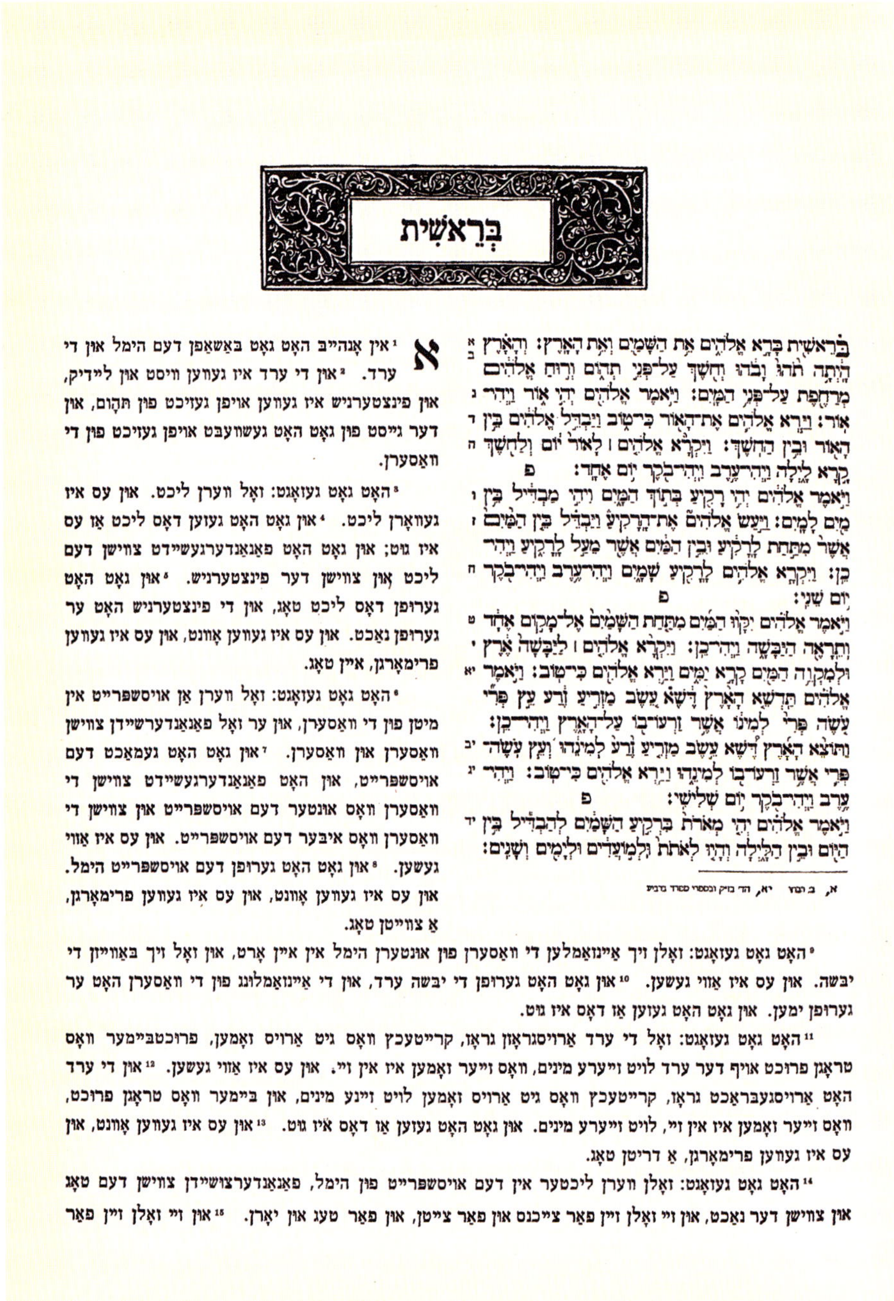

בְּרֵאשִׁית

א ב בְּרֵאשִׁית בָּרָא אֱלֹהִים אֵת הַשָּׁמַיִם וְאֵת הָאָרֶץ׃ וְהָאָרֶץ
הָיְתָה תֹהוּ וָבֹהוּ וְחֹשֶׁךְ עַל־פְּנֵי תְהוֹם וְרוּחַ אֱלֹהִים
ג מְרַחֶפֶת עַל־פְּנֵי הַמָּיִם׃ וַיֹּאמֶר אֱלֹהִים יְהִי אוֹר וַיְהִי־
ד אוֹר׃ וַיַּרְא אֱלֹהִים אֶת־הָאוֹר כִּי־טוֹב וַיַּבְדֵּל אֱלֹהִים בֵּין
ה הָאוֹר וּבֵין הַחֹשֶׁךְ׃ וַיִּקְרָא אֱלֹהִים ׀ לָאוֹר יוֹם וְלַחֹשֶׁךְ
קָרָא לָיְלָה וַיְהִי־עֶרֶב וַיְהִי־בֹקֶר יוֹם אֶחָד׃ פ
ו וַיֹּאמֶר אֱלֹהִים יְהִי רָקִיעַ בְּתוֹךְ הַמָּיִם וִיהִי מַבְדִּיל בֵּין
ז מַיִם לָמָיִם׃ וַיַּעַשׂ אֱלֹהִים אֶת־הָרָקִיעַ וַיַּבְדֵּל בֵּין הַמַּיִם
אֲשֶׁר מִתַּחַת לָרָקִיעַ וּבֵין הַמַּיִם אֲשֶׁר מֵעַל לָרָקִיעַ וַיְהִי־
ח כֵן׃ וַיִּקְרָא אֱלֹהִים לָרָקִיעַ שָׁמָיִם וַיְהִי־עֶרֶב וַיְהִי־בֹקֶר
יוֹם שֵׁנִי׃ פ
ט וַיֹּאמֶר אֱלֹהִים יִקָּווּ הַמַּיִם מִתַּחַת הַשָּׁמַיִם אֶל־מָקוֹם אֶחָד
י וְתֵרָאֶה הַיַּבָּשָׁה וַיְהִי־כֵן׃ וַיִּקְרָא אֱלֹהִים ׀ לַיַּבָּשָׁה אֶרֶץ
יא וּלְמִקְוֵה הַמַּיִם קָרָא יַמִּים וַיַּרְא אֱלֹהִים כִּי־טוֹב׃ וַיֹּאמֶר
אֱלֹהִים תַּדְשֵׁא הָאָרֶץ דֶּשֶׁא עֵשֶׂב מַזְרִיעַ זֶרַע עֵץ פְּרִי
עֹשֶׂה פְּרִי לְמִינוֹ אֲשֶׁר זַרְעוֹ־בוֹ עַל־הָאָרֶץ וַיְהִי־כֵן׃
יב וַתּוֹצֵא הָאָרֶץ דֶּשֶׁא עֵשֶׂב מַזְרִיעַ זֶרַע לְמִינֵהוּ וְעֵץ עֹשֶׂה־
יג פְּרִי אֲשֶׁר זַרְעוֹ־בוֹ לְמִינֵהוּ וַיַּרְא אֱלֹהִים כִּי־טוֹב׃ וַיְהִי־
עֶרֶב וַיְהִי־בֹקֶר יוֹם שְׁלִישִׁי׃ פ
יד וַיֹּאמֶר אֱלֹהִים יְהִי מְאֹרֹת בִּרְקִיעַ הַשָּׁמַיִם לְהַבְדִּיל בֵּין
הַיּוֹם וּבֵין הַלָּיְלָה וְהָיוּ לְאֹתֹת וּלְמוֹעֲדִים וּלְיָמִים וְשָׁנִים׃

א, ב רבתי   יא, הד׳ בזיק וכספרי ספרד מרביע

א 1 אין אָנהייב האָט גאָט באַשאַפן דעם הימל און די ערד. 2 און די ערד איז געווען וויסט און ליידיק, און פינצטערניש איז געווען אויפן געזיכט פון תּהום, און דער גייסט פון גאָט האָט געשוועבט אויפן געזיכט פון די וואַסערן.

3 האָט גאָט געזאָגט: זאָל ווערן ליכט. און עס איז געוואָרן ליכט. 4 און גאָט האָט געזען דאָס ליכט אַז עס איז גוט; און גאָט האָט פאַנאַנדערגעשיידט צווישן דעם ליכט און צווישן דער פינצטערניש. 5 און גאָט האָט גערופן דאָס ליכט טאָג, און די פינצטערניש האָט ער גערופן נאַכט. און עס איז געווען אָוונט, און עס איז געווען פרימאָרגן, איין טאָג.

6 האָט גאָט געזאָגט: זאָל ווערן אַן אויסשפּרייט אין מיטן פון די וואַסערן, און ער זאָל פאַנאַנדערשיידן צווישן וואַסערן און וואַסערן. 7 און גאָט האָט געמאַכט דעם אויסשפּרייט, און האָט פאַנאַנדערגעשיידט צווישן די וואַסערן וואָס אונטער דעם אויסשפּרייט און צווישן די וואַסערן וואָס איבער דעם אויסשפּרייט. און עס איז אַזוי געשען. 8 און גאָט האָט גערופן דעם אויסשפּרייט הימל. און עס איז געווען אָוונט, און עס איז געווען פרימאָרגן, אַ צווייטן טאָג.

9 האָט גאָט געזאָגט: זאָלן זיך אײַנזאַמלען די וואַסערן פון אונטערן הימל אין איין אָרט, און זאָל זיך באַווייזן די יבשה. און עס איז אַזוי געשען. 10 און גאָט האָט גערופן די יבשה ערד, און די אײַנזאַמלונג פון די וואַסערן האָט ער גערופן ימען. און גאָט האָט געזען אַז דאָס איז גוט.

11 האָט גאָט געזאָגט: זאָל די ערד אַרויסגראָזן גראָז, קרײַטעכץ וואָס גיט אַרויס זאָמען, פרוכטביימער וואָס טראָגן פרוכט אויף דער ערד לויט זייערע מינים, וואָס זייער זאָמען איז אין זיי. און עס איז אַזוי געשען. 12 און די ערד האָט אַרויסגעבראַכט גראָז, קרײַטעכץ וואָס גיט אַרויס זאָמען לויט זײַנע מינים, און ביימער וואָס טראָגן פרוכט, וואָס זייער זאָמען איז אין זיי, לויט זייערע מינים. און גאָט האָט געזען אַז דאָס איז גוט. 13 און עס איז געווען אָוונט, און עס איז געווען פרימאָרגן, אַ דריטן טאָג.

14 האָט גאָט געזאָגט: זאָלן ווערן ליכטער אין דעם אויסשפּרייט פון הימל, פאַנאַנדערצושיידן צווישן דעם טאָג און צווישן דער נאַכט, און זיי זאָלן זײַן פאַר צייכנס און פאַר צייטן, און פאַר טעג און יאָרן. 15 און זיי זאָלן זײַן פאַר

4.13 *Torah, Nevi'im, Ketuvim* (Gen. 1:1–10), New York: Yehoash Farlag, 1941. Widener Library, Harvard University.

of contemporary American Jewish Bible translations mirrors Jewry's fragmentation in contemporary American society.

I will conclude this survey by mentioning the first "modern" translation of the Bible into Yiddish, which appeared only in the twentieth century. Its author, Solomon Bloomgarden (1870–1927), better known by his pen name Yehoash, began his project of translating the Bible into Yiddish in the first decade of the century, in the heyday of secularist Yiddish cultural nationalism.[99] Dissatisfied with his initial work, Yehoash began the translation anew several years later, and finally published it in the years between 1926 and 1936 (much of the work, in other words, after his death). This initial publication contained only the Yiddish text of the translation, set out in a single column across the page in a fairly modern Yiddish typeface; there was no Hebrew on the page. Yehoash's stated purpose, however, was not to replace the Hebrew Bible with a Yiddish one but, as he explained in a preface published later, to create a work that would serve as the "backbone" for a new high Yiddish literature, as a classic source of secularist Yiddish culture, its language a synthesis of the Yiddish language in all its stages and dialects.[100] In other words, Yehoash wanted his Bible to be a literary and cultural monument, not a religious document, and he wanted it to do for Yiddish what the King James Bible had done for English literary culture.[101]

Even so, when the translation was republished in 1941, it had a decidedly different shape and meaning, as can be seen in its page layout (fig. 4.13). The Masoretic Hebrew text of the Bible (with cantillation notes) was restored to the center of the page with the Yiddish translation surrounding it (like the Targum) in a slightly smaller font. For all the author's radical secularizing ambitions, the translation survived in a page format that is instantly recognizable as that of a traditional Jewish Bible. Yehoash's freestanding secular monument, the foundation for a new Yiddish culture, had resumed its role as a supplement to the Hebrew Bible. Tradition in the form of page layout, one might say, trumped the forces of secular modernization.

As this brief survey has demonstrated, the history of Jewish Bible translations since the sixteenth century provides a virtual index of the differing responses of Jewish communities throughout the world toward the larger host cultures in which the translations were produced. The responses embodied in these translations are analogous to the ways in which, before the sixteenth century, the material shapes of the Hebrew Bible reflected the varied responses of different Jewish communities to the gentile host cultures in which the Jewish producers of the Bibles lived. For all the differences between manuscript and print, similar dynamics have fueled the history of the Jewish Bible even in its translations. Never simply surrogates or replacements for the Hebrew Bible, translation has always been a medium through which Jews have participated in the process of cultural exchange between themselves and their many diasporas.

The Zionist Bible

From its inception, Zionism seized upon the Bible as an antidote to the "Talmudism" that, it claimed, had defined and dominated diasporic Jewish culture for two thousand years. In Zionist literary culture, Biblicism once again became a stylistic ideal for the newly reborn Hebrew language and its burgeoning literature. Zionists exploited biblical geography for a vision of an idealized homeland rooted in ancient landscapes. In cultural Zionist circles, particularly in Germany, the Bible became an active source of artistic inspiration for artists like E. M. Lilien (1874–1927). Working in the distinctive style of *Jugendstil*, German Art Nouveau, Lilien created a utopian biblical landscape featuring monumental Grecian-like figures posed heroically against dramatic backgrounds, and highly eroticized portraits of naked women (and men) seductively gesturing toward a symbolic future. The result was like nothing that had ever appeared in a Jewish Bible.

Fig. 4.14 comes from Lilien's three-volume Bible in German translation, published in 1908, the first modern Jewish Bible illustrated by a Jewish artist (to the best of my knowledge).[102] The intensely black-and-white, double-page opening illustrates the expulsion of Adam and Eve from the Garden of Eden. Note, however, the fearsome angel standing at the gates of Paradise, clearly a bearded likeness of Theodor Herzl (whose iconic portrait Lilien had drawn in a widely disseminated print), with a very manly sword dramatically thrust down between his thighs. By presenting the biblical scene in this way, Lilien effectively allegorized the expulsion as a more modern story of the exile of the Jews from Zion into the Diaspora. Herzl, representing Zionism, would oversee their reentrance to Paradise just as he oversaw their departure. In this way, Lilien effectively turned the Bible into a politicized document in the service of Zionism, still another aspect of the Jewish cultural Bible.

In British Palestine, the newly founded Bezalel School of Arts and Crafts, under the direction of Boris Schatz (1866–1932), continued on Lilien's path and cultivated an idiosyncratic Orientalist biblical style. Schatz himself illustrated editions of the Song of Songs and Ruth as well as a printed Esther scroll.[103] The most striking Zionist accomplishment in terms of the history of the Bible as a book was, however, the invention of a new Hebrew typography. Early on, even before the establishment of the state in 1949, a number of figures in the Zionist leadership had sought to initiate production of a new edition of the Hebrew Bible. In the 1940s, these figures approached Eliyahu Koren (born Korngold, 1907–2001), one of the leading designers and typographers in British Mandate Palestine, with a request to design a new font for the Bible.[104] The initiative never came to fruition, but Koren continued to pursue its realization on his own, and in 1962, he finally published *The Koren TaNaKh*, the first Hebrew Bible since the incunable period to be designed, edited, printed, and bound wholly by Jews. "Israel is redeemed from shame," David Ben Gurion declared upon the publication of the book. The Koren Bible soon became the all

4.14 *Die Bücher der Bible, herausgegeben von F. Rahlwes; Zeichnungen von E. M. Lilien, nach der Übersetzung von [Eduard] Reuss* (Braunschweig: Georg Westermann, 1908), 1:40–41. Widener Library, Harvard University.

but official Bible of the state of Israel: presidents of Israel were sworn into office with it, and copies were distributed to all new inductees into the army.

The new font that Koren designed for the Bible, pictured in fig. 4.15, is indeed one of the most beautiful typefaces in the history of Jewish printing. Based on a medieval Sephardic square script, the font was both classical and modern, combining an astonishing clarity and elegance to produce a remarkably legible letter. By reinventing the medieval script, Koren simultaneously performed an act of cultural retrieval and produced a truly Israeli Bible distinguished by its typeface. In more explicitly polemical ways, Koren emphasized the Jewishness of his edition. He downplayed the division into chapters and verses because it was a Christian invention (even if it was eventually adopted by Jews); he restored the open and closed sections (*petuḥot* and *setumot*) and the *sedarim* as the primary organizational devices in the biblical text; and he printed the historical books—Samuel, Kings, and Chronicles—as single units (although, for the sake of his readers' convenience, he did not remove the divisions that Christians had placed to divide these books into two parts, e.g., 1 Samuel and 2 Samuel). As the reader will recall, the use of

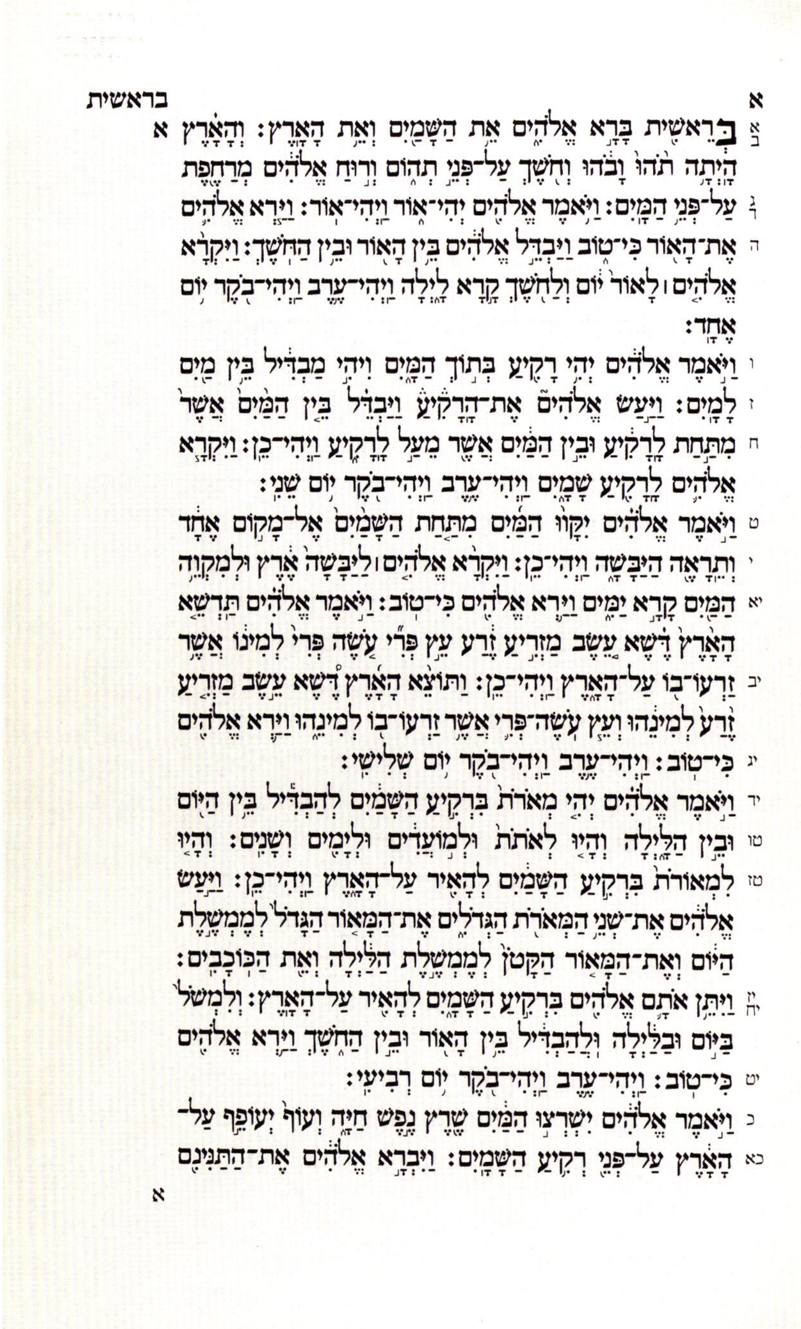

א בראשית

א ב בראשית ברא אלהים את השמים ואת הארץ: והארץ א
היתה תהו ובהו וחשך על־פני תהום ורוח אלהים מרחפת
ג ד על־פני המים: ויאמר אלהים יהי־אור ויהי־אור: וירא אלהים
ה את־האור כי־טוב ויבדל אלהים בין האור ובין החשך: ויקרא
אלהים לאור יום ולחשך קרא לילה ויהי־ערב ויהי־בקר יום
אחד:
ו ויאמר אלהים יהי רקיע בתוך המים ויהי מבדיל בין מים
ז למים: ויעש אלהים את־הרקיע ויבדל בין המים אשר
ח מתחת לרקיע ובין המים אשר מעל לרקיע ויהי־כן: ויקרא
אלהים לרקיע שמים ויהי־ערב ויהי־בקר יום שני:
ט ויאמר אלהים יקוו המים מתחת השמים אל־מקום אחד
י ותראה היבשה ויהי־כן: ויקרא אלהים ליבשה ארץ ולמקוה
יא המים קרא ימים וירא אלהים כי־טוב: ויאמר אלהים תדשא
הארץ דשא עשב מזריע זרע עץ פרי עשה פרי למינו אשר
יב זרעו־בו על־הארץ ויהי־כן: ותוצא הארץ דשא עשב מזריע
זרע למינהו ועץ עשה־פרי אשר זרעו־בו למינהו וירא אלהים
יג כי־טוב: ויהי־ערב ויהי־בקר יום שלישי:
יד ויאמר אלהים יהי מארת ברקיע השמים להבדיל בין היום
טו ובין הלילה והיו לאתת ולמועדים ולימים ושנים: והיו
טז למאורת ברקיע השמים להאיר על־הארץ ויהי־כן: ויעש
אלהים את־שני המארת הגדלים את־המאור הגדל לממשלת
היום ואת־המאור הקטן לממשלת הלילה ואת הכוכבים:
יז יח ויתן אתם אלהים ברקיע השמים להאיר על־הארץ: ולמשל
ביום ובלילה ולהבדיל בין האור ובין החשך וירא אלהים
יט כי־טוב: ויהי־ערב ויהי־בקר יום רביעי:
כ ויאמר אלהים ישרצו המים שרץ נפש חיה ועוף יעופף על־
כא הארץ על־פני רקיע השמים: ויברא אלהים את־התנינם

א

4.15 *Torah, Nevi'im, Ketuvim* (Gen. 1) (Jerusalem: Koren, 1965), p. 1. Widener Library, Harvard University.

these divisions in the Hebrew Bible was first introduced by a Jewish convert to Christianity, Felix Pratensis, in the First Rabbinic Bible published by Daniel Bomberg in 1517.

Koren's Bible was only one of many new Bible editions produced in the state of Israel. There have also appeared editions with new commentaries that have sought to convey a modern Jewish interpretation of the Bible drawing upon both traditional sources and contemporary biblical scholarship, as well as many school editions tailored to the Israeli educational curriculum. And now there is even a translation of the Bible into contemporary modern Hebrew (*'ivrit bat yameinu*), *Tanakh Ram*.[105] Laid out in parallel columns, with the biblical text on the right and modern Israeli Hebrew on the left, the edition acknowledges the unhappy fact that, for most Israelis today, biblical Hebrew is a foreign language.

The Rediscovery of the Ancient Manuscripts

The story of the modern Hebrew Bible—in the state of Israel and the contemporary Diaspora—is not limited to translations, new editions, and commentaries. There is another part to that story that is less known: the rediscovery of the ancient manuscripts and their impact upon the Jewish Bible.

This narrative begins long before the establishment of the state of Israel. As we have seen, already in the late eighteenth century, the medieval heritage of the Hebrew Bible was being retrieved by Christian Bible scholars in Europe. In the eighteenth century in England, Benjamin Kennicott collected and collated some six hundred manuscripts in search of variants, while in Italy the scholar and bibliophile Giovanni Bernardo De Rossi (1742–1831) amassed an impressive collection of Bibles that he, too, studied for variants. The manuscripts these scholars studied, however, were nearly all late codices, no earlier than the thirteenth century, and the variants they contained typically were either scribal errors or those copied from previous errors made in transcription.

This situation changed radically in the middle of the nineteenth century, when an entirely new corpus of Hebrew Bible manuscripts came to light that was truly early. In the 1840s, the Karaite leader, polemicist, collector, and reputed forger, Avraam Samuilovich Firkovich (1787–1875), began to travel through the Near East and Crimea in search of documents and artifacts to support claims that Firkovich (and other Karaite leaders) wished to make for the antiquity of the Karaites as the original Israelites. In the course of his travels, Firkovich came across numerous early Hebrew manuscripts (and fragments of lost codices) and managed to persuade their owners to give them to him as "a donation."[106] Among the horde of manuscripts Firkovich amassed were many sections and fragments of early tenth- and eleventh-century Masoretic Bibles and one complete Masoretic Bible, still the earliest existing complete copy of the entire Hebrew Bible. This Bible was written, probably in the land of Israel, in 1008–9 and contains the complete *masorah magna* and *parva*. Today it is known as the Leningrad Codex (or, among scholars, by its shelf mark, St. Petersburg Heb. MS 1 B 19a).

In 1862–63, Firkovich sold his collection, the greatest collection of its kind, to the Imperial Public Library in Saint Petersburg, today the National Library of Russia, where it is known today as the First Firkovich Collection (because he later sold them a second collection). After Firkovich's collection became part of the Imperial Library, word of its existence gradually spread; among the Western scholars who heard of it was a highly accomplished German Semitic philologist, Paul Kahle (1875–1964). In 1925, Kahle was in Leningrad studying Hebrew Bible manuscripts from the Firkovich Collection—Kahle was particularly interested in Babylonian Masoretic texts—when he received a letter from the eminent biblicist and editor of the *Biblia Hebraica*, Rudolph Kittel, asking his advice as to which Bible text he should use in preparing a new edition of the *Biblia Hebraica*, which was already considered the standard critical edition by most scholars.[107] In the first two editions, Kittel had based his text on Jacob ben Ḥayyim ibn Adoniyahu's Second Rabbinic Bible of 1525. As it happened, Kahle had just discovered the Leningrad Codex for himself and, convinced of its status as a trustworthy representative of the Ben Asher tradition, he proposed to Kittel that he base his new edition on it. Kittel agreed, and with the publication of the third edition of *Biblia Hebraica* in 1937, for the first time in more than four hundred years, the Leningrad Codex replaced Ibn Adoniyahu's Second Rabbinic Bible as the definitive scholarly text of the Hebrew Bible.

In the late 1940s, the Dead Sea Scrolls were discovered. As the earliest fragments of the Hebrew Bible known to scholars, they have almost totally transformed our understanding of the early development of the Hebrew text. The data culled from the scrolls has, equally importantly, given us a glimpse into the world of early Jewish scribal practice. That knowledge has in turn reshaped our ideas about the history of the Bible as a material text. Much of that knowledge underlies my discussion of the early history of the Torah scroll in chapter 1. Indeed, the very possibility of writing a material history of the Hebrew Bible was enabled by the Qumran discoveries.

In the late 1950s, the *Biblia Hebraica* was revised yet again to incorporate the many variants found in the biblical texts recovered from the scrolls. This edition, known as *Biblia Hebraica Stuttgartensia* or *BHS* (1969–77), included for the first time a complete edited text of the Masorah based on the Masorah in the Leningrad Codex. With this edition, the contents of the Second Rabbinic Bible were fully replaced. Currently, a fifth edition, the *Biblia Hebraica Quinta* (*BHQ*), is in production, with several volumes already in print, thus further consolidating the authority of the Leningrad Codex.[108] Fig. 4.16 is the first page of the book of Ruth, the first volume of *BHQ* to be published (1997). Unlike previous editions of *Biblia Hebraica*, whose editors were mainly German Protestants, *BHQ*'s editorial board is truly international, with scholars from Spain, England, the United States, and Israel; its board also includes (for the first time) Jews and Catholics. *BHS*'s text

RUTH רות

1 וַיְהִי בִּימֵי שְׁפֹט הַשֹּׁפְטִים וַיְהִי רָעָב בָּאָרֶץ וַיֵּלֶךְ אִישׁ מִבֵּית לֶחֶם ה̇ . ב̇ חד מל̇ וחד חס̇
2 יְהוּדָה לָגוּר בִּשְׂדֵי מוֹאָב הוּא וְאִשְׁתּוֹ וּשְׁנֵי בָנָיו׃ וְשֵׁם הָאִישׁ ל̇
אֱלִימֶלֶךְ וְשֵׁם אִשְׁתּוֹ נָעֳמִי וְשֵׁם שְׁנֵי־בָנָיו ׀ מַחְלוֹן וְכִלְיוֹן אֶפְרָתִים
3 מִבֵּית לֶחֶם יְהוּדָה וַיָּבֹאוּ שְׂדֵי־מוֹאָב וַיִּהְיוּ־שָׁם׃ וַיָּמָת אֱלִימֶלֶךְ
4 אִישׁ נָעֳמִי וַתִּשָּׁאֵר הִיא וּשְׁנֵי בָנֶיהָ׃ וַיִּשְׂאוּ לָהֶם נָשִׁים מֹאֲבִיּוֹת שֵׁם ב̇ . מ̇ג̇ . ל̇ וחס̇
5 הָאַחַת עָרְפָּה וְשֵׁם הַשֵּׁנִית רוּת וַיֵּשְׁבוּ שָׁם כְּעֶשֶׂר שָׁנִים׃ וַיָּמוּתוּ ל̇
גַם־שְׁנֵיהֶם מַחְלוֹן וְכִלְיוֹן וַתִּשָּׁאֵר הָאִשָּׁה מִשְּׁנֵי יְלָדֶיהָ וּמֵאִישָׁהּ׃ ל̇
6 וַתָּקָם הִיא וְכַלֹּתֶיהָ וַתָּשָׁב מִשְּׂדֵי מוֹאָב כִּי שָׁמְעָה בִּשְׂדֵה מוֹאָב ל̇ וחס̇ . ב̇ כתב ה
7 כִּי־פָקַד יְהוָה אֶת־עַמּוֹ לָתֵת לָהֶם לָחֶם׃ וַתֵּצֵא מִן־הַמָּקוֹם אֲשֶׁר
הָיְתָה־שָׁמָּה וּשְׁתֵּי כַלֹּתֶיהָ עִמָּהּ וַתֵּלַכְנָה בַדֶּרֶךְ לָשׁוּב אֶל־אֶרֶץ ב̇ חד מל̇
8 יְהוּדָה׃ וַתֹּאמֶר נָעֳמִי לִשְׁתֵּי כַלֹּתֶיהָ לֵכְנָה שֹּׁבְנָה אִשָּׁה לְבֵית אִמָּהּ ב̇ . ב̇ . ב̇ בנתי בנתי
9 יַעֲשֶׂה יְהוָה עִמָּכֶם חֶסֶד כַּאֲשֶׁר עֲשִׂיתֶם עִם־הַמֵּתִים וְעִמָּדִי׃ יִתֵּן יעשׂ ק̇
יְהוָה לָכֶם וּמְצֶאןָ מְנוּחָה אִשָּׁה בֵּית אִישָׁהּ וַתִּשַּׁק לָהֶן וַתִּשֶּׂאנָה ב̇

[1:1] תרין פסוק̇ מיחדין ולית זוגה ויהי רעב בארץ ב̇ בטע̇ וירד אברם . וילך איש :o:

1:1 בִּימֵי שְׁפֹט הַשֹּׁפְטִים 4QRuth[a] G[Mss] (V) (T) | ἐν τῷ κρίνειν τοὺς κριτάς G | ܒܝܘ̈ܡܝ ܕܝ̈ܢܐ S (facil-synt) ✣ • וּשְׁנֵי בָנָיו׃ 4QRuth[a] 4QRuth[b] G[Mss] V T | καὶ οἱ υἱοὶ αὐτοῦ G S (implic) • **2** וְשֵׁם[1] 4QRuth[a] G S T | ש]ם 4QRuth[b] | *ipse vocabatur* V (transl) • אֱלִימֶלֶךְ G[Mss] V S T | Ἀβιμέλεχ G • וַיִּהְיוּ־ G T | וישבו 4QRuth[a] (assim-1:4?) | *morabantur* V (transl) | ܠܡܥܡܪ S (transl) ✣ • **3** אִישׁ נָעֳמִי G V S T | *vir eius* La • **5** מִשְּׁנֵי יְלָדֶיהָ וּמֵאִישָׁהּ׃ 4QRuth[a] V T | ἀπὸ τοῦ ἀνδρὸς αὐτῆς καὶ ἀπὸ τῶν δύο υἱῶν αὐτῆς G S (harm-chron) ✣ • **6** וְכַלֹּתֶיהָ T | prec δύο G (V) S • **7** בַדֶּרֶךְ G V (T) | > La S ✣ • **8** לִשְׁתֵּי G[Mss] T | > G S | V (indet) • אִמָּהּ G T | τοῦ πατρὸς αὐτῆς G[Mss] (assim-cultur) | *matris vestrae* La V (assim-ctext) | *patris vestri* V[Mss] (assim-cultur + assim-ctext) | ܐܒܘܟܝܢ S (assim-cultur + assim-ctext) • יַעֲשֶׂה | יעשׂה M[ket] | יַעַשׂ M[qere] | G V S T (indet) • **9** לָכֶם G V | foll ἔλεον G[L] S (ampl) | foll ... אגר טב שלים T (midr) ✣ •

4.16 *Biblia Hebraica Quinta: Megillot* (Ruth 1:1–9) (Stuttgart: Deutsche Bibelgesellschaft, 1997), p. 1. Widener Library, Harvard University.

has also been used in many other editions, including the *JPS TANAKH*, thereby making the text in the Leningrad Codex the most widely used in the world.

But the story of recovery of the past does not end here. One biblical manuscript escaped Firkovich's clutches (though not for want of trying): *Keter Aram Tzova*, the Aleppo Codex, with whose story we began our history of the Hebrew Bible as a codex.[109] Since the early Middle Ages, Jewish scholars have considered *Keter Aram Tzova* to be the early biblical codex with the most accurate documentation of the Tiberian Masoretic textual tradition, and therefore representative of the most accurate biblical text. The reason for the preference shown to the Aleppo Codex is that it is the only early Masoretic Bible in which the biblical text in the codex and the accompanying Masorah almost entirely agree.[110] (In contrast, there are hundreds of discrepancies between text and Masorah in the Leningrad Codex, in addition to many visible corrections on its pages.)[111] The care and accuracy with which *Keter Aram Tzova* was written have been called virtually "super-human."[112] Indeed, according to Moshe Goshen-Gottstein, the Aleppo Codex was "the greatest event in the history of the Tiberian Bible text," the earliest complete codex of the Bible to incorporate the full Masoretic system perfected by the family of Aaron Ben Asher.[113] This unique achievement was recognized even in its own time by having the title *al-Taj*, "the crown," bestowed upon it. This Arabic title was later translated into Hebrew as *Ha-Keter*, hence its present title, *Keter Aram Tzova,* "the Crown of Aleppo."[114] Today there is almost complete agreement among scholars that the Aleppo Codex was the Bible to which Maimonides referred as the most accurate copy in his famous statement in the *Mishneh Torah* (*Hilkhot Sefer Torah*, chap. 8).[115] To be sure, the Aleppo Codex is currently missing most of the Pentateuch and the last books of the Writings. The Leningrad Codex still remains the earliest complete Hebrew Bible.[116]

In our account of *Keter Aram Tzova*'s history, we related the amazing story of how, in the 1950s, the codex was spirited out of Syria to the state of Israel. A large part of the reason why Israeli scholars, including Yitzhak Ben-Zvi, the state's first president (who had seen the codex in Aleppo years earlier), were so eager to bring the *Keter* to Israel was their hope that it might provide a basis for a new scholarly edition of the Hebrew Bible. Almost immediately upon the Bible's arrival in 1958, this project was put into action with the establishment of the Hebrew University Bible Project (HUBP), whose purpose was to produce that definitive edition.[117] In addition to using *Keter Aram Tzova* as its base text, HUBP also differs from *BHQ* in recording and taking account of citations of biblical variants from rabbinic sources that have never appeared in any earlier modern critical edition or in *BHQ*.

And yet, in their material form, *BHQ* and the HUBP edition look remarkably similar, as one can easily see by juxtaposing their pages (figs. 4.16 and 4.17). They both share the page format of a typical modern scholarly critical edition whose manifest purpose is to represent to the reader the accurate text with all its variants. That page format, with the

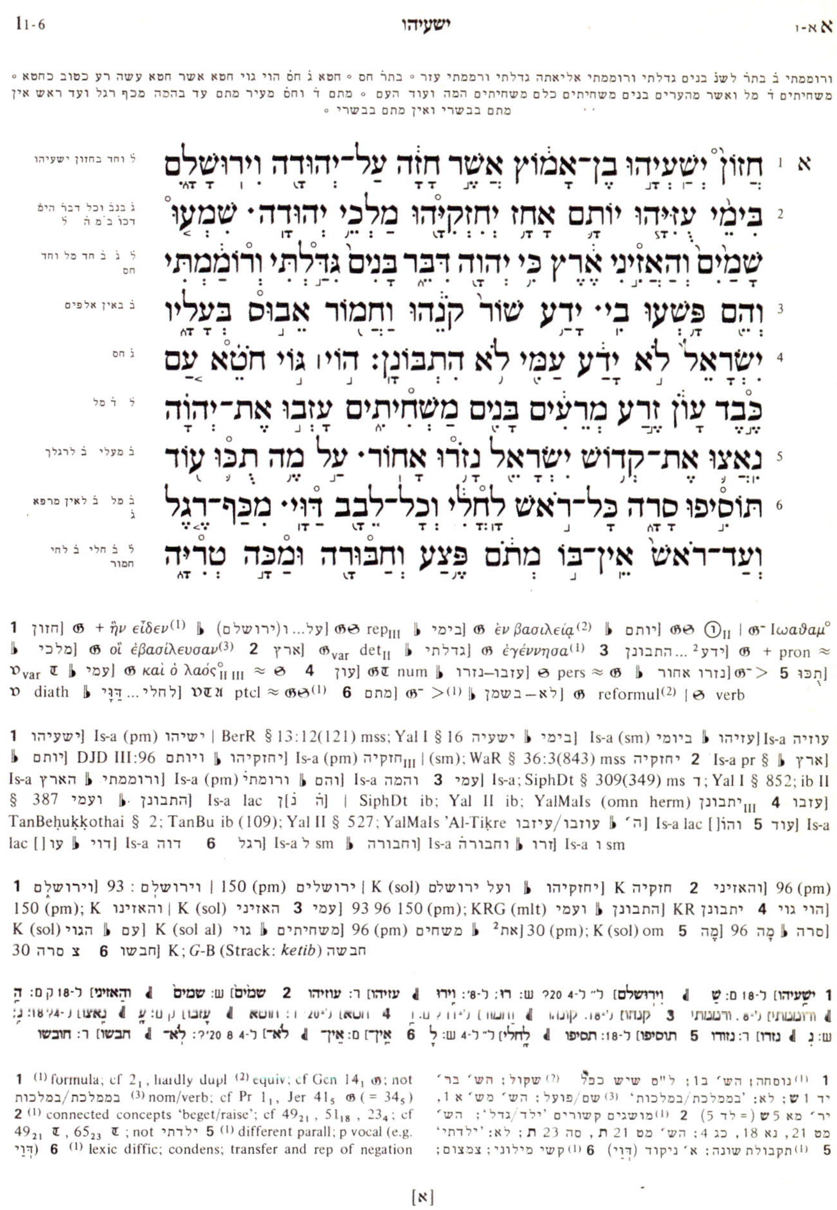

4.17 *The Hebrew University Bible* (Isa. 1:1–6), *The Book of Isaiah*, ed. Moshe H. Goshen-Gottstein (Jerusalem: Magnes, 1975), p. 1. Widener Library, Harvard University.

biblical text at the top of the page, critical apparatus beneath it, and notes at the bottom of the page, is a typical Western page format first developed for critical editions of classical Greek and Latin texts. The page format is neither Jewish nor Christian. And the rivalry between the two Bibles continues.

And so we end our history in the contemporary moment with a contest between two competing scholarly editions, each based on a different early Tiberian Masoretic codex, Leningrad and Aleppo. For anyone except a scholar with an intense interest in the Masorah and its bearing on the biblical text, the differences between the two codices are so minor—mainly matters of accentuation or slightly different orthography or vocalization—that they might well appear ridiculous. But the two Bibles are nonetheless different, and their differences continue to pose the question: which one should serve as the basis for the Bible? This question, which revolves around philological and textual issues, is complicated by the fact that the rivalry between the two editions, even if it sometimes seems almost denominational, can no longer be characterized in Jewish-Christian terms. Jews are among the editors of BHQ, and important Jewish editions—the *JPS TANAKH* is the most prominent example—have used the Leningrad Codex as their base text.[118] Yet however their rivalry is construed, its very existence testifies to the fact that, even today, the Hebrew Bible remains a book in contestation.

EPILOGUE

THE FUTURE OF THE JEWISH BIBLE

This book on the material history of the Jewish Bible is a child of its times: the digital age. I say this not only on account of the fact that the text of this book was written on a laptop computer, but because the scholarly field out of which this book emerged, the history of the book, came into existence with the glimmering of the digital age and the recognition that a new age of writing technology had begun. That awareness, along with the anxiety that accompanied it, led scholars to turn to the past to understand earlier changes in the technologies of writing and reading. They doubtless did this with the hope that studying the past might help in navigating the present transition. By appreciating the ways the book has changed, we might better understand the ways it *will* change. And so, a new scholarly field came into existence. And thus, too, the history of the Jewish book, and this book.

How will the digital text change the Jewish book? In the case of some classic Jewish books, the transition to an electronic text has already significantly, even radically, transformed them. Study of the Talmud has undergone massive changes. Now that its text, a massive work of some one and a half million words, has been digitalized, sophisticated search engines and databases have enabled all sorts of heretofore impossible textual analyses—locating parallel passages, searching for combinatory phrases and motifs—

which have changed our entire conception of how the Talmud evolved. Digitalized manuscripts dispersed in libraries and collections all over the world can now be compared on screen, and with the new technology, fragments of a single text can be virtually joined and thus restored to their original complete state. By looking at manuscripts and early printings on screen, students in even the most orthodox, antimodern *yeshivot* have been persuaded that sometimes a difficult text was difficult because it was simply incorrect.

In the cases of the prayer book and especially the Passover Haggadah, the changes wrought by the digital revolution have been even more widespread and have touched an even wider audience of Jews. Just google *homemade* or *do-it-yourself haggadah* and you will find numerous sites, including some that instruct users—laypersons—on how to make their own Haggadah. Anyone dissatisfied with the traditional text or wishing to make a more personal one can now do it on a laptop. So far there has been no proliferation of self-produced *siddurim*, but it is not difficult to foresee a time in the not distant future when any rabbi will be able to create a different service for his or her congregation every Sabbath morning or tailor the conventional service to a specific occasion, adding links and images that congregants, using e-book readers in the synagogue, will be able to pray from in place of the printed prayer book.

With the Bible, it is much more difficult to predict the kind of transformation the technological shift will bring. On the one hand, the capacity of digital technology to gather and supply the reader or user with access to previously dispersed or unavailable sources related to the Bible is virtually unlimited. A website like *Sefaria: A Living Library of Jewish Texts Online* (www.sefaria.org), which posts classical Jewish texts in Hebrew and in English translation, includes the Bible, rabbinic midrash, and virtually every medieval commentary, as well as forums for readers' comments and contemporary interpretations, and seems destined to replace the *Miqraot Gedolot* as the definitive locus for Bible study. For laypersons, if not for scholars, sites like *Sefaria* enable an unprecedented interactive engagement with the text and with a community of other readers and students, a community that crosses every conceivable border and boundary. Indeed, the most dramatic transformations that the new technology can effect will likely be in the study of the Bible rather than in the text itself.

To be sure, one can imagine more radical changes. As scholars of the digital humanities have noted, the electronic platform can be profoundly destabilizing, particularly in the virtually unconstrained power over the text that it bestows upon the reader or user. Any individual with a word processor can now cut, paste, edit, and—this is the key point—publish on the Internet his or her own version of the Bible. In fact, such attempts are not unprecedented. Thomas Jefferson literally cut and pasted his own version of the gospels out of the Authorized New Testament.[1] In 1990, Harold Bloom and David Rosenberg presented an English translation with commentary on what they considered the "original" Bible, the so-called Yahwist document, stripped of all the detritus of later documents, which, they argued, sought to domesticate and cast a legal shadow over the radical originality of the Yahwist.[2]

The likelihood of many more such projects, however, seems low. The Torah scroll will continue to be written by trained scribes and chanted in the traditional Torah service in the synagogue as it has been for the last millennium or longer. Digitalized texts of Bibles are already being used by laypersons as well as scholars for more advanced and quicker searches, but biblical concordances, databases, and other cross-referencing tools have been available in printed form for centuries (and in any case, the biblical text is not so huge that it's impossible to know it by heart). Indeed, the Masorah, with its attention to the enumeration and description of every minor orthographic, syntactic, and lexical eccentricity, uncannily anticipated a thousand years ago the tools now available electronically. If anything, the Masorah suggests that the digital revolutionary may not be quite as revolutionary as often thought.

As we have seen in the course of this study, the story of the Masorah is key to the Jewish Bible's history, or better yet, the key to its Jewishness. This book's most important contribution may be its attempt to restore the Masorah to its rightful place at the heart of the Jewish Bible's history. It is no exaggeration to say that the Masorah has figured as the main protagonist of the Bible's story from its initial appearance in the earliest codices of the Hebrew Bible (which, as we saw, were produced for the purpose of guaranteeing the accuracy of the text in Torah scrolls). The Masorah's prominence was maintained through its ubiquitous, almost necessary presence in medieval manuscripts as a mark of the Bible's Jewishness, and later through its critical role in the religious contests over ownership of the Bible that have dominated its history since the sixteenth century. Those contests have not ended. Even today, the Bible remains a contested book with two rival editions, each distinguished by its own Masoretic text, each competing for absolute authority as the Bible's definitive text. By itself the digitalized Bible will not resolve that contest.

The most profound contribution digital technology may make to our understanding of the Bible is a greater appreciation of its materiality. Looking back on the Bible's career as traced in this study, it is hard not to be saddened by how diminished and visually impoverished the Bible as a material artifact has become in the course of history. The splendor, the monumentality, the symbolic aura of manuscript Bibles, and the typographical complexity and variety of early printed Bibles have all been lost in the modern, contemporary Bible which is, to be generous, an undistinguished, unmemorable material object that conveys little of the religious and cultural grandeur of the Bible. As more manuscripts and early printed books are digitalized and published on the Web, the material Bible, in its full historical splendor, will now become visible for everyone to view and study, if only virtually. And what they will see is what we have shown repeatedly through this book. The Bible may still be contested as a text, but its material history demonstrates how the books of the Jews—the books that Jews have actually held in their hands—have been consistently shaped by those of the gentile host cultures in which they have lived even while their Jewish producers have sought to differentiate them from their gentile counterparts. The monumental Torah scroll of the rabbis was both like and unlike the scrolls of surrounding Near Eastern cultures; similarly, it intentionally differed from the scrolls used by nonrabbinic Jews like the Samaritans. The early biblical codices were intimately informed by their producers' knowledge of Islamic books, Qur'ans in particular, and yet Judaized through features like micrography. And throughout the Middle Ages, as Jews struggled with Christians over ownership of the Bible, over claims to being its sole true heir and correct interpreter, the material shapes of their Bibles continuously reflected those of that other religious tradition, and consequently had to be marked and designated with their Jewish identity. That contest has continued down to the present day in translations of the Bible, with the struggle over ownership still being played out in the vernacular languages of translation, languages that Jews and their books inevitably share with the dominant culture and its books. And in each of the stages of its history, the meaning of the Bible for Jews has changed. As scroll or codex, as a hand-written or a printed or a digital text, the Jewish Bible, as a material artifact, has always been more than just a book.

NOTES

Introduction

1 Bamidbar Rabbah 13:15–16; cf. *Mishnat R. Eliezer. O, Midrash Sheloshim u-Shetayim Midot*, ed. H. G. Enelow (New York: Blokh, 1933), 45. For a history of the phrase, see Mack, "Seventy Faces."

2 The literature in this field is now vast. For a helpful overview, see the many articles and essays in Finkelstein and McCleary, *Book History Reader*. The scholars whose work has been especially formative for me are Donald McKenzie, Roger Chartier, and Peter Stallybrass. The many sessions of the Workshop on the Material Text in Van Pelt Library at the University of Pennsylvania, led by Stallybrass, got me into the field and have consistently served as a source of inspiration.

3 For the best introductions to their work, see Beit-Arié, *Hebrew Manuscripts of East and West*; and Sirat, *Hebrew Manuscripts of the Middle Ages*. Numerous articles and studies by both scholars are cited throughout this volume.

Chapter 1. The Torah Scroll

1 The history of the Bologna Torah scroll in the subsequent paragraphs is drawn from Perani, "Il più antico Sefer Torah"; and De Tatta, "L' occhio dello studiosa." I wish to thank Professor Perani for supplying me with English translations of both Italian articles, and Elena Fratta for working with me on the original Italian version.

2 Especially noteworthy are the four Erfurt Torah scrolls, on which see Penkower, "Ashkenazi Pentateuch Tradition," 124, 140. A thirteenth-century (CA 1270) scroll, reputed to be the oldest complete Ashkenazic Sefer Torah, was sold at Sotheby's on December 22, 2015; for a full description, see Sotheby's, *Important Judaica* (New York: Sotheby's, 2015), 8–11. A number of other purportedly medieval scrolls have been shown to be fakes; the most famous of these is the Sefer Torah, reputed to have been written by R. Nissim of Gerondi in NLI, about which see Zucker, "On the Margins," which replaces Havlin, "A Sefer-Torah."

3 On the word *sefer*, see Hurwitz, "The Origins and Development of 'Megillat-Sefer.'"

4 For a good summary of the history of the term through the rabbinic period, see Kugel, "Torah," esp. 996–98.

5 On the question of how many books actually are in the Hebrew Bible—whether it is twenty-four or twenty-two—and on the possible analogy to the twenty-four books in each Homeric epic, see Darshan, "Twenty-Four or Twenty-Two Books of the Bible."

6 My colleague Jeffrey Tigay has called to my attention Daniel 9:2, which refers to studying *ba-sefarim*, which the Vulgate translates as *biblia*.

7 There is as yet no complete or comprehensive history of the Hebrew Bible, either as a scroll or as a codex. Currently, for the best short survey, see Olszowy-Schlanger, "Hebrew Bible."

8 The following discussion draws heavily on the groundbreaking research by Menahem Haran in the series of articles cited below. For an earlier treatment of some of the same material, see Ludwig Blau, *Studien*.

9 Note that in Exodus 34:1, God says that he will inscribe the text on the second set in the same way he did it on the first set; in contrast, 34:28 states that Moses wrote the Ten Commandments (*devarim*). The two versions seems to present an unresolved contradiction. There is a similar discrepancy between Exodus 31:18 and 32:16, according to which both sets were written by the finger of God while, in contrast, Moses himself appears to have inscribed "the book of the covenant" (*sefer ha-brit*) in Exodus 24:4 (cf. 24:7) and 2 Kings 23:2,21. Whether the scribe was divine or human, stone was regularly used in the ancient Near East for texts of great importance which required long-term preservation, but exactly why two tablets were necessary for a relatively short text like the Decalogue is not clear.

10 Isa. 10:1; Jer. 17:1,17.

11 Note that *sefer ha-brit* is only one name in a series of changing names for the Decalogue "tablets of testimony" (*luḥot ha-'edut* in Exod. 31:18, 32:16) and "tablets of the covenant" (*luḥot ha-brit* in Deut. 9:11,15); "the book of the covenant" (*sefer ha-brit*) in Exod. 24:4 (cf. 24:7) and 2 Kings 23:2,21. So, too, in relation to a text whose precise content is unclear: "the *torah* of Moses" (*torat moshe*) in 1 Kings 2:3; "the book of the *torah* of Moses" (*sefer torat moshe*) in 2 Kings 14:6; "the book of the Torah" (*sefer ha-torah*) in 2 Kings 22:8,11; and "book of Moses" (*sefer moshe*) in Neh. 13:1; 2 Chron. 25:4 (*torah sefer moshe*) and 35:12. On the significance of this changing vocabulary, see Demsky, *Literacy*, 232–37.

12 Tov, *Scribal Practices*, 40n78; Tigay, *The JPS Torah Commentary: Deuteronomy*, 248. The debate over the contents of the text continued into the Middle Ages. According Mishnah Sotah 7 (and compare B. Sotah 36a), the stones contained, in addition to the Hebrew text, translations into all seventy languages the gentile nations speak.

13 See Jer. 17:1 for a tablet (*luaḥ libam*) and Isa. 29:11 for a scroll (*sefer*).

14 The Nash Papyrus contains the Ten Commandments (Exod. 20:2–17) and the beginning of the *Shema'* (Deut. 6:5–21); for discussion, see Tov, *Textual Criticism*, 118. For an example of a biblical narrative pointing to the use of papyrus, see Jer. 36, in which King Jehoiakim destroys a scroll containing Jeremiah's prophecies of doom by cutting it into shreds with a scribe's knife and then throwing it into a fire until it is consumed (23). As Haran ("Book-Scrolls in Israel," 167–68) points out, the scene makes sense only if the scroll were made of papyrus, which can be both easily shredded with a knife and quickly burned in a fire; Haran (168–70) also points

to the use of the Hebrew verb *maḥah* (wipe off) rather than *garad* (scrape) for erasure, which suggests that the process was done by using water and wiping the slate clean, as it were; such a technique only works with papyrus, not parchment, where the mistake must be scraped off.

15 Haran, "Book-Scrolls in Israel" and "Book-Scrolls at the Beginning of the Second Temple Period."

16 For discussion of lengths of papyrus and skin rolls in the biblical period, see Niditch, *Oral World*, 73–74. The Harris Papyrus (twelfth century BCE), the longest preserved papyrus roll, is 133 feet long and contains 79 sheets of papyrus. 4QIsa[a], the longest scroll found at Qumran, is about 24 feet in length and consists of 54 columns on 17 skin sheets.

17 Haran, "Book-Scrolls in Israel," 166–67; "Book-Scrolls at the Beginning of the Second Temple Period," 112–19.

18 Haran, "Book-Scrolls in Israel," 167.

19 See Haran, "Book-Scrolls at the Beginning of the Second Temple Period."

20 On this in particular, see Haran, "Bible Scrolls in Eastern and Western Communities," 22–23; and Haran, "Book-Size," 167–72.

21 Hurwitz, "Megillat-Sefer," 45*–46*.

22 Haran, "Book-Scrolls at the Beginning of the Second Temple Period," 112.

23 The most recent discussion of this transition in transcription is Price and Naeh, "On the Margins of Culture," esp. 275–84; cf. Naveh, *Alphabet*, 112–24; Tov, *Scribal Practices*, 237–48; Mathews, "Palaeo-Hebrew," 552; and for a different perspective, Diringer, "Early Hebrew Script."

24 On Paleo-Hebrew's development, see Mathews, "Palaeo-Hebrew," 552. On the Samaritans' use of Paleo-Hebrew, see Crown, *Samaritan Scribes*; and Naveh, *Alphabet*, 123–24.

25 On the scroll, see *Valmadonna Trust Library*, 18–19. I wish to thank Stefan Schorch for informing me about the importance of this scroll and its dating. On the Abisha scroll, see Crown, "Abisha Scroll."

26 Mathews, "Palaeo-Hebrew," 552–54.

27 *Letter of Aristeas*, 176, in Charlesworth, *The Old Testament Pseudepigrapha*, 2:24.

28 Significantly, later rabbinic law (Sifre Deut., par. 36; B. Shabbat 103b; Masekhet Sefer Torah [ed. Higger] 1:7; Masekhet Soferim [ed. Higger] 1:8) explicitly prohibits extravagant decoration of Torah scrolls, citing the Alexandrian case as a precedent *not* to be followed. See Siegel, *Scribes of Qumran*, 217–20; and Tov, *Scribal Practices*, 54, who connects writing in gold letters to the use of red ink and rubrics; he also notes that the rabbinic prohibition is specifically against writing God's name in gold (although he assumes that they prohibited writing anything else in gold as well).

29 Josephus, *Against Apion*, 1:36–42; and see the enlightening discussion in Wyrick, *The Ascension of Authorship*, 111–25.

30 For the references in Josephus to the Temple scroll, see Josephus, *Works, Jewish Antiquities* 3.38, 4.303, and 5.61 (though note the comment of H. St. J. Thackeray in *Josephus* [Cambridge, MA: LCL, 1930] 4.622 note, who argues that the references are not to the Bible but to a book of hymns and other selected texts kept in the Temple). For the scroll taken to Rome, see Josephus, *Jewish War*, Bk. VII, 7.5,7; cf. Siegel, "Scribes of Qumran," 185–86. The source for the Severus scroll is Moshe Hadarshan's *Midrash Bereishit Rabbati*, ed. C. Albeck (Jerusalem:

H. Vagshall, 1983/84), 209; on the variants, see Lieberman, *Hellenism*, 23–27; and Siegel, "Scribes of Qumran," 183–216.

31 For one scroll, see M. Kelim 15:6; for three, Sifre Deut. 356 (ed. Finkelstein, p. 423); and on the entire question, Lieberman, *Hellenism*, 22, who argues that such "accurate" (*akribēs*) official scrolls were characteristic of general Hellenistic book culture.

32 Tov, *Textual Criticism*, 29–36; for a general outline of the early history of the biblical text, and for Qumran in particular, 101–16. Tov points to three types of textual traditions documented in the fragments found at Qumran: a proto-Masoretic tradition, a pre-Samaritan one, and a third that does not affiliate with either of the first two. On the pre-Samaritan, see 84–100. Note should also be made of the fragments that Tov designates as "popular," that is, texts written much less carefully, either on inferior parchment or on papyrus, and that seem to have been produced specifically for private use by individuals. On Ezra and Nehemiah, see Tov, *Textual Criticism*, 103.

33 Tov, *Textual Criticism*, 35.

34 In particular, see Tov, *Scribal Practices* and his earlier article, "Scribal Practices"; Siegel, "Scribes of Qumran"; Haran, "Bible Scrolls in Eastern and Western Jewish Communities"; and Glatzer, "Book of Books," 61–68. My discussion of scribal culture at Qumran is strongly indebted to Tov's magisterial study, *Scribal Practices*.

35 On the background to the scribal culture generally in the late biblical and Hellenistic periods in Israel, see Tov, *Scribal Practices*, 7–16; on more universal scribal practices in contrast to those specific to Qumran, 260–76 and the tables in appendix 1, 277–88.

36 Haran, "Book-Size," 169.

37 There may have been a few scrolls containing two books (e.g., Genesis and Exodus), a fact possibly reflected in the later prohibition (Soferim 3:4) against writing scrolls for two books alone.

38 For an example of *ḥomesh*, see T. Megillah 3:20. The word *ḥomesh* literally means "a fifth," and should be distinguished from the similarly spelled (and pronounced) *ḥumash*, which in the Middle Ages became the term for a liturgical Pentateuch codex (on which see chapter 2 of this book). Note as well that the term *sefer Torah* in early rabbinic sources often refers to a *ḥomesh*; see for example M. Yoma 7:1; M. Sota 7:7; M. Yevamot 16:7; B. Sotah 41a; and Haran, "Torah and Bible Scrolls," 94–95 and 99–102.

39 Sirat, "Les rouleaux bibliques," esp. the tables on 421–27. Please note that the lengths of the scrolls are all based on reconstructions. For the general size of scrolls at Qumran, see Tov, *Scribal Practices*, 79–82.

40 The single possible candidate for an entire Pentateuch is Mur 1 but the evidence is ambiguous; see Tov, *Scribal Practices*, 75, 79. For a list of scrolls that may have contained more than one Pentateuchal book, see 75.

41 No fragment of Ezra has, in fact, been found at Qumran, although it is likely that this is simply a matter of no copy having survived, not a statement about the book's canonicity.

42 Tov, *Scribal Practices*, 126–28.

43 For a full description, see Talmon, *Masada VI*, 76–90.

44 Khan, *Short Introduction*, 21–22 and, for earlier scholarship, 21n18.

45 Haran, "Torah and Bible Scrolls," 94–95, 99–102, and on the technological advances, 96. Aside from the improved technology for producing thinner parchment, Haran also notes the increasing use of two rollers for the monumental Sefer Torah, which made using it much easier than with a single roller. The exact history of the transition from the *ḥomesh* to the Sefer Torah as the prescribed scroll to read in the synagogue is difficult to reconstruct, and the terminology used to describe the different types of Bible scrolls is perplexing. References to single scrolls holding the entire Pentateuch begin to appear in the Tosefta and in post-Mishnaic *beraitaot* preserved in the Talmud, and it was not until the end of the Talmudic period that the single monumental Torah scroll appears to have completely displaced the small *ḥomashim*. M. Megillah 3:1 speaks of a Torah and *sefarim*; the former presumably means a Sefer Torah with all five books, but it is not clear whether *sefarim* refers to *ḥomashim* or scrolls of the Prophets and the Writings. T. Megillah 20, which deals with what scrolls may be placed atop one another, explicitly distinguishes between Sifrei Torah (with all five books) and *ḥomashim*, but there is no statement as to whether only one or both were permitted to be used in the synagogue (although see T. Megillah 3:18, which suggests that *ḥomashim* were still being used in the synagogue at the time of the Tosefta). I wish to thank my colleague Bernard Septimus for pointing me to these last sources.

46 Olszowy-Schlanger, "Hebrew Bible," 34; but see Sarna, "Ancient Libraries," 57, who suggests that these lists may have served as catalogs for libraries. As we will see in the next chapter, the sequence of books in a pandect Bible codex remained in flux even in the Middle Ages.

47 Tov, *Textual Criticism*, 80–101; cf. Crown, *Samaritan Scribes*, 1–39, for further background.

48 On the rabbinic stricture, see the discussion later in this chapter.

49 See Price and Naeh, "On the Margins of Culture," 283n93, who note that, from the third century on, each of the separate religious communities in the area of Palestine identifies itself through a separate script: rabbinic Jews, Aramaic; Samaritans, Paleo-Hebrew; and gentiles and Christians, Syrian Aramaic script (Syriac).

50 Tov, *Scribal Practices*, 252, and 51, table 9, a list of the papyrus fragments.

51 Haran, "Bible Scrolls in Eastern and Western Jewish Communities," 38; cf. Tov, *Scribal Practices*, 34–35, and other bibliography listed there.

52 Glatzer, "The Book of Books," 63–64.

53 The statements in this paragraph are all based on Tov, *Scribal Practices*.

54 See Mathews, "Background of the Palaeo-Hebrew Texts"; Tov, *Scribal Practices*, 238–47, esp. 243, table 1.

55 For a recent review and reassessment of the scholarship on the scribal composition and transmission of this scroll, see Williamson, "Scribe and Scroll."

56 Tov, *Scribal Practices*, 218; and Mathews, "Background of the Palaeo-Hebrew Texts," 551.

57 Tov, *Scribal Practices*, 131–32; note, however, that texts in Paleo-Hebrew use dots. As Tov notes, Naḥmanides (*Commentary on the Torah*, ed. C. B. Chavel [Jerusalem: Mosad Harav Kuk, 1959], 1:5–6) claimed that the Torah was originally written with no word spaces and the text in its entirety consisted of the divine name.

58 These definitions of the *petuḥot* and the *setumot* are taken from Siegel, "Scribes of Qumran," 73, quoted in Tov, *Scribal Practices*, 144–45.

59 Tov, *Scribal Practices*, 145–47.

60 Tov, *Scribal Practices*, 106–8. Curiously, as Tov notes (105), texts in Paleo-Hebrew both break words at the left margin and have left justification, practices that continue in later Samaritan scribal tradition. In contrast, later rabbinic tradition maintained left justification much more strictly and prohibited breaking words at the end of the line.

61 Tov, *Scribal Practices*, 138–40.

62 David Carr, in *Writing on the Tablet*, 140–41, has argued that one can see these separate roles of the Bible delineated as early as the book of Deuteronomy, in which the Bible is represented both as public testimony to be read aloud before the entire nation (by either the priests or the king) as a record of Israel's covenant with God (with the public reading being a kind of reenactment of the original covenant ceremony at Sinai) and as a private study text to be recited aloud repeatedly by individuals.

63 On the ten *nequdot*, see the next section. On the phenomenon generally, see Saul Lieberman, *Hellenism*, 38–43. The other famous case is that of the *antisigma* and *sigma*, which became the famous inverted *nuns* found in Numbers 10:35–36 and in Psalm 107, and which were probably originally meant to signify that the bracketed text was in an incorrect place. This original functional meaning was not entirely forgotten by the rabbis, but some sages understood the bracket-like signs as marking the section's specialness, even as a separate book in the Pentateuch; cf. Sifre Num. 84 (ed. Horowitz, p. 80) to Num. 10:35 and its parallel, B. Shabbat 115a–116a. In subsequent rabbinic tradition, the eighty-five letters in the section became the minimum length of a biblical fragment that requires the special treatment accorded to a holy text.

64 The best single comparative study of Qumran and rabbinic scribal practice is Tov, "Scribal Practices"; cf. *Scribal Practices*, 214–18 and 274–76.

65 The earliest known fragment of a Torah scroll, T-S NS 3.21, a large partially preserved sheet containing sections of Gen. 13–17, has been dated by different scholars to either the fifth–sixth centuries or the eighth. For an excellent reproduction of the fragment, see Brown, *In the Beginning*, 110–11, 248–49. For other early fragments, see Sirat, "Rouleaux de la Tora"; Sirat, *Hebrew Manuscripts*, 27–28; Birnbaum, "A Sheet of an Eighth Century Synagogue Scroll"; Paul Sanders, "The Ashkar-Gilson Manuscript" (which deals with a different section of the same scroll from which Birnbum's sheet derived); Penkower, "A Sheet of Parchment"; and Olszowy-Schlanger, "An Early Palimpsest Scroll."

66 Masekhet Sefer Torah also served as the basis for the later compilation, Masekhet Soferim, to be discussed later in the section on the Middle Ages.

67 Esther's obligatory status was understood to be stipulated in the scroll itself, in Esther 9:28.

68 There is some irony in the fact that Esther became the model biblical text given its somewhat ambiguous status within the biblical canon. As is well known, Esther is the only book in the Bible not represented in a single manuscript at Qumran; it is also the only book in the Bible in which the divine name is not found.

69 Thus the Kaufmann Codex of the Mishnah. Parma 138 reads *'al ha'or*, "on the skin/leather."

70 Compare, for example, M. Gittin 4:6 and T. Avodah Zarah 3:7, which either imply or explicitly state that one can use and buy Torah scrolls written by gentiles, with B. Gittin 45b and B. Menahot 42b, both of which implicitly or explicitly forbid doing so (even though there are dissenting opinions, even in regard to idolaters); cf. as well as Soferim 1:14, which lists all

persons disqualified from writing a Torah scroll, including heretics, informers, converts, slaves, and minors (but not gentiles!), and Maimonides, *Hilkhot Sefer Torah*, 1:3; see Heczer, *Jewish Literacy*, 480–81 and notes. On requiring the scroll to be written with the proper intention (*kavvanah* or *li-shemah*), see B. Gittin 54b (which states that skins must be tanned *li-shemah* and that all divine names [*hazkarot*] be written with *kavvanah*) and such passages as Berakhot 5:1, which forbids a person to interrupt while he is writing God's name(s) in a scroll even if a king greets him. Again, compare Maimonides, *Hilkhot Sefer Torah*, 1:13 and 1:15, and 10:1, which connects the two issues; so far as I can tell, Soferim does not deal with intentionality.

71 Aside from Y. Megillah 1:71b–72a, discussed in the text, see the following sections in the Babylonian Talmud: B. Megillah, esp. 8b–9a, 24b–27a, 92a; B. Menahot 29b–32a (mainly about permissible corrections); B. Shabbat 103a–105a (on correct orthography and spacing); B. Bava Batra 13b–14b (on binding different parts of scripture together, leaving spaces between books, and correct rolling of scrolls); B. Gittin 60a–b (which discourages and prohibits writing *ḥomashim* as well as mini-scrolls of sections solely for the education of children).

72 For a complete list and discussion, see Tov, *Scribal Practices*, 274–76.

73 Tov, *Scribal Practices*, 251.

74 See Soferim 1:15; Sifre Deut. 135; B. Shabbat 103b; and other sources cited in Soferim, 109.

75 On this general tendency and the incorporation of paratextual elements in rabbinic scrolls, see Tov, *Scribal Practices*, 214–18. The classic discussion of the attitude of the rabbis toward the *nequdot*, the inverted *nuns*, and other aspects of what the rabbis call *tikunei soferim* remains that of Saul Lieberman, *Hellenism*, 28–46; cf. as well the still useful monograph by Romain Butin, *Ten Nequdoth*.

76 For this particular interpretation, see B. Bava Mezi'a 87a and ARN A, ch. 34 (ed. Schechter, pp. 100–101); Sifre Numbers 69 (ed. Horowitz, p. 64); Ber. R. 48.9 (ed. Theodor-Albeck, p. 492). On the passage as a whole, see Butin, *Ten Nequdoth*, 62–67.

77 Tov, *Scribal Practices*, 254, and more generally, 274–76.

78 According to B. Menahot 29b and Y. Megillah 71c, two or three corrections per column are permitted; according to Soferim 3:10, one to three. The divine name cannot be erased under any circumstances although the rabbis devote considerable attention to prefixes and suffixes of the divine name and other epithets for God; see Y. Megillah 71d, and both Soferim and Sefer Torah, chaps. 4–5. For a great midrash on Deut. 12:4 explaining why it is forbidden to erase the divine name, see Sifre Deut. 61 (= Soferim/Sefer Torah 5.9 and B. Makkot 22a.)

79 For its origins in the period of the return from Babylonia, see Tigay, "Torah Scroll," 328–29, and his quotation from Y. Kaufmann there.

80 Jaffee, *Torah in the Mouth*, 80 and 189n55; cf. Hayes, "Halakhah Le-Moshe Mi-Sinai." For examples of its use in Tannaitic sources, see M. Yadayim 4:3; M. Eduyyot 8:7; M. Peah 2:6; and T. Sukkah 3:1. For more discussion, see S. Safrai in *Literature of the Sages*, 2:182–83; M. Jaffee, *Torah in the Mouth*, 80–83 and 188–89n55; and Danzig, "Ruling of Sacred Books," 283n1. Note, too, that ruling (*sirtut*, *sirgul*) is added by the Yerushalmi; it is not mentioned in the Mishnah. See as well Maimonides, *Hilkhot Tefillin*, 1:8–9.

81 Note that the expression is also found in Sefer Torah 1:1 (= Soferim 1:1). Depending on the dating of Sefer Torah, the assignation of the formula to scribal rules may have begun earlier

than the Yerushalmi, although it is equally likely, given the structure of the passage, that the expression may be a gloss inserted later; further study is required.

82 Note that the one thing that is not stated in this passage as "a law given to Moses at Sinai" is the fact that the text has to be written in Assyrian letters.

83 Not that the rabbis entirely deny the fact that changes in the Torah's material form occurred historically. They are clearly cognizant of the difference between their Assyrian script and the Paleo-Hebrew script; as the rabbinic discussions (B. Sanhedrin 21b) indicate, the rabbis were at least aware of the fact that the Assyrian script's appearance was late and came up with Ezra from Assyria with the return from the Babylonian exile, even if they also sought to show that it was the original script in which the Torah was given and had been lost until Ezra recovered it. The discussion in B. Gittin 60a about the permissibility of using *ḥomashim* in the synagogue lection also displays an awareness among some rabbis that there were different types of Sifrei Torah.

84 This rule is never stated explicitly in the Talmud, but it is implicit in many passages. The locus classicus is the passage in B. Gittin 60a cited in the previous note, where the use of *ḥomashim* for liturgical chanting in the synagogue is prohibited, as well as the writing of fragmentary scrolls or sections of the Torah for teaching children.

85 On these Genesis fragments and their size, see Sirat, "Les rouleaux bibliques de Qumran," 426.

86 On the Laurenziana fragments, see Sirat, "Rouleaux de la Tora." For a list of other fragments from before the tenth century, see Penkower, "A Sheet of Parchment."

87 Sirat, "Les rouleaux bibliques de Qumran," 428.

88 On the dating and provenance of Soferim and Sefer Torah, see pro tem Blank, "It's Time to Take Another Look," which supersedes most previous treatments, like Strack and Stemberger, *Introduction*, 227–28 and 232. In his critical edition of the text, Higger argues that the standard compilation is Palestinian with its first part closely based upon Sefer Torah (Masekhet Soferim, p. i); Higger also published a fragmentary Babylonian recension of the first several chapters. Blank's far more methodologically sophisticated study has rejected the view of a Palestinian provenance for the entirety of the composition. As she shows (4–5n10), Soferim chapters 10–21 were almost certainly composed outside of Palestine, probably in Europe, possibly in Italy or Byzantium. Chapters 1–5, which are closely connected to Sefer Torah, are probably Palestinian and perhaps as early as the third century, and chapters 6–9 are very likely much later from the period of the seventh through tenth centuries. Chapters 10–21 were probably appended to the first nine chapters "in an effort to compile an all-purpose handbook for the laws of scrolls," and this composite text was then taken to Ashkenaz, where it was accepted as authoritative; in some cases, its rulings even trump those of the Babylonian Talmud. In addition to Soferim and Sefer Torah, there existed still another compilation, *Sefarim*, which is a kind of abridgment of Soferim; this text, which survives only in a single manuscript, was published by S. Shenblum in *Sheloshah Sefarim Niftahim* (Lvov, 1877), but see the comments of Danzig, "Ruling," 287n10. See as well Adler, *An Eleventh Century Introduction.*

89 Penkower, "A Sheet of Parchment." Note that the Oriental (Near Eastern) codices that Penkower cites are mainly from the tenth and eleventh centuries while the Yemenite manuscripts are from the fifteenth and sixteenth centuries.

90 On scripts in the Middle Ages as they differ in geocultural areas and historical periods, see Yardeni, *Book of Hebrew Script*, 84–100, 209–59.

91 There does not yet exist a serious study of the *tagin* and other scribal flourishes, but pro tem see Yardeni, *Book of Hebrew Script*, 210–15; and Razhabi, *Ha-otiot Ha-meshunot Ba-Torah*, 78–93. As Yardeni notes, the *tagin* or "crowns" (in the form we know them as short horizontal lines with balls on the tops of certain letters), though mentioned in rabbinic literature (B. Menahot 29a), are actually a fairly late phenomenon, no earlier than the Geonic period. There exists a work called *Sefer Tagei* (or *Tagin*), probably composed in the Geonic period; for a preliminary critical edition, see Yaakov Besser, *Sefer Tagei and Sefer Tagin* [in Hebrew] (Israel: n.p., 1970); and Perani, "Il più antico Sefer Torah." (One of the anomalous features of the Bologna Torah Scroll is its ubiquitous use of *tagin*.)

92 On the peculiar letters and other oddities, see Razhabi, *Ha-otiot Ha-meshunot Ba-Torah*, particularly 94–180, which includes charts illustrating the differing shapes of the unusual letters in different regions.

93 For a helpful and brief summary of this literary genre, see the description of the fifteenth-century Ashkenazic Torah scroll in the catalog of *Important Judaica* (no. 809), sold at Sotheby's in New York, Dec. 15, 2010.

94 Leiman, "Masorah and Halakhah," 303, following a suggestion made by Israel Ta-Shma.

95 See Yardeni, *Book of Hebrew Script*, 268–77, with charts illustrating the scripts.

96 See Birnbaum, "A Sheet of an Eighth Century Synagogue Scroll"; Sanders, "The Ashkar-Gilson Manuscript"; Sirat, "Rouleaux de la Tora" and "An Announcement"; Penkower, "A Sheet of Parchment," esp. 263, and his observations on pp. 263–64 regarding the number of lines per column in these scrolls, in contrast to the recommended numbers in Maimonides and in the Shulḥan ʿArukh. Virtually all Bible scrolls studied and described to date are Pentateuch scrolls. For a recent study of a (probably) eleventh-century scroll containing sections from other parts of the Bible, probably a *haftarah* scroll used for the prophetic readings in the synagogue, see Olszowy-Schlanger, "An Early Palimpsest Scroll."

97 For the dots, see the Jews College scroll discussed by Birnbaum as well as T-S NS 2.16 and Laurenziana (Florence) 74.17, discussed by Sirat in both "Rouleaux de la Tora" and "Announcement," and her additional article, "Les rouleaux bibliques de Qumran," esp. 427–29 and table 5. The Laurentian scroll has all the features cited in the text. Note, too, that Sirat dates the Jews College scroll much later than Birnbaum does, to the eleventh or twelfth century, but see now Sanders, "The Ashkar-Gilson Manuscript," 2, for a seventh–eighth century dating based on a carbon-14 analysis.

98 On the scroll's many anomalies, see Perani, "Il più antico Sefer Torah"; Perani and Corazzol, *Nuovo Catalogo*, 30–34; and De Tatta, "L'occhio dello studiosa." I also wish to thank Professor Jordan Penkower for first drawing my attention to the scroll in a thrilling lecture he delivered at the University of Pennsylvania in 2013.

99 For a concise description of the different layers, see Glatzer, "The Book of Books," 63–68.

100 The classic Talmudic source is B. Shabbat 79b and parallels; the best recent exposition is Glatzer, "The Book of Books," 63–68; for a more technical discussion, see Haran, "Bible Scrolls." Exactly what part of the skin was *klaf* and what part *dukhsustos* is debated by Easterners

(mainly Babylonians and Spanish authorities like Maimonides and Naḥmanides) and Westerners (Ashkenaz, Italy, and North Africa).

101 On different types of skins, B. Shabbat 79a; B. Gittin 22a; B. Megillah 19a. For dog dung, see B. Berakhot 25a; B. Ketubot 77a. On the entire process, see Haran, "Bible Scrolls," esp. 34–37.

102 Haran, "Bible Scrolls," 47–62.

103 Haran, "Bible Scrolls, 47–62. As Haran shows, Jews living in the Arabic/Islamic worlds, who still possessed a living tradition of leather preparation, were familiar with the differences between the skins; as a result, they went to considerable lengths in their legal deliberations to respond to the discrepancies (to legitimize purchasing the local *raq* from its gentile producers). The Jews in Christian Europe, on the other hand, no longer possessed their own traditions of leather preparation and were already accustomed to purchasing their skins from gentiles; as a result, halachic authorities had to obfuscate the differences between the Talmudic requirements and the contemporary parchment by exploiting ambiguities in some Talmudic texts and, for the most part, avoiding the problem as much as they could.

104 The classic and still definitive study of the Kaifeng community remains Leslie, *The Survival of the Chinese Jews*, upon which my brief discussion is based.

105 For the Torah scrolls, see Pollack, *The Torah Scrolls of the Chinese Jews*, in particular 37–42 and 87–115; and Pollack, "A Preliminary Study." It seems likely that most of the surviving scrolls were written after the flood of 1642; they date therefore from the period of the community's decline, which may partly explain why nearly all of them are riddled with spelling and calligraphic errors and omissions. The use of a brush is a conjecture based on the appearance of the script.

106 On the origins of the synagogue, see Levine's *The Ancient Synagogue*, 19–41, and on the place of Torah reading in the earliest stages of the synagogue's emergence, 35–38, where Levine connects the origins of the Torah reading with the *ma'amadot* described in M. Taanit 4:2.

107 Levine, *The Ancient Synagogue*, 138.

108 For alternative Torah readings not stated in the Mishnah, see Tosefta Megillah 3:1–9, and such passages as B. Megillah 31b, which list special readings that have not been maintained in later tradition. See Levine, *The Ancient Synagogue*, 506.

109 For individual ownership of scrolls, specifically *ḥomashim*, see the sources cited in note 38 above; obviously, a *ḥomesh* would have been much easier for individuals to own, and may even have been a desirable possession on account of belief in its amuletic power. Despite the Talmud's exhortation that every Jew should write his own personal Torah scroll from which to read in the synagogue, or at least hire a scribe to write one for him (B. Sanhedrin 21b; Maimonides, *Sefer Hamitzvot*, Positive Commandments, #18; *Mishneh Torah*, Laws of Tefillin, Mezuzah, and Sefer-Torah, 7:1), there is no evidence to support wide observance of the practice even though it is known that a number of medieval sages, including Maimonides, did indeed write Sifrei Torah for themselves. For extensive discussion of Maimonides's rationale, see Kapach, *Mishneh Torah*, 2:384–86. For a list of other medieval and early modern sages who are reported to have "written" Torah scrolls for themselves (though some of them may have commissioned scribes to do the writing), see Havlin, "Sefer Torah," 10–13. Note that the vast majority of the sages cited by Havlin are Sephardi.

110 I know of no source in rabbinic literature explicitly documenting the absence of a Sefer Torah in a community, but see the story in T. Megillah 2:4 about R. Meir who found himself on Purim in a town without an Esther scroll, cited and discussed in Hezser, *Jewish Literacy,* 467; on the considerable cost of a scroll, see 145–50 for a good overview of the economics of ownership.

111 For the text and annotations, see Blau, *Teshuvot Ha-Rambam,* 2:550–653. Maimonides responded that it was permissible to do so; see Kapach's discussion in his edition of the *Mishneh Torah* (*Sefer Torah*), p. 416.

112 On study of the Torah from "aural" acquisition of the text, see David Stern, "First Jewish Codices," 176–87.

113 On the history of the divisions, see Katznellenbogen, "The Division of the Sections of the Torah"; Stulberg, "The Last Oral Torah."

114 See Naeh, "Cycles of Torah Reading," 182–87, for a very suggestive reading of T. Sotah 7:9–12 as relating to an early "rabbinic" *hakheil* ceremony.

115 On the history of the name, see Ya'ari, *Toledot ḥag,* 28–31, which shows that *Simḥat Torah* was originally the name for a ceremony celebrating the completion of the Torah; it did not become the name for the holiday until the eleventh century, when it is attested for both Spain (where the name for the holiday was probably coined) and Ashkenaz. In fact, the term already occurs in a *piyyut* by Eliezer Kalir in the sixth century; the *piyyut* was published and discussed by Fleischer, "A List of the Annual Holidays," who used the poem to prove that the annual cycle already existed in Palestine and was not a late Babylonian invention.

116 Levine, *Ancient Synagogue,* 139, suggests that the translation of the Bible into Greek (the ancestor of the Septuagint) in the third century BCE may be evidence that a regular reading of the Torah was already in place at that time, thereby justifying the need for a translation for an audience that could not understand the Hebrew text.

117 The discussion in this and the following paragraphs is based largely on Levine, *Ancient Synagogue,* 219–21, 327–32; Hachlili, *Ancient Jewish Art,* 166–87; Fine, "From Meeting House to Sacred Realm," 36–38; Langer, "Study of Scripture," 52–54. Eric Meyer, in "The Torah Shrine," dates the introduction of a *fixed aedicule* in both the Diaspora (e.g., Dura Europos) and the land of Israel (Khirbet Shema and Nabratein) to the mid-third century.

118 Levine, *Ancient Synagogue,* 329; Gutmann, "Programmatic Painting," 148.

119 On the orientation toward Jerusalem, see T. Berakhot 3:15–16; M. Berakhot 5:5; and other sources cited in Levine, *Ancient Synagogue,* 180–81. Also see Langer, "From Study of Scripture," 53.

120 For the clearest summary of the current state of scholarship, see Levine, *Ancient Synagogue,* 327–32.

121 Levine, *Ancient Synagogue,* 136. Some scholars have suggested that the chancel screen (*meḥitzah, soreig*) found in several fourth- to sixth-century Palestinian synagogues was used to separate the *bimah* and ark from the rest of the synagogue interior, thus creating a kind of "realm of Torah" (Fine, "From Meeting House to Sacred Realm," 38); see Branham, "Vicarious Sacrality," 331–35. Levine (317–18) disputes this suggestion.

122 In addition to the work of the scholars mentioned later in this paragraph, see Tigay, "Torah Scroll," which is the most extensive discussion to date of the topic.

123 Van der Toorn, "The Iconic Book," esp. 239–48.

124 Van der Toorn, "The Iconic Book," 241.

125 Van der Toorn, "The Iconic Book," 242.

126 See Tigay, "Torah Scroll," 325–326n5, for a critique of van der Toorn.

127 See, for example, the portrait of the Torah in Bereishit (Genesis) Rabbah 1:1.

128 Van der Toorn, "The Iconic Book," 245–47.

129 For Langer's excellent series of articles, see Langer, "From Study of Scripture" and "Early Stages" (which deal with the earliest stages through Soferim), and "Sinai, Zion," which treats its subsequent medieval development.

130 On Ashkenazic attitudes to God's presence in the synagogue, see Woolf, "And I Shall Dwell in Their Midst," esp. 317. Except for the passage treated on this page, Woolf does not deal with the Torah rite, but it clearly fits the overall pattern he describes.

131 Langer, "Early Stages," 105–6.

132 See, for example, Mekhilta Shirta 3 (very beginning) and 9; Sifre Deut. 343; and Vayikra R. 31:5.

133 For the problematics of the text in Masekhet Soferim (particularly 14:5–8), see Langer, "Early Stages," 110–18.

134 See Langer's extensive discussion in "Sinai, Zion," esp. on the German pietistic period, 128–33, and on later centuries, 135–58.

135 On this liturgy and its invocations of God, see Tigay, "Torah Scroll," 339.

136 On the rabbinic imagery, see Wolfson, "Female Imaging," 1–6. These images are not exclusive. The Torah could be God's daughter whom he gives as a bride to either Israel or Moses.

137 On the mystical conceptions, see Idel, "Concepts of Scripture"; and Wolfson's two articles, "Female Imaging" and "Mystical Significance of Torah Study."

138 See Wolfson, "Mystical Significance of Torah Study," 73–75.

139 Langer, "Sinai, Zion," 159.

140 On the important distinction between the two, see Tigay, "Torah Scroll," 340.

141 This is not the case with rabbinic or medieval Jewish thought in general, where the Torah is frequently, almost typically, viewed as a feminine figure. On these conceptions, see Wolfson, "Mystical Significance of Torah Study," and "Female Imaging." As Wolfson notes ("Mystical Signficance of Torah Study," 20–23), in post-Zoharic Kabbalah, the Torah is associated with the *sefirah* of *tiferet*, which is masculine, but in Hasidism, the feminine personification returns with a vengeance, as it were. It is worth speculating that the difference in gendered personification may owe to the distinction between the Sefer Torah as a ritual artifact and the Torah as a text to be studied; where the former is generally masculine, the latter is typically feminine.

142 For the midrash, see Midrash Tannaim *ad* 33:4, and Shemot Rabbah 33:7; for further discussion, Shalev-Eyni, "Human Faces of the Torah," 153–62, esp. 156. As she points out, the conception of the Torah as Israel's bride also underlies the ritual of the *ḥatan Torah* on the festival of Simḥat Torah and may have facilitated the misunderstanding of the original term *ḥatam Torah*; on this ritual, see my short history of the Torah crown below.

143 Shalev-Eyni, "Human Faces of the Torah," 142.

144 On the custom, see Shulḥan 'Arukh, Oraḥ Ḥayyim 149, 1; and Piskei Teshuvot 2, p. 209. See as well *Sefer Ta'amei Ha-Minhagim*, 64–65.

145 On the Christian rituals, see Parmenter, "The Iconic Book," 69–70.

146 Moshe Isserles, Shulḥan 'Arukh, Oraḥ Ḥayyim 149, citing Isaac of Vienna's *Or Zaru'a*.

147 For histories of the different items that make up the Torah's garb, see Vivian Mann, "Torah Ornaments"; Yaniv, *Ma'aseh Hosheiv*, 16–26, nearly all of which appears in English translation in her article, "Regional Variations"; and Yaniv, *Ma'ase Rokem*. For an earlier, though still helpful treatment of European cases and ornaments, see Landsberger, "The Origin of European Torah Decorations" and "Old-Time Torah Curtains."

148 For the *teivah*, *mitpaḥat*, and *tik*, see B. Megillah 14a and 26a–b; for silk coverings, B. Shabbat 133b; for decorated colored cloths, M. Kelim 28:4. For the best recent overview, see Yaniv, *Ma'aseh Hosheiv*, 19. Both Mann, "Torah Ornaments," 2; and Fine, "From Meeting House," 25, point to textiles found in the Judaean desert as the remains of such woven coverings, though it is not clear to me how these remains can be identified as having been Torah coverings. In any case, Mann notes that the designs on these coverings resemble those of Coptic textiles of the period; as she also notes, these textiles were used by Egyptian Christians to wrap their holy writings. Eventually, Egyptian monks ended up missionizing in Ireland and Northumbria, where, according to scholars, the textiles became the models for so-called carpet pages in Insular gospel books as well as in other tenth-century Islamic and Christian books. As we will see in the next chapter, these Islamic carpet pages became models adapted in early Jewish books of the period.

149 Yaniv, "Regional Variations," 40–41.

150 The word *me'il* as well as the term *avneit*, which is used for the "belt" with which the Torah scroll is tied beneath the *me'il*, and the word *tas*, a shield that is hung over the *me'il*, are elsewhere associated with the garments of the high priest; as a result, it is sometimes mistakenly believed that this mode of Torah dressing is based upon the priestly garb. In fact, it is not, as shown by Joseph Gutmann in "Priestly Vestments," which argues persuasively that this model has no basis whatsoever in reality and derives solely from a mistranslation in the King James Bible of *tas* as "breastplate."

151 On the *avneit*, *yeri'ah*, and *wimpel*, see Yaniv, *Ma'ase Rokem*, 73–104. On the *wimpel*, see Weber, Friedlander, and Armbruster, *Mappott*, particularly the essay by Joseph Gutmann (65–69); Kirschenblatt-Gimblett, "The Cut That Binds"; Feuchtwanger-Sarig, "Danish Torah Binders"; and Shalev-Eyni, "Human Faces of the Torah," 146–53, which argues that these binders add an additional layer of meaning to the representation of the Torah as a child.

152 The surviving examples of *tikkim* are all late—from the fifteenth century—and there are few *me'ilim* from before the seventeenth century, but the cultures that produced these objects were all so traditional that even the late evidence reflects much earlier artifacts.

153 See the photograph of the Great Synagogue in Bukhara, 1896, originally published in E. N. Adler, *Jews in Many Lands* (London, 1912); and reproduced in Yaniv, "Regional Variation," plate 8.

154 For this and the remainder of the paragraph, see Landsberger, "Origin of European Torah Decorations," 88–89, 92–93; and Vivian Mann, "Torah Ornaments," 8–15.

155 Maimonides's reference clearly indicates that the *rimmonim* were by his time a conventional accoutrement of the Torah scroll. See Vivian Mann, "Torah Ornaments," 9, which cites a

passage from Gregory of Tours (569 CE) discussing a synagogue robbery involving *rimmonim*.

156 For a superb survey of *rimmonim* across Jewish cultures, see Gross, *50 Rimmonim*. In resembling the towers of their cultures, the *rimmonim* follow the pattern evident in European *besamim* or spice towers; on the latter, see Gross, "Bemer the Slow." For the common visual vocabulary of Jews and Christians in this sphere of material medieval culture, see Vivian Mann, "Torah Ornaments," 9.

157 The responsum is preserved in Isaac ben Judah Ibn Ghiyyat (Spain, 1038–89), *Shaare Simhah* (Fürth, 1861–62), 117; translated and discussed in Landsberger, "Origin of European Torah Decorations," 94–95. Other testimonies from the thirteenth century attest to the similar and continuing use of a crown on Simḥat Torah in both Ashkenaz—see Abraham ben Nathan Hayarchi of Lunel's *Sefer Hamanhig* (1204) (ed. Goldberg, Berlin 1855, p. 72; also cited and translated by Landsberger, "Origin of European Torah Decorations," 95–96); and Sepharad—see Solomon ben Aderet, *Teshuvot U-She'eilot Ha-Rashba* (Rome, 1470), #73. On these passages, see Landsberger's discussion (94–98), including many other early references to the use of Torah crowns; Vivian Mann, "Origin of European Torah Ornaments," 11–12; and Yaniv, *Ma'aseh Hosheiv*, 29. See also Goitein, "The Synagogue Building," 94–96, Doc. 10, for a list dated 1159 CE of all valuables in the synagogues in Old Cairo (Fustat), which includes several silver Torah crowns, one gilt, and one in niello.

158 In actuality, Simḥat Torah, like Shemini Atzeret, the holiday celebrated on the previous day, is its own holiday, not part of Sukkot.

159 The last phrase is a well-known Talmudic formula. The Hebrew term used most commonly for the person who is called for the reading of the final section of the Torah is *ḥatan torah*, but as Ya'ari (*Toledot Hag*, 80–84) notes, the correct phrase is *ḥatam torah*, "the one who finishes the Torah." Once *ḥatam* was replaced by *ḥatan*, the phrase was mistranslated as "the bride-groom of the Torah." See as well Sperber, *Minhagei Yisrael*, 135–37, which cites additional sources confirming Ya'ari and notes that the *m/n* transference is common in rabbinic Hebrew.

160 See *Sefer Ha-manhig*, paragraph 59 (ed. Y. Raphael, Jerusalem, 1978, part 2, 317–18), quoted in Sperber, *Minhagei Yisrael*, 128.

161 For these midrashim, see Dunsky, *Midrash Shir Ha-Shirim Rabba* (3:11), 97; Grunhut, *Midrash Shir Hashirim* (3:11), 76–77; and Midrash Mishlei 1:8. Landsberger, "Origin of European Torah Decorations," 95, mentions the verse but does not elaborate.

162 It is also possible that the Torah itself is being crowned as the "bride" of either Israel or God. Brides in the ancient world, including Jewish brides, were typically adorned with a wreath on their wedding day; for full exposition, see Feuchtwanger, "Coronation." The notion of the Torah as a bride is rabbinic; on the other hand, as noted above in note 154, the idea that Simḥat Torah celebrates a marriage (between God or Israel and the Torah) is based mainly on the misunderstanding of *ḥatan torah* as a "bride-groom."

163 On the shape of the Torah crown, see Yaniv, "Regional Variations," 45–46, and the accompanying plates that show how Torah crowns mirror the crowns of the surrounding culture.

164 On the *tas*, see Vivian Mann, "Origin of European Torah Ornaments," 13–15. As she explains, the *tas* originated as a plaque to indicate which Torah scroll was to be used on special Sabbaths

and holidays for specific readings; at a later point, it also came to serve as a dedicatory medium. In some cases, the *tas* is decorated with the Urim ve-Tumim, the priestly breastplate, which lends the regal costume a priestly note as well.

165 The *parokhet* goes back to the early synagogue; traces of holes for hooks to hang such a curtain have been found at Dura Europos and at the synagogue remains in Beit Alpha; see Landsberger, "Old-Time Torah Curtains," 130–31. The name *parokhet* clearly alludes to the curtains for the biblical tabernacle named in 2 Chronicles 3:14, and was part of the early project to identify the synagogue with the Temple. Most surviving *parokhot* date from the seventeenth and eighteenth centuries, when the use of the crown and *keter Torah* as identifying features of the Sefer Torah became typical. For the history of the *parokhet*, see Yaniv, *Ma'ase Rokem*, 157–203; for an excellent catalog of *parokhot* with illustrations (as well as other textiles including *me'ilim)*, see Swetschinski, *Orphaned Objects*.

166 See Landsberger, "Origin of European Torah Decorations," 101–4; and most recently, Feuchtwanger, "Chanting to the Hand." As both Landsberger and Feuchtwanger note, the original practice was simply to cover the hand with a cloth (usually the *mitpaḥat*, a practice still observed in some North African Jewish communities) when touching the scroll, out of respect for its holiness.

167 On the Mishnaic phrase, see Goodman, "Sacred Scripture"; Friedman, "Holy Scriptures Defile the Hands"; Haran, *The Biblical Collection*, 201–75; and Albert Baumgarten, "Sacred Scriptures."

168 Thus B. Shabbat 14a: "He who holds a Torah-scroll naked [i.e., with his bare hands] will be buried naked."

169 For the hierarchy of placement, see B. Megillah 27a. The hierarchy may reflect the placement of different types of scrolls within a Torah ark of the sort depicted in the Dura Europos synagogue wall painting.

170 For the sale of a Torah scroll only under specific circumstances, see B. Megillah 27a, and for burial, sometimes in an earthenware vessel, next to a sage, B. Megillah 26b; the same passage also relates that worn-out *mitpaḥot sefarim*, cloth wrappers for a Torah, are to be used for shrouds. The Hebrew root usually translated as "bury" in such contexts is *g-n-z*, which actually means "taken out of circulation" (or "removed" or "hidden away") and is also used to refer to the treatment of "heretical books" (*sifrei minim*); in other words, it is not mere burial, although the Talmudic statements are certainly the origin of the (medieval Jewish) practice of genizah. On the latter, see "Genizah" in Zevin, *Encylopaedia Talmudit*, 6:232–39; and now, more extensively, Beit-Arié, "Genizot." One wonders, however, if the practice referred to in the Talmudic statement does not reflect the ancient (universal?) practice of burying personal property, articles of wealth, and the tools of their trade along with the dead, particularly distinguished dead persons; hence, the emphasis on burying the Torah scroll next to the sage (thereby killing two birds, as it were, with one stone—giving the dead sage his own Torah for the world-to-come and burying the used scroll with proper respect).

171 Most of the information in the following section is drawn from Trachtenberg, *Jewish Magic*, 104–13, esp. 105–6; Patai, "Massekhet Segulot"; and in particular, Sabar, "Torah and Magic."

172 See as well Midrash Tehillim 3:2, cited in Sabar, "Torah and Magic," 151 (who also quotes the Sanhedrin passage).

173 Fine, "From Meeting House," 33.

174 I have borrowed the term "artifactual power" from Kalman Bland, *The Artless Jew*, 83–84.

175 *Patrologia Graecae* 48, 852:40,44; translation in Wendy Mayer and Pauline Allen, *John Chrysostom* (London: Routledge, 2000), 160. The passage is cited and discussed in both Levine, *The Ancient Synagogue*, 187; and Fine, "From Meeting House to Sacred Realm," 40. See as well the discussion in Wilken, *John Chrysostom*, 79–81.

176 Jacob Mann, *Texts and Studies*, 2:50, on the basis of texts 3 and 9, published there in Appendix I on pp. 75 and 79; cited in Yaniv, *Ma'aseh Hoshein*, 29. Daniel attacks the Rabbanites both for prostrating before the Torah and for using an ark, which he calls a *matzevah* (monument or statue) and thus an idol. See Tigay, "Torah Scroll," 134 and note 34, where he calls attention to *Midrash Mishlei* (ed. Visotzky), 6, lines 40–44, and Soferim 14:8, which both mention bowing to the Torah; cf. Bar-Ilan, "The Book-Case," 62–63.

177 Sabar, "Torah and Magic"; cf. Goldberg, *Jewish Passages*, 96–97. I wish to thank Eva Frojmovich for discussing this image with me and expressing her reservations about the interpretation linking the image and the folk custom.

178 For discussion of the custom, Kirschner's illustration, and additional references in other Christian Hebraist "ethnographic" works of the period, and for rabbinic criticism of the practice, see Sabar, "Torah and Magic," 153–58.

179 For this and related practices, see Patai, "Massekhet Segulot," 485–86.

180 Jordan, *French Monarchy*, 57. The gentiles' insistence upon Jews using the Torah scroll when making oaths is in fact paralleled in Jewish tradition; see B. Shavuot 38b, discussed in Tigay, "Torah Scroll," 332; and Libson, "Use of a Sacred Object," 53–60. According to the thirteenth-century kabbalist Jacob ben Sheshet of Girona (cited in Idel, "Concepts of Scripture," 160), the Torah scroll must be held when making oaths "by the name of God" because "the Torah is God's name."

181 G. Durando, *Rationale divinorum officiorum a G. Durando*, ed. V. d'Avino (Naples, 1859), caput III, p. 25; English translation in Durandus, *The Symbolism of Churches and Church Ornaments: A Translation of the 'Rationale Divinorum Officiarum' Written by William Durandus*, ed. J. M. Neale and B. Webb (Leeds, 1843), 51, cited in Camille, "Visual Signs," 111, who also notes that the scroll/codex binary for Judaism/Christianity has a long prior tradition in Christian iconography. For an enlightening survey of (mainly) later medieval illustrations depicting the scroll-codex binary, see Stallybrass, "Books and Scrolls."

182 Lipton, *Images of Intolerance*, 57ff.

183 Lipton, *Images of Intolerance*, 62–63.

184 For a superb treatment of the iconicization of the Christian book, with its striking parallels to the processes that the Torah scroll underwent, see Parmenter, "Iconic Book." Cf. Claudia Rapp, "Holy Texts," for more observations on the increasingly iconic dimension of Christian books and Christian scribal culture more generally, but compare the very insightful comments of Frances Young, "Books and Their 'Aura,'" regarding the aniconic beginnings of the Christian book.

185 See, however, Fine, "Open Torah Ark," which argues that in the Greek-speaking Diaspora, the open Torah ark did become a kind of symbol of Jewish identity as a way of illustrating

Jewish devotion to the Law. In Roman and Byzantine Palestine, in contrast, most depictions of the Torah ark picture it as closed, either with doors or a curtain across its front.

186 On the history of the Decalogue and its shape in both Jewish and Christian tradition, see Sarfatti, "Tables of the Covenant"; and Mellinkoff, "Round-Topped Tablets of the Law." On the Magen David/Seal of Solomon, see Scholem, "Star of David." The Decalogue is especially relevant to our discussion because its symbolic use first appeared in Christian art as a negative image of Judaism, as a symbol of the Synagoga, as in the famous statue on the west façade of Notre Dame in Paris where the Jews are portrayed as a despondent, sometimes blindfolded woman holding in her hands the broken tablets. As Sarfatti shows, Jewish tradition later appropriated the image and revalued it as a positive emblem of Jewishness, which is how it appears embroidered on the *parokhet* covering the front of many Torah arks since at least the nineteenth century.

Chapter 2. The Hebrew Bible in the Age of the Manuscript

1 For summaries of the codex's history, see Ofer, "History and Authority of the Aleppo Codex"; Shammosh, *Haketer*; and Friedman, *Aleppo Codex*.

2 For a different version of the recent history of the codex and its mutilation, see Shamosh, *Haketer*; and Friedman, *Aleppo Codex*.

3 The enumeration of the early codices and their descriptions throughout this chapter are based upon the comprehensive and definitive study of Beit-Arié, Sirat, and Glatzer, *Codices Hebraicis Litteris*.

4 Personal communications from Malachi Beit-Arié and Jordan Penkower. Most of these leaves and fragments of lost codices are in the Firkovich collections in Saint Petersburg. On the story of the modern rediscovery of the codices, see chapter 4.

5 The estimated number is that of Goshen-Gottstein, in "Biblical Manuscripts in the United States," 35–42, who provides the classification I use and the estimated percentages: (1) Masoretic codices; (2) study books; and (3) "listener's copies," by which he means what I call popular Bibles. On the latter, see Khan, *Short Introduction to the Tiberian Masoretic Bible*, 7–9, which notes that these copies were not always written carelessly by scribes but simply with greater freedom from the traditional Tiberian readings, sometimes in accordance with more popular reading traditions. Cf. as well Olszowy-Schlanger, "Hebrew Bible," 33, who calls the last type "private" Bibles.

6 The best account of the Masorah is Khan, *Short Introduction to the Tiberian Masoretic Bible*; for more extensive treatments, see Dotan, "Masorah"; and Yeivin, *Introduction to the Tiberian Masorah*.

7 The scholarship on the transition from scroll to codex and on the invention of the codex is immense. The classic work is Roberts and Skeat, *Birth of the Codex*. For an accessible account of the multiple origins of the wax tablet and the transition to the codex across antiquity, see Avrin, *Scribes, Script and Books*, s.v. "wax tablet" and "codex," and especially 173–75.

8 Lieberman, *Hellenism*, 203–5. For references, see M. Shabbat 12:5; M. Avot 3:16; T. Sotah 15:1; Bereishit Rabbah 81:1; and Lieberman, *Hellenism*, for further references.

9 M. Kelim 24:7.

10 The classic account of the transition remains Roberts and Skeat, *Birth of the Codex*, but see as well Bagnall, *Early Christian Books*.

11 For the most recent assessment of the question, see Bagnall, *Early Christian Books,* 70–90.

12 Roberts and Skeat, *Birth of the Codex*, 35–37.

13 For the classic discussion of reasons for the ancient Jewish resistance to the codex, see Lieberman, *Hellenism*, 203–8.

14 For the argument that the scroll served as an icon of self-identification by Jews, see Resnick, "The Codex"; cf. Stroumsa, "Early Christianity." Given what we now know about the likelihood that Greek-speaking Jews used the codex, the argument that it was an especially if not exclusively Christian writing medium has lost much of its force. On the latter question, see Treu, "Significance of Greek," 138–44; and the various papers collected in Kraft, "Files and Information."

15 Note, however, that the fragment scholars consider to be from the very earliest known Jewish codex, the Cambridge Codex (T-S 6 H 9-H21, eighth century?), is a liturgical text, not a Bible; on this codex, see Sirat, *Les papyrus,* 69–80. (This codex is noteworthy also because most other early liturgical texts, particularly *piyyutim*, are written on *rotuli*, scrolls written vertically, not horizontally, like a Torah scroll.) On the Jewish adaption of the codex, see Beit-Arié, *Hebrew Manuscripts,* 11–12; "How Hebrew Manuscripts Are Made," 35–37. It was long believed that the earliest dated manuscript with a colophon was the famous Prophets Codex preserved in the Karaite synagogue Moussa Dar'i in Old Cairo, with a colophon stating that the manuscript was written by Moshe Ben Asher in 894/5, possibly in Tiberias, but it is now widely accepted that this colophon was copied from an earlier colophon; according to Beit-Arié, the manuscript was copied before 1129–30 (*Codices Hebraicis* 1:28). Aside from the Aleppo Codex, there survive fourteen other Bible manuscripts that were copied between 903/4 and 1008 (as described in *Codices* 1); five others between 1020 and 1044 (*Codices* 2); and one additional manuscript in 1122 (*Codices* 3). All these Bibles are Masoretic Bibles. With the exception of the Moussa Dar'i codex, the Aleppo Codex, the fragments of codices rescued from the Cairo Genizah and currently preserved mainly at the Cambridge University Library, and two other codices today in a private collection, the rest of the surviving codices and fragments are nearly all part of the various Firkovich collections in the Russian National Library in Saint Petersburg.

16 On the Islamic background to the Jews' adaption of the codex form, see Khan, *Short Introduction to the Tiberian Masoretic Bible*, 6. The inscription of the Qur'an in the codex form is usually associated with the recension of the text undertaken at the behest of the caliph Uthman (ruled 644–56 CE). On the Qur'an's early history, see Schoeler, *Genesis of Literature*, 32.

17 Beit-Arié, "How Hebrew Manuscripts Are Made," 36. The earliest reference in Jewish literature to *miṣḥaf* is found in *Hilkhot Re'u*, an early translation into Hebrew by the students of Yehudai Gaon of his *Halakhot Pesuko*t (late eighth or early ninth century); see A. L. Schlossberg, *Sefer Halakhot Pesukot O Hilkhot Re'u*. For a thorough discussion of the text and its use of the term, see Glatzer, "Aleppo Codex," 260–61. The other term used by Jews for a codex, *diftar*, is borrowed from the Greek *diphthera*, "animal skin," but this term could also refer to a scroll.

18 The most exhaustive study of every aspect of the material dimensions of the Aleppo Codex is Glatzer, "Aleppo Codex." Inasmuch as the Aleppo Codex is representative of all the early codices, Glatzer's study is the best introduction to the entire group.

19 Ben-Hayyim, "Masorah u-mesoret"; but compare Dotan, "Masorah," 1418–19; and Khan, *Short Introduction to the Tiberian Masoretic Bible*, 1n1.

20 On the Aleppo page in fig. 2.1, there are two *Qeri* notes in the margin to the right of the middle column: two lines from the top (*ad* Deut. 28:27), the reader is told to substitute *u-va-teḥorim* for *u-va-ʿfolim*, while closer to the middle of the column (*ad* 28:30), the word *yishkavenah* is substituted for *yishgalenah*.

21 On the Aleppo Codex page, for example, such a *lamed* appears on the far right margin about a third of the way down the column as well as twice six lines down to the right of the middle column, and then once in the next line down. In each case, the notation refers to the word or phrase in the adjacent column with a small circle above it.

22 For example, on the far right margin, roughly two-thirds of the way down the page, the letter *daled* appears twice, with a *gimel* beneath it to note that the referenced word appears three times in the same form in the Bible. Directly beneath the middle *bet*, another *gimel* indicates that its reference occurs three times. In the middle of the same column, another note *yud-aleph be-taʿam* indicates that the word *ʿad* (Deut. 28:23) appears eleven times in the Bible with this accent.

23 On the far left margin in the middle of the column, the abbreviation *bet ḥas[er]* indicates that the word *ha-tolaʿat* (Deut. 28:39) is spelled defectively twice in the Bible.

24 Frensdorff, *Ochlah W'ochlah*.

25 Frensdorff, *Ochlah W'ochlah*, supplement 2, p. 173; cf. the acerbic remarks of Levita, *Massoreth ha-massoreth*; and Ginsburg's own helpful explanation in *The Massorah*, #553, p. 71. On the *simanim* more generally, see Dotan, "Masorah," 16:1424–25. There are also Aramaic *simanim*, about which see now David Marcus, *Scribal Wit*.

26 For the colophons, see Beit-Arié, Sirat, and Glatzer, *Codices*, for example, MSS 5 (St. Petersburg EBP.IIB17); 6 (Aleppo Codex; Yad Ben Zvi MS 1); 29 (St. Petersburg EBPIIB124). The Leningrad Codex (MS 17, St. Petersburg EBP1B19a) is an example of a manuscript composed by a single individual, Samuel ben Yaakov, who did everything himself. On the process of composition, see Yeivin, *Tiberian Masorah*, 122–25; Dotan, "Masorah," 1426.

27 As noted in the previous chapter, the rabbis discouraged the writing of nonkosher scrolls (that is, those not according with halacha), and especially partial scrolls, even for the purpose of teaching. Doubtless such scrolls existed, even many of them, and these as well as those unsuitable for liturgical use could have been used for writing Masoretic notes. On this, see Yeivin, *Tiberian Masorah*, 7; Dotan, "Masorah," 1416. For examples of later scrolls with Masoretic notes, mainly preserved in the Genizah, see Davis and Outhwaite, *Hebrew Bible Manuscripts*, 4:414–17: fragments T-S AS 63.50, 63.61, 63.88, 63.98, 63.102, 63.154, 63.172.

28 Yeivin, *Tiberian Masorah*, 131–36; Dotan, "Masorah," 1405–14.

29 B. Megillah 3a = Y. Megillah 4:1 (74d), both in reference to Nehemiah 8:8.

30 Dotan, "Masorah," 1414. Compare Yeivin, *Tiberian Masorah*, 35.

31 Freedman and Cohen, "The Masoretes as Exegetes," specifically 35. Cf. as well Kogut, *Correlations*; and most recently, Revell, "Interpretive Value."

32 See Yeivin, "Masorah," 153–55; Dotan, *Tiberian Masorah*, 1471–75; and Khan, "Contribution of the Karaites," specifically 298.

33 On the Uthmanian recension, see Schoeler, *Genesis*, 30–35. It should be noted that Kahle, in *Cairo Genizah*, 78–94, was the first to point to the Islamic/Qur'anic background to the Masoretic project.

34 Khan, "Standardization and Variation," 57. Note as well Khan's comment in *A Short Introduction to the Tiberian Masoretic Bible*, 64n56, which draws a parallel between the Masoretic counting of verses and the command of Hajjaj ibn Yusuf, the governor of Iraq (died 717 CE), ordering that the letters of the Qur'an be counted so as to determine the exact midpoint of the text (although Khan thinks Ibn Yusuf might have gotten the idea for his order from the Jews).

35 On the grammatical connection, see Khan, *Early Karaite Traditions*, 14–22; cf. Yeivin, *Tiberian Masorah*, 35–36; for the other connections, see Dotan, "Masorah," 1414–15.

36 Davis and Outhwaite, *Hebrew Bible Manuscripts*, 2:266. The *serugin* phenomenon requires further study. On the Palestinian vocalization system, see Revell, *Hebrew Texts*.

37 On this very unusual manuscript, see Wernberg-Møller, "Prolegomenon."

38 Ofer, *Babylonian Masora of the Pentateuch*, 17.

39 For the most extensive account of the rise of the Tiberian system and the decline of the Babylonian, see Chiesa, *Hebrew Biblical Pointing*, 17–35, which translates many of the primary Judeo-Arabic sources; cf. Yeivin, *Tiberian Masorah*, 9–31; Dotan, "Masorah," 1425–27. Eventually, of course, Babylonian rabbinic Judaism also claimed the Tiberian tradition as their own; see Chiesa, *Hebrew Biblical Pointing*, 9–13; Drory, *Models and Contacts*, 126–57; and her earlier Hebrew volume, *Reishit Hamaga*, 134–49.

40 Quoted in translation in Chiesa, *Reishit Hamaga*, 19. See also Khan, "Al-Qirqisani's Views."

41 Thus Drory, *Models and Contacts*, 139, who also argues that the Karaites were the first to adapt the Tiberian system for themselves as a way of rejecting Babylonian Rabbanite tradition (as they called the Babylonian rabbinic establishment); as Chiesa notes (*Hebrew Biblical Pointing*, 41), the Tiberian system emerged roughly at the same time that the first Iraqi Karaites settled in Palestine.

42 Chiesa, *Hebrew Biblical Pointing*, 22, citing Qirqisani.

43 The statement praising the Tiberians' Hebrew was made by the tenth-century Karaite David b. Abraham al-Fāsī, cited in Chiesa, *Hebrew Biblical Pointing*, 9. Drory (*Models and Contacts*, 126–57; *Reishit Hamaga*, 134–49); and Chiesa, *Hebrew Biblical Pointing*, 9–13, both point to the parallel between the high estimation of the "classical purity" attributed to the Hebrew of Tiberias and the way pre-Islamic Arabic poetry was idealized in early Islamic culture.

44 This point was suggested to me by Malachi Beit-Arié, personal communication.

45 Dotan, "Masorah," 1416.

46 The codex in which Moses ben Asher is named is the famous Prophets (*Nevi'im*) preserved in the Karaite synagogue Moussa Dar'i in Old Cairo, and discussed above in note 16. On Aaron ben Asher, see Dotan, "Masorah," 1472–73.

47 Maimonides, *Mishneh Torah*, Sefer Torah 8:4. Penkower, "Maimonides and the Aleppo Codex," 39–128.

48 Goshen-Gottstein, "Rise of the Tiberian Bible Text," 86–87.

49 See Dotan, *Ben Asher's Creed*; Zer, "Masorete of the Keter"; and most recently, Rustow, *Heresy and the Politics of Community*, 36–57.

50 In fact, Anan himself was not a Karaite, but he was appropriated by later Karaite tradition and cast in the role of founder. The key study on Anan and his appropriation by Karaites is Ben-Shammai, "Between Annanites and Karaites," esp. 22–23. For a recent and insightful analysis of the issues involved, see Rustow, *Heresy*, 52–57. Furthermore, recent scholarship has shown that the famous slogan attributed to him was both more traditional and less rebellious than it sounds. The first half parallels frequent rabbinic injunctions to investigate the Torah thoroughly while the second should be understood as encouraging a tempered rationalism that resists unquestioning obedience to authority. It was not a call for wholesale rejection of tradition. For a superb dissection of the slogan's prehistory, see Frank, *Search Scripture*, 22–32.

51 On the origins of Karaism, see Gil, "Origins of the Karaites," which reviews both past and contemporary views; Astren, "Islamic Contexts"; and Rustow, *Heresy*, 52–57, for helpful and broader overviews of the larger social and political conditions of the movement's emergence. There have been many discussions about possible ties of Karaism to earlier Jewish sectarian movements, like the Qumran community; for discussion, see Erder, "The Karaites and the Second Temple Sects."

52 See Gil, "Origins of the Karaites," esp. 100–11; and Wasserstrom, *Between Muslim and Jew*, 33–45.

53 Drory, *Models and Contacts*, 138–43; Goldstein, "Beginnings of the Transition."

54 Rustow, *Heresy*, 46.

55 For the early Masoretic Bibles that were donated to Karaite synagogues, see Beit-Arié, Sirat, and Glatzer, *Codices*, I, #1 (p. 27), Cairo Prophets Codex (probably written before 1129/30 and dedicated by its original patron, Yavetz ben Shlomo, to the Karaite community of Jerusalem, then plundered by the Crusaders, and eventually rededicated to the Karaite synagogue in Cairo); II, #23 (p. 61), Cairo Prophets (written in 1028), now in the Karaite synagogue in Cairo; III, #60 (p. 89), First Prophets, St. Petersburg EBP III c144 (no date; taken from a Karaite synagogue in Crimea).

56 On the use of the codex in the Karaite synagogue, see Allony, "Torah Scrolls"; and Fleischer, *Eretz-Israel Prayer*, 293–320. In a personal communication, however, Geoffrey Khan has pointed out to me that there is no hard evidence for the use of codices in Karaite synagogues in the Middle Ages. Strangely, there is very little information or documentation about Karaite liturgical reading of the Torah in their synagogues; the one book on the topic is a late Karaite text, *Sefer Patshegen Ketav Ha-Dat*, written by Calev Apendopulo (fifteenth century, Constantinople), which already shows the "rabbinization" of Karaism. Because all the known rules governing the production of a kosher Sefer Torah are rabbinic, it is hard to believe that Karaites accepted them, even by default.

57 See Khan, *Karaite Bible Manuscripts*, 20.

58 I want to thank Meira Polliack for pointing this out to me.

59 The Karaites' preference for the reading over the writing tradition is exemplified in the transliterations—not translations—they made of the Hebrew text of the Bible into Arabic. For one such manuscript, see fig. 4.5 and the discussion in that chapter.

60 Rustow, *Heresy*, 46.

61 See Polliack, "Rethinking Karaism," esp. 86–91, on what she calls the "Scripturalist" orientation in Judaism.

62 On this process in both Karaism and Rabbanism, see Rustow, *Heresy*, 47–56.

63 The classic source for rabbis who knew the Torah by heart is Y. Megillah 4:1 (= B. Megillah 18b). See as well T. Megillah 2:5, for the injunction against chanting the Torah from memory and the story of R. Meir, who once wrote the Scroll of Esther entirely from memory. The very fact that the Tosefta felt it necessary to prohibit chanting from memory is a good indication that a number of people could do it. On all these sources, see Naeh, "Art of Memory," 556–60.

64 James Kugel, "Two Introductions," 93ff.

65 Maria Subtelny of the University of Toronto has pointed out to me that the column form within elaborate frames is also found in roughly contemporary Persian poetic texts. For further discussion, see Stern, "First Jewish Codices," 189–91.

66 Firkovich Collection, Russian National Library, St. Petersburg BPIIB8 (= *CHL* 2:27ff.).

67 The stichography is already mentioned in B. Megillah 16b. For some discussion of possible scribal antecedents, see Yeivin, *Tiberian Masorah,* 43–44 (par. 77); and Tov, *Scribal Practices,* 174–75.

68 The phrase is not attested in the best early manuscripts of the Mishnah representing the Palestinian text tradition, like the Kaufmann Codex (early thirteenth century, Library of the Hungarian Academy of Sciences, Budapest, Collection Kaufmann A 50); see Sharvit, *Tractate Avot,* 135. It does appear, however, in Avot de-Rabbi Natan B, chap. 33, as *seyag la-torah masoret,* so the provenance of the saying must be ancient even if not originally Mishnaic. I want to thank Professor Jacob Elbaum for directing me to this reference.

69 For a medieval commentary on the passage, see Mahzor Vitry (N. France, eleventh to twelfth century) in its commentary on Avot, ad locum (Hürwitz, *Maḥzor Vitry*, 513). On the "original" meaning of *masoret* and medieval uses of the word, see Ben-Hayyim, "Masorah u-mesoret," 283–92. For the Masoretic poem, see the Leningrad Codex (fol. 490v) as reconstructed in Dotan, *Ben Asher's Creed,* 68–71 and 72–79.

70 On aspects of the Masorah as a fence, see Weber, "Masoret Is a Fence."

71 On this manuscript's colophon, see note 15 above.

72 Lyons, *Cumulative Masora, 65–66.* For more on the geometric illustrations and designs in the Cairo Prophets Codex, see Avrin, *Illuminations,* 157–61.

73 On the Jewish-Islamic connections, see Milstein, "Hebrew Book Illumination"; and now Mann, "A Shared Tradition," for an even more extensive discussion. See Milstein, "Hebrew Book Illumination," 435, for discussion of the designs on the folios from St. Petersburg II Firkovich B116. On the symbolic significance of Temple/sanctuary representations in Spanish Jewish art, see Gutmann, *Hebrew Manuscript Painting,* 18–19, 50–57; Gutmann, "Masorah Figurata in the Mikdashyah," 71–83; Yaffa Levy, "Ezekiel's Plan," 68–85; Narkiss, *Hebrew Illuminated Mss* 1: index s.v. "Sanctuary Implements" and "Temple of Jerusalem," esp. 17, 21, 24–27, 101–4; Stern, "Hebrew Bible in the Middle Ages"; Stern, "The Hebrew Bible in Spain," 49–85. For the Karaite background to the symbol, see Naftali Wieder, "'Sanctuary' as a Metaphor for Scripture," 165–75.

74 For examples, see Avrin, "*Micrography*," plates 9 (Pentateuch, 929 CE, Russian National Library, St. Petersburg, Firkovich II B 17, fol. 5v) and 15 (Firkovich II B 116).

75 Avrin, "Micrography," 43–44, also differentiates Jewish micrographic art from the *poema figurata*, where the lines of a poem (or other text) are laid out on the page so that they fill the shape of an object.

76 On the use of such devices in later medieval literature, see Carruthers, *Book of Memory*, 221–57. Note the comments of Joseph ibn Aknin (*Sefer Musar*, 97) and Menachem Meiri (*Beit Ha-Beḥirah*, 134), both of whom suggest that the word *masoret* refers to mnemonic techniques used to remember Torah. Cf. Ben-Hayyim, "Masorah u-mesoret," 384–85, where he cites S. D. Luzatto's similar view.

77 On such expressions of individuality, though mainly in relation to scribal practice in later centuries, see Beit-Arié, *Unveiled Faces*, 42–45.

78 Grabar, *Mediation of Ornament*, 190, and more generally, 155–93.

79 Grabar, *Mediation of Ornament*, 186.

80 The strongest case for Jewish-Muslim cooperation in the production of both Bibles and Qur'ans has been made by Vivian Mann, "A Shared Tradition." See as well Milstein, "Hebrew Book Illumination."

81 On the carpet page in Islamic books, see Ettinghausen, *Islamic Art*, 76–78.

82 On the history of the Magen David, see Scholem, "The Star of David."

83 These pages have not yet been studied in depth. The best (and so far as I know, only) codicological study of the codex is in Beit-Arié, Sirat, and Glatzer, *Codices*, 1:114–19. As the editors note (114), the final folios of the codex, ff. 471–91, which include all the carpet pages, have been preserved as single sheets, not as parts of quires, and their present placement (the codex is no longer bound, but the folios are numbered) is incorrect. As the manuscript is currently foliated, there are no carpet pages at its beginning (although there is a full-page colophon on 1r, which must have been written after the manuscript was completed because it lists the date of completion as well as the other conventional information), while all the carpet pages are currently at the codex's conclusion, grouped in two sections (as noted above) among the Masoretic rules. Six of these decorated pages are also colophons, albeit brief ones. Because of the current state of the codex, it is impossible to reconstruct its original structure, but it is likely that a number of the carpet pages, particularly those with gates, were originally at the codex's beginning.

84 For this definition of ornament and the characterization of the overall shape, see Schapiro, *Language of Form*, 29–34.

85 Ettinghausen, *Islamic Art*, 76.

86 Ettinghausen, *Islamic Art*, 76.

87 Penkower, "Sheet of Parchment." As the subtitle of Penkower's article (in which he lists the four geocultural-based text traditions) indicates, there are also Oriental examples (drawn mainly from tenth- to eleventh-century texts) and Yemenite (fifteenth- to sixteenth-century) traditions aside from Ashkenazic and Sephardic (thirteenth to fourteenth centuries).

88 On the codicological and paleographic distinctions between the books produced in these different areas, see Beit-Arié, *Hebrew Manuscripts*, 26–35. Both Byzantium and the Near East tended to follow Sepharad after the twelfth century. The distinct features of Italian Bibles

emerge only after the late thirteenth century; before that time, most Italian Bibles resemble those of Ashkenaz.

89 Dukan, *La Bible hébraïque*, 10.

90 The contemporary "genizot" that scholars are, admirably, working to reconstruct—like the Italian Genizah or the German one—are not "genizot" in the traditional sense: the fragments they are collecting, mainly from book bindings and other secondary uses, are mainly those of luxury codices that had the unlucky fate of falling into the hands of Christians who reused them for secondary purposes.

91 Mention should also be made of Bibles produced in Byzantium, the Near East, and North Africa. While the books of these regions have some distinct features, they generally follow the Sephardic model.

92 On the question of sequence, see *Encyclopedia Judaica,* 3:580–82. There does not appear to be any geographical rationale for the differences in sequence in different manuscripts.

93 The most common appendices are lists of the differences between the schools of Ben Asher and Ben Naftali; among post-Masoretic texts, Kimḥi's grammatical treatise *Sefer Mikhlol* was also copied, albeit much less commonly. As we will see, Ashkenazic Masoretic Bibles include the Aramaic Targum, often written interverse; on the practice, see my discussion in this chapter.

94 See, for example, the fragmentary Pentateuch (Ms. Vatican ebr. 448), which contains both the Masorah and the Targum, the latter vocalized with Tiberian vowel signs, which are, however, supralinear—above rather than below the consonants—a typical feature of early Babylonian texts, suggesting a Babylonian origin for the manuscript, which probably dates from the late eleventh century. For discussion, see Diez Macho, "Introductory Remarks." See as well Parma 2004, formerly de Rossi 12 (Parma Catalogue 74), a Pentateuch with Targum whose colophon states that it was copied from an earlier Pentateuch brought from Babylonia that contained supralinear vowel points—apparently very much like Vatican 448—and that it was "corrected" to conform to the normative Tiberian sublinear vocalization by a R. Nathan bar Makhir bar Menahem from Ancona, the son of R. Samuel bar Makhir from the province of Oria, who was possibly an ancestor of the great sage Gershom ben Judah (ca. 960–1028), known as Rabbeinu Gershom Meir Ha-Golah, "Our teacher Gershom, the Light of the Exile." Gershom himself may have been born in Ancona; he later settled in Mainz and was largely responsible for making that community the earliest center of Ashkenazi Jewry.

95 Christian Bibles of this sort come in multiple types. Aside from notations like *capitula*, or chapter cues that identify the order and location of readings, there are many types of collections of readings: epistolaries (Pauline and Catholic epistles and Acts), evangelistaries (the gospels), and larger Mass lectionaries that contained both the epistle and gospel readings. All these types appear to have been in use simultaneously going back to the eighth century, although they reached the height of their use during the thirteenth and fourteenth centuries. On the subject, see Richard Gyug, "Early Medieval Bibles," esp. 35–38. I also wish to thank Mr. Andrew Irving for sharing with me his knowledge about Latin Bibles.

96 I will not deal with these books here, but the subject of Jewish Psalters and their relation to Christian books of the same kind deserves a full study in its own right. On haftarah books, see now Kogel, "Reconstruction of a *Sefer Haftarot*," and especially her caveat on 48–49 noting

that (1) haftarot collections are very rare and (2) it is very difficult to determine whether those that do exist were originally written as separate books in their own right or whether they were once part of larger, multivolume *ḥumashim* from which they were later pulled and extracted.

97 For a good sketch of the historical background, see Kogman-Appel, *Jewish Book Art*, 10–56.

98 The Toronto Pentateuch is actually a composite volume consisting of sections from several codices. Its first half (Gen.–Exod.) is from a tenth- to eleventh-century Near Eastern Masoretic Bible; the second half (Lev.–Deut.), the Sephardic Pentateuch, with two supplementary manuscripts that fill in gaps in the two major sections. For a brief description, see Walfish, *"As It Is Written,"* 11–12. I want to thank Barry Walfish for calling this codex to my attention. This reference also corrects my statement in Stern, "Hebrew Bible in Europe," 12, that the earliest Spanish Hebrew Bible (Paris, Bibliothèque Nationale de France [BnF], cod. Héb. 105) was written in Toledo in 1197.

99 On their accuracy, Zimmels, *Ashkenazim and Sepharadim*, 138; Sarna, "Hebrew and Bible Studies," 329–31, 345–46; Sarna, "Introductory Remarks."

100 The statement about the superior Spanish and Tiberian books is found in *Teshuvot Talmidei Menahem Le-Dunash*, ed. S. G. Stern (1879), 67–68, cited in Sarna, "Introductory Remarks." For Meir of Rothenberg, see his glosses to Maimonides's *Mishneh Torah, Hilkhot Sefer Torah*, 8:2–4.

101 Meiri, *Kiryat Sefer*, 48.

102 This tendency is already evident in the earliest surviving dated Hebrew Bibles from Spain, including both the 1188 Girona Pentateuch (Toronto, Friedberg MSS 9-005) mentioned earlier and described in note 98 and the Toledo 1197 Bible (Paris, Bibliothèque Nationale de France [BnF] cod. Héb. 105); by 1197, Toledo had been under Christian rule for more than a century (since 1085 CE). For a reproduction of a page from the latter codex, see Beit-Arié and Engel, *Specimens of Mediaeval Hebrew Script,* plate 14. In the Toledo 1197 Bible, the biblical text is written in two rather than three columns. Most Spanish Masoretic Bibles like the Girona 1188 Pentateuch use three columns, though there are a number with two. For the influence of the Islamic book on these Bibles, see Kogman-Appel, *Jewish Book Art*, 38–50.

103 Exceptions to the Islamicizing Bibles are some of the great Bibles of the late thirteenth century, like the Cervera Bible and the Kennicott Bible, as well as a number of the Bibles associated with Joshua Ibn Gaon, which also show the strong influence of Gothic books produced in Christian environments. On these Bibles, see Kogman-Appel, *Jewish Book Art*, 98–130, 212–19; Narkiss, *Hebrew Illuminated Manuscripts in the British Isles*, 22–35, 152–68.

104 The relationship between the aniconic designs in the Castilian Bibles and the representational miniatures in the Catalonian Haggadah is discussed in Kogman-Appel, *Illuminated Haggadot*, 187–223, where she attributes the differences to social class and religious ideology. For a very different view, see Frojmovic, "Jewish Mudejarismo," which argues that both tendencies can be seen as characteristic of Mudejarismo, not as emanating from two separate social groups. In an unpublished paper, I propose a third alternative that pins part of their differences on the generic stances required by the books—Bibles on the one hand, Haggadoth on the other—and the polemical strategies appropriate to the genre that each one adopts in responding to Christian hegemony.

105 On BnF héb. 25, see Sed-Rajna, *Les manuscrits hébreux enluminés*, 5–7. The early Masoretic Bible referred to is Saint Petersburg EBP II B8 (f. 56v–57r), pictured in figure 2.4. The wall-like frame also appears in an undated and unlocalized manuscript, London, British Library, MS Or. 2363. Margoliouth, *Catalogue*, 1:39 describes this Bible as either Persian or Babylonian and dates it to sometime between the eleventh and thirteenth centuries, but Kogman-Appel, *Jewish Book Art*, 46–47, appears less certain. See also Leveen, *Hebrew Bible in Art*, 70–71.

106 For a description, see Sed-Rajna, *Manuscrits hébreux de Lisbonne*.

107 For another example of a liturgical Pentateuch from the Lisbon workshop, see the Almanzi Pentateuch, Lisbon, 1480–90, BL Add. 27167, with pages reproduced in Tahan, *Hebrew Manuscripts*, 64–65.

108 Note, however, that the use of the semicursive for the biblical text also becomes quite common in Italian Bibles of the late fourteenth and early fifteenth centuries; see my discussion later in this chapter.

109 Gross, "Rashi and the Tradition of Study," 37 and note 44.

110 Abrahams, *Hebrew Ethical Wills*, 65–66.

111 Gross, "Rashi and the Tradition of Study"; Penkower, "Process of Canonization." I should add, however, that the evidence of the codices themselves does not entirely reflect the textual sources. Most Spanish liturgical Pentateuchs do not have either Targum or Rashi, though for an exception, see New York, JTSA Lutzki 191, a fragment of a large quarto-sized liturgical Pentateuch written in fourteenth-century Spain in which each verse is followed by the Targum, then Saadiah, then Rashi. The biblical verse is written in large square Sephardic script, the Targum and Saadiah in a significantly smaller semicursive, and then Rashi in an even smaller semicursive.

112 For the Rabbeinu Asher citation, see his novellae (*ḥiddushim*) for B. Berakhot 1:8, and the work Orḥot Ḥayyim, attributed to him and cited in Penkower, "Process of Canonization," 143n86. For Jacob Ba'al Ha-Turim, see Tur Oraḥ Ḥayyim #285.

113 Gross, "Rashi," 37–40; and Penkower, "Process of Canonization," esp. 138–46.

114 The most recent and extensive study, on which my own comments are based, is Kogman-Appel, *Jewish Book Art*. An older but still useful account of the development of the Sephardic Bible can be found in Narkiss, *Hebrew Illuminated Manuscripts*, 20–41, 101–20, 153–76.

115 The classic article is Dodds, "Mudejar Tradition," now updated by Frojmovic, "Jewish Mudejarismo."

116 On this Bible and others composed in the same period (and probably in geographical proximity), see Kogman-Appel, *Jewish Book Art*, 131–40.

117 On Christian appropriations of Mudejar style, see Ecker, *Caliphs and Kings*, 6–8, and esp. 57–65, including the amazing baptismal font (Toledo, ca. 1400) pictured on p. 59. The use of Mudejar designs in Jewish architecture (e.g., the El Transito Synagogue in Toledo) and textiles has often been noted. See Dodds, "Mudejar Tradition"; cf. Gerber, "World of Samuel Halevi"; and Frojmovich, "Jewish Mudejarismo."

118 See note 103 above on exceptions to the Islamicizing tendencies.

119 See Kogman-Appel, *Jewish Book Art*, 175–85.

120 I wish to thank Professor Raymond Scheindlin for reminding me of this important fact.

121 My argument here is very close to that of Frojmovich, "Messianic Politics" and "Jewish Mudejarismo," which present a far more textured and rich presentation of the idea.

122 On the idea and the architecture in particular, see Dodds, "Mudejar Tradition"; and Gerber, "World of Samuel Halevi."

123 Williams, "Castilian Tradition"; Kuenel, "Jewish and Christian Art," esp. 13–14; Nordström, "Temple Miniatures," all of which agree that the Madrid manuscript illustrations were directly based on Jewish models.

124 For other linkages between contemporaneous Jewish exegesis and the symbolism of the Temple implements, particularly in respect to iconography, see Kogman-Appel, "Sephardic Ideas in Ashkenaz."

125 Chavel, *Peirush R. Bahya,* 2:268.

126 Chavel, *Peirush R. Bahya,* 2:288–89.

127 Note, however, that these Temple implement illustrations cannot be called truly aniconic, either, since they clearly have a representational dimension. On this dimension, see Frojmovic's comments on the cherubim in the Perpignan Bible (fol. 12v), in Frojmovic, "Jewish Mudijarismo," 250–51.

128 Wieder, "Sanctuary," 171, where he cites the colophon to the Jerusalem Mikdashyah, a deluxe illuminated Bible, written by Elisha Crescas in 1366–83, in which the scribe describes the book as "ha-sefer shel arba'ah ve-'esrim ha-mekhuneh be-fi he-hamon [called by the masses] Mikdashyah." The "official" formal name for a Bible was *ha-sefer shel arba'ah ve-'esrim* (the book of the twenty-four).

129 In a Bible written in northern Italy in 1499 (Parma 2516, Cat. #24), the Spanish scribe Moshe Akrish used the biblical term *mishkan* (Tabernacle) in the colophon as his designation for the Bible.

130 Wieder, "Sanctuary," esp. 166–68. Wieder notes that the analogy is a metaphor for equivalent *sancta*, but given the exceptional literacy of the Qumran sectarians and their devotion to the Bible, as evidenced by the huge number of biblical fragments found among the Dead Sea Scrolls, it is tempting to think that the Bible and attention to biblical study may actually have served them as a surrogate sanctuary and mode of worship.

131 Abraham Ibn Ezra, *Sefer Moznayim* (Venice, 1546), 196; quoted in Wieder, "Sanctuary," 168–69. He uses the metaphor in describing the Masoretes as "guardians of the Sanctuary [*miqdash*]" who "prevent the stranger [*ha-zar*] from approaching the gates of righteousness."

132 On Duran and *Ma'aseh Efod*, see now the exemplary study of Kozodoy, *Secret Faith of Maestre Honoratus*, esp. 161–203. For previous scholarship, see Gutwirth, "Religion and Social Criticism"; Bland, *Artless Jew*, 82–91; Zwiep, "Jewish Scholarship"; and most recently, Fishman, "Hebrew Bible"; and Josef Stern, "Profayt Duran's *Ma'aseh Efod*."

133 Duran, *Ma'aseh Efod*, 13–14.

134 For a complete discussion of the term, see Kozodoy, *Secret Faith*, 188–91. For "occult virtue," see 190. See as well Josef Stern, "Profayt Duran's *Ma'aseh Efod*," the first serious study of Duran's grammatical theory. Previous treatments have focused almost exclusively on the book's introduction; Stern's study significantly shifts the focus. According to Stern, Duran essentially argues that by understanding the structure of the Hebrew language, the student can

understand the structure of God's world and through this understanding actualize the artifactual power of scripture. I wish to thank Josef Stern for allowing me to read his article in manuscript form even though he thinks my interpretation is "completely wrong," as he once told me.

135 Duran, *Ma'aseh Efod*, 10, on which see Kozodoy, *Secret Faith*, 175–77.

136 Duran, *Ma'aseh Efod*, 13.

137 Duran, *Ma'aseh Efod*, 11.

138 Duran, *Ma'aseh Efod*, 14. On *shimush tehillim*, see Kozodoy, *Secret Faith*, 193–95.

139 Kozodoy, *Secret Faith*, 1–11. According to Kozodoy, he converted sometime after 1391.

140 Kozodoy, *Secret Faith*, 176.

141 On the capacity of Torah meditation to draw down divine emanation, see Kozodoy, *Secret Faith*, 192–93; cf. as well Fishman, "Hebrew Bible and the Senses," for an even more expansive view of Torah study in Duran as a talisman.

142 Duran, *Ma'aseh Efod*, 19.

143 Duran, *Ma'aseh Efod*, 21.

144 Duran, *Ma'aseh Efod*, 21.

145 Frojmovich, "Jewish Mudejarismo," 241–46.

146 Frojmovich, "Jewish Mudejarismo," 244.

147 Thus the Ambrosian Bible (Milan, Ambrosian Library, ms. B30–32), a three-volume illustrated Bible composed probably in the region around Würzberg in 1236–38, and the Wroclaw Bible (Universitätsbibliothek Breslau Ms. M 1106), composed in 1238. On the Ambrosian Bible, see Narkiss, *Hebrew Illustrated Manuscripts*, pl. 25; and Ottolenghi, *Hebraica Ambrosiana, II*, 119–25. On the Wroclaw Bible, Metzger, *Die Bibel*; and on their common scribe, Joseph Qalonymus, see Gutmann, "Joseph Ben Kalonymus." Interverse Targum is also found in the two "giant" Bibles from Erfurt as well as in BnF Héb. 5–6 (S. Germany or S. Switzerland, 1294–95) and 8–10 (S. Germany, 1304), both of which are multivolume Masoretic Bibles like the Ambrosian and contain the interverse Targum in the Pentateuch volume. Both are also large if not giant codices (53.4 × 37.5 cm and 44.5 × 32.5 cm, respectively). On the entire phenomenon, see Weber, "Masoret Is a Fence."

148 On these fragments, see Klein, *Genizah Manuscripts of Palestinian Targum*, 1:xxii, and 2:MS B (plates 4–9), MS C (plates 10–19), and MS D (plates 20–49). On the significance of the scribal practice of writing Targum interverse, see the important remarks of Steven Fraade, "Rabbinic Views," 264–65 and note 31. I wish to thank Professor Fraade for calling my attention to the Palestinian texts and for allowing me to read the unpublished material he has written on the subject.

149 On this manuscript and on the question of the Babylonian origins of the liturgical Pentateuch, see my discussion in note 94 above.

150 On this manuscript, Beit-Arié, *Only Dated Medieval Hebrew Manuscript*; and Olszowy-Schlanger, *Les manuscrits hébreux*, 238–42. Note as well that the Valmadonna Pentateuch also has the Masorah, which is sometimes found in Ashkenazic liturgical Pentateuchs but not always.

151 For French Pentateuchs that leave out the Targum altogether, see BnF Héb. 53 (Sed-Rajna, *Manuscrits hébreux enluminés*, #60); Héb. 19 (#64); Héb. 4 (#69); it may be significant that

all three manuscripts also have Masorah. For French Pentateuchs that substitute Rashi for Targum, see BnF Héb. 1349 (#59) and London, BL Ms. Or. 2696. For Rashi's place as a commentator, see the section below on study Bibles. The first medieval sage to mention the substitution of Rashi for the Targum was the French Tosafist Moses of Coucy (first half of the thirteenth century) in Sefer Mitzvot Gadol, end of Positive Commandments #19, where he already mentions that his teachers had advised reading Rashi over the Targum as being more profitable. See as well Gross, "Rashi and the Tradition of Study," 37.

152 For a description of the page, see Sassoon, *Ohel Dawid*, 19–21. Note that in the picture inside the roundel Eve has no breasts, while in the larger portrait next to the roundel she does. This iconography is found in a number of Byzantine Octateuchs, on which see Meyer, "Eve's Nudity." Whether or not this iconography is to be found in any Western manuscripts remains to be determined.

153 For some speculations on the possible ceremonial use of the Targum in these Bibles, see Weber, "Masoret Is a Fence," esp. 12–13.

154 See Maimonides, *Teshuvot Ha-Rambam*, no. 294. On the history of the problem as summarized below, see Ta-Shma, *Early Franco-German Ritual*, 171–81. Note that in his responsum, Maimonides refers to "our *ḥumashim*," with certain reference to codices; this would appear to be one of our earliest sources for the use of the term in connection with liturgical Pentateuchs. In B. Gittin 60a, which Maimonides uses as a source for his view, the word *ḥo[u]mashim* refers to scrolls containing single books of the Bible; see Rashi's comment on the passage in Gittin 60a.

155 For an insightful suggestion as to the original meaning and significance of this direction, see Fraade, "Rabbinic Views," 264–65.

156 Meir of Rothenburg, *Sefer Minhagim*, Kriyah Be-Ḥumashim, 13.

157 Isaac bar Moshe, *Sefer Or Zaru'a*, part 1, "The Laws of Kri'at Shema,'" par. 11; cf. Shalev-Eyni, *Jews among Christians*, 9–10. The same practice was already predicated as normative law in *Maḥzor Vitry* of Simha ben Samuel (d. 1105), par. 117, which was especially influential in northern France; for the text, see Hürwitz, *Maḥzor Vitry*, 1:88. For more contextualization, see Weber, "Masoret Is a Fence," 11–12.

158 See Saenger, "Reading in the Later Middle Ages."

159 Saenger, "Reading in the Later Middle Ages," 133.

160 For the larger picture, see de Hamel, *The Book*, 64–139; for the early Italian giant Bibles, Cahn, *Romanesque Bible Illumination*, 101–6, and for the subsequent history of the giant Bible, 121–66, and the separate essays in Boynton and Reilly, *Practice of the Bible*, esp. Richard Gyeg, "Early Medieval Bibles, Biblical Books, and the Monastic Liturgy in the Benevantan Region," 34–60; Diane J. Reilly, "Lectern Bibles and Liturgical Reform in the Central Middle Ages," 105–25; Lila Yawn, "The Italian Giant Bibles," 126–56; and Laura Light, "The Bible and the Individual," 228–46. The first scholar to connect the Hebrew Bibles to their Latin counterparts in Germany was Shalev-Eyni in *Jews among Christians*, esp. 1–10.

161 Chistopher de Hamel, *The Book*, 135–39; and now esp. Light, "The Bible and the Individual."

162 For a preliminary survey of the sizes of Ashkenazic Bibles, see Attia, "Targum Layouts." While she does not realize that most of the books with Targum that she surveys are *ḥumashim*, her survey is nonetheless valuable and demonstrates the range of sizes as well as formats and

other codicological features. For how these changes in size affected Jewish books more generally, see Sirat, "Le livre hébreu"; and on the Bible in particular, Shalev-Eyni, *Jews among Christians*.

163 This is in decided contrast to Sephardic Bibles, whose size varies between a quarto and a medium-sized folio. For Spanish Bibles before 1280, see Dukan, *La Bible hébraïque*, 187–222, and particularly the helpful table on 222; most of the codices are either in what she calls "grand format" (between 369 × 295 mm and 299 × 277 mm) or "format intermédiare" (283 × 275 mm to 197 × 178 mm). My preliminary survey suggests that most fourteenth-century Spanish Bibles continue to adhere to these rough proportions.

164 On Erfurt 1, see Hahn et al., "Erfurt Hebrew Giant Bible"; for illustrations and a short description, see *Kitwe-Jad*, 18–25. The other giant Bibles include Erfurt 2 (SBB Ms. Or. Fol. 1212), and approximately fourteen other codices whose height exceeds 500 mm (= 19.7 inches). Among thirteenth-century Bibles, the Ambrosian Bible of 1236–38 and the Wroclaw Bible of 1238 measure, respectively, 453 × 344 mm (= 18 × 13.5 inches) and 488 × 360 mm (= 19.2 × 14 inches). On these Bibles, see Weber, "Masorah Is a Fence"; and Fronda, "Attributing of Three Ashkenazi Bibles."

165 For some discussion, see Weber, "Masorah Is a Fence."

166 Reilly, *Art of Reform*; Reilly, "Lectern Bibles"; and Yawn, "The Italian Giant Bibles."

167 De Hamel, *The Book*, 37–38; Reilly, "Lectern Bibles," 108–9.

168 See Beit-Arié, "The Individualistic Nature." The best-known cases of individuals dedicating their books to synagogues nearly all relate to Karaites and the Karaite community. An exceptional case in Ashkenaz may be that of Mahzor Worms; see Beit-Arié, "The Worms Mahzor," 16–17, which suggests that the patron may already have intended, at the time he commissioned the book, to bequeath it to the community after his death.

169 Hahn et al., "Erfurt Hebrew Giant Bible," 18.

170 For the Schocken Bible and a reproduction of its famous opening initial word page for Bereishit, see Narkiss, *Hebrew Illustrated Manuscripts*, pl. 31. The liturgical Pentateuchs include the Duke of Sussex German Pentateuch (BL Add MS 15282), also from Lake Constance, ca. 1300, on which see Shalev-Eyni, *Jews among Christians*, 105–29.

171 Paris, BnF MS Héb. 33, described in Sirat, "Le livre hébreu," 246–47 and illustration 9.

172 These include (1) BnF Héb. 36, liturgical Pentateuch written in Poligny in 1300 (reproduced and described in Garel, *D'une main forte*, 105), in which (fol. 283v) the menorah, located at the end of Deuteronomy before the Scrolls section of the codex, is surrounded by scenes of Aaron, the Binding of Isaac, and the Judgment of Solomon; the page is reproduced in Narkiss, *Hebrew Illustrated Manuscripts*, pl. 24; (2) the Regensburg Pentateuch (Bavaria [Regensburg]), ca. 1300 (Jerusalem, Israel Museum, Ms. 180/52, fol. 155v–156r), which contains the array of Temple implements plus Aaron kindling the menorah (fol. 155v–156r), about which see Kogman-Appel, *Jewish Book Art*, 156–60; and now Kogman-Appel, "Sephardic Ideas in Ashkenaz," who has correctly characterized the difference in the shapes of the utensil in Ashkenazic and Sephardic manuscripts; the latter follow Maimonides's description, the former seem to follow Rashi's; (3) BL Ms. Add. 11639, fol. 114r, the so-called French Miscellany, northern France, ca. 1288–98, about which see my discussion below under the liturgical Pentateuch in Ashkenaz; (4) BnF Héb. 5–6 (S. Germany/S. Switzerland, 1294–95, fol. 118v), reproduced in

Garel, *D'une maine forte*, with its very interesting full-page micrographic drawing of an olive tree from which (presumably) Aaron is picking olives and others are pressing them to make olive oil for the menorah; the olive tree itself is depicted as resembling a seven-branched menorah. There are also several Italian Bibles with a picture of the menorah: (1) BL Ms. Harley 5710, vol. 1, fol. 136r, Rome, Italy, around 1300, reproduced in Tahan, *Hebrew Manuscripts*, 30; and found also at the end of Deuteronomy. (Note that in Margoliouth's British Library catalog, this manuscript is incorrectly dated to 1240 on the basis of an owner's inscription; Bezalel Narkiss, in the unpublished "Catalogue of the Hebrew Illuminated Manuscripts in the British Isles," vol. 2, "Italian Manuscripts," corrected the date to 1340. I wish to thank Ms. Anna Nizza for the reference.) (2) Parma 1849, #64 in Richler's Parma Palatina catalog, written in 1304, contains pictures of the Temple implements within an opening of two folio pages (fol. 91a), placed between Exodus and Leviticus. Reproduced in Ottolenghi, "Un gruppo," 157, this illustration is more like a map of the Temple structure, and bears little similarity to the design of the Spanish carpet-page-like illustrations of the Temple implements. To the best of my knowledge, neither of these Italian Bibles has figured in past scholarship about the history of Temple implement imagery.

173 Halperin, "Decorated Masorah."

174 On the emergence of initial word panels in biblical manuscripts, as part of the development of modes of structural design and transparency to aid readers, see Beit-Arié, *Unveiled Faces*, 51–59, and on biblical manuscripts in particular, 55–57.

175 On the first illustrated initial word panels in Jewish books, in Munich Cod. Heb. 5 (the Rashi *kuntras*, on which see my discussion on study Bibles), see Frojmovic, "Jewish Scribes and Christian Illuminators."

176 Garel, *D'une main forte*, #70, pp. 102–3. For similar images in contemporary Christian books, see Randall, *Images in the Margins*, LXV, no. 315 (Verdun, Bibliothèque Municipale, MS 107, fol. 19v, early fourteenth-century France) and no. 316 (London BL Royal MS 10 E.IV, ff. 65v. early fourteenth-century England). For another example of a similar illustration in an early fourteenth-century book, see the Luttrell Psalter (London BL Add. MS 42130), 10. For a general treatment of the motif of the Jewish knight in medieval Hebrew manuscripts, see Sara Offenberg, "A Jewish Knight," which does not, however, treat our image.

177 On such initials and their micrographic illustrations, see Fronda, "Attributing of Three Ashkenazi Bibles," particularly in reference to the Erfurt Bibles; cf. as well Weber, "Masoret Is a Fence," 12–17.

178 For an excellent illustration of the parallels between Christian and Jewish book-art grotesques, see Reeve, *Sacred*, 150–51, which counterposes a folio from the Duke of Sussex's German Pentateuch (a liturgical Pentateuch), Germany ca. 1300 (BL Add. MS 15282, f. 45v) with marginal grotesques, and an opening from the English Luttrell Psalter, fourteenth century (BL Add. MS 42130, ff. 179v–180r). The Pentateuch's monsters are, of course, micrographic pen drawings, while the Luttrell Psalter's are painted.

179 See, for example, BnF Héb. 1, fol. 104v, a Pentateuch written in 1286, possibly in the Rhineland, which contains a micrographic depiction of the red heifer that directly illustrates the text on the page, Numbers 19; reproduced in Garel, *D'une main fort*, 123. For other examples, see Berlin, SBB Ms. Or quarto 9 (Rouen, 1233), fol. 19a, with a picture of Jacob's ladder to illustrate

Genesis 28:10–22, reproduced in *Kitwe-Jad*, 28–29; and BnF MS Héb. 85 (Lorraine, Franche Comte, ca. 1280–1300), fol. 112v, reproduced in Garel, *D'une main fort*, 104, which has a jousting scene between knights identified as "David" and "Naval" to illustrate their "contest" over Abigail in 1 Samuel 25; the figures are very similar to the jousting knights in BnF Héb. 4 discussed above.

180 Wistinetzki, *Sefer Hasidim*, par. 709 (= Parma #3280, p. 137); Bologna ed. #282. For a more complete translation of the entire passage and discussion, see Fronda, "Attributing of Three Ashkenazi Bibles," 45–47. On the prohibition and its background, see Beit-Arié, "Individualist Nature," 565; and Shalev-Eyni, *Jews among Christians*, 4–5. Note, however, that Judah—whether or not he was aware of it—does not complain that these images derive from Christian books. For micrographic trees, see BnF Héb. 5–6, described above in n. 172.

181 Frojmovic, "Jewish Mudejarismo," 244–45.

182 Sitbon, "L'espace," and "Intersections."

183 Grabar, *Mediation of Ornament*, 155–93, in particular 190.

184 On dragons, Epstein, *Dreams of Subversion*, 70–95, and on the problematic presence of such images, see his comments on 82ff; and now, Rodov, "Dragons," which despite its subtitle deals extensively with dragons in manuscript art as well.

185 The key work here is Camille, *Image on the Edge*, which is about the Luttrell Psalter.

186 Camille, *Image on the Edge*, 9.

187 On hybrids and marginality, cf. Shalev-Eyni, *Jews among Christians*, 79–83.

188 Marcus, *Rituals of Childhood*, 11–12.

189 For examples of such recent scholarship, Marcus, *Rituals of Childhood*; Elisheva Baumgarten, *Mothers and Children*; and the various chapters in Biale, *Cultures of the Jews*.

190 In the case of Sepharad, I am speaking about the overall strategy of resistance to the hegemonic Christian culture of the Iberian kingdoms. The micrographic Masoretic decorations that borrow elements of Mudejar design and reflect Islamic aniconism are, in fact, similar instances of inward acculturation.

191 This manuscript and its importance particularly for Rashi studies have been hotly debated over the past twenty years. See, in particular Grossman, *ḥakhmei Tsarfat Harishonim*, 184–93, which summarizes his earlier debate with Eliezer Touitou in Touitou, "Does Ms. Leipzig 1." Cf. Penkower, "Rashi's Corrections," and Penkower's other articles on the Masoretic notes in the codex listed in the bibliography.

192 For more on this topic, see Stern, "The First Jewish Codices."

193 The following discussion draws on Mordechai Breuer, "Keep Your Children from *Higgayon*"; Talmage, "Keep Your Sons from Scripture"; Kanarfogel, "On the Role of Bible Study"; and Gross, "Rashi." For the best overall survey of the variety of types of medieval Jewish biblical exegesis, see the numerous chapters in Saebo, *Hebrew Bible/Old Testament*, vol. 1, part 2.

194 The Prophets and Hagiographa were often considered the proper subject of "advanced" biblical study, particularly in the Mediterranean area, and were therefore studied alone; see Talmage, "Keep Your Sons from Scripture," 85.

195 See, for example, the manuscripts in the Bodleian Library listed in Neubauer, *Catalogue of the Hebrew Manuscripts*, cols. 19–20, ##119–28.

196 Kanarfogel, *Jewish Education*, 79–85; Kanarfogel, "On the Role of Bible Study"; and Grossman, *Ḥakhmei Tsarfat Harishonim*, 457–506.

197 Kanarfogel, *Jewish Education*, 15–32.

198 Touitou, "Concerning the Presumed Original Version of Rashi's Commentary."

199 On this, see Grossman, *Ḥakhmei Tsarfat Harishonim*, 184–93; Touitou, "Does Ms. Leipzig 1"; and Penkower, "Rashi's Corrections."

200 Smith, "Jews and Christians Imagining the Temple," 104.

201 Munich, BSB, Cod. Hebr. 5. For a description of the manuscript and its background, see Beit-Arié, *Hebrew Manuscripts of East and West*, 21 and 111n53, where he cites R. Suckale's study of the Latin instructions; and for analysis of the significance of the very complex and multiple dimensions of the Jewish-Christian collaboration in the manuscript, see Frojmovic, "Jewish Scribes and Christian Illuminators."

202 Cited from Paris BnF Ms. Héb. 184 in Simon, "Interpreting the Interpreter," 92; see as well the quote from Judah ibn Mosconi cited on the same page of Simon's article.

203 On this particular manuscript, see de Hamel, *Glossed Books of the Bible*, 24–25.

204 For the definitive treatment of the process of its development, see de Hamel, *Glossed Books of the Bible*, 14–27; and Parkes, "Folia librorum quaerere."

205 To the best of my knowledge, the first person to identify Christian glossed Bibles as the source of the Talmudic page format—as noted in the text, it appears first in study Bibles—was Colette Sirat, in *Hebrew Manuscripts*, 60. For further discussion of the entire phenomenon and its background, see Sirat, "Notes sur la circulation" and "En vision globale"; and Shatzmiller, *Cultural Exchange*, 25–26 and 162–63.

206 I hope to treat the history of this page format in detail in my study of the Talmud's material history. For other examples of the format in medieval Hebrew manuscripts, see Vienna, Österreichische Nationalbibliothek Cod. Hebr. 9, Ashkenaz, fourteenth century; Oxford, Bodleian Ms. Kennicott 5, Segovia, Spain 1487 (Former Prophets with Targum, Rashi, Kimḥi, and Gersonides), all of which are reproduced in Beit-Arié, *Hebrew Manuscripts of East and West* (figs. 37, 38, and 39). For another remarkable example from Spain, see the "Rabbinic Bible" (San Lorenzo de El Escorial, Real Biblioteca, MS G-I-5), described and reproduced in Alfonso et al., eds., *Biblias de Sefarad*, 288–91. One should also note the case of glossed Psalters. While most medieval Psalters were liturgical books and do not have commentaries, there are a sufficient number that do, the most famous being the Parma Psalter (Parma 1870 [De Rossi 510]), a lavishly illustrated late thirteenth-century (ca. 1280) codex from northern Italy, with the commentary of Abraham Ibn Ezra written in the three outer margins around the text. Interestingly, this particular page format parallels the Byzantine form used for some Christian Psalters rather than the glossed form (with columns) used more widely; see Gibson, "Psalters," 91–96 and plates 5.7–5.8.

207 On this manuscript, see the Bodleian catalogs of Neubauer and Beit-Arié, no. 129 (pp. 20 and 16 respectively). On transparent layout, see Beit-Arié, *Unveiled Faces*, 49–59.

208 Sirat, "Le livre hébreu," 247.

209 Simon, "Interpreting the Interpreter," esp. 93–94. For examples of pages with a super-commentary using the *Glossa Ordinaria* format, see Sirat, *Hebrew Manuscripts*, 128–31, in

particular fig. 58 (Paris, Séminaire Israélite de France, MS 1); and esp. fig. 59 (Nîmes, Bibliothèque Municipale, MS hébr. 22).

210 The glossed format appears already in the 1472 Bologna Pentateuch, but the page reaches its fuller form first in the Second Rabbinic Bible (Venice, 1523–24).

211 The earliest European manuscript is Ms. Vatican ebr. 31, probably written in Apulia (very likely in Otranto) in 1072/3. In contrast, the earliest dated Ashkenazic manuscript is a Babylonian Talmud, Florence, Biblioteca Nazionale Centrale Ms. II 7, written in 1177.

212 Beit-Arié, "Making of the Book," 29–32, 63, 78.

213 On the Sephardic communities in Italy, primarily in the south and the Kingdom of Naples in particular (until 1541), see Bonfil, *Rabbis and Jewish Communities*, 145–50, 155. Recent scholarly research by Joseph Hacker and Fabrizio Lelli has revised Bonfil's picture and pointed to much more widespread Sephardic emigration to Spain and more significant communities, which included many scribes among their populations.

214 The quantitative information in this passage was graciously supplied to me by Professor Malachi Beit-Arié, based on the data in Sfardata.

215 On the development of the humanist text, see the excellent article by Davies, "Humanism in Script and Print," 49–51.

216 This attitude also makes them very different from other "plain" Hebrew Bibles, such as those produced in Yemen and the Near East, despite their codicological similarity.

217 On the different modes of script and the increasing preference for the semicursive mode, see Beit-Arié, *Unveiled Faces*, 75–81.

218 See, for example, BnF héb. 27, a Bible copied in 1294/95 in a semicursive script in two columns, again with headlines in a large square script.

219 Beit-Arié, *Unveiled Faces*, 80.

220 Thus Parma 1679 (De Rossi 509, Cat. 24), which has been attributed to Isaac b. Ovadiah b. David of Forli, on whom see below and the articles of Nurit Pasternak.

221 Calkins, *Illuminated Books of the Middle Ages*, 273.

222 The three books are all annotated with a special system of *te'amim* or accents that distinguish them from the rest of the Bible. Although its original purpose is not known, this special system fostered the idea that these books are poetic—indeed, in medieval and Renaissance treatments, these books were commonly believed to epitomize the essence of biblical poetry. Their status as poetry also probably lay behind the special ways they are spaced (with a division in the middle of each verse) in medieval manuscripts. On the history of these books as poetry laid out on the page, Kugel, *The Idea of Biblical Poetry*, esp. 114–15 and 125–26, and for their later treatment, see the references in the index, s.v. *Sifrei EMeT*.

223 In terms of numbers, to give one example, the Parma collection alone contains nine Psalters written in Italy from 1391 through the end of the fifteenth century, and twelve Sifrei EMeT.

224 Exactly how or why this view of the books developed is not clear, but perhaps it had something to do with their common title *Sifrei EMeT* (originally an anagram of Iyov [Job], Mishlei [Proverbs], and Tehillim [Psalms]), understood as "Books of Truth," that is, philosophical truth.

225 Lelli, "Christian and Jewish Iconographies of Job," 216.

226 For a near contemporary account, see Henri Estienne's colorful picture of his father Robert's publishing house, quoted and translated in Grafton, *Bring Out Your Dead*, 142–43, and Grafton's analysis, 141–47; for a secondhand, and somewhat overvividly imagined but charming picture of the multicultural scene in Daniel Bomberg's early sixteenth-century Venetian printing house, see Amram, *Makers of Hebrew Books*, 175–77. Cf. Eisenstein, *Printing Press*, 75–76, 250–54. For further bibliography and discussion, see Stern, "Rabbinic Bible," 77, 253n2.

227 Pasternak, "A Meeting Point," 185 and passim; Pasternak, "Isaac ben Ovadiah ben David of Forli"; and Pasternak, "Together and Apart." My remarks are largely drawn from Pasternak's seminal work on Isaac ben Ovadiah.

228 Pasternak, "A Meeting Point," 199.

229 As Pasternak notes, sixteen of Isaac's extant works are biblical in genre. These include five full Bibles, several liturgical Pentateuchs, Psalters, and several Sifrei EMeT.

230 I wish to express my gratitude to Eva Frojmovic for identifying these images for me (and for correcting the incorrect explanations I provided for them in the original publication of this material).

231 For a brief overview, see Muchawsky-Schnapper, *The Yemenites*, 13–14; Golb, *Spertus College of Judaica Yemenite Manuscripts*, v–xv.

232 Morag, *Ha-'Ivrit*, 16–17.

233 Morag, *Ha-'Ivrit*, 17–19; Morag, *Masorot*, 65–73.

234 Morag, *Ha-'Ivrit*, 20–21; Morag, *Masorot*, 76–77; and especially, Spiegel, "Yemenite Rite," which deals at length with the significant differences that remained in Yemenite pronunciation and cantillation practice even after the adaption of the Tiberian system.

235 A comprehensive study of Yemenite scribal culture remains a desideratum but see Ratsaby, *Bem'agloth Teman*, 86–103; Riegler, "Colophons"; Riegler, "Benayah Ha-Sofer."

236 Yardeni, *Hebrew Script*, 256–63.

237 Riegler, "Benayah Ha-Sofer." See as well Ratzaby, "An Early Scribal Poem"; but cf. Beit-Arié, "*Emunah Yotzrah Etzlo Amanah.*" Whether or not the poem was composed by Benayah, the history of its transcription and copying exemplifies the dynastic element of Yemenite scribal culture.

238 Penkower, "Sheet of Parchment." For nine unique spellings of words in Yemenite *Tajim*, see Morag, "A Few Words," 2.

239 Morag, *Masorot*, 77; and Morag, *Ha-'Ivrit*, 22 and note 1, where he cites Goitein, the first scholar to float this idea; see also Stern, "On the Term *Keter*." As Morag also notes, some early Yemenite Bible manuscripts even state in their colophons that their texts follow "the Bible from Egypt masorited by Ben-Asher."

240 Greidi, "Introductory Note," 1.

241 Greidi, "Introductory Note," 1. For an atypical example of a *Taj*, see Hibshoosh, *Hibshoosh Family Pentateuch*, written by David Ben Benayah in 1485. As its English title indicates, it is only a Pentateuch with haftarot; the latter are accompanied by the Targum Pseudo-Jonathan, transcribed interverse with Babylonian supralinear vocalization. The volume also contains at its beginning the *Sefer Ti'jan* in both Hebrew and Judeo-Arabic. On its contents, see the introduction by Morag.

242 Greidi, "Introductory Note," 2–3. Morag, *Ha-'Ivrit*, 22 and note 1; Morag, *Masorot*, 77. As Morag notes there as well, the term *Taj* has also been appropriated by printers as a title for what is in fact a *parashah* (or *ḥumash*); see the edition of the Pentateuch printed in Jerusalem in 1886–91.

243 Greidi, "Introductory Note," 2–3.

244 See Ettinghausen, "Yemenite Bible Manuscripts"; and Katz, "Yemenite Manuscripts."

Chapter 3. The Jewish Bible in the Early Age of Print

1 The exact number of Hebrew incunabula is unknown; undoubtedly, some editions never survived, while new ones occasionally surface, and scholars have voiced different views on several editions. Offenberg, *Hebrew Incunabula*, enumerates 139 books; Tishby, "Hebrew Incunables," 808, states that he has more than 140 in his possession; Iakerson, *Catalogue*, 1:v, suggests a number between 140 and 150 separate editions.

2 The debate began with the publication of Eisenstein, *The Printing Press*; was fully ignited by Johns in *The Nature of the Book*; and continued with the exchange between Eisenstein and Johns in *American Historical Review* 107 (2002): 87–121. For a vivid description of the differences in reading practice caused by print, see Anthony Grafton, "The Humanist as Reader"; and Cavallo and Chartrier, *History of Reading*, 22–33, for important cautionary remarks on applying the term *revolution* to the invention of print.

3 The classic article on this subject remains Beit-Arié, "Relationship between Early Hebrew Printing and Handwritten Books."

4 The literature on Christian Hebraism has exploded over the last several decades. The classic and still comprehensive study remains Secret, *Les kabbalistes chrétiens*, but since the 1980s the literature has been enormously enriched by monographs and articles on specific figures and aspects of the movement. For some sense of the new complexities of the field and the varieties of research being done in it, see the essays in Coudert and Shoulson, eds., *Hebraica Veritas*.

5 As Shimon Iakerson points out in "Early Hebrew Printing," 125–26, even the Italian edition, which was printed by the Sephardi Abraham ben Garton in Reggio di Calabria (which was strongly under the political and cultural influence of Aragon), was actually "Sephardic in all respects." For early printed Hebrew Bibles between 1477 and 1528, Ginsburg's survey in *Introduction to the Massoretico* remains the most extensive discussion but must be supplemented by Zafren, "Bible Editions"; the relevant entries in Berkowitz, *In Remembrance of Creation*, esp. items 121–49 and 165–71; and the excellent survey by Schenker, "From the First Printed Hebrew, Greek, and Latin Bibles." Still useful is the shorter survey by Gottheil, "Bible Editions" (with a useful chart diagramming a stemma of influences).

6 Zafren, "Bible Editions," *240–41. Among the earliest dated Hebrew books printed in Italy and Spain were commentaries on the Bible by Rashi.

7 See Zafren, "Bible Editions"; and Alexander Marx, "Choice of Books," 156.

8 Our knowledge of early Hebrew printing, specifically how the *niqud* and *te'amim* were printed along with the letters, is sparse. In the meantime, see Lubell, "Sixteenth-Century Hebrew

Typography," 332–33, where he cites the suggestion of Scott-Martin Kosofsky that the vocalization and accents may have been added by hand even though this would have been "an extremely consuming process." It is also possible that some of the diacritics may have been printed and others added by hand; in short, anything is possible. The argument made by Goldschmidt, *Earliest Editions*, 12–13, that it was the "religious awe which this Holy Book inspired" and that "mechanical reproduction might have been regarded as profanation" has no basis in evidence. I wish to thank Steven Lubell, Scott-Martin Kosofsky, Marvin Heller, Shimon Iakerson, Emile Schrijver, and Jordan Penkower for helping me deal with this vexed, as yet unexplained question.

9 For reproductions of select pages, see Freimann and Marx, *Thesaurus*, #25, pp. 34–35; and for description, Ginsburg, *Introduction*, 783–84.

10 The quote is from Roth, "A Jewish Printer in Naples," 64; see that page and the following for the history of the frame. The first book in which Soncino used the frame was his Rashi edition of 1487; later he used it in several Talmudic tractates (Niddah and Hulin, 1489), the *Mishneh Torah* (1490), and the Tur (1490?).

11 For this number, see Zafren, "Bible Editions," 242*–245*. I have excluded from my survey books of Psalms alone or other individual books.

12 These are Proverbs with Gersonides and Menahem Meiri (1492), and Former Prophets with Gersonides and David Kimḥi (1494).

13 This is not to suggest that it is—or was—impossible to distinguish between Hebrew books produced primarily for Jews and those produced primarily for Christians; on the latter, see Burnett, "Christian Hebrew Printing." My point is only that the once clear-cut category had become decidedly blurred.

14 The original title of the 1517 edition on its title page is *Arba'ah ve-'esrim*, namely, "the Twenty-Four" books of the Hebrew Bible. The title page of the 1524–25 edition has *Sha'ar Adonai he-ḥadash* (The New Gate of the Lord), and then simply lists its contents as *ḥumash (Pentateuch)*. . . *Nevi'im rishonim*. . . *Nevi'im aḥaronim*. . . *U-ketuvim*. Penkower ("Jacob Ben Ḥayyim," 1; and "The First Edition of the Hebrew Bible," 601–2n68) has shown that the earliest sign of the later title, *Miqraot gedolot*, is in the 1548 Venice edition, where its title appears as *'Esrim ve-arba' gadol*, the "large" (i.e., folio-size) "Twenty Four" books; beginning from that period, the edition was sometimes referred to as the *Miqra gedola* (The Large Scripture). Penkower also cites two occurrences of the plural form *Miqraot gedolot* in the 1595 Mantua censorship list, where the phrase means "copies of the Miqra Gedolah." The earliest appearance of the phrase as the title of the Bible in its entirety is to be found in the Lemberg (?) 1808 edition; for an illustration of the page, see *Encyclopaedia Judaica* 2:783. The term *Rabbinic Bible* (*Biblia Rabbinica*) appears to be a Christian Hebraist name; it is not clear when it first came into usage.

15 The following pages draw heavily upon Penkower, "Jacob Ben Ḥayyim," the definitive work to date on the first two rabbinic Bibles and, unfortunately, not published as yet. In the meantime, see Penkower, "Rabbinic Bible." Penkower's work is complemented by B. Levy, "Rabbinic Bibles," the initial part of a work in progress on the history of the RB in its entirety; I wish to express my gratitude to Professor Levy for allowing me to read his unpublished manuscript. See as well Levy's earlier book, *Fixing God's Torah*. Earlier works that remain valuable are

Ginsburg, *Jacob Ben Chajim Ibn Adonijah's Introduction*, which includes both a Hebrew text of Jacob ben Ḥayyim's introduction and an English translation as well as a long introductory essay; Ginsburg, *Introduction to the Massoretico*, with full descriptions of all the early printings; Goldschmidt, *Earliest Editions of the Hebrew Bible*; Marx, "Soncino's Wanderyears," esp. 442–45; Bloch, *Venetian Printers of Hebrew Books*; Amram, *Makers of Hebrew Books*, 146–224; Schwarzbach, "Les éditions de la Bible hébraïque"; and Tamani, "Le prime edizioni della Bibbia Ebraica."

16 For the most recent important study, part of a work in progress, see Nielsen, "Daniel van Bombergen," which now updates Habermann, *Printer Daniel Bomberg*; Mehlmann, "Printing House of Daniel Bomberg"; Berliner, "Hebrew Publishing House of Daniel Bomberg"; and Goshen-Gottstein, "Introduction." For more on Bomberg, see as well the pages in Bloch and Amram cited in the previous note.

17 On Venetian printing in general in the early sixteenth century, see Richardson, *Printing, Writers and Readers*; Pettegree, *Book in the Renaissance.*

18 The little known about Pratensis is best summed up in Kahle, "Felix Pratensis"; epitomized in Kahle, *Cairo Geniza*, 69n3; and Kahle, "The Hebrew Text," 742–44.

19 The two kabbalistic works were Abraham Abulafia's *Imrei Shefer* and *Sefer Ha-Temunah*, a kabbalistic interpretation of the Hebrew alphabet. Both translations were apparently Pratensis's. See Penkower, "First Edition," 597n51.

20 Penkower, "First Edition," 598–99.

21 On the difference between privileges and patents, see Witcomb, *Copyright in the Renaissance*, 21–22, and for Pratensis and Bomberg, 43–44. It should be noted that receiving either the right to publish or a copyright could not be taken for granted by anyone, not even Bomberg. Gershom Soncino, the greatest of all Jewish early printers of Hebrew books, had tried unsuccessfully to receive a privilege to publish in Venice; it is not known for certain whether his failure to receive the privilege was due to Christian suspicions about the contents of Jewish books and their threat to the Christian faith, or if his request was blocked by Aldus Manutius, the leading printer in Venice at the time, who also aspired to print Hebrew books (in addition to the Greek texts for which he became famous). On Soncino and this episode, see Marx, "Soncino's Wanderyears," 441–42 and 445–56. On Aldus's Hebrew ambitions, see Davies, *Aldus Manutius*, 50–55; and Marx, "Soncino's Wanderyears," 441–42 and 445–56.

22 The English translation and original Latin are taken from Ginsburg, *Introduction to the Massoretico*, 945–46.

23 Ginsburg, *Introduction to the Massoretico*, 945–46. This last claim has been the subject of much debate. Ginsburg vehemently criticizes it as misleadingly hyperbolic (945–47), but see Kahle's explanation in *Cairo Geniza*, 123; and Penkower's explanation of Pratensis's statement in "Jacob Ben Ḥayyim," 187–88, and now, his post on January 11, 2009, on Tradition Seforim Blog (http://seforim.traditiononline.org/index.cfm/2009/1/11 /A-Note-on-the-Latin-Dedication-in-the-Rabbinic-Bible-of-Venice-15). See as well the comments of Houtman, "Targum Isaiah," 201–2, in regard to his text of the Targum.

24 Penkower, "Rabbinic Bible," 362.

25 In apparent deference to Christian readers, several passages in Kimḥi's commentary on Psalms that refuted Christological interpretations of certain verses were censored, although

in some copies a separate single folio containing the censored sections was inserted in the Hagiographa volume immediately after Psalms. See Schwarzbach, "Les éditions de la Bible hébraïque," 38–39 and 54; cf. the brief history of the text in A. Darom's edition of R. David Kimḥi, *Ha-perush ha-shalem 'al Tehilim* (Jerusalem: Mosad Harav Kook, 1979), 5–6. The specific verses in Psalms are 2:12, 19:10, 21:1, 22:32, 45:18, 72:20, 110:7.

26 Penkower, "Chapter Divisions," 353–60, where he studies the variants in the divisions as based on the Vulgate, as established (if not introduced) by Stephen Langton in the thirteenth century. Verse numbers, also based on Christian enumerations, were not introduced into a Jewish Bible until the 1548 reprinting of the Rabbinic Bible in which every fifth verse is marked in the text. See Penkower, "Verse Divisions." As Jacob ben Ḥayyim ibn Adoniyahu states near the end of his introduction (translation in Ginsburg, *Jacob Ben Chajim Ibn Adonijah's Introduction,* 80–81), he adapted the chapter divisions from R. Isaac Nathan's biblical concordance, *Nativ Meir* (written in 1437–45, first published by Bomberg, with Adoniyahu's editing, in 1523), which in turn adapted the chapter and verse numberings from Arlotti's Latin concordance (ca. 1290); Isaac Nathan compiled his work to assist Jews in rebutting Christian polemical attacks. See, however, Penkower, "Chapter Divisions," 362–65, where he shows that Ibn Adoniyahu actually took the numerations from the chapter list at the beginning of the concordance.

27 This estimate is primarily based upon the figures and reasoning in Baruchson, "Money and Culture," esp. 28 and 28n9, with additional bibliography on print runs in contemporary Christian printing houses; see as well her complementary article, Baruchson-Arbib, "The Prices of Hebrew Printed Books." The most up-to-date study of book prices is Nielsen, "A Note about Book Prices," but he does not discuss print runs. In an older study, Habermann (*Toledot ha-sefer ha'Ivri*, 79) gives a range of 800–1,500 for the output of sixteenth-century Hebrew presses; in his later work, "The Printer Daniel Bomberg," 21, he proposes a range of 500–1,000 copies. Cf. Heller, *Printing the Talmud*, 159, and especially 191, for some important economic considerations determining the size of print runs. For print runs of non-Jewish Hebrew books in early sixteenth-century Italy, the most extensive discussion remains Hirsch, *Printing, Selling, and Reading*, 61–68, which concludes with a quote from F. Kapp (*Geschichte des deutschen Buchhandels*): "Up to the middle of the XVIth century no rule can be established for the size of editions. Available data are too incomplete." See as well Richardson, *Printing, Writers and Readers*, 21, where he estimates the norm to have been about one thousand copies.

28 On the 1521 edition, see Heller, *Sixteenth-Century Hebrew Book*, 1:143.

29 See the material collected and analyzed by Penkower, "Jacob Ben Ḥayyim," 8–12, and in his appendices on 396–99.

30 The two kabbalistic commentaries are the *Tzror Ha-Mor* by Abraham Saba (Venice, 1522–23) and the "Commentary on the Torah" by Menaḥem Recanati (Venice, 1523). For the most complete list of the books Ibn Adoniyahu worked on, see Penkower, "Jacob Ben Ḥayyim," 7, which supersedes the listings in Habermann, *The Printer Daniel Bomberg*. On *Nativ Meir*, see Penkower, "Jacob Ben Ḥayyim," 389–91.

31 For a detailed investigation, see Penkower, "Jacob Ben Ḥayyim," chap. 4 in its entirety, 148–90, and for a summary, 177–78.

32 Penkower, "Jacob Ben Ḥayyim," 52–53. As Penkower notes, Ibn Adoniyahu did not, strictly speaking, invent the *masorah finalis* (*Masorah sofit*). The term had been used throughout the Middle Ages to describe the Masoretic material, e.g., lists of differences, treatises, etc., that were copied at the back of Masoretic codices. What he did invent was a new use for the term and a new form for it.

33 For a single indication of the importance attributed to Ibn Adoniyahu's text, see the statement in 1897 by Ginsburg in *Introduction to the Massoretico*, 963–64, that Ibn Adoniyahu's text "is the only Massoretic recension. No textual redactor of modern days who professes to edit the Hebrew text according to the Masorah can deviate from it without giving conclusive justification for so doing." In his own edition of the Hebrew Bible, Ginsburg (who was a Jewish convert to Christianity) exactly reproduced the 1524–25 text, as did the first two editions of Rudolph Kittel's *Biblia Hebraica* (1906, 1913). Not until the third edition (1929–37) was Ibn Adoniyahu's text replaced with the text of the Leningrad Codex (B 19a); on the switch, see Kahle, *Cairo Geniza*, 72–78, and my discussion in the final chapter of this book.

34 For a discussion of whether Jewish complaints against the 1517 edition on account of Pratensis's editorship motivated Bomberg to publish the Second Rabbinic Bible, see Penkower, "Jacob Ben Ḥayyim," 410–12.

35 Penkower, "Jacob Ben Ḥayyim," 8–14; Penkower, "Rabbinic Bible," 362. Penkower's primary explicit evidence for Ibn Adoniyahu's belief in the kabbalistic significance of the Masorah is his note on Exodus 10:5 in which he used kabbalistic (Zoharic) notions to determine whether the word *lir'ot* is written plene or defectively (with or without a *vav*).

36 As translated by Ginsburg, *Jacob Ben Chajim Ibn Adonijah's Introduction*, 77–78, with slight stylistic revisions.

37 Cf. the somewhat astonished remark of Joseph Hakohen (in *Divre Ha-Yamim le-Malkhei Tsarfat u-vet Otoman ha-Tugar* [Sabionetta, 1554], 137b, quoted in Habermann, *The Printer Daniel Bomberg*, 12) that, for all his beneficence toward Jews, Bomberg did not have "a drop of Jewish seed" in him." For a collection of other encomia paid to Bomberg by his Jewish correctors, editors, and printers, see Habermann, *The Printer Daniel Bomberg*, 16–17.

38 Hebrew: *Ke-derekh he-'arukh*; the translation follows Ginsburg, *Jacob Ben Chajim Ibn Adonijah's Introduction*, 40.

39 Ginsburg, *Jacob Ben Chajim Ibn Adonijah's Introduction*, 41

40 On Ibn Adoniyahu's conversion, see Ginsburg, *Jacob Ben Chajim Ibn Adonijah's Introduction*, 11–14; the main evidence for his conversion is Elijah Levita's famous slur in his poetic introduction to *Massoreth ha-massoret*, 94, where he refers to Ibn Adoniyahu as one "whose name was formerly Jacob, let his soul be bound up in a bag with holes." See also Penkower, "Jacob Ben Ḥayyim," 412–14n12.

41 The main scholar to raise this speculation is Mehlmann, "Printing House," 18–19; but see as well Benayahu, *Copyright*, 17 and note 4; and Heller, *Printing the Talmud*, 138–39, for an overview of the positions.

42 I need to emphasize that I am not making a historical claim here but solely addressing Ibn Adoniyahu's self-perception and representation of himself vis-à-vis a specific Christian, Daniel Bomberg. For the historical "reality," and the complications in speaking about it, see Bonfil, *Jewish Life*, 101–24.

43 Like the 1517 edition, the only thing the Second Rabbinic Bible lacked was the convenience of the haftarot in the Pentateuch volume, but see Penkower, "First Edition," 591–92, where he argues convincingly that RB 1517 began as a folio-size liturgical Pentateuch, with the haftarot, Five Scrolls, Targum, and Rashi, which was then expanded into the RB on the entire Bible; the only complete copy of this edition that Penkower was able to locate is preserved today in two separate volumes in the Bodleian, Opp. fol. 23 and Opp. fol. 41.

44 Note that Rashi is printed in Spanish and Portuguese imprints like Toledano's 1491 Lisbon Pentateuch, not to mention Italian editions like the 1482 Bologna Pentateuch. On Rashi in Sepharad, see my discussion in the previous chapter; Gross, "Rashi and the Tradition of Study"; and Penkower, "The Process of Canonization."

45 Reiner, "Liturgy versus Text." I wish to thank Professor Reiner for allowing me to read and cite his important article before publication.

46 According to Jerome Friedman, *Most Ancient Testimony*, 13–14, between the years 500 and 1500 there may have been no more than a few dozen Christians who could read Hebrew with any real facility, even the Hebrew text of the Bible, let alone postbiblical writings. Cf. Burnett, "Later Christian Hebraists"; and Hamilton, "Humanists and the Bible."

47 Burnett, "The Strange Career of the *Biblia Rabbinica*." I wish to thank Professor Burnett for allowing me to read this article before its publication.

48 For a particularly fascinating example of Christian Hebraic literacy in the early sixteenth century, see Penkower, "A 14th C. Ashkenazi Hebrew Bible," and his brilliant analysis of the Latin inscriptions in this codex (Dessau, George 187.2°–188.2°) by Martin Luther (1483–1546), Philip Melanchthon (1497–1560), Bernhard Ziegler (1496–1556), and Justus Jonas (1493–1555), who translate and debate passages in Isaiah and, in addition to their sophisticated discussion of the Hebrew text of the Bible and its pointing (and whether or not Jews changed the pointing), demonstrate knowledge of Tanna de-Bei Eliyahu, the Babylonian Talmud, and David Kimḥi. However, for a cautionary statement about overestimating Hebraic literacy among Christian Hebraists, see Burnett, "Strange Career of the *Biblia Rabbinica*"; and Burnett, "Christian Hebrew Printing."

49 On Muenster, see Rosenthal, "Sebastian Muenster's Knowledge." Note too that Muenster was not alone. According to Mesguich, "Early Christian Hebraists," 267n59, Pellican translated into Latin both Ibn Ezra's commentary on the Pentateuch and Rashi on Genesis and Exodus, although the translations were never published; so, too, the Hebraist Wolfgang Fabricius Caputo (1478–1541) was familiar with Ibn Ezra's biblical commentary and used him in his work (268).

50 Probably the most famous of Bomberg's Christian readers, albeit in a period preceding the Rabbinic Bible, was the great German Hebraist and Christian kabbalist Johannes Reuchlin, who, in 1519, wrote to Bomberg and requested a copy of his edition of Psalms, Proverbs, and Ecclesiastes; the two continued to correspond until 1521. For the correspondence and generous translations into English of the Latin texts, see Amram, *Makers of Hebrew Books*, 164–67; and for additional correspondence, Penkower, "Jacob Ben Ḥayyim," 298n90. I wish to thank Professor Jordan Penkower for reminding me of this correspondence.

51 For the complete exposition of this point, see Stern, "Rabbinic Bible," 101–6.

52 Part of this was due to the expert testimony to its excellence by scholars of the Masorah like Elias Levita (1469–1549), particularly in his laudatory poem appended to the last volume of the 1524–25 Rabbinic Bible; and still later by Menaḥem di Lonzano (1550–before 1624), author of *Or ha-Torah*, and Yedidyah Norzi (1560–1626), author of the *Minḥat shai*. Both di Lonzano and Norzi made many corrections and emendations of Ibn Adoniyahu's text and the accompanying Masorah; they nonetheless used it as the standard. See Breuer, *Aleppo Codex*, xxvi–xxviii; and Penkower, "Jacob Ben Ḥayyim," 44–45, the latter for discussion of a responsum written by R. Jacob b. Israel Levi in Venice in 1614.

53 It is also worth noting Penkower's observation (personal communication) that, by virtue of its authoritative printed status, the 1524–25 Rabbinic Bible also marked the triumph of the Sephardic text type of the Bible over the Ashkenazic text type, a victory of one biblical textual tradition over all its rivals. Such a victory could never have occurred in the centuries of handwritten transmission of the biblical text.

54 The history of the various editions and their multiple commentaries is treated in B. Barry Levy's work in progress on the Rabbinic Bible/*Miqraot Gedolot* as well as the question of the definition of the genre.

55 On these editions, see B. Levy, "Rabbinic Bibles"; and his forthcoming book mentioned in the previous note. Cf. as well Penkower, "Rabbinic Bible."

56 Which was the case with the Babylonian Talmud; after Bomberg's 1521–23 edition, virtually all editions of the Babylonian Talmud follow both Bomberg's pagination and the exact page format of nearly every page that begins and ends with the same word.

57 For images of miniature codices, see Bromer, *Miniature Books*, 84–85; for Torah scrolls and Esther scrolls, see David Stern, *Chosen*, 75–76. As Stern notes there, the Jews have always been a tiny people.

Chapter 4. The Jewish Bible since the Sixteenth Century

1 Sheehan, *Enlightenment Bible,* for a concise summary, xi–xiv.

2 For primary texts, including rabbinic responsa, see Vivian Mann, *Jewish Texts*, 19–34; Kalman Bland, "Defending, Enjoying, and Regulating the Visual." The locus classicus for rabbinic opposition to the making of images in books in particular is the famous responsum of Meir of Rothenburg (1215–93) (*Responsa Maharam of Rothenburg* [Jerusalem, 1986], no. 56, translated in Vivian Mann, *Jewish Texts*, 111–12), in which he objects to illustrations because they are distracting and detract from concentrating upon prayers; however, he explicitly states that illustrations are not prohibited on account of idolatry. As noted in chapter 2, the same criticism is often made of micrography, as evidenced by the remarks of R. Judah He-Ḥasid quoted and discussed in the earlier chapter.

3 Thus, for example, the Cervera and Kennicott Bibles, discussed in chapter 2.

4 A rare exception is the Holkham Bible (Oxford, Bodleian Holkham c. 1), a hand-painted copy of the Bible printed by Joshua Solomon Soncino in Naples in 1491 or 1492.

5 On the illustrated ketubah, see Sabar, *Ketubbah*, esp. 12–25; and Landsberger, "Illuminated Marriage Contracts," specifically 377–78 for a responsum written by Abraham Ḥiyya di Boton of Salonika (1560–1603).

6 To date there exists no comprehensive study of the illustrated Esther scroll. The best recent overview is the section titled "Esther Imagined: The Art and History of Decorated Megillot," in Cohen, *Journey through Jewish Worlds*, 226–88, also translated in Schrijver and Wiesemann, *Schöne Seiten*, 250–327; and David Stern, *Chosen*, 62–69. For earlier treatments, see Wischnitzer-Bernstein, "Esther Story in Art"; and Namenyi, "Illumination of Hebrew Manuscripts," 431–39. For illustrations that capture the range of Esther scrolls, see the catalog *O Svitku*. The scroll written by Estellina is now in the Braginsky Collection; for illustrations and description, see *Schöne Seiten*, 256–59.

7 On the artistic connections between the two genres, see Sabar, *Ketubbah*, 14–16; and Landsberger, "Illuminated Marriage Contracts," 407–8.

8 See Maimonides, *Mishneh Torah, Zemanim*, Laws of the Megillah 2:9–10, where he permits missing and blurred letters in an Esther scroll, something that would never be permitted in a Torah scroll. Compare Shulḥan ʿArukh, Oraḥ Ḥayyim Laws of Megillah, Section 691, where he permits using a vocalized scroll. While the Talmud already distinguished between a Torah scroll and mezuzot and tefillin in terms of strictness, it does not explicitly distinguish between Torah and Esther scrolls in this regard. See, however, B. Megillah 19a, where, as Bernard Septimus has called to my attention, the Talmud notes that an Esther scroll is called both a *sefer* (i.e., Sefer Torah, Torah scroll) and an *igeret* (a letter, such as a diplomatic letter); as Rashi notes, that is why the laws of an Esther scroll are not as rigorous as those governing a Torah scroll. Nonetheless, the grounds for the distinction are unclear. The sole early modern rabbinic text that I have seen dealing with problems associated with the Esther scroll is a responsum from Moses Provenzali (1503–1575) dealing with the permissibility of using an Esther scroll printed on parchment; for the text, see Vivian Mann, "Printing, Patronage, and Prayer," 91–94. An explanation often cited for the laxity afforded the Esther scroll attributes it to the absence of the Divine Name from the book's text, but I have found no written testimony to this explanation. The lack of halachic source material dealing with the permissibility of illustrating an Esther scroll is truly surprising, especially because the practice was so widespread. I wish to thank Aviel Slae for helping me explore this topic.

9 See, for example, Kogman-Appel, "Tree of Death."

10 On Salom d'Italia and for a complete description of this type of Esther scroll with its iconographic background, see Assaf and Bilski, *Salom Italia's Esther Scrolls*; and Sabar, "A New Discovery."

11 For a good analysis of modernizing, see Assaf and Bilski, *Salom Italia's Esther Scrolls*; and for midrashic interpretations, the comments of Evelyn Cohen on the *megillot* in Stern, *Chosen*, 62–69.

12 On the material history of the (Christian) Bible in the West during and after the Reformation, see de Hamel, *The Book*, 216–45.

13 Witness the introduction in Hebrew by Sebastian Muenster to his Hebrew-Latin edition of the Bible, *Mikdash Adonai* (Basel, 1534–35).

14 For general introductions to the Septuagint and Old Greek translations, see Tov, "Septuagint"; and Wevers, "Interpretive Character." For the best recent treatment of the role of Hebraic illiteracy as its motivation, see Wasserstein and Wasserstein, *Legend,* 6–18.

15 On the history of this legend, see Wasserstein and Wasserstein, *Legend*, esp. 51–83.

16 Translated in Wasserstein and Wasserstein, *Legend*, 55–56, where it is cited as a *beraita* and attributed to R. Judah b. Ilai, a second-century sage; as the Wassersteins point out (57), R. Judah appears to be already familiar with the legend, hence it probably predates him. It is worth noting that Irenaeus, bishop of Lyon at the end of the second century, is already familiar with the legend of the Septuagint's divine inspiration (*Against Heresies*, 3.31.2, cited in Eusebius, *Ecclesiastical History*, 5.8.11–15).

17 For the full argument, see Treu, "Significance of Greek," 138–44; and Kraft, "Files and Information."

18 Masekhet Sefer Torah 1:8–9 (ed. Higger, 1930, I.6) and Masekhet Soferim I, 7–8 (ed. Higger, I:7–8). Masekhhet Sefer Torah is an early work, possibly dating to the third century; Soferim is a post-Talmudic composition partly based on Sefer Torah. For discussion of these texts, with translations, and the rabbinic disavowal of the Septuagint, see Wasserstein and Wasserstein, *Legend*, 69–83, cf. as well 81, for discussion of the fast day observed on either the eighth or eighteenth of the month of Tevet, "the day the Torah was written in Greek in the days of king Ptolemy, and darkness descended upon the world for three days." For an alternative to the "appropriation by Christians" theory, see Adler, "What the Hebrews Say."

19 The Aquila fragments are all found on palimpsests from the Cairo Genizah and were already published in the late nineteenth and early twentieth centuries; for bibliography and discussion, see de Lange, "Jewish Greek Bible Versions." For the rabbinic portrait of Aquila (and the confusion between him and Onkelos), see Smelik, *Rabbis, Language, and Translation,* 434–99.

20 On Theodotion and Symmachus, along with Aquila, the *kaige* tradition, and other revisions to the Septuagint, see de Troyer, "Septuagint," 280–86.

21 See de Lange, "Jewish Greek Bible Versions."

22 The main evidence for the Latin translations are inscriptions on sarcophagi at Beth-Shearim; see Cassuto, "Jewish Translation"; and Kedar, "Latin Translations," 308–9. Scholars have also speculated about a Jewish *Vorlage* to the Syriac *Peshitta*, which is a Christian translation produced by and for Jews living in the Syriac-speaking world; see Dirksen, "Peshitta," 261–84; and Weitzman, "Interpretive Character," 601–3.

23 For introductions to the Targum, see Alexander, "Jewish Aramaic Translations"; and Levine, "Targums." For rabbinic control of the Targum in the synagogue, see Alexander, "Targums and Rabbinic Rules"; and Fraade, "Rabbinic Views." The rabbis' attempts to control the oral performance of Targum in the synagogue—or translations into Greek, for that matter—does not mean that the rabbis had a single view on the matter; as usual, there were many differences among them. On this, see Smelik, *Rabbis, Language, and Translation,* 170–219.

24 Alexander, "Jewish Aramaic Translations," 241; cf. Smelik, "Orality," 64–66, on the transition from orality to textual inscription of the Targumim.

25 For the history of the codex, see Diez Macho, *Neophyti*, introduction.

26 Fraade, "Rabbinic Views," 258–60; Smelik, *Rabbis, Language, and Translation*, 100–71, esp. 141, where he notes that the semantic range of the word *targum* varies from "translation (into any language)" to "Aramaic Bible translation," "interpretive statement," and "declamation."

27 See my discussion in chapter 2 on the origins of this scribal practice and its format. Cf. Smelik, "Orality," 71–75.

28 For a general overview of Judeo-Arabic (and Jewish Arabic) translations, see Griffith, *Bible in Aramaic*, 102–3, 122–25, and esp. 155–74. On Saadiah's *Tafsir*, see Steiner, *Biblical Translation*. On the question as to whether Saadiah originally wrote the translation in Hebrew or Arabic script, see the statement of Abraham Ibn Ezra in his commentary on Genesis 2:11, and the discussion in Blau and Hopkins, "Ancient Bible Translations," 7–8. As Blau notes, Saadiah explicitly writes that he composed his translation for non-Jews—that is, contemporary Muslims—as well as for Jews. The former would not have known how to read Hebrew script, while the latter certainly felt more comfortable in Judeo-Arabic.

29 Blau and Hopkins, "Ancient Biblical Translations," 9–11; Polliack, *The Karaite Tradition of Arabic Bible Translation*, 10–13.

30 Scholars have speculated about the Karaite origins of a ninth-century translation of Proverbs, partly because it is also written in Arabic script.

31 The phrase is Simon Hopkins's, cited in Steiner, *Biblical Translation*, 126 and note 44.

32 Khan, *Karaite Bible Manuscripts*, esp. 20–21 for the rationale behind this practice.

33 Khan, *Karaite Bible Manuscripts*, 21. For discussion of the rabbinic prohibition, see chapter 1 of this book (on the Sefer Torah).

34 Khan, *Karaite Bible Manuscripts*, 21.

35 The introduction was originally discovered by Haggai Ben-Shammai; see Ben-Shammai, "New and Old," 200–202, and Steiner, *Biblical Translation*, 1–3.

36 Translation taken from Steiner, *Biblical Translation*, 1.

37 Steiner, *Biblical Translation*, 76–93.

38 Steiner, *Biblical Translation*, esp. 15; and Blau and Hopkins, "Ancient Bible Translations."

39 Steiner, *Biblical Translation*, 135–43.

40 All these medieval translations with transcriptions and scholarly apparatuses and commentary are now available on an ambitious website, Biblia Medieval, http://www.bibliamedieval.es, which is managed by Professor Andrés Enrique-Arias.

41 On the Arragel Bible, see Avenoza, "The Bible in Spanish," esp. 296–97; Fellous, *Histoire de la Bible*; Sáenz-Badillos, "Luis de Guzmán's Patronage"; and the various essays in the companion volume to the facsimile edition edited by Schonfield, *La Biblia de Alba*, in particular Fellous's essay on the art in the Bible. The family of the Duke of Alba has owned the manuscript since 1688. Professor Luis Girón-Negrón of Harvard University is currently directing a team of scholars who are producing a critical annotated translation and edition of the Bible. I wish to thank Professor Girón-Negrón for reviewing this section and offering valuable suggestions.

42 See Genesis Rabba 68:11 and Girón-Negrón's commentary for further sources and discussion. I wish to thank Professor Girón-Negrón for allowing me to read this section of his work in progress.

43 For discussion of this illustration, see Fellous, *Histoire de la Bible*, 176–80.

44 For the most complete account of Arragel's methodology and procedure, see Sáenz-Badillos, "Luis de Guzmán's Patronage." Note that the translation was edited by Christians after Arragel completed it, so the text as we have it in the Alba codex may not be exactly what Arragel wrote.

45 The most striking of these codicological features in the Alba Bible is that the writing of the text hangs from the ruled lines rather than resting upon them. See Avenoza, "Jews and the Copying of Books," 352–53.

46 On the Complutensian, see Chinchilla, "The *Complutensian Polyglot Bible*"; and Ortega-Monasterio, "Patronage." The *conversos* involved in the Complutensian were Alfonso de Zamora, Pablo Coronel, and Alfonso de Alcalá. It is worth pointing out that Augustino Giustiniani, bishop of Nebbio in Corsica, the sponsor and editor of the other famous, near contemporary Polyglot, a volume of Psalms with Latin, Hebrew, Greek, Aramaic, and Arabic texts (Genoa, 1516)—Giustiniani intended to publish a complete Bible but drowned shortly after completing the Psalterium—expressly prohibited Jews from participating in its preparation.

47 For an extensive, groundbreaking analysis of Zamora's "de-Masoratized" Hebrew text with a companion study of how Arias Montano restored the Masoretic text in his edition, see Dunkelgrün, "Multiplicity of Scripture."

48 For an initial foray into comparison, which touches upon many of the more bibliographic and historical differences between the two Bibles, see Van Nes, "The 'Jewish' Rabbinic Bibles."

49 For a comparison of their biblical texts, see Kahle, "The Hebrew Text of the Complutensian Polyglot."

50 On the edition, see Heller, *The Sixteenth-Century Hebrew Book*, 324–25. The Judeo-Persian polyglot translation was done by Jacob ben Joseph Tavus (sixteenth century) but draws on a lengthy history of Judeo-Persian translation, about which see Paper, "Judeo-Persian Bible Translations."

51 See Lazar, *Ladino Bible*; Rypins, "Ferrara Bible."

52 Rypins, "Ferrara Bible," 250–55.

53 Rypins, "Ferrara Bible," 251–52; Berkowitz, *In Remembrance*, 114–15.

54 On the history of the term, see Banitt, *Rashi*, 6, which notes that *le'az* originally referred to the Greek translation of the Bible (B. Megillah 18a).

55 Banitt, *Rashi*, esp. 4, for the postulation of an Old French Vulgate version of the Bible (*la'az ha'am*). Valmadonna 1, the Anglo-Norman liturgical Pentateuch written in 1189 and discussed in chapter 2, contains a marginal list of Hebrew words, accompanied by their Old French translation, for the unclean birds listed in Leviticus 11:13–19. For a complete description and translation of the marginal note, see Beit-Arié, *The Only Dated Medieval Hebrew Manuscript*, 137; and for an illustration of the marginal note, *Valmadonna Trust Library: Part I*, 39.

56 For a succinct summary of Judeo-Italian translations and bibliography, see the article by Seth Jerchower on Judeo-Italian at http://www.jewish-languages.org/judeo-italian.html.

57 The following discussion is based on Turniansky, "To the History of the 'Taytsch-Khumesh'"; Turniansky, "Reception and Rejection"; and Baumgarten, *Old Yiddish Literature*, 82–127. The classic although dated study of this literature is Staerk and Leitzmann, *Die Jüdisch-Deutschen Bibelübersetzungen*.

58 The earliest text cited in Staerk and Leitzmann is Cod. Hebr. Karlsruhe 8 (= Cod. Reuchl. XIII), which they date to the fourteenth to fifteenth century. Baumgarten, *Old Yiddish Literature,* 104, refers to fourteenth-century manuscripts and in note 45 lists several manuscripts, although none appear to be that early. For a collection of fifteenth- and (mainly) sixteenth-century manuscripts and early printings, see Turniansky and Timm, *Yiddish in Italia*, 2–11, and Turniansky's comments on p. 193 on the use of these codices.

59 Turniansky, *Yiddish in Italia,* 193.

60 Cited from the Cremona edition published by Leyb Bresh in 1560, translated in Baumgarten, *Old Yiddish Literature*, 106.

61 Baumgarten, *Old Yiddish Literature*, 105.

62 On these various books and their relation to *Taytsch-ḥumash*, see Turniansky, "To the History of the 'Taytsch-Khumesh,'" 48–56; and Baumgarten, *Old Yiddish Literature*, 105–12.

63 Baumgarten, *Old Yiddish Literature*, 113–21, and bibliography cited there.

64 On the illustrations, see Heyd, "Illustrations."

65 On the Christian provenance of the *Tse'ena Ure'enah*'s illustrations (as well as those in most early modern Jewish books), see Wiesemann, "*Kommt heraus und schaut,*" 24–32; Wiesemann, *Ondanks*, 14–31; and Gross, "Biblical Illustrations on Judaica Objects," 143–44.

66 Turniansky, "To the History," 56–57.

67 On the two translations, see Timm, "Blitz and Witzenhausen"; Aptroot, "In *galkhes*"; Aptroot, "Yiddish Bibles"; and Berger, "Bibles and Publishers."

68 See Turniansky, "Reception and Rejection," 18. As Turniansky notes, the *Taytsch-ḥumash* remained the primary translation used in elementary education within traditional East European culture until the time of the Holocaust; even today it continues to be used in Yiddish-speaking communities in Israel and America.

69 For a fuller account, see Breuer, *Limits of Enlightenment*; Burnett, "Later Christian Hebraists"; and Breuer, "Jewish Study of the Bible." My account is based on these sources.

70 The copy is now in the Deutsche Staatsbibliothek in Berlin. For an image of its pages, see de Hamel, *The Book*, 219; and Berkowitz, *In Remembrance*, 86.

71 Sheehan, *Enlightenment Bible*, esp. xiii–xiv.

72 On Kennicott, see Burnett, "Later Christian Hebraists," 795–801.

73 Cited in Edward Breuer, *Limits of Enlightenment*, 97. On Michaelis in general, see Legaspi, *Death of Scripture*; and Sheehan, *Enlightenment Bible*, 199–211.

74 I wish to thank Edward Breuer for reviewing this section and helping me understand the complexity of the issues surrounding Mendelssohn's translation. I also wish to thank Breuer for allowing me to read in manuscript his soon to be published introduction to the *Be'ur.*

75 Cited in Edward Breuer, "Jewish Study," 1016.

76 On the page format, see Gilman, "Between Religion and Culture," 101–5.

77 On the German translations, see Bechtoldt, *Jüdische deutsche Bibelübersetzungen*; and on Zunz in particular, Gilman, "Jewish Quest." For an innovative and illuminating study of the changing nature of the Mendelssohn Bible's audience, see Lowenstein, "Readership."

78 On the Buber-Rosenzweig translation, see Benjamin, *Rosenzweig's Bible*, esp. 103–70; Fox, "The Book in Its Contexts"; Rosenwald, "Buber and Rosenzweig's Challenge"; and Gilman, "Between Religion and Culture."

79 Fox, "The Book in Its Contexts," xv–xx; and Gilman, "Between Religion and Culture," 114. This ambition—to Hebraize the German language—was not without a polemical side. The true precursor that the Buber-Rosenzweig translation sought to overthrow was not Mendelssohn's translation but Luther's, and not for its emendations of the Hebrew text but for the fact that it had, in the translators' view, Christianized the German language. Buber and Rosenzweig intended their translation to appeal to both Jews and Christians, but its intent was to show that the Jewish Bible was the original and universal Bible. On this side of the translation, see Benjamin, *Rosenzweig's Bible,* 107–21. As she acutely notes (105), "For Rosenzweig, the Bible represented the locus of Jewish and Christian struggle with one another to win a privileged position vis-à-vis the text."

80 Fox, "The Book in Its Contexts," xv, xxi–xxii. As Benjamin points out (*Rosenzweig's Bible,* 146), the word *Leitwort* was Buber's neologism.

81 Fox, "The Book in Its Contexts," xxiii.

82 Gilman, "Between Religion and Culture," 109; and Benjamin (citing Peter Gordon and Gerald Bruns), *Rosenzweig's Bible,* 112–25.

83 To be sure, there are references to the verse numbers on the top left-hand corner of the page, but by removing them from their usual position as part of the punctuation, Buber and Rosenzweig further differentiated the page from other Bibles and made it harder to use as a mere reference book, clearly one of the translators' aims.

84 The divisions marked by the cola bear no relation to the Masorah's division of verses, although it should be noted that Buber and Rosenzweig did accept and employ the Masoretic text, if only because they felt that they had no other choice. On their attitude to the Masorah, see Benjamin, *Rosenzweig's Bible,* 129–30.

85 The Italian edition was I. Reggio's *Sefer Torat Ha-Elohim* (1821), and the French, Samuel Cahan's *La Bible* (1831–51); see Breuer and Gafni, "Jewish Biblical Scholarship," 292–93; and on Cahan's translation, Berkovitz, *Rites and Passages*, 184–87.

86 Cited in Ruderman, *Jewish Enlightenment,* 87; and for extensive discussion of Levi's context and battles against Kennicott et al., 23–88; on Levi's and other English translations by Jews, see 219–31.

87 Ruderman, *Jewish Enlightenment*, 230–31.

88 Ellenson, "Vindication of Judaism," 67. On the book, see Meirovich, *Vindication of Judaism*; and Skloot, "Moses of Hamilton Terrace."

89 The characterization of biblical criticism is taken from Hertz's preface to the first edition (1937).

90 To be fair, it should be noted that Hertz asked the Jewish Publication Society for permission to reprint the 1917 translation and was initially turned down, but by the time of the second edition of Hertz's Pentatuech in 1938, the society had relented and their translation was substituted for the Revised Authorized Version.

91 Cited in Sussman, "Another Look," 179.

92 Sussman, "Another Look," 174.

93 Sussman, "Another Look," esp. 172–78; cf. Sarna, *JPS Torah*, 95–96.

94 For a detailed retelling of the history of the translation, see Sarna, *JPS Torah*, 97–120; and Greenspoon, "Book 'Without Blemish.'" On Margolis himself, see Greenspoon, "On the Jewishness."

95 Margolis, “Preface,” vii.

96 On the JPS *TANAKH*, see Sarna, *JPS Torah*, 233–47. “Intelligibility” as a criterion is Harry Orlinsky’s intervention; see Orlinsky, *Essays*, 355. “Intrinsically” is borrowed from Sarna, *JPS Torah*, 243.

97 The Reform volume, *The Torah: A Modern Commentary*, edited by W. Gunther Plaut, appeared in 1981; the Conservative movement’s Bible, *Etz Hayim*, edited by David L. Lieber, in 2001. Orthodox translations include Arye Kaplan’s popular *The Living Torah: The Five Books of Moses* (New York: Moznayim, 1981); and the Artscroll *Tanach*, ed. Nosson Scherman (Brooklyn: Mesorah, 1996).

98 For example, Everett Fox’s *The Five Books of Moses: Genesis, Exodus, Leviticus, Numbers, Deuteronomy: A New Translation with Introductions, Commentary and Notes* (New York: Schocken, 1995); and Robert Alter’s *The Five Books of Moses: A Translation with Commentary* (New York: Norton, 2004), followed by several volumes of additional books from the Prophets and Writings. Mention should also be made of *The Book of J*, translated by David Rosenberg and interpreted by Harold Bloom (New York: Grove Wiedenfeld, 1990).

99 On Yehoash, see Orlinsky, “Yehoash’s Yiddish Translation”; and Berger, “Religion, Culture, Literature.”

100 Berger, “Religion, Culture, Literature,” 627. Interestingly, as Berger points out (525), Yehoash’s early translations—of Isaiah, Job, the Song of Songs, Ruth, and Ecclesiastes, all published in 1910—were very literal word-by-word translations, in the mold of the *Taytsch-ḥumash*.

101 Orlinsky, “Yehoash’s Yiddish Translation,” 176.

102 *Die Bücher der Bible, herausgegeben von F. Rahlwes: Zeichnungen von E.M. Lilien, nach der Übersetzung von [Eduard] Reuss* (Braunschweig: Georg Westermann, 1908). On Lilien, see Gelber, *Melancholy Pride*, esp. 100–124.

103 On Bezalel and the Bible as well as on Schatz, see Manor, “Biblical Zionism.”

104 On Koren and history of the Koren Bible, see Friedman, “Prayer Type”; and Yardeni, *Book of Hebrew Script*, 120.

105 *Tanakh Ram*, translated by Abraham Ahuviyah (Herzliya: RAM Publishing, 2010).

106 On Firkovich’s acquisitions, see Harviainen, “Abraham Firkovich”; and Shapira, *Avraham Firkowicz*, 67–93.

107 Kahle, *Cairo Geniza*, esp. 60–62, 72–77.

108 For a clear statement about the principles and methodology underlying *BHQ* as well as its differences from its predecessors, see the general introduction in the *Megillot* volume, English text, vii–xxvi. For an insightful overview and comparison of *BHQ* with other contemporary critical editions, including the Hebrew University Bible Project discussed below, see Richard D. Weis, “*Biblia Hebraica Quinta* and the Making of Critical Editions of the Hebrew Bible,” http://rosetta.reltech.org/TC/v07/Weis2002.html.

109 On Firkovich and the Aleppo Codex, see Harviainen, “Abraham Firkovich.”

110 Mordechai Breuer, *Aleppo Codex*, xxiv–xxv.

111 Mordechai Breuer, *Aleppo Codex*, xvii.

112 Mordechai Breuer, *Aleppo Codex*, xliv.

113 Goshen-Gottstein, “Rise of the Tiberian Bible Text,” 87–89.

114 For an attempt to explain the background of this title, see David Stern, “On the Term *Keter*.”

115 On Maimonides and the Aleppo Codex, see Penkower, "Maimonides"; on the superiority of the Aleppo Codex, see Penkower, *Nusaḥ HaTorah*, 56–61; and Mordechai Breuer, *Aleppo Codex*, xi–xii, xxx–xxxi.

116 Thus Revell, "Leningrad Codex," xliii.

117 There were, of course, many other important editions printed in Israel. In addition to the Koren and HUBP editions, mention should be made of (1) *Torah, Nevi'im U-Ketuvim*, ed. Aron Dotan (Tel Aviv: ADI Publishers, 1973); revised and retypeset as *Biblia Hebraica Leningradensia: Prepared according to the Vocalization, Accents, and Masora of Aaron ben Moses ben Asher in the Leningrad Codex*, ed. Aron Dotan (Peabody, MA: Hendrickson, 2001); and (2) *Torah, Nevi'im Ketuvim/ Mugahim 'al pi ha-Nusaḥ ve-ha-Mesorah shel Keter Aram Tsovah ve-Kitvei Yad Ha-Kerovim lo* [edited according to the text and Masorah of the Aleppo Codex and manuscripts similar to it], ed. Mordechai Breuer (Jerusalem: Mosad Ha-Rav Kuk, 1977–82); reprinted in *Torat ḥayim: ḥamishah ḥumashei Torah*, ed. Mordechai Breuer, Yosef Kapaḥ, and M. L. Katsenelenbogen (Jerusalem: Mosad Ha-Rav Kuk, 1986); and *Keter Yerushalayim: Tanakh Ha-Universitah Ha-'Ivrit be-Yerushalayim*, ed. Yosef Ofer (Jerusalem: Ben Zvi, 2000).

118 Thus Dotan's edition cited in the previous note. The Koren edition was essentially based on the Wolf Heidenheim revised edition of RB 1525; see Mordechai Breuer, *The Aleppo Codex*, xxviii.

Epilogue

1 Thomas Jefferson, *The Jefferson Bible: The Life and Morals of Jesus of Nazareth Extracted Textually from the Gospels in Greek, Latin, French & English* (Washington, DC: Smithsonian Books, 2011).

2 David Rosenberg and Harold Bloom, *The Book of J* (New York: Grove Weidenfeld, 1990).

BIBLIOGRAPHY

Abrahams, Israel, ed. *Hebrew Ethical Wills*. Philadelphia: Jewish Publication Society, 1926.

Adler, Elkan Nathan, ed. *An Eleventh Century Introduction to the Hebrew Bible (Ginzei Mitsrayim Hilkhot Sefer Torah)*. Oxford, private circulation, 1897.

———. "Professor Blau on the Bible as a Book." In *About Hebrew Manuscripts*, 51–64. 1905. Reprint, New York: Hermon Press: 1970.

Adler, William. "'What the Hebrews Say': Translation, Authority, and the Story of Susanna and the Elders." In *Studies and Texts in Jewish History and Culture*, edited by Bernard D. Cooperman, 19–39. Bethesda: University Press of Maryland, 2002.

Alexander, Philip S. "Jewish Aramaic Translations of the Hebrew Scriptures." In *Mikra: Text, Translation, Reading and Interpretation of the Hebrew Bible in Ancient Judaism and Early Christianity*, edited by Martin J. Mulder, 217–54. Philadelphia: Van Gorcum and Fortress, 1988.

———. "The Targums and Rabbinic Rules for the Delivery of the Targum." In *Congress Volume: Salamanca, 1983 (Supplements to Vetus Testamentum, 36)*, edited by J. A. Amerton, 14–28. Leiden: Brill, 1985.

Alfonso, Esperanza, Javier del Barco, M. Teresa Ortega Monasterio, and Arturo Prats, eds. *Biblias de Sefarad / Bibles of Sepharad*. Madrid: CSIC/Bibliotheca National de España, 2012.

Allony, Nehemia. "Torah Scrolls and the Codex in the Public Lectionary Reading in the Rabbanite and Karaite Communities." *Beit Mikra* 78 (1979): 321–35.

Amram, David Werner. *The Makers of Hebrew Books in Italy: Being Chapters in the History of the Hebrew Printing Press*. 1909. Reprint, London: Holland Press, 1963.

Aptroot, Marion. "'In *galkhes* they do not say so, but the *taytsh* is as it stands here': Notes on the Amsterdam Yiddish Bible Translations by Blitz and Witzenhausen." *Studia Rosenthaliana* 27 (1993): 136–58.

———. "Yiddish Bibles in Amsterdam." In *The Bible in/and Yiddish*, edited by Shlomo Berger, 42–60. Amsterdam: Menasseh ben Israel Institute, 2007.

Assaf, Sharon, and Emily D. Bilski. *Salom Italia's Esther Scrolls and the Dutch Golden Age*. Amsterdam: Menasseh ben Israel Institute and the Jewish Historical Museum Amsterdam, 2011.

Astren, Fred. "Islamic Contexts of Medieval Karaism." In *Karaite Judaism: A Guide to Its History and Literary Sources*, edited by Meira Polliack, 145–78. Boston: Brill, 2003.

Attia, Elodie. "Targum Layouts in Ashkenazi Manuscripts: Preliminary Methodological Observations." In *A Jewish Targum in a Christian World*, edited by Alberdina Houtman, Eveline van Staalduine-Sulman, and Hans-Martin Kirn, 99–122. Boston: Brill, 2014.

Avenoza, Gemma. "The Bible in Spanish and Catalan." In *The New Cambridge History of the Bible, Vol. 2: From 600 to 1450*, edited by Richard Marsden and E. Ann Matter, 288–306. Cambridge: Cambridge University Press, 1912.

———. "Jews and the Copying of Books in the Iberian Peninsula in the Fourteenth and Fifteenth Centuries." In *Patronage, Production, and Transmission of Texts in Medieval and Early Modern Jewish Cultures*, edited by Esperanza Alfonso and Jonathan Decter, 341–60. Turnhout: Brepols, 2014.

Avrin, Leila. "Micrography as Art." In *La lettre hébraïque et sa signification and Micrography as Art*, edited by Collette Sirat and Leila Avrian, 43–47. Paris: Editions de CNRS, 1981.

———. *Scribes, Script and Books: The Book Arts from Antiquity to the Renaissance.* Chicago: American Library Association, 1991.

Bagnall, Roger S. *Early Christian Books in Egypt*. Princeton, NJ: Princeton University Press, 2009.

Banitt, Menachem. *Rashi: Interpreter of the Biblical Letter*. Tel Aviv: Chaim Rosenberg School of Jewish Studies, Tel Aviv University, 1985.

Bar-Ilan, Meir. "The Book-Case (Ark) in Ancient Synagogues" [in Hebrew]. In *Libraries and Book-Collections,* edited by J. Kaplan and M. Sluhovsky, 49–64. Jerusalem: Merkaz Zalman Shazar, 2006.

Baron, Salo Wittmayer. *A Social and Religious History of the Jews.* 18 vols. 2d ed. New York: Columbia University Press, 1965.

Baruchson, Zipora. "Money and Culture: Financing Sources and Methods in the Hebrew Printing Shops in Cinquecento Italy." *La Bibliofilia* 92 (1990): 23–39.

Baruchson-Arbib, Shifra Z. "The Prices of Hebrew Printed Books in Cinquecento Italy." *La Bibliofilia* 97 (1995): 149–61.

Baumgarten, Albert I. "Sacred Scriptures Defile the Hands." *Journal of Jewish Studies* 67 (2016): 46–67.

Baumgarten, Elisheva. *Mothers and Children: Jewish Family Life in Medieval Europe.* Princeton, NJ: Princeton University Press, 2004.

Baumgarten, Jean. *Introduction to Old Yiddish Literature*. Edited and translated by Jerold C. Frakes. New York: Oxford University Press, 2005.

Bechtoldt, Han-Joachim. *Jüdische deutsche Bibelübersetzungen vom ausgehenden 18. bis zum Beginn des 20. Jahrhunderts*. Stuttgart: Kohlhammer, 2005.

Beit-Arié, Malachi. "*Emunah Yotzrah Etzlo Amanah:* A Poem That Was Customary to Copy at the End of a Torah Codex in Yemen" [in Hebrew]. In *Shai le-Heiman, A. M. Habermann Jubilee Volume: Studies in Medieval Hebrew Literature*, edited by Z. Malachi, 37–50. Jerusalem: Reuben Mass, 1997.

———. "Genizot: Depositories of Consumed Books as Disposing Procedure in Jewish Society." *Scriptorium* 50 (1996): 407–14.

———. *Hebrew Manuscripts of East and West: Towards a Comparative Codicology.* London: British Library: 1992.

———. "How Hebrew Manuscripts Are Made." In *A Sign and a Witness: 2,000 Years of Hebrew Books and Illuminated Manuscripts*, edited by Leonard Singer Gold, 35–46. New York: Oxford University Press, 1989.

———. "The Individualistic Nature of the Hebrew Medieval Book: Production and Consumption" [in Hebrew]. *Zion* 65 (2000): 441–51.

———. "The Making of the Book: A Codicological Study." In *The Barcelona Haggadah (MS British Library Additional 14761)*, edited by Jeremy Schonfeld, commentary volume, 14–23. London: Facsimile Editions, 1992.

———. *The Only Dated Medieval Hebrew Manuscript Written in England (1189 CE) and the Problem of Pre-expulsion Anglo-Hebrew Manuscripts.* London: Valmadonna Trust Library, 1985.

———. "The Relationship Between Early Hebrew Printing and Handwritten Books: Attachment or Detachment." In *The Makings of the Medieval Hebrew Book*, 251–76. Jerusalem: Magnes, 1993.

———. *Unveiled Faces of Medieval Hebrew Books: The Evolution of Manuscript Production—Progression or Regression?* Jerusalem: Magnes, 2003.

———. "The Worms Mahzor-MS Jerusalem, Jewish National and University Library Heb 4° 781/1: Wuerzburg? (Germany), 1272." In *The Makings of the Medieval Hebrew Book*, 152–80. Jerusalem: Magnes, 1993.

Beit-Arié, Malachi, and Edna Engel. *Specimens of Mediaeval Hebrew Script.* 2 vols. Jerusalem: Israel Academy of Sciences and Humanities, 2002.

Beit-Arié, Malachi, C. Sirat, and M. Glatzer, eds. *Codices Hebraicis Litteris Exarati Quo Tempore Scripti Fuerint Exhibentes* (*Monumenta Paleographica Medii Aevi, Series Hebraica*). Jerusalem, 1997 (vol. 1), 1999 (vol. 2), 2002 (vol. 3).

Benayahu, Meir. *Copyright, Authorization and Imprimatur for Hebrew Books Printed in Venice* [in Hebrew]. Jerusalem: Makhon Ben-Zvi and Mosad Harav Kook, 1971.

Ben-Hayyim, Ze'ev. "Masorah u-mesoret" [in Hebrew]. *Leshoneinu* 21 (1957): 283–92.

Benjamin, Mara, *Rosenzweig's Bible: Re-inventing Scripture for Jewish Modernity.* Cambridge: Cambridge University Press, 2009.

Ben-Shammai, Haggai. "Between Annanites and Karaites: Observations on Early Medieval Jewish Sectarianism." In *Studies in Muslim-Jewish Relations*, edited by Ronald L. Nettler, 19–29. Chur: Harwood Academic, 1993.

———. "New and Old: 'The Long Introduction' and 'The Short Introduction' to R. Saadiah Gaon's Translation of the Torah" [in Hebrew]. *Tarbiz* 69 (2000): 199–210.

Berger, Shlomo. "Bibles and Publishers: Yiddish Paratexts in Amsterdam." In *Paratexts: The Fuzzy Edges of Literature*, edited by C. Dauven et al., 127–39. Amsterdam: Institute of Culture and History, University of Amsterdam, 2004.

———. "Religion, Culture, Literature: On Yehoyesh's Preface to His Yiddish Bible Translation." In *Leket: Yiddish Studies Today*, edited by Marion Aptroot et al., 619–34. Düsseldorf: Düsseldorf University Press, 2012.

Berkovitz, Jay R. *Rites and Passages: The Beginnings of Modern Jewish Culture in France (1650–1860).* Philadelphia: University of Pennsylvania Press, 2004.

Berkowitz, David Sandler. *In Remembrance of Creation: Evolution of Art and Scholarship in the Medieval and Renaissance Bible.* Waltham, MA: Brandeis University Press, 1968.

Berliner, A. "The Hebrew Publishing House of Daniel Bomberg" [in Hebrew]. In *Ketavim Nivharim (Selected Essays)*, 1:163–75. Jerusalem: Mosad Harav Kook, 1969.

Biale, David, ed. *Cultures of the Jews.* New York: Schocken: 2002.

Birnbaum, S. A. "A Sheet of an Eighth Century Synagogue Scroll." *Vetus Testamentum* 9 (1959): 122–29.

Bland, Kalman. *The Artless Jew: Medieval and Modern Affirmations and Denials of the Visual.* Princeton, NJ: Princeton University Press, 2000.

———. "Defending, Enjoying, and Regulating the Visual." In *Judaism in Practice: From the Middle Ages Through the Early Modern Period*, edited by Lawrence Fine, 281–97. Princeton, NJ: Princeton University Press, 2001.

Blank, Debra Reed. "It's Time to Take Another Look at 'Our Little Sister' Soferim: A Bibliographical Essay." *Jewish Quarterly Review* 90 (1999): 1–26.

Blau, Joshua, ed. *Teshuvot Ha-Rambam.* 3 vols. Jerusalem: Mekitzei Nirdamim, Reuven Mass, 1986.

Blau, Joshua, and Simon Hopkins. "Ancient Bible Translations to Judeo-Arabic." *Pe'amim* 83 (2000): 4–14.

Blau, Ludwig. *Studien zum althebraische Buchwesen und zur biblischen Literaturgeschichte.* Budapest: Landes-Rabbiner Schule, 1902.

Bloch, Joshua. *Venetian Printers of Hebrew Books.* New York: New York Public Library, 1932.

Bonfil, Robert. *Jewish Life in Renaissance Italy.* Translated by Anthony Oldcorn. Berkeley: University of California Press, 1991.

———. *Rabbis and Jewish Communities in Renaissance Italy.* London: Littman Library, 1993.

Boynton, Susan, and Diane J. Reilly, eds. *The Practice of the Bible in the Middle Ages: Production, Reception and Performance in Western Christianity.* New York: Columbia University Press, 2011.

Branham, Joan. "Vicarious Sacrality: Temple Space in Ancient Synagogues." In *Ancient Synagogues: Historical Analysis and Archaeological Discovery*, edited by Dan Urman and Paul V. M. Flesher, 2:319–45. Leiden: Brill, 1995.

Breuer, Edward. "Jewish Study of the Bible Before and During the Jewish Enlightenment." In *Hebrew Bible / Old Testament: The History of Its Interpretation*, edited by M. Sæbø, 2:1006–23. Göttingen: Vandenhoeck & Ruprecht, 2000.

———. *The Limits of Enlightenment: Jews, Germans, and the Eighteenth-Century Study of the Bible.* Cambridge, MA: Harvard University Center for Jewish Studies, 1996.

Breuer, Edward, and Chanan Gafni. "Jewish Biblical Scholarship Between Tradition and Innovation." In *Hebrew Bible / Old Testament: The History of Its Interpretation*, edited by Magne Sæbø, 3:262–303. Göttingen: Vandenhoeck & Ruprecht, 2013.

Breuer, Mordechai. *The Aleppo Codex and the Accepted Text of the Bible* [in Hebrew]. Jerusalem: Mosad Harav Kook, 1976.

———. "Keep Your Children from *Higgayon*" [in Hebrew]. In *Mikhtam Le-David: Sefer Zikhron Harav David Ochs*, edited by Y. Gilat and E. Stern, 242–64. Ramat Gan: Bar Ilan University Press, 1978.

Bromer, Anne C., and Julian I. Edison. *Miniature Books: 4,000 Years of Tiny Treasures*. New York: Abrams, 2007.

Brown, Michelle P., ed. *In the Beginning: Bibles Before the Year 1000*. Washington, DC: Smithsonian Institution, 2006.

Burnett, Stephen G. "Christian Hebrew Printing in the Sixteenth Century: Printers, Humanism, and the Impact of the Reformation." *Helmantica* 11 (2000): 13–42.

———. "Later Christian Hebraists." In *Hebrew Bible / Old Testament: The History of Its Interpretation*, edited by M. Sæbø, 2:785–801. Göttingen: Vandenhoeck & Ruprecht, 2000.

———. "The Strange Career of the *Rabbinica* Among Christian Hebraists, 1517–1620." In *Shaping the Bible in the Reformation: Books, Scholars and Readers in the Sixteenth Century*, edited by Matthew McLean and Bruce Gordon. Leiden: Brill, 2012.

Butin, Romain. *The Ten Nequdoth of the Torah, with a Prolegomenon by Shemaryahu Talmon*. 1906. Reprint, New York: Ktav, 1969.

Cahn, Walter. *Romanesque Bible Illumination*. Ithaca, NY: Cornell University Press, 1982.

Calkins, Robert G. *Illuminated Books of the Middle Ages*. Ithaca, NY: Cornell University Press, 1983.

Camille, Michael. *Image on the Edge: The Margins of Medieval Art*. Cambridge, MA: Harvard University Press, 1992.

———. "Visual Signs of the Sacred Page: Books in the *Bible Moralisée*." *Word and Image* 5 (1989): 111–30.

Carr, David. *Writing on the Tablet of the Heart: Origins of Scripture and Literature*. New York: Oxford, 2005.

Carruthers, Mary. *The Book of Memory: A Study of Memory in Medieval Culture*. Cambridge: Cambridge University Press, 1990.

Cassuto, U. "The Jewish Translation of the Bible in Latin and Its Importance for the Study of the Greek and Aramaic Versions." In *Biblical and Oriental Studies*, 1:285–309. Jerusalem: Magnes, 1973.

Cavallo, G., and R. Chartrier, eds. *A History of Reading in the West*. Translated by L. G. Cochrane. Amherst: University of Massachusetts Press, 2003.

Charlesworth, J., ed. *The Old Testament Pseudepigrapha*. 2 vols. Garden City, NJ: Doubleday, 1985.

Chavel, C., ed. *Peirush R. Bahya ʿal Hatorah*. 5 vols. Jerusalem: Mosad Harva Kuk, 1966–68.

Chiesa, Bruno. *The Emergence of Hebrew Biblical Pointing: The Indirect Sources*. Frankfurt a.M.: Lang, 1979.

Chinchilla, Rosa Helena. "The *Complutensian Polyglot Bible* (1520) and the Political Ramifications of Biblical Translation." In *La traducción en España ss. XIV–XVI*, 169–80. Leon: Universidad de Leon, 1995.

Cohen, Evelyn M., Sharon Lieberman Mntz, and Emile G. L. Schrijver. *A Journey Through Jewish Worlds: Highlights from the Braginsky Collection of Hebrew Manuscripts and Printed Books*. Amsterdam: Bijzondere Collecties, Universiteit van Amsterdam, 2009.

Coudert, Allison P., and Jeffrey S. Shoulson. *Hebraica Veritas: Christian Hebraists and the Study of Judaism in Early Modern Europe*. Philadelphia: University of Pennsylvania Press, 2004.

Crown, Alan D. "Abisha Scroll." In *A Companion to Samaritan Studies*, edited by Alan D. Crown, Reinhard Pummer, and Abraham Tal, 4–6. Tubingen: Mohr Siebeck, 1993.

———. *Samaritan Scribes and Manuscripts*. Tubingen: Mohr Siebeck, 2001.

Danzig, Nahman (Neil). "The Ruling of Sacred Books: The Origins of the Halakhah and Its Repercussions" [in Hebrew]. In *Atara L'Haim: Studies in the Talmud and Medieval Rabbinic Literature in Honor of Professor Haim Zalman Dimitrovsky*, edited by Daniel Boyarin et al., 283–359. Jerusalem: Magnes, 2000.

Darshan, Guy. "Twenty-Four or Twenty-Two Books of the Bible and the Homeric Corpus" [in Hebrew]. *Tarbitz* 77 (2007): 5–22.

Davies, Martin. *Aldus Manutius: Printer and Publisher of Renaissance Venice*. Tempe: Arizona Center for Medieval and Renaissance Studies, 1999.

———. "Humanism in Script and Print." In *The Cambridge Companion to Renaissance Humanism*, edited by Jill Kraye, 47–62. Cambridge: Cambridge University Press, 1996.

Davis, M. C., and Ben Outhwaite. *Hebrew Bible Manuscripts in the Cambridge Genizah Collections*. Vol. 4. Cambridge: Cambridge University Press, 2003.

de Hamel, Christopher. *The Book: The History of the Bible*. London: Phaedon, 2001.

———. *Glossed Books of the Bible and the Origins of the Paris Book Trade*. Dover, NH: Brewer, 1984.

de Lange, Nicholas. "The Greek Bible Translations of the Byzantine Jews." In *The Old Testament in Byzantium*, edited by Paul Magdalino and Robert S. Nelson, 39–54. Dumbarton Oaks, CA: Dumbarton Oaks Research Library and Collection, 2010.

———. "Jewish Greek Bible Versions." In *The New Cambridge History of the Bible*, edited by Richard Marsden and E. Ann Matter, 2:56–68. Cambridge: Cambridge University Press.

Demsky, Aaron. *Literacy in Ancient Israel* [in Hebrew]. Jerusalem: Mossad Bialik, 2012.

De Tatta, Rita. "L'occhio dello studiosa e la lente del bibliotecario: Breve storia del rotulo ebraico della Biblioteca Universitaria di Bologna." In *Il Rotulo 2 della Biblioteca Universitaria di Bologna*, edited by Biancastella Antonino, Rita De Tata, and Mauro Perani, 22–35. Bologna: Biblioteca Universitaria di Bologna, 2015.

de Troyer, Kristin. "The Septuagint." In *The New Cambridge History of the Bible*, edited by James Carleton Paget and Joachim Schaper, 1:267–88. Cambridge: Cambridge University Press, 2013.

Diez Macho, Alejandro. "Introductory Remarks" [in Hebrew]. *The Pentateuch with Masorah Parva and the Masorah Magna and with Targum Onkelos, Ms. Vat. Heb. 448*. Jerusalem: Makor, 1977.

———. *Neophyti 1: Targum Palestinense MS de la Biblioteca Vaticana*. Vol. 1, *Genesis: Edición Príncipe, Inroducción General y Versión Castellana*. Madrid: Consejo Superior de Investigaciones Científicas, 1968.

Diringer, D. "Early Hebrew Script Versus Square Hebrew Script." In *Essays and Studies Presented to Stanley Arthur Cook*, edited by D. Winton Thomas, 35–49. London: Taylor's Foreign Press, 1950.

Dirksen, Peter B. "The Old Testament Peshitta." In *Mikra: Text, Translation, Reading and Interpretation of the Hebrew Bible in Ancient Judaism and Early Christianity*, edited by Martin J. Mulder, 255–98. Philadelphia: Van Gorcum and Fortress, 1988.

Dodds, Jerrilyn D. "Mudejar Tradition and the Synagogues of Medieval Spain: Cultural Identity and Cultural Hegemony." In *Convivencia: Jews, Muslims, and Christians in Medieval Spain*, edited by Vivian B. Mann et al., 113–32. New York: George Braziller, 1992.

Dotan, Aaron. *Ben Asher's Creed: A Study of the History of the Controversy*. Translated by Raphael Posner. Missoula: Scholars Press, 1977.

———. "Masorah." In *Encyclopaedia Judaica*, 16:1401–82. 3d ed. Jerusalem: Keter, 1974.

Drory, Rina. *Models and Contacts: Arabic Literature and Its Impact on Medieval Jewish Culture*. Leiden: Brill, 2000.

———. *Reishit Hamaga'im shel Hasifrut Hayehudit 'im Hasifrut Ha'aravit Vemeiah He'asirit (The Emergence of Jewish-Arabic Literary Contacts at the Beginning of the Twelfth Century)*. 2d ed. Tel Aviv: Porter Institute for Poetics and Semiotics, Tel Aviv University, HaKibbutz Hameuhad, 1999 [1988].

Dukan, Michele. *La Bible hébraïque: Les codices copiés en Orient et dans le zone sefarade avant 1280* (*Bibliologia* 22). Turnhour: Brepols, 2006.

Dunkelgrün, Theodore W. "The Multiplicity of Scripture: The Confluence of Textual Traditions in the Making of the Antwerp Polyglot Bible (1568–1573)." PhD diss., University of Chicago, 2012.

Dunsky, S., ed. *Midrash Shir Ha-Shirim Rabba*. Jerusalem: Dvir, 1980.

Duran, Profiat. *Ma'aseh Efod: Einleitung in das Studium und Grammatik der Hebräischen Sprache von Profiat Duran*. Edited by J. Friedländer and Jakob Kohn. Vienna: J. Holzwarth, 1865.

Ecker, Heather. *Caliphs and Kings: The Art and Influence of Islamic Spain*. Washington, DC: Smithsonian Institution, 2004.

Eisenstein, Elizabeth. *The Printing Press as an Agent of Change*. 2 vols. Cambridge: Cambridge University Press, 1979.

Ellenson, David. "A Vindication of Judaism: The Polemics of the Hertz Pentateuch: A Review Essay." *Modern Judaism* 21 (2001): 67–77.

Encyclopaedia Judaica. Detroit: Macmillan Reference USA, 2007.

Epstein, Mark M. *Dreams of Subversion in Medieval Jewish Art and Literature*. University Park: Pennsylvania State University Press, 1997.

Erder, Yoram. "The Karaites and the Second Temple Sects." In *Karaite Judaism: A Guide to Its History and Literary Sources*, edited by Meira Polliack, 119–44. Boston: Brill, 2003.

Ettinghausen, Richard. *Islamic Art and Architecture 650–1250*. 2d ed. New Haven, CT: Yale University Press, 2001.

———. "Yemenite Bible Manuscripts of the XVth Century." *Eretz-Israel* 7 (1964): 32*–39*.

Fellous, Sonia. *Histoire de la Bible de Moïse Arragel*. Paris: Somogy Éditions d'Art, 2001.

Feuchtwanger, Naomi. "Chanting to the Hand: Some Preliminary Observations on the Origins of the Torah Pointer." *Studia Rosenthaliana* 37 (2004): 3–27.

———. "The Coronation of the Virgin and of the Bride." *Jewish Art* 12/13 (1986/87): 213–24.

Feuchtwanger-Sarig, Naomi. "The Danish Torah Binders." In *Danish Jewish Art—Jews in Danish Art*, edited by M. Gelfer Jørgensen, 362–411. Copenhagen: Rhodos International Science, 1999.

Fine, Steven. "From Meeting House to Sacred Realm: Holiness and the Ancient Synagogue." In *Sacred Realm: The Emergence of the Synagogue in the Ancient World*, 21–47. Oxford: Oxford University Press, 1966.

———. "The Open Torah Ark: A Jewish Iconographic Type in Late Antique Rome and Sardis." In *Viewing Ancient Jewish Art and Archaeology: VeHinnei Rachel—Essays in Honor of Rachel Hachlili*, edited by Ann E. Killebrew and Gabrielle Fassbeck, 121–34. Boston: Brill, 2016.

Finkelstein, David, and Alistair McCleary, eds., *The Book History Reader*. 2d ed. New York: Routledge, 2006.

Fishman, Talya. "The Hebrew Bible and the Senses in Late Medieval Spain." In *Jewish Culture in Early Modern Europe: Essays in Honor of David B. Ruderman*, edited by Richard I. Cohen, Natalie B. Dohrmann, Adam Shear, and Elchanan Reiner, 75–84. Pittsburgh: University of Pittsburgh Press, 2014.

Fleischer, Ezra. "Annual and Triennial Reading of the Bible in the Old Synagogue" [in Hebrew]. *Tarbiz* 61 (1992), 27–43.

———. *Eretz-Israel Prayer and Prayer Rituals* [in Hebrew]. Jerusalem: Magnes, 1988.

———. "A List of the Annual Holidays in a Piyyut of R. Eliezer b. Kilir." *Tarbiz* 52 (1983): 243–46.

———. "Remarks Concerning the Triennial Cycle of the Torah Reading in Eretz Israel" [in Hebrew]. *Tarbiz* 73 (2004): 83–124.

Fox, Everett. "The Book in Its Contexts." In Martin Buber and Franz Rosenzweig, *Scripture and Translation*, xiii–xxvii. Translated by Lawrence Rosenwald with Everett Fox. Bloomington: Indiana University Press, 1994 (1936).

Fraade, Steven D. "Rabbinic Views on the Practice of Targum, and Multilingualism in the Jewish Galilee of the Third–Sixth Centuries." In *The Galilee in Late Antiquity*, edited by Lee I. Levine, 253–86. Cambridge, MA: Harvard University Press, 1992.

Frank, Daniel. *Search Scripture Well: Karaite Exegetes and the Origins of the Jewish Bible Commentary in the Islamic East*. Leiden: Brill, 2004._

Freedman, D. B., and M. B. Cohen. "The Masoretes as Exegetes: Selected Example." *Masoretic Studies* 1 (1974): 35–46.

Freimann, Aron, and Moses Marx. *Thesaurus Typographiae Hebraicae Saeculi XV: Hebrew Printing During the Fifteenth Century*. 1924–31. Reprint, Jerusalem: Universitas Booksellers, 1967–69.

Frensdorff, S. *Das Buch Ochlah W'ochlah*. 1864. Reprint, New York: Ktav, 1972.

Friedman, Jerome. *The Most Ancient Testimony: Sixteenth-Century Christian-Hebraica in the Age of Renaissance Nostalgia*. Athens: Ohio University Press, 1983.

Friedman, Joshua J. "Prayer Type: How Eliyahu Koren Used Typography to Encourage a New Way to Pray." *Tablet*, June 30, 2009.

Friedman, Matti. *The Aleppo Codex*. Chapel Hill, NC: Algonquin, 2012.

Friedman, Shamma. "The Holy Scriptures Defile the Hands: The Transformation of a Biblical Concept in Rabbinic Theology." In *Minḥah le-Naḥum: Biblical and Other Studies Presented to Nahum M. Sarna in Honour of His 70th Birthday*, 117–32. Sheffield: JSOT Press, 1993.

Frojmovic, Eva. "Jewish Mudejarismo and the Invention of Tradition." In *Late Medieval Jewish Identities: Iberia and Beyond*, edited by Carmen Caballero-Navas and Esperanza Alfonso, 233–58. New York: Palgrave Macmillan, 2010.

———. "Jewish Scribes and Christian Illuminators: Interstitial Encounters and Cultural Negotiation." In *Between Judaism and Christianity: Art Historical Essays in Honor of Elisheva (Elizabeth) Revel-Neher*, edited by Katrin Kogman-Appel and Mati Meyer, 281–305. Leiden: Brill: 2009.

———. "Messianic Politics in Re-Christianized Spain: Images of the Sanctuary in Hebrew Bible Manuscripts." In *Imagining the Self, Imagining the Other: Visual Representation and Jewish-Christian Dynamics in the Middle Ages and Early Modern Period*, edited by Eva Frojmovic, 91–128. Leiden: Brill, 2002.

Fronda, Rahel. "Attributing of Three Ashkenazi Bibles with Micrographic Images." *Ars Judaica* 9 (2013): 45–56.

Garel, Michel. *D'une main forte: Manuscrits hébreux des collections françaises.* Paris: Bibliothèque Nationale, 1991.

Gelber, Mark H. *Melancholy Pride: Nation, Race, and Gender in the German Literature of Cultural Zionism.* Tübingen: Max Niemeyer, 2000.

Gerber, Jane S. "The World of Samuel Halevi: Testimony from the El Transito Synagogue of Toledo." In *The Jew in Medieval Iberia 1100–1500*, edited by Jonathan Ray, 33–59. Boston: Academic Studies Press, 2012.

Gibson, Margaret. "Carolingian Glossed Psalters." In *The Early Medieval Bible*, edited by Richard Gameson, 78–100. Cambridge: Cambridge University Press, 1994.

Gil, Moshe. "The Origins of the Karaites." In *Karaite Judaism: A Guide to Its History and Literary Sources*, edited by Meira Polliack, 73–118. Leiden: Brill, 2003.

Gilman, Abigail. "Between Religion and Culture: Mendelsohnn, Buber, Rosenzweig and the Enterprise of Biblical Translation." In *Studies and Texts in Jewish History and Culture*, edited by Bernard D. Cooperman, 93–114. Bethesda: University of Maryland Press, 2002.

———. "The Jewish Quest for a German Bible: The Nineteenth-Century Translations of Joseph Johlson aand Leopold Zunz." SBL Form Archive, http://www.sbl-site.org/publications/article.aspx?articleId=829.

Ginsburg, Christian D. *Introduction to the Massoretico—Critical Edition of the Hebrew Bible.* 1897. Reprint, New York: Ktav, 1966.

———. *Jacob Ben Chajim Ibn Adonijah's Introduction to the Rabbinic Bible.* 1867. Reprint, New York: Ktav, 1968.

———. *The Massorah.* Vienna: G. Brög, 1897–1905.

Glatzer, M. "The Aleppo Codex: Codicological and Palaeographical Aspects" [in Hebrew]. *Sefunot* 19 (1989): 167–276.

———. "The Book of Books—from Scroll to Codex and into Print." In *Keter Yerushalayim, Jerusalem Crown: The Bible of the Hebrew University of Jerusalem,* edited by Mordechai Glatzer, companion volume, 61–101. Jerusalem: Ben-Zvi Printing, 2002.

Goitein, S. D. "The Synagogue Building and Its Furnishings According to the Records of the Cairo Geniza" [in Hebrew]. *Eretz Israel* 7 (1964), 81–97.

Golb, Norman. *Spertus College of Judaica Yemenite Manuscripts: An Illustrated Catalogue.* Chicago: Spertus College of Judaica, 1972.

Gold, Leonard Singer, ed. *A Sign and a Witness: 2,000 Years of Hebrew Books and Illuminated Manuscripts.* Oxford: Oxford University Press, 1988.

Goldberg, Harvey. *Jewish Passages: Cycles of Jewish Life.* Berkeley: University of California Press, 2003.

Goldschmidt, Lazarus. *The Earliest Editions of the Hebrew Bible with a Treatise on the Oldest Manuscripts of the Bible by Paul Kahle.* New York: Aldus, 1950.

Goldstein, Miriam. "The Beginnings of the Transition from *Derash* to *Peshat* as Exemplified in Yefet Ben Eli's Commentary on Ps. 44:24." In *Exegesis and Grammar in Medieval Karaite Texts*, edited by Geoffrey Khan, 41–64. Oxford: Oxford University Press, 2001.

Goodman, Martin. "Sacred Scripture and 'Defiling the Hands.'" *Journal of Theological Studies* 41 (1990): 99–107.

Goshen-Gottstein, Moshe. "Biblical Manuscripts in the United States." *Textus* 2 (1962): 28–59.

———. "Introduction." In *Biblia Rabbinica*, 3–20. Jerusalem: Makor, 1972.

———. "The Rise of the Tiberian Bible Text." In *Biblical and Other Studies*, edited by A. Altmann, 79–122. Cambridge, MA: Harvard University Press, 1963.

Gottheil, Richard. "Bible Editions." In *The Jewish Encyclopaedia*, 3:154–62. New York: Funk & Wagnalls, 1903.

Grabar, Oleg. *The Mediation of Ornament.* Princeton, NJ: Princeton University Press, 1992.

Grafton, Anthony. *Bring Out Your Dead: The Past as Revelation.* Cambridge, MA: Harvard University Press, 2001.

———. "The Humanist as Reader." In *A History of Reading in the West*, edited by G. Cavallo and R. Chartrier, translated by L. G. Cochrane, 179–212. Amherst: University of Massachusetts Press, 2003.

Greenspoon, Leonard. "A Book 'Without Blemish': The Jewish Publication Society's Bible Translation of 1917." *Jewish Quarterly Review* 79 (1988): 1–21.

———. "On the Jewishness of Modern Jewish Biblical Scholarship: The Case of Max Margolis." *Judaism* 39 (1990): 82–92.

Greidi, Shimon. "Introductory Note on the Parasha-Tag Tradition of Yemenite Jewry." In *The Pentateuch: A Yemenite Manuscript.* Jerusalem: Makor, 1978.

Griffith, Sidney H. *The Bible in Arabic: The Scriptures of the "People of the Book" in the Language of Islam.* Princeton, NJ: Princeton University Press, 2013.

Gross, Abraham. "Rashi and the Tradition of Study of Written Torah in Sepharad." In *Rashi Studies*, edited by Z. A. Steinfeld, 27–55. Ramat Gan: Bar Ilan University Press, 1993.

Gross, William. *50 Rimmonim.* Tel Aviv: Tel Aviv University, 1998.

———. "Bemer the Slow: A Seventeenth Century Architect and the Classic Galician Spice Tower." In *Eshkolot: Essays in Memory of Rabbi Ronald Lubofsky*, edited by Anna Rosner Blay, 165–74. Melbourne: Hybrid, 2002.

———. "Biblical Illustrations on Judaica Objects: The Gross Family Collection." In "*Kommt heraus und schaut." Jüdische und christliche Illustrationen zur Bibel in alter Zeit,* edited by Falk Wiesemann, 143–48. Essen: Klartext Verlag, 2002.

Grossman, Abraham. *Ḥakhmei Tsarfat Harishonim* (*The Early Sages of France*). Jerusalem: Magnes, 1996.

Grunhut, Eliezer Halevi, ed. *Midrash Shir Hashirim.* 1897. Reprint, Jerusalem: Ktav Yad VaSefer Institute, 1981.

Günzburg, Baron David, and Vladimir Stassoff. *Illuminations from Hebrew Bibles of Leningrad.* Jerusalem: Bialik Institute, 1990.

Gutmann, Joseph. *Hebrew Manuscript Painting.* New York: George Braziller, 1978.

———. "Joseph Ben Kalonymus—the Enigma of a Thirteenth-Century Hebrew Scribe." In *A Crown for a King: Studies in Jewish Art, History, and Archaeology in Memory of Stephen A. Kayser*, edited by Shalom Sabar et al., 147–51. Jerusalem: Gefen, 2000.

———. "Masorah Figurata in the Mikdashyah." In *VIII International Congress of the International Organization for Masoretic Studies (Chicago 1988)*, 71–77. Atlanta: Scholars Press for the Society of Biblical Literature and the International Organization for Masoretic Studies, 1990.

———. "Priestly Vestments, Torah Ornaments and the King James Bible." In *Beauty in Holiness: Studies in Jewish Customs and Ceremonial Art*, edited by Joseph Gutmann, 122–24. New York, Ktav, 1970.

———. "Programmatic Painting in the Dura Synagogue." In *The Dura-Europos Synagogue: A Re-evaluation (1932–1972)*, edited by J. Guttmann, 137–55. Missoula: American Academy of Religion & Society of Biblical Literature, 1973.

Gutwirth, Eliezer. "Religion and Social Criticism in Late Medieval Rousillon: An Aspect of Profayt Duran's Activities." *Michael: On the History of the Jews in the Diaspora* 12 (1991): 135–56.

Gyug, Richard. "Early Medieval Bibles, Biblical Books, and the Monastic Liturgy in the Beneventan Region." In *The Practice of the Bible in the Middle Ages*, edited by Susan Boynton and Diane J. Reilly, 34–60. New York: Columbia University Press, 2011.

Habermann, A. M. *The Printer Daniel Bomberg and the List of Books Published by His Press* [in Hebrew]. Safed: Museum of Printing Art, 1978.

———. *Toledot ha-sefer ha'Ivri*. Jerusalem: Rubin Mass, 1945.

Hachlili, Rachel. *Ancient Jewish Art and Archaeology in the Land of Israel*. Leiden: Brill, 1988.

Hahn, O., with T. Wolff, H.-O. Feistel, I. Rabin, and M. Beit-Arié. "The Erfurt Hebrew Giant Bible and the Experimental XRF Analysis of Ink and Plummet Composition." *Gazette du livre médiéval* 51 (2007): 16–28.

Halperin, Dalia-Ruth. "Decorated Masorah on the Openings Between Quires in Masoretic Bible Manuscripts." *Journal of Jewish Studies* 45 (2014): 323–48.

Hamilton, Alastair, "Humanists and the Bible." In *The Cambridge Companion to Renaissance Humanism*, edited by Jill Kraye, 100–117. Cambridge: Cambridge University Press, 1996.

Haran, Menahem. "Book-Scrolls at the Beginning of the Second Temple Period: The Transition from Papyrus to Skins." *Hebrew Union College Annual* 54 (1983): 111–22.

———. "Bible Scrolls in Eastern and Western Jewish Communities from Qumran to the High Middle Ages." *Hebrew Union College Annual* 56 (1985): 21–61.

———. *The Biblical Collection: Its Consolidation to the End of the Second Temple Times and Changes of Form to the End of the Middle Ages* [in Hebrew]. Jerusalem: Magnes Press, 1996.

———. "Book-Scrolls in Israel in Pre-Exilic Times." *Journal of Jewish Studies* 33 (1982): 161–73.

———. "Book-Size and the Thematic Cycles in the Pentateuch." In *Die Hebraeische Bibel and ihre zweifache Nachgeschichte*, edited by Erhard Blum et al., 165–76. Neukirchen: Neukirchen Verlag, 1990.

———. "Torah and Bible Scrolls in the First Centuries in the Common Era" [in Hebrew]. *Shnaton: An Annual for Biblical and Ancient Near Eastern Studies* 10 (1990): 93–106.

Harviainen, Tapani. "Abraham Firkovich, the Aleppo Codex, and Its Dedication." In *Jewish Studies at the Turn of the Twentieth Century*, edited by Judit Targarona Borrás and Angel Sáenz-Badillos, 1:131–36. Leiden: Brill, 1999.

Havlin, S. Z. "A Sefer-Torah that Rabbeinu Nissim Gerondi Wrote for Himself." *Alei Sefer* 12 (1986): 5–36.

Hayes, Christine. "'Halakhah Le-Moshe Mi-Sinai' in Rabbinic Sources: A Methodological Case Study." In *The Synoptic Problem in Rabbinic Literature*, edited by Shaye J. D. Cohen, 61–117. Providence, RI: Brown Judaica Series, 2000.

Heller, Marvin J. *Printing the Talmud: A History of the Earliest Printed Editions*. Brooklyn: Am Hasefer, 1992.

———. *The Sixteenth-Century Hebrew Book: An Abridged Thesaurus*. 2 vols. Boston: Brill, 2004.

Heyd, Milly. "Illustrations in Early Editions of the Tsene-U'Rene: Jewish Adaptations of Christian Sources." *Journal of Jewish Art* 10 (1984): 64–81.

Hezser, Catherine. *Jewish Literacy in Roman Palestine*. Tübingen: Mohr, 2001.

Hibshoosh, Yehiel. *The Hibshoosh Family Pentateuch: Facsimile Edition of an Exquisite Yemenite Manuscript Copied in the Year 1485*. Tel Aviv: private publisher, 1985.

Higger, M., ed. *Masekhet Soferim*. 1937. Reprint, Jerusalem: Makor, 1970.

Hirsch, Rudolph. *Printing, Selling, and Reading: 1450–1550*. Wiesbaden: Otto Harrassowitz, 1967.

Houtman, Alberdina. "Targum Isaiah According to Felix Pratensis." In *Journal for the Aramaic Bible* 1 (1999): 191–202.

Hurwitz, Avi. "The Origins and Development of 'Megillat-Sefer'—a Chapter in the Development of Writing Terminology in the Biblical Period" [in Hebrew]. In *Texts, Temples, and Traditions: A Tribute to Menahem Haran*, edited by M. V. Fox et al., 37*–46*. Winona Lake: Eisenbrauns, 1996.

Hürwitz, S., with A. Berliner, eds. *Maḥzor Vitry*. Nürenberg, 1923.

Iakerson, Shimon. *Catalogue of Hebrew Incunabua from the Collection of the Library of the Jewish Theological Seminary of America*. 2 vols. New York: Jewish Theological Seminary of America, 2005.

———. "Early Hebrew Printing in Sepharad (ca. 1475–1491)." In *Biblias de Sefarad / Bibles of Sepharad*, edited by Esparanza Alfonso et al., 125–48. Madrid: CSIC, 2012.

Idel, Moshe. "Concepts of Scripture in Jewish Mysticism." In *Jewish Concepts of Scripture: A Comparative Introduction*, edited by Benjamin D. Sommer, 157–78. New York: New York University Press, 2012.

Isaac bar Moshe of Vienna. *Sefer Or Zaru'a*. Zhitomir, 1862.

Jaffee, Martin. *Torah in the Mouth: Writing and Oral Tradition in Palestinian Judaism 200 BCE–400 CE*. Oxford: Oxford University Press, 2001.

Johns, Adrian. *The Nature of the Book: Print and Knowledge in the Making*. Chicago: University of Chicago Press, 1998.

Jordan, William Scott. *The French Monarchy and the Jews: From Philip Augustus to the Last Capetians*. Philadelphia: University of Pennsylvania Press, 1989.

Josephus. *Works*. Translated by H. J. St. Thackeray. 10 vols. Cambridge, MA: Harvard University Press, 1934–76.

Kahle, Paul E. *The Cairo Geniza*. London: British Academy, 1947.

———. "Felix Pratensis—a Prato Felix, Der Bearbeiter der ersten Rabbinerbibel, Venedig, 1516–17." *Die Welt des Orients* 1 (1947): 32–36.

———. "The Hebrew Text of the Complutensian Polyglot." In *Homenaje a Millas-Vallicrosa*, 742–44. Barcelona: Consejo Superior de Investigaciones Cientificas, 1954.

Kanarfogel, Ephraim. *Jewish Education and Society in the High Middle Ages*. Detroit, MI: Wayne State University Press, 1992.

———. "On the Role of Bible Study in Medieval Ashkenaz." In *The Frank Talmage Memorial Volume*, edited by Barry Walfish, 1:151–66. Hanover, NH: University Press of New England, 1993.

Kapach, Yosef, ed. *The Mishneh Torah*. Jerusalem: Machon Mishnat HaRambam, 1983.

Karasik, Ber. *Me'ir 'Einei Soferim*. Vilna: Rosenkrantz, 1898/99.

Katz, K. I. "Yemenite Manuscripts and an Ethiopic Manuscript Parallel" [in Hebrew]. *Eretz-Israel* 7 (1964): 135–37.

Katznellenbogen, Ilana. "The Division of the Sections of the Torah According to the Number of Seven Persons Called Up to Read" [in Hebrew]. *Sinai* 119 (1997): 224–45.

Kedar, Benjamin. "The Latin Translations." In *Mikra: Text, Translation, Reading and Interpretation of the Hebrew Bible in Ancient Judaism and Early Christianity*, edited by Martin J. Mulder, 299–338. Philadelphia: Van Gorcum and Fortress, 1988.

Khan, Geoffrey. "Al-Qirqisani's Views About the Biblical Text and Parallel Islamic Views About the Qur'an" [in Hebrew]. *Encounters in Medieval Judaeo-Arabic Culture*, edited by J. Blau, H. Ben-Shammai, et al., 69–80. Tel Aviv: Tel Aviv University Press, 1998.

———. "The Contribution of the Karaites to the Study of the Hebrew Language." In *Karaite Judaism: A Guide to Its History and Literary Sources*, edited by Meira Polliack, 291–318. Boston: Brill, 2003.

———. *The Early Karaite Traditions of Hebrew Grammatical Thought*. Leiden: Brill, 2000.

———. *Karaite Bible Manuscripts from the Cairo Genizah*. Cambridge: Cambridge University Library, 1990.

———. *A Short Introduction to the Tiberian Masoretic Bible and Its Reading Tradition*. Piscataway, NJ: Gorgias Press, 2012.

———. "Standardization and Variation in the Orthography of Hebrew Bible and Arabic Qur'an Manuscripts." In *Manuscripts of the Middle East*, edited by Francois Deroche, Adam Gancik, and Jan Jist Witkam, 5:53–58. Leiden: Ter Lugt Press, 1990–91.

Kirschenblatt Gimblett, Barbara. "The Cut That Binds: The Western Ashkenazic Torah Binder as Nexus Between Circumcision and Torah." In *Celebration: Studies in Festivity and Ritual*, edited by Victor Turner, 136–46. Washington, DC: Smithsonian Institution Press, 1982.

Kittel R., and P. Kahle. *Biblia Hebraica*. 1929–37. Reprint, Stuttgart: W. Rudolph and K. Elliger, 1967–77.

Kitwe-Jad: Jüdischer Handschriften Restaurieren, Bewahren, Praesentieren. Berlin: Staadtsbibliothek zu Berlin-Preussischer Kulturbesitz, 2002.

Klein, Michael. *Genizah Manuscripts of Palestinian Targum to the Pentateuch*. 2 vols. Cincinnati, OH: Hebrew Union College Press, 1986.

Kogel, Judith. "The Reconstruction of a *Sefer Haftarot* from the Rhine Valley: Towards a Typology of Ashkenazi Pentateuch Manuscripts." In *Books Within Books: New Discoveries in Old Book Bindings*, edited by Andreas Lenhardt and Judith Olszowy-Schlanger, 43–68. Boston: Brill, 2014.

Kogman-Appel, Katrin. *Illuminated Haggadot from Medieval Spain*. University Park: Pennsylvania State University Press, 2006.

———. *Jewish Book Art Between Islam and Christianity: The Decoration of Hebrew Bibles in Medieval Spain*. Leiden: Brill, 2004.

———. "Sephardic Ideas in Ashkenaz—Visualizing the Temple in Medieval Regensburg." *Simon Dubnow Institute Yearbook* 8 (2009): 245–77.

———. "The Tree of Death and the Tree of Life: The Hanging of Haman in Medieval Jewish Manuscript Painting." In *Between the Picture and the Word: Manuscript Studies from the Index of Christian Art*, edited by Colum Hourihane, 187–208. University Park: Pennsylvania State University Press, 2005.

Kogut, Simcha. *Correlations Between Biblical Accentuation and Traditional Jewish Exegesis* [in Hebrew]. Jerusalem: Ktav, 1994.

Kozodoy, Maude. *The Secret Faith of Maestre Honoratus: Profayt Duran and Jewish Identity in Late Medieval Iberia*. Philadelphia: University of Pennsylvania Press, 2015.

Kuehnel, Bianca. "Jewish and Christian Art in the Middle Ages: The Dynamics of a Relationship." In *Juden und Christen zur Zeit der Kreuzzuege*, 1–15. Sigmaringen: Jan Thorbecke, 1999.

Kugel, James. *The Idea of Biblical Poetry: Parallelism and Its History*. New Haven, CT: Yale University Press, 1981.

———. "Torah." In *Contemporary Jewish Religious Thought*, edited by Arthur A. Cohen and Paul Mendes-Flohr, 995–1005. New York: Free Press, 1987.

———. "Two Introductions to Midrash." In *Midrash and Literature*, edited by G. Hartman and S. Budick, 77–104. New Haven, CT: Yale University Press, 1986.

Landsberger, Franz. "Illuminated Marriage Contracts, with Special Reference to the Cincinnati Ketubahs." In *Beauty in Holiness: Studies in Jewish Customs and Ceremonial Art*, edited by Joseph Gutmann, 370–413. New York: Ktav, 1970.

———. "Old-Time Torah Curtains." In *Beauty in Holiness: Studies in Jewish Customs and Ceremonial Art*, edited by Joseph Gutmann, 125–66. New York: Ktav, 1970.

———. "The Origin of European Torah Decorations." In *Beauty in Holiness: Studies in Jewish Customs and Ceremonial Art*, edited by Joseph Gutmann, 87–105. New York: Ktav, 1970.

Langer, Ruth. "Early Stages in the Development of the Torah-Ceremony in the Synagogue in the Middle Ages." In *Kenishta*, edited by J. Tabory, 99–118. Ramat Gan: Bar-Ilan University Press, 2003.

———. "From Study of Scripture to a Reenactment of Sinai: The Emergence of the Synagogue Torah Service." *Worship* 72 (1998): 43–67.

———. "Sinai, Zion, and God in the Synagogue: Celebrating Torah in Ashkenaz." In *Liturgy in the Life of the Synagogue*, edited by R. Langer and S. Fine, 121–59. Winona Lake, IN: Eisenbrauns, 2005.

Lazar, Moshe. *The Ladino Bible of Ferrara [1553]*. Culver City, CA: Labyrinthos, 1992.

Legaspi, Michael C. *The Death of Scripture and the Rise of Biblical Studies.* New York: Oxford University Press, 2010.

Leiman, Sid Z. "Masorah and Halakhah: A Study in Conflict." In *Tehillah le-Moshe: Biblical and Judaic Studies in Honor of Moshe Greenberg,* edited by Mordechai Cogan, Barry L. Eichler, and Jeffrey H. Tigay, 291–306. Winona Lake, IN: Eisenbrauns, 1997.

Lelli, Fabrizio. "Christian and Jewish Iconographies of Job in Fifteenth Century Italy." In *Jewish Biblical Interpretation and Cultural Exchange: Comparative Exegesis in Context,* edited by Natalie B. Dohrmann and David Stern, 214–35. Philadelphia: University of Pennsylvania Press, 2008.

Leslie, Donald Daniel. *The Survival of the Chinese Jews.* Leiden: Brill, 1972.

Leveen, Jacob. *The Hebrew Bible in Art.* London: Oxford University Press, 1944.

Levine, Etan. "The Targums: Their Interpretive Character and Their Place in Jewish Text Tradition." In *Hebrew Bible / Old Testament: The History of Its Interpretation,* edited by Magne Sæbø, 1:323–31. Goettingen: Vandenhoek & Ruprecht, 2000.

Levine, Lee. *The Ancient Synagogue: The First Thousand Years.* New Haven, CT: Yale University Press, 2000.

Levita, Elias. *The Massoreth ha-massoreth of Elias Levita.* Edited by C. D. Ginsburg. 1867. Reprint, New York: Ktav, 1968.

Levy, B. Barry. *Fixing God's Torah: The Accuracy of the Hebrew Bible Text in Jewish Law.* New York: Oxford, 2001.

———. "Rabbinic Bibles, *Mikra'ot Gedolot,* and Other Great Books." *Tradition* 25 (1991): 65–81.

Levy, Yaffa. "Ezekiel's Plan in an Early Karaite Bible." *Journal of Jewish Art* 20 (1993/94): 68–85.

Libson, G. "The Use of a Sacred Object in the Administration of a Judicial Oath." *Jewish Law Association Studies* 1 (1985): 53–60.

Lieberman, Saul. *Hellenism in Jewish Palestine.* New York: Jewish Theological Seminary of America, 1950.

———. *The Tosefta: The Order of Zeraim* [in Hebrew]. New York: Jewish Theological Seminary, 1955.

Light, Laura. "The Bible and the Individual: The Paris Bible." In *The Practice of the Bible in the Middle Ages: Production, Reception and Performance in Western Christianity,* edited by Susan Boynton and Diane J. Reilly, 228–46. New York: Columbia University Press, 2011.

Lipton, Sara. *Dark Mirror: The Medieval Origins of Anti-Jewish Iconography.* New York: Henry Holt, 2014.

———. *Images of Intolerance: The Representation of Jews and Judaism in the* Bible Moralisée. Berkeley: University of California Press, 1999.

Lowenstein, Steven. "The Readership of Mendelssohn's Bible Translation," *Hebrew Union College Annual* 53 (1982): 179–213.

Lubell, Stephen. "Sixteenth-Century Hebrew Typography: A Typographical and Historical Analysis Based on the Guillaume I Le Bé documents in the Bibliothèque Nationale de France." PhD diss., University of London, School of Advanced Study, Institute of English Studies, 2014.

Lyons, David. *The Cumulative Masora: Text, Form, and Transmission.* Beer Sheva: Ben Gurion University Press, 1999.

Mack, Hananel. "The Seventy Faces of the Torah—on the Development of an Expression" [in Hebrew]. In *Rabbi Mordechai Breuer Festschtift: Collected Papers in Jewish Studies*, 2:449–62. Jerusalem: Akademon, 1992.

Maimonides. *Teshuvot Ha-Rambam*. Edited by J. Blau. Jerusalem: Mekitsei Nirdamim, 1957–61.

Mann, Jacob. *The Bible as Read and Preached in the Old Synagogue*. 2 vols. Cincinnati, OH: Hebrew Union College Press, 1940–66.

———. *Texts and Studies in Jewish History and Literature*. 2 vols. Philadelphia: Jewish Publication Society, 1935.

Mann, Vivian. *Jewish Texts on the Visual Arts*. Cambridge: Cambridge University Press, 2000.

———. "A Shared Tradition: The Decorated Pages of Medieval Bibles and Qur'ans." In *The Edinburgh Companion to the Bible and the Arts*, edited by Stephen Prickett, 161–74. Edinburgh: Edinburgh University Press, 2014.

———. "Torah Ornaments Before 1600." In Rafi Grafmann, *Crowning Glory: Silver Torah Ornaments of the Jewish Museum, New York*, edited by Vivian B. Mann, 1–16. Boston, MA: David R. Godine, 1996.

Mann, Vivian, with Daniel D. Chazin. "Printing, Patronage and Prayer: Art Historical Issues in Three Responsa." *Images* 1 (2007): 91–97.

Manor, Dalia. "Biblical Zionism in Bezalel Art." *Israel Studies* 6, no. 9 (2001): 55–75.

Marcus, David. *Scribal Wit: Aramaic Mnemonics in the Leningrad Codex*. Piscataway, NJ: Gorgias Press, 2013.

Marcus, Ivan. *Rituals of Childhood: Jewish Acculturation in Medieval Europe*. New Haven, CT: Yale University Press, 1996.

Margoliouth, G. *Catalogue of the Hebrew and Samaritan Manuscripts in the British Museum*. 4 vols. 1905. Reprint, London: British Museum, 1965.

Margolis, Max. "Preface." In *The Holy Scriptures According to the Masoretic Text*. Philadelphia: Jewish Publication Society of America, 1917

Marx, Alexander. "The Choice of Books by the Printers of Hebrew Incunabula." In *To Doctor R.: Essays Here Collected and Published in Honor of the Seventieth Birthday of Dr. A. S. W. Rosenbach, July 22, 1946*, 155–57. Philadelphia: n.p., 1946.

Marx, Moses. "Gershom (Hieronymus) Soncino's Wanderyears in Italy, 1492–1527: Exemplar Judaicae Vitae." *Hebrew Union College Annual* 11 (1936): 427–501.

Mathews, K. A. "The Background of the Palaeo-Hebrew Texts at Qumran." In *The Word of the Lord Shall Go Forth: Essays in Honor of David Noel Freedman in Celebration of His Sixtieth Birthday*, edited by C. L. Meyers and M. O'Connor, 549–68. Winona Lake, IN: Eerdsmans, 1983.

Mehlmann, Yisrael. "The Printing House of Daniel Bomberg in Venice" [in Hebrew]. In *Genuzot sefarim*, 13–42. Jerusalem: Jewish National and University Library, 1976.

Meiri, Menachem. *Kiryat Sefer*. Edited by M. Hirschler. Jerusalem: n.p., 1996.

Meirovich, Harvey. *A Vindication of Judaism: The Polemics of the Hertz Pentateuch*. New York: Jewish Theological Seminary of America, 1998.

Mellinkoff, Ruth. "The Round-Topped Tablets of the Law: Sacred Symbol and Emblem of Evil." *Journal of Jewish Art* 1 (1974): 28–43.

Mesguich, Sophie Kessler. "Early Christian Hebraists." In *Hebrew Bible / Old Testament: The History of Its Interpretation*, edited by Magne Sæbø, 2:254–75. Gottingen: Vandenhoeck & Ruprecht, 2008.

Metzger, Therese. *Die Bibel von Meschullam und Joseph Qalonymos*. Wuerzberg: Schoeningh, 1994.

Meyer, Eric M. "The Torah Shrine in the Ancient Synagogue: Another Look at the Evidence." In *Jews, Christians and Polytheists in the Ancient Synagogue*, edited by Steven Fine, 201–23. New York: Routledge, 1999.

Meyer, Mati. "Eve's Nudity: A Sign of Shame or Precursor of Christological Economy." In *Between Judaism and Christianity: Art Historical Essays in Honor of Elisheva (Elisabeth) Revel-Neher*, edited by Katrin Kogman-Appel and Mati Meyer, 243–58. Leiden: Brill, 2009.

Milstein, Rachel. "Hebrew Book Illumination in the Fatimid Era." In *L'Egypte Fatimide: Son art et son histoire*, edited by M. Barrucand, 429–40. Paris: Presses de l'Université de Paris-Sorbonne, 1999.

Morag, Shelomo. "A Few Words About the Manuscript" [in Hebrew]. In *Taj Keter Torah shel Mishpaḥat ḥabashush*. Tel Aviv: n.p., 1985.

———. *Ha-'Ivrit She-be-fi Yehudie Teiman* (The Spoken Hebrew of the Yemenite Jews). Jerusalem: Academy for the Hebrew Language, 1958.

———. *Masorot Ha-lashon Ha-'Ivrit Veha-lashon Ha-Aramit Shebe-fi Yehude Teman*. Tel Aviv: Afikim, 1902.

Muchawsky-Schnapper, Ester. *The Yemenites: Two Thousand Years of Jewish Culture*. Jerusalem: Israel Museum, 2000.

Naeh, Shlomo. "The Art of Memory: Structures of Memorization and Constructs of Text in Rabbinic Literature" [in Hebrew]. In *Meḥqerei Talmud: Talmudic Studies Dedicated to the Memory of Professor Ephraim E. Urbach, III*, edited by Yaakov Sussman and David Rosenthal, 543–89. Jerusalem: Magnes, 2005.

———. "Cycles of Torah Reading in Eretz Israel: A New Look" [in Hebrew]. *Tarbiz* 67 (1998): 167–87.

Namenyi, Ernest M. "The Illumination of Hebrew Manuscripts after the Invention of Printing." In *Jewish Art*, edited by Cecil Roth, 425–54. New York: McGraw-Hill, 1961.

Narkiss, Bezalel. *Hebrew Illuminated Manuscripts in the British Isles: A Catalogue Raisonné*. Vol. 1, *The Spanish and Portuguese Manuscripts*. London: Oxford University Press, 1982.

Naveh, Joseph. *Early History of the Alphabet: An Introduction to West Semitic Epigraphy and Palaeography*. Jerusalem: Magnes, 1982.

Neubauer, Adolph. *Catalogue of the Hebrew Manuscripts in the Bodleian Library*. Oxford: Clarendon, 1886.

Niditch, Susan. *Oral World and Written Word*. Louisville, KY: Westminster John Knox Press, 1996.

Nielsen, Bruce. "Daniel van Bombergen, a Bookman of Two Worlds." In *The Hebrew Book in Early Modern Italy*, edited by Adam Shear and Joseph Hacker, 56–75, 230–52. Philadelphia: University of Pennsylvania Press, 2011.

———. "A Note About Book Prices in the Sixteenth Century." In *The Valmadonna Trust Library: Part I Magnificent Manuscripts and the Bomberg Talmud*, 65–66. New York: Sotheby's, 2015.

Nordstrom, Carl-Otto. "The Temple Miniatures in the Peter Comestor Manuscript at Madrid." In *No Graven Images*, edited by Joseph Guttman, 39–74. New York: Ktav, 1971.

Ofer, Yosef. *The Babylonian Masora of the Pentateuch, Its Principles and Methods.* Jerusalem: Magnes, 2001.

———. "The History and Authority of the Aleppo Codex up to the Present." In *Keter Yerushalayim, Jerusalem Crown: The Bible of the Hebrew University of Jerusalem*, edited by Mordechai Glatzer, companion volume, 26–50. Jerusalem: Ben-Zvi, 2002.

Offenberg, A. K. *Hebrew Incunabula in Public Collections: A First International Census.* Nieuwkoop: de Graaf, 1990.

Offenberg, Sara. "A Jewish Knight in Shining Armour: Messianic Narrative and Imagination in Ashkenazic Illuminated Manuscripts." *Toronto Journal of Jewish Thought* 4 (2014).

Olszowy-Schlanger, Judith. "An Early Palimpsest Scroll of the Book of Kings from the Cairo Genizah." In *"From a Sacred Source": Genizah Studies in Honour of Professor Stefan C. Reif*, edited by Ben Outhwaite and Siam Bhayro, 237–47. Leiden: Brill, 2010.

———. "The Hebrew Bible." In *The New Cambridge History of the Bible*, edited by Richard Marsdekn and E. Ann Matter, 2:19–40. Cambridge: Cambridge University Press, 2012.

———. *Les manuscrits hébreux dans l'Angleterre médiévale: Étude historique et paléographique.* Louvain: Peeters, 2003.

Orlinsky, Harry M. *Essays in Biblical Culture and Bible Translation.* New York: Ktav, 1974.

———. "Yehoash's Yiddish Translation of the Bible." *Journal of Biblical Literature* 60 (1941): 173–77.

Ortega-Monasterio, Maria Teresa. "Patronage of the Bible in Sixteenth-Century Spain: A Defense of the Faith or an Attack on Heresy." In *Patronage, Production, and Transmission of Text in Medieval and Early Modern Jewish Cultures*, edited by Esperanza Alfonso and Jonathan Decter, 199–227. Turnhout: Brepols, 2014.

O Svitku / Form of the Scroll. Prague: Jewish Museum in Prague, 2006.

Ottolenghi, Luisa Mortara. "Un gruppo di manoscritti ebraici romani del sec. XIII e XIV e la loro decorazione." In *Studi sull'Ebraismo Italiano in memoria di Cecil Roth*, edited by E. Toaff, 139–58. Italy: Barulli Editore, 1974.

———. *Hebraica Ambrosiana, II: Description of Decorated and Illuminated Hebrew Manuscripts in the Ambrosian Library.* Milan: Edizioni il Polifilo, 1972.

Paper, Herbert H. "Judeo-Persian Bible Translations." In *Translation of Scripture*, 139–60. Philadelphia: Jewish Quarterly Review Supplement, 1990.

Parkes, Malcolm. "*Folia librorum quaerere:* Medieval Experience of the Problems of Hypertext and the Index." In *Fabula in tabula: Una storia degli indici dal manoscritto al testo elettronico*, edited by Claudio Leonardi, Marcello Morelli, and Francesco Santi, 23–41. Spoleto: Centro Italiano di Studi Sull'Alto Medioevo, 1995.

Parmenter, Dorina Miller. "The Iconic Book: The Image of the Bible in Early Christian Rituals." In *Iconic Books and Texts*, edited by James W. Watts, 63–92. Sheffield: Equinox, 2013.

Pasternak, Nurit. "Isaac ben Ovadiah ben David of Forli: An Esteemed Jewish Scribe Who Converted to Christianity?" [in Hebrew]. *Tarbiz* 68 (1999): 411–28.

———. "A Meeting Point of Hebrew and Latin Manuscript Production: A Fifteenth-Century Florentine Hebrew Scribe, Isaac ben Ovadiah of Forli." In *Scrittura e Civilta* 25 (2001): 185–200.

———. "Together and Apart: Hebrew Manuscripts as Testimonies to the Encounters of Jews and Christians in Fifteenth-Century Florence: The Makings, the Clients, Censorship." PhD diss., Hebrew University of Jerusalem, 2009.

Patai, Raphael. "Massekhet Segulot" [in Hebrew]. *Sefer Hashanah Liyehudei Amerika* 10–11 (1949): 472–87.

Penkower, Jordan. "The Ashkenazi Pentateuch Tradition as Reflected in the Erfurt Hebrew Bible Codices and Torah Scrolls." In *Erfurter Schriften zur Jüdischen Geschichte, Band 3: Zu Bild und Text im jüdisch-christlichen Kontext im Mittelalter*, edited by F. Bussert, S. Laubenstein, M. Stürzebecher, 118–41. Erfurt: Landeshauptstadt Erfurt, 2015.

———. "The Chapter Divisions in RB 1525." *Vetus Testamentum* 48 (1998): 350–74.

———. "The First Edition of the Hebrew Bible That Bomberg Published and the Beginning of His Publishing House" [in Hebrew]. *Kiryat Sefer* 58 (1983): 586–604.

———. "A Fourteenth-Century Ashkenazi Hebrew Bible Codex with Later Inscriptions in Latin and Hebrew by Luther, Melanchthon, Jonas and Ziegler." *Codices Manuscripti* 82–83 (2012): 43–60.

———. "Jacob Ben Ḥayyim and the Rise of the Biblia Hebraica (*Yaakov ben ḥayyim Utsemihut Mahadurat HaMiqraot Hagedolot*)." 2 vols. PhD diss., Hebrew University of Jerusalem, 1982.

———. "Maimonides and the Aleppo Codex." *Textus* 9 (1981): 39–129.

———. *Nusah HaTorah Beketer Aram-Tsovah (New Evidence for the Pentateuch Text in the Aleppo Codex)*. Ramat Gan: Bar-Ilan Press, 1992.

———. "The Process of Canonization of Rashi's Commentary to the Torah." In *Study and Knowledge in Jewish Thought*, edited by Howard Kreisel, 2:123–46. Beer-Sheva: Ben Gurion University of the Negev Press, 2006.

———. "Rabbinic Bible." In *The Dictionary of Biblical Interpretation*, edited by John H. Hayes, 2:361b–364a. Nashville, TN: Abingdon Press, 1999.

———. "Rashi's Corrections to His Commentary on the Pentateuch." *Jewish Studies* 6 (2007): 141–86.

———. "A Sheet of Parchment from a 10th or 11th Century Torah Scroll: Determining Its Type Among Four Traditions (Oriental, Sefardi, Ashkenazi, Yemenite)." *Textus* 21 (2002): 235–64.

———. "Verse Divisions in the Hebrew Bible." *Vetus Testamentum* 50 (2000): 279–393.

Perani, Mauro. "Il più antico Sefer Torah intero del sec. XII–XIII riscoperto nella Biblioteca Universitaria di Bologna" / "The Oldest Known Entire Torah Scroll from 12th–13th Century Rediscovered at the Bologna University Library." In *Il Rotulo 2 della Biblioteca Universitaria di Bologna*, edited by Biancastella Antonino, Rita De Tata, and Mauro Perani, 37–62, 63–78. Bologna: Biblioteca Universitaria di Bologna, 2015.

Perani, Mauro, and G. Corazzol. *Nuovo Catalogo dei manoscritti ebraici della Biblioteca Universitaria di Bologna* (BUB, Ricerchi e cataloghi sui Fondi della Biblioteca Universitaria di Bologna). Argelato: Minerva Edizioni, 2013.

Pettegree, Andrew. *The Book in the Renaissance*. New Haven, CT: Yale University Press, 2010.

Pollak, Michael. "A Preliminary Study of the Twelve Detached Skins from a Centuries-Old Chinese Torah Scroll." *Studies in Bibliography and Booklore* 21 (2001): 83–104.

———. *The Torah Scrolls of the Chinese Jews*. Dallas: Bridwell Library, Southern Methodist University, 1975.

Polliak, Meira. *The Karaite Tradition of Arabic Bible Translation: A Linguistic and Exegetical Study of Karaite Translations of the Pentateuch from the Tenth and Eleventh Centuries.* Leiden: Brill, 1997.

———. "Rethinking Karaism: Between Judaism and Islam." *AJS Review* 30 (2006): 67–93.

Price, Jonathan, and Shlomo Naeh. "On the Margins of Culture: The Practice of Transcription in the Ancient World." In *From Hellenism to Islam: Cultural and Linguistic Change in the Roman Near East*, edited by Hannah M. Cotton et al., 257–88. Cambridge: Cambridge University Press, 2009.

Randall, Lilian M. C. *Images in the Margins of Gothic Manuscripts.* Berkeley: University of California Press, 1966.

Rapp, Claudia. "Holy Texts, Holy Men, and Holy Scribes: Aspects of Scriptural Holiness in Late Antiquity." In *The Early Christian Book*, edited by William E. Klingshirn and Linda Safran, 194–222. Washington, DC: Catholic University of America Press, 2007.

RaSHBA. *Sheelot Uteshuvot HaRaSHBA (Rabbi Shlomo Ben Aderet)*, parts 1–3. 1808 (Piotrokov), 1868 (Warsaw), 1884 (Vilna). Reprint, Bnei Brak: n.p., 1958–59.

Ratzaby, Yehuda. *Bem'agloth Teman (Yemen Paths): Selected Studies in Yemenite Culture.* Tel Aviv: 'Am Oved, 1987.

Razhabi, Yitzhak. "An Early Scribal Poem for the Torah" [in Hebrew]. *'Alei Sefer* 3 (1976): 54–62.

———. *Ha-otiot Ha-meshunot Ba-Torah.* In *Humash Torah Shelemah.* Vol. 29. Edited by Menachem M. Kasher. 1947. Reprint, Jerusalem: Bet Torah Shelemah, 1992.

Reeve, John, ed. *Sacred: Books of the Three Faiths: Judaism, Christianity, Islam.* London: British Library, 2007.

Reilly, Diane J. *The Art of Reform in Eleventh-Century Flanders: Gerard of Cambrai, Richard of Saint-Vanne and the Saint-Vaast Bible.* Boston: Brill, 2006.

———. "Lectern Bibles and Liturgical Reform in the Central Middle Ages." In *The Practice of the Bible in the Middle Ages*, edited by Susan Boynton and Diane J. Reilly, 105–25. New York: Columbia University Press, 2011.

Reiner, Elhanan. "Liturgy Versus Text: A Dispute over the Printed Hebrew Bible in 16th C. Ashkenaz." Unpublished manuscript.

Resnick, I. M. "The Codex in Early Jewish and Christian Communities." *Journal of Religious History* 17 (1992): 1–17.

Revell, E. J. *Hebrew Texts with Palestinian Vocalization.* Toronto: University of Toronto Press, 1970.

———. "The Interpretive Value of the Massoretic Punctuation." In *Hebrew Bible / Old Testament*, edited by M. Sæbø, 1:105–25. Göttingen: Vandenhoek & Ruprecht, 2000.

———. "The Leningrad Codex as a Representative of the Masoretic Text." In *The Leningrad Codex: A Facsimile Edition*, edited by David Noel Freedman. Grand Rapids, MI: Eerdsmans, 1998.

Richardson, Brian. *Printing, Writers and Readers in Renaissance Italy.* Cambridge: Cambridge University Press, 1999.

Riegler (Rigler), Michael. "Benayah Ha-Sofer ve-Tze'etzeav." *Pe'amim* 64 (1995): 54–65.

———. "The Colophons of Manuscripts as a Historical Source: The Book and Scribes in Yemen" [in Hebrew]. In *Meḥkarim ba-Sifrut 'Am Yisrael u-be-Tarbut Teiman: Sefer Ha-Yovel le-Yehuda Ratzaby*, edited by Yehudit Dishon and Ephraim Hazan, 161–79. Ramat-Gan: Bar-Ilan University Press, 1991.

Roberts, Colin H., and T. C. Skeat. *The Birth of the Codex*. London: British Academy, 1983.

Rodov, Ilia. "Dragons: A Symbol of Evil in European Synagogue Decoration?" *Ars Judaica* 1 (2005): 63–84.

Rosenthal, E. I. J. "Sebastian Muenster's Knowledge and Use of Jewish Exegesis." In *Essays in Honor of the Very Reverend J. H. Hertz*, edited by I. Epstein et al., 351–69. London: Goldston, 1943.

Roth, Cecil. "A Jewish Printer in Naples." In *Studies in Books and Booklore*, 59–70. New York: Gregg International, 1972.

Ruderman, David. *Jewish Enlightenment in an English Key*. Princeton, NJ: Princeton University Press, 2000.

Rustow, Marina. *Heresy and the Politics of Community: The Jews of the Fatimid Caliphate*. Ithaca, NY: Cornell University Press, 2008.

Rypins, Stanley. "The Ferrara Bible at Press." *Library* 10 (1955): 244–69.

Sabar, Shalom. *Ketubbah: Jewish Marriage Contracts of Hebrew Union College Skirball Museum and Klau Library*. Philadelphia: Jewish Publication Society, 1990.

———. "A New Discovery: The Earliest Illustrated Esther Scroll by Shalom Italia." *Ars Judaica* 12 (2012): 1–18.

———. "Torah and Magic: The Torah Scroll and Its Accessories in Jewish Culture in Europe and in Muslim Countries" [in Hebrew]. *Pe'amim* 85 (2000): 149–79.

Sæbø, Magne. *Hebrew Bible / Old Testament: The History of Its Interpretation*. Göttingen: Vandenhoek & Ruprecht, 2000.

Saenger, Paul. "Reading in the Later Middle Ages." In *A History of Reading in the West*, edited by Guglielmo Cavallo and Roger Chartier, translated by L. G. Cochrane, 120–48. Boston: University of Massachusetts Press, 1999.

Sáenz-Badillos, Angel. "Luis de Guzmán's Patronage and the Spanish Translation and Commentary of the Bible by Arragel." In *Patronage, Production, and Transmission of Texts in Medieval and Early Modern Jewish Cultures*, edited by Esperanza Alfonso and Jonathan Decter, 361–82. Turnhout: Brepols, 2014.

Safrai Shmuel, ed. *The Literature of the Sages*. 2 vols. Philadelphia: Fortress Press, 1987/2006.

Sanders, James A. "The Hebrew University Bible and *Biblia Hebraica Quinta*." *Journal of Biblical Literature* 118 (1999): 518–26.

Sanders, Paul. "The Ashkar-Gilson Manuscript: Remnant of a Proto-Masoretic Model Scroll of the Torah." *Journal of Hebrew Scriptures* 14 (2014): 1–25.

Sarfatti, Gad B. "The Tables of the Covenant as a Symbol of Judaism." In *The Ten Commandments in History and Tradition*, edited by Ben-Zion Segal and Gershon Levi, 383–418. Jerusalem: Magnes, 1990.

Sarna, Nahum. "Ancient Libraries and the Ordering of the Biblical Books." In *Studies in Biblical Interpretation*, 53–66. Philadelphia: Jewish Publication Society, 2000.

———. "Hebrew and Bible Studies in Medieval Spain." In *The Sephardi Heritage*, edited by R. D. Barnett, 323–66. New York: Ktav, 1971.

———. "Introductory Remarks." In *The Pentateuch: Early Spanish Manuscript (Codex Hillely) from the Collection of the Jewish Theological Seminary*. Jerusalem: Makor, 1977.

———. *The JPS Torah Commentary: Exodus*. Philadelphia: Jewish Publication Society, 1991.

Sassoon, David Solomon, ed. *Ohel Dawid: Descriptive Catalogue of the Hebrew and Samaritan Manuscripts in the Sassoon Library, London*. London: Oxford University Press, 1932.

Schapiro, Meyer. *The Language of Forms: Lectures on Insular Manuscript Art*. New York: Pierpont Morgan Library, 2005.

Schenker, Adrian. "From the First Printed Hebrew, Greek, and Latin Bibles to the First Polyglot Bible, the Complutensian Polyglot: 1477–1517." In *Hebrew Bible / Old Testament: The History of Its Interpretation*, edited by Magne Sæbø, 2:276–91. Göttingen: Vandenhoeck & Ruprecht, 2008.

Schlossberg, A. L., ed. *Sefer Halakhot Pesukot O Hilkhot Re'u*. 1886. Reprint, Jerusalem, 1967.

Schoeler, Gregor. *The Genesis of Literature in Islam: From the Aural to the Read*. Translated by Shawkat M. Toorawa. Edinburgh: Edinburgh University Press, 2009.

Scholem, Gershom. "The Star of David: History of a Symbol." In *The Messianic Idea in Judaism, and Other Essays on Jewish Spirituality*, 257–81. New York: Schocken, 1971.

Schonfield, Jeremy, ed. *La Biblia de Alba: An Illustrated Manuscript Bible in Castilian by Rabbi Mosses Arragel*. Madrid: Fundación Amigos de Sefarad, 1992.

Schrijver, Emile, and Falk Wiesemann. *Schöne Seiten: Jüdische Schriftkultur aus der Braginsky Collection*. Zürich: Scheidegger & Spiess, 2011.

Schwarzbach, Bertram Eugene. "Les éditions de la Bible hébraïque au xvi siècle et la création du texte massorétique." In *La Bible imprimée dans l'Europe moderne*, edited by B. E. Schwarzbach, 16–67. Paris: Bibliothèque Nationale de France, 1999.

Secret, François. *Les kabbalistes chrétiens de la Renaissance*. Paris: Dunod, 1963.

Sed-Rajna, Gabrielle. *The Hebrew Bible in Medieval Illuminated Manuscripts*. Translated by Josephine Bacon. New York: Rizzoli, 1987.

———. *Manuscrits hébreux de Lisbonne: Un atelier de copistes et d'enlumineurs au XVe siècle*. Paris: Éditions du Centre National de la Recherche Scientifique, 1970.

———. *Les manuscrits hébreux enluminés des bibliothèques de France*. Leuven: Peeters, 1994.

Shalev-Eyni, Sarit. "The Human Faces of the Torah and Medieval Art" [in Hebrew]. *Zion* 73 (2008): 139–71.

———. *Jews among Christians: A Hebrew School of Illumination of the Lake Constance Region*. London: Harvey Miller, 2010.

Shalom, Rahamim Sar. "Customs of Dividing the Torah Sections for Seven Readers." *Sinai* 122 (1998): 214–19.

Shamosh, Amnon. *Haketer: Sipuro shel Keter Aram Tsova*. Jerusalem: Machon Ben-Zvi, 1987.

Shapira, Dan. *Avraham Firkowicz in Istanbul (1830–1832): Paving the Way for Turkic Nationalism*. Ankara: KaraM, 2003.

Sharvit, Shimeon. *Tractate Avot Through the Ages: A Critical Edition, Prologomena, and Appendices*. Jerusalem: Mosad Bialik, 2004.

Shatzmiller, Joseph. *Cultural Exchange: Jews, Christians, and Art in the Medieval Marketplace*. Princeton, NJ: Princeton University Press, 2013.

Sheehan, Jonathan. *The Enlightenment Bible: Translation, Scholarship, Culture*. Princeton, NJ: Princeton University Press, 2007.

Siegel, Jonathan P. "The Scribes of Qumran: Studies in the Early History of Jewish Scribal Customs, with Special Reference to the Qumran Biblical Scrolls and to the Tannaitic Traditions of *Massekheth Soferim*." PhD diss., Brandeis University, 1971.

Simon, Uriel. "Interpreting the Interpreter: Supercommentaries on Ibn Ezra's Commentaries." In *Abraham Ibn Ezra*, edited by I. Twersky and J. Harris, 86–128. Cambridge, MA: Center for Jewish Studies, Harvard, 1993.

Sirat, Colette. "An Announcement About the Discovery of Remnants of Six Torah Scrolls Written Before the Year 1000" [in Hebrew]. *Kirjat Sefer Collected Essays* 68 suppl. (1998): 105–10.

———. "En vision globale: Les juifs médiévaux et les livres latins." *Bibliologia* 20 (2003): 15–19.

———. *Hebrew Manuscripts of the Middle Ages*. Edited and translated by Nicholas de Lange. Cambridge: Cambridge University Press, 2002.

———. "Le livre hébreu: Rencontre de la tradition juive et de l'esthétique française." In *Rashi et la culture juive en France du nord au Moyen Âge*, edited by G. Nahon and C. Touati, 242–59. Paris: Peeters, 1997.

———. "Notes sur la circulation des livres entre juifs et chrétiens au Moyen Âge." *Bibliologia* 18 (2001): 183–403.

———. *Les papyrus en caractères hébraïques trouvés en Egypte*. 2 vols. Paris: Éditions du Centre National de la Recherche Scientifique, 1985.

———. "Les rouleaux bibliques de Qumran au Moyen Âge: Du livre au Sefer Tora, de l'oreille à l'oeil." *Comptes rendus de l'Académie des Inscriptions & Belles-lettres*, 417–32. Paris: Diffusion de Boccard, 1991.

———. "Rouleaux de la Tora anterieurs à l'an mille." *CRAI* 5 (1994): 861–87.

Sitbon, Suzy. "L'espace, les formes dessinées par la lettre, le texte dans les bibles hébraïques espagnoles du XIIIe siècle." In *Jewish Studies at the Turn of the Twentieth Century*, edited by Judit Targarona Borrás and Angel Sáenz-Badillos, 2:163–68. Leiden: Brill, 1999.

———. "Intersections Between Artistic Visual Creation and Cosmogony in Some Spanish Bibles." *Iggud: Selected Essays in Jewish Studies* 3 (2007): 99*–113*.

Skloot, Joseph. "Moses of Hamilton Terrace: The Hertz Torah Commentary in Context and Interpretation." AB thesis, Princeton University, 2005.

Smelik, Willem. "Orality, Manuscript Reproduction, and the Targums." In *Paratext and Megatext as Channels of Jewish and Christian Traditions: The Textual Markers of Contextualization*, edited by A. Den Hollander, Ulrich Schmid, and Willem Smelik, 49–81. Leiden: Brill, 2003.

———. *Rabbis, Language, and Translation in Late Antiquity*. Cambridge: Cambridge University Press, 2013.

Smith, Leslie. "Jews and Christians Imagining the Temple." In *Crossing Borders: Hebrew Manuscripts as a Meeting-Place of Cultures*, edited by Piet van Boxel and Sabine Arndt, 99–114. Oxford: Bodleian Library, 2009.

Sotheby's. *Important Judaica*. New York: Sotheby's, 2015.

Sperber, Daniel. *Minhagei Yisrael: Mekorot Vetoledot*. Jerusalem: Mosad Harav Kuk, 1989.

Sperling, Abraham Isaac, ed. *Sefer Ta'amei Ha-Minhagim*. Jerusalem: Shai La-Mora, 1999.

Spiegel, Mira. "The Yemenite Rite for Reading the Torah." *Pe'amim* 77 (1988): 43–67.

Staerk, W., and A. Leitzmann. *Die Jüdisch-Deutschen Bibelübersetzungen*. Frankfurt a.M.: Kauffman Verlag, 1923.

Stallybrass, Peter. "Books and Scrolls." Unpublished article.

Steiner, Richard C. *A Biblical Translation in the Making: The Evolution and Impact of Saadiah Gaon's* Tafsir. Cambridge, MA: Harvard University Center for Jewish Studies, 2010.

Steinschneider, Moritz. *Verzeichniss der hebræischen Handschriften*. 2 vols. Berlin: G. Vogt, 1878–97.

Stern, David. *Chosen: Philadelphia's Great Hebraica*. Philadelphia: Rosenbach Museum & Library, 2007.

———. "The First Jewish Codices and the Early History of Jewish Reading." *Jewish Quarterly Review* 98 (2008): 163–202.

———. "The Hebrew Bible in Europe in the Middle Ages: A Preliminary Typology." *Jewish Studies Internet Journal* 11 (2012): 1–88.

———. "The Hebrew Bible in Spain: An Introduction." In *Biblias de Sefarad / Bibles of Sepharad*, edited by Esparanza Alfonso et al., 49–86. Madrid: CSIC, 2012.

———. "'Jewish' Art and the Making of the Medieval Prayerbook." *Ars Judaica: A Journal of Jewish Art* 6 (2010): 23–44.

———. "On the Term *Keter* as a Title for Bibles: A Speculation About Its Origins." In *Festschrift for Menahem Schmelzer*, edited by Evelyn Cohen and Emile Schrijver. Leiden: Brill, 2017.

———. "The Rabbinic Bible in Its Sixteenth Century Context." In *The Hebrew Book in Early Modern Italy*, edited by Adam Shear and Joseph Hacker, 78–108. Philadelphia: University of Pennsylvania Press.

Stern, Josef. "Profayt Duran's *Ma'aseh Efod*: The Philosophical Grammar of a Converso." In *The Origin and Nature of Language and Logic in Medieval Islamic, Jewish, and Christian Thought*, edited by Steven Harvey and Nadja Germann. Turnhout: Brepols, forthcoming.

Strack, H. L., and Gunter Stemberger. *Introduction to the Talmud and Midrash*. Translated by M. Bockmuehl. Minneapolis: Fortress, 1996.

Stroumsa, Guy G. "Early Christianity—a Religion of the Book?" In *Homer, the Bible, and Beyond*, edited by M. Finkelberg and G. G. Stroumsa, 153–73. Boston: Brill, 2003.

Stulberg, Ephraim. "The Last Oral Torah: The Division of the Torah into 'Aliyot." *Jewish Studies Internet Journal* 8 (2009): 183–202.

Sussman, Lance. "Another Look at Isaac Leeser and the First Jewish Translation of the Bible in the United States." *Modern Judaism* 5 (1985): 159–90.

Swetschinski, Daniel, et al. *Orphaned Objects: Facets of the Textiles Collection of the Joods Historisch Museum, Amsterdam*. Amsterdam: Waanders, 1997.

Tahan, Ilana. *Hebrew Manuscripts: The Power of Script and Image*. London: British Library, 2007.

Talmage, Frank. "Keep Your Sons from Scripture: The Bible in Medieval Jewish Scholarship and Spirituality." In *Understanding Scripture*, edited by C. Thoma and M. Wyschograd, 81–101. New York: Paulist Press, 1987.

Talmon, Shemaryahu. *Masada VI: Yigael Yadin Excavations (1963–1965) Hebrew Fragments*. Jerusalem: Hebrew University of Jerusalem, 1999.

Tamani, Giuliano. "Le prime edizioni della Bibbia Ebraica." In *Bibel in jüdischer und christlicher tradition*, 259–74. Frankfurt: Anton Hain, 1993.

Ta-Shma, Israel. *Early Franco-German Ritual and Custom* [in Hebrew]. Jerusalem: Magnes, 1994.

Tigay, Jeffrey H. *The JPS Torah Commentary: Deuteronomy*. Philadelphia: Jewish Publication Society, 1996.

———. "The Torah Scroll and God's Presence." Unpublished manuscript.

Timm, Erika. "Blitz and Witzenhausen." In *Studies in Jewish Culture in Honour of Chone Shmeruk*, edited by I. Bartal, E. Mendelsohn and C. Turniansky, 39*–66*. Jerusalem: Zalman Shazar Center, 1993.

Tishby, Peretz. "Hebrew Incunables: A Detailed Bibliographic Description of Hebrew Books Printed Before 1500, with Photographs of Watermarks and Facsimiles of Exceptional Pages" [in Hebrew]. *Kirjat Sepher* 58 (1983): 808–57.

Touitou, Elazar. "Concerning the Presumed Original Version of Rashi's Commentary on the Pentateuch" [in Hebrew]. *Tarbiz* 56 (1987): 211–42.

———. "Does Ms. Leipzig 1 Reflect the Original Text of Rashi's Commentary to the Torah?" [in Hebrew]. *Tarbiz* 61 (1992): 315.

Tov, Emanuel. *Scribal Practices and Approaches Reflected in the Texts Found in the Judean Desert*. Boston: Brill, 2004.

———. "Scribal Practices Reflected in the Documents from the Judean Desert and in the Rabbinic Literature: A Comparative Study." In *Texts, Temples, and Traditions: A Tribute to Menahem Haran*, edited by M. V. Fox, V. A. Hurowitz, M. L. Klein, B. J. Schwartz, and N. Shudak, 383–403. Winona Lake: Eisenbrauns, 1996.

———. "The Septuagint." In *Mikra: Text, Translation, Reading and Interpretation of the Hebrew Bible in Ancient Judaism and Early Christianity*, edited by Martin J. Mulder, 161–88. Philadelphia: Van Gorcum and Fortress, 1988.

———. *Textual Criticism of the Hebrew Bible*. Minneapolis: Fortress, 1992.

Trachtenberg, Joshua. *Jewish Magic and Superstition: A Study in Folk Religion*. New York: Behrman's, 1939.

Treu, Kurt. "The Significance of Greek for Jews in the Roman Empire." *Kairos* NF 15 (1973): 123–44.

Turniansky, Chava. "Reception and Rejection of Yiddish Renderings of the Bible." In *The Bible in/and Yiddish*, edited by Shlomo Berger, 7–20. Amsterdam: Menasseh ben Israel Institute, 2007.

———. "To the History of the 'Taytsh-Khumesh'—'Khumesh mit Khiber'" [in Hebrew]. In *Devarim Sheneemru Be-erev likhvod Dov Sadan Bimlot Lo Shmonim Ve-hamesh Shana*, 21–58. Jerusalem: Israel Academy of Sciences and Humanities, 1988.

Turniansky, Chava, and Erika Timm. *Yiddish in Italia: Yiddish Manuscripts and Printed Books from the 15th to the 17th Century*. Milano: Associazione Italiana Amici dell'Università do Gerusalemme, 2003.

Valmadonna Trust Library: Part I, Magnificent Manuscripts and the Bomberg Talmud. New York: Sotheby's, 2015.

van der Toorn, Karel. "The Iconic Book: Analogies Between the Babylonian Cult of Images and the Veneration of the Torah." In *The Image and the Book*, edited by Karel Van Der Toorn, 229–48. Leuven: Peeters, 1997.

Van Nes, Hans, and Eveline van Staalduine-Sulman. "The 'Jewish' Rabbinic Bibles Versus the 'Christian' Polyglot Bibles." In *A Jewish Targum in a Christian World*, edited by Alberdina Houtman, Eveline van Staalduine-Sulman, and Hans-Martin Kirn, 185–207. Boston: Brill, 2014.

Walfish, Barry Dov. *"As It Is Written": Judaic Treasures from the Thomas Fisher Rare Book Library.* Toronto: Thomas Fisher Rare Book Library, University of Toronto, 2015.

Wasserstein, Abraham, and David J. Wasserstein. *The Legend of the Septuagint: From Classical Antiquity to Today.* Cambridge: Cambridge University Press, 2006.

Wasserstrom, Steven M. *Between Muslim and Jew: The Problem of Symbiosis Under Early Islam.* Princeton, NJ: Princeton University Press, 1995.

Weber, Annette. "'The Masoret Is a Fence to the Torah': Monumental Letters and Micrography in Medieval Ashkenazic Bibles." *Ars Judaica* 11 (2015): 7–30.

Weber, Annette, Evelyn Friedlander, and Fritz Armbruster. *Mappott . . . Blessed Be Who Comes: The Band of Jewish Tradition.* Osnabrück: Secolo Verlag, 1997.

Weitzman, Michael. "The Interpretive Character of the Syriac Old Testament." In *Hebrew Bible / Old Testament: The History of Its Interpretation*, edited by Magne Sæbø, 1:587–611. Göttingen: Vandenhoek & Ruprecht, 2000.

Wernberg-Møller, P. "Prolegomenon." In *The Hebrew Bible—Latter Prophets, the Babylonian Codex of Petrograd*, edited by Hermann L. Strack, vii–xv. 1876. Reprint, New York: Ktav, 1971.

Wevers, John W. "The Interpretive Character and Significance of the Septuagint Version." In *Hebrew Bible / Old Testament: The History of Its Interpretation*, edited by Magne Sæbø, 1:84–107. Goettingen: Vandenhoek & Ruprecht, 2000.

Wieder, Naphtali. "'Sanctuary' as a Metaphor for Scripture." *Journal of Jewish Studies* 8 (1957): 165–75.

Wiesemann, Falk. *"Kommt heraus und schaut." Jüdische und christliche Illustrationen zur Bibel in alter Zeit.* Essen: Klartext Verlag, 2002.

———. *Ondanks het Tweede Gebod/Despite the Second Commandment.* Amsterdam: Bijbels Museum, 2003.

Wilken, Robert. *John Chrysostom and the Jews.* Berkeley: University of California Press, 1983.

Williams, John. "A Castilian Tradition of Bible Illustration." *Journal of the Warburg and the Courtauld Institutes* 28 (1965): 66–85.

Williamson, H. G. M. "Scribe and Scroll: Revisiting the Great Isaiah Scroll from Qumran." In *Making a Difference: Essays on the Bible and Judaism in Honor of Tamara Cohn Eskenazi*, edited by David J. A. Clines, H. K. Richards, and J. L. Wright, 329–42. Sheffield: Sheffield Phoenix Press, 2012.

Wischnitzer-Bernstein, Rachel. "The Esther Story in Art." In *The Purim Anthology*, edited by Philip Goodman, 222–49. Philadelphia: Jewish Publication Society, 1949.

Wistinetzki, Judah, ed. *Sefer Hasidim.* Jerusalem: Wahrmann, 1969.

Witcomb, Christopher L. C. E. *Copyright in the Renaissance: Prints and the Privilegio in Sixteenth-Century Venice and Rome.* Leiden: Brill, 2004.

Wolfson, Elliot. "Female Imaging of the Torah: From Literary Metaphor to Religious Symbol." In *Circle in the Square: Studies in the Use of Gender in Kabbalistic Symbolism*, 1–28. Albany: SUNY Press, 1995.

———. "The Mystical Significance of Torah Study in German Pietism." *Jewish Quarterly Review* 84 (1993): 43–77.

Woolf, Jeffrey R. "And I Shall Dwell in Their Midst: God's Presence in the Medieval Ashkenazic Synagogue." *Journal of Jewish Studies* 65 (2014): 302–22.

Wyrick, Jed. *The Ascension of Authorship: Attribution and Canon Formation in Jewish, Hellenistic, and Christian Traditions*. Cambridge, MA: Harvard University Dept. of Comparative Literature, 2004.

Ya'ari, A. *Toledot Hag Simhat-Torah*. Jerusalem: Mosad Harav Kuk, 1964.

Yaniv, Bracha. *Ma'aseh Hosheiv: Hatik Lesefer Tolrah Vetoldotav* [The Torah Case: Its History and Design] [in Hebrew]. Jerusalem: Bar Ilan University Press, 1997.

———. *Ma'ase Rokem: Textile Ceremonial Objects in the Ashkenazi, Sephardi, and Italian Synagogue* [in Hebrew]. Jerusalem: Hebrew University, 2009.

———. "Regional Variations of Torah Cases from the Islamic World." In *For Everything a Season: Proceedings of the Symposium on Jewish Ritual Art*, edited by J. Gutmann, 38–75. Cleveland, OH: Cleveland State University, 2002.

Yardeni, Ada. *The Book of Hebrew Script*. Jerusalem: Carta, 1997.

Yawn, Lila. "The Italian Giant Bibles." In *The Practice of the Bible in the Middle Ages*, edited by Susan Boynton and Diane J. Reilly, 126–56. New York: Columbia University Press, 2011.

Yeivin, Israel. *Introduction to the Tiberian Masorah*. Translated and edited by E. J. Revell. N.p., 1980.

Young, Frances. "Books and Their 'Aura': The Functions of Written Texts in Judaism, Paganism and Christianity During the First Centuries CE." In *Religious Identity and the Problem of Historical Foundation: The Foundational Character of Authoritative Sources in the History of Christianity and Judaism*, edited by Judith Frishman, Willemien Otten, and Gerard Rouwhorst, 535–52. Leiden: Brill, 2004.

Zafren, Herbert C. "Bible Editions, Bible Study and the Early History of Hebrew Printing." *Eretz-Israel* 16 (1982): *241–*51.

Zer, Raphael Yitzhak (Zinger). "Was the Masorete of the Keter a Rabbanite or a Karaite?" [in Hebrew]. *Sefunot* 8 (2003): 573–87.

Zevin, S. Y., ed. *Encyclopaedia Talmudit* [in Hebrew]. Jerusalem: Encyclopaedia Talmudit Publications, 1954.

Zimmels, H. J. *Ashkenazim and Sephardim*. London: Oxford University Press, 1958.

Zucker, Shlomo. "On the Margins of Historical Research: Forged Documents" [in Hebrew]. *Tarbiz* 80 (2012): 623–37.

Zwiep, Irene E. "Jewish Scholarship and Christian Tradition in Late-Medieval Catalonia: Profiat Duran on the Art of Memory." In *Hebrew Scholarship and the Medieval World*, 224–39. Cambridge: Cambridge University Press: 2001.

INDEX OF PRIMARY SOURCES

Hebrew Bible

Dead Sea Scrolls

Masada

Rabbinic Literature

INDEX OF MANUSCRIPTS

GENERAL INDEX

Note: Early printed editions discussed in the book are listed under the names of their publishers, printers, or editors.

THE SAMUEL & ALTHEA STROUM LECTURES IN JEWISH STUDIES

The Yiddish Art Song, performed by Leon Lishner, basso, and Lazar Weiner, piano (stereophonic record album)

The Holocaust in Historical Perspective, Yehuda Bauer

Zakhor: Jewish History and Jewish Memory, Yosef Hayim Yerushalmi

Jewish Mysticism and Jewish Ethics, Joseph Dan

The Invention of Hebrew Prose: Modern Fiction and the Language of Realism, Robert Alter

Recent Archaeological Discoveries and Biblical Research, William G. Dever

Jewish Identity in the Modern World, Michael A. Meyer

I. L. Peretz and the Making of Modern Jewish Culture, Ruth R. Wisse

The Kiss of God: Spiritual and Mystical Death in Judaism, Michael Fishbane

Gender and Assimilation in Modern Jewish History: The Roles and Representation of Women, Paula E. Hyman

Portrait of American Jews: The Last Half of the 20th Century, Samuel C. Heilman

Judaism and Hellenism in Antiquity: Conflict or Confluence? Lee I. Levine

Imagining Russian Jewry: Memory, History, Identity, Steven J. Zipperstein

Popular Culture and the Shaping of Holocaust Memory in America, Alan Mintz

Studying the Jewish Future, Calvin Goldscheider

Autobiographical Jews: Essays in Jewish Self-Fashioning, Michael Stanislawski

The Jewish Life Cycle: Rites of Passage from Biblical to Modern Times, Ivan Marcus

Make Yourself a Teacher: Rabbinic Tales of Mentors and Disciples, Susan Handelman

Writing in Tongues: Yiddish Translation in the Twentieth Century, by Anita Norich

Agnon's Moonstruck Lovers: The Song of Songs in Israeli Culture, by Ilana Pardes

A Best-Selling Hebrew Book of the Modern Era: The Book of the Covenant *of Pinḥas Hurwitz and Its Remarkable Legacy,* by David B. Ruderman

The Jewish Bible: A Material History, by David Stern